A Critique of Emotional Intelligence:
What Are the Problems and How Can They Be Fixed?

D1566875

Gregory Bedny and David Meister
The Russian Theory of Activity: Current Applications to Design and Learning

Winston Bennett, David Woehr, and Charles Lance
Performance Measurement: Current Perspectives and Future Challenges

Michael T. Brannick, Eduardo Salas, and Carolyn Prince
Team Performance Assessment and Measurement: Theory, Research, and Applications

Jeanette N. Cleveland, Margaret Stockdale, and Kevin R. Murphy
Women and Men in Organizations: Sex and Gender Issues at Work

Aaron Cohen
Multiple Commitments in the Workplace: An Integrative Approach

Russell Cropanzano
Justice in the Workplace: Approaching Fairness in Human Resource Management, Volume 1

Russell Cropanzano
Justice in the Workplace: From Theory to Practice, Volume 2

James E. Driskell and Eduardo Salas
Stress and Human Performance

Sidney A. Fine and Steven F. Cronshaw
Functional Job Analysis: A Foundation for Human Resources Management

Sidney A. Fine and Maury Getkate
Benchmark Tasks for Job Analysis: A Guide for Functional Job Analysis (FJA) Scales

J. Kevin Ford, Steve W. J. Kozlowski, Kurt Kraiger, Eduardo Salas, and Mark S. Teachout
Improving Training Effectiveness in Work Organizations

Jerald Greenberg
Organizational Behavior: The State of the Science, Second Edition

Uwe E. Kleinbeck, Hans-Henning Quast, Henk Thierry, and Hartmut Häcker
Work Motivation

Laura Koppes
Historical Perspectives in Industrial and Organizational Psychology

Ellen Kossek and Susan Lambert
Work and Life Integration: Organizational, Cultural, and Individual Perspectives

Martin I. Kurke and Ellen M. Scrivner
Police Psychology Into the 21st Century

Joel Lefkowitz
Ethics and Values in Industrial–Organizational Psychology

Manuel London
Job Feedback: Giving, Seeking, and Using Feedback for Performance Improvement, Second Edition

Manuel London
How People Evaluate Others in Organizations

Manuel London
Leadership Development: Paths to Self-Insight and Professional Growth

Robert F. Morrison and Jerome Adams
Contemporary Career Development Issues

Michael D. Mumford, Garnett Stokes, and William A. Owens
Patterns of Life History: The Ecology of Human Individuality

Kevin Murphy
A Critique of Emotional Intelligence: What Are the Problems and How Can They Be Fixed?

Kevin R. Murphy
Validity Generalization: A Critical Review

Kevin R. Murphy and Frank E. Saal
Psychology in Organizations: Integrating Science and Practice

Susan E. Murphy and Ronald E. Riggio
The Future of Leadership Development

Margaret A. Neal and Leslie Brett Hammer
Working Couples Caring for Children and Aging Parents: Effects on Work–Family Fit, Well-Being, and Work

Steven A. Y. Poelmans
Work and Family: An International Research Perspective

Robert E. Ployhart, Benjamin Schneider, and Neal Schmitt
Staffing Organizations: Contemporary Practice and Theory, Third Edition

Erich P. Prien, Jeffrey S. Schippmann, and Kristin O. Prien
Individual Assessment: As Practiced in Industry and Consulting

Ned Rosen
Teamwork and the Bottom Line: Groups Make a Difference

Heinz Schuler, James L. Farr, and Mike Smith
Personnel Selection and Assessment: Individual and Organizational Perspectives

John W. Senders and Neville P. Moray
Human Error: Cause, Prediction, and Reduction

Frank J. Smith
Organizational Surveys: The Diagnosis and Betterment of Organizations Through Their Members

George C. Thornton III and Rose Mueller-Hanson
Developing Organizational Simulations: A Guide for Practitioners and Students

George C. Thornton III and Deborah Rupp
Assessment Centers in Human Resource Management: Strategies for Prediction, Diagnosis, and Development

Yoav Vardi and Ely Weitz
Misbehavior in Organizations: Theory, Research, and Management

---

For more information on LEA titles, please contact Lawrence Erlbaum Associates, Publishers, at www.erlbaum.com

A Critique of Emotional Intelligence:
What Are the Problems and How Can They Be Fixed?

Edited by

Kevin R. Murphy
Pennsylvania State University

2006

LAWRENCE ERLBAUM ASSOCIATES, PUBLISHERS
Mahwah, New Jersey   London

Lawrence Erlbaum Associates, Inc., Publishers
10 Industrial Avenue
Mahwah, New Jersey 07430
www.erlbaum.com

Cover design by Tomai Maridou

Library of Congress Cataloging-in-Publication Data

A critique of emotional intelligence : what are the
problems and how can they be fixed? / edited by Kevin
R.Murphy.
    p. cm.

Includes bibliographical references and index.
ISBN 0-8058-5317-0 (cloth : alk. paper)
ISBN 0-8058-5318-9 (pbk. : alk. paper)
1. Emotional intelligence. I. Murphy, Kevin R., 1952-
BF576.C75 2006
152.4—dc22   2005044676
                                                   CIP

Contents

Series Foreword   ix
Jeanette N. Cleveland and Edwin A. Fleishman

Preface   xi

I.   The Definition and Measurement of EI   1

1   What Is This Thing Called Emotional Intelligence?   3
    Gerald Matthews, Amanda K. Emo, Richard D. Roberts,
    and Moshe Zeidner

2   The Two EIs   37
    Kevin R. Murphy and Lori Sideman

3   Can Emotional Intelligence Be Measured?   59
    Jeffrey M. Conte and Michelle A. Dean

II.   The Relationships Between EI and Other Constructs   79

4   The Long, Frustrating, and Fruitless Search   81
    for Social Intelligence: A Cautionary Tale
    Frank J. Landy

5   Emotional Intelligence in Classrooms and in Schools: 125
    What We See in the Educational Setting
    Jennifer Allen and Jonathan Cohen

6   Explaining the Popularity of Emotional Intelligence   141
    Adrian Furnham

7   Beyond *g*   161
    Nathan Brody

III.   The Limits of EI   187

8   Evaluating the Claims: Emotional Intelligence   189
        in the Workplace
        Peter J. Jordan, Claire E. Ashton-James,
        and Neal M. Ashkanasy

9   EI in the Business World   211
        Mark J. Schmit

10 Multiplying Intelligences: Are General, Emotional,   235
        and Practical Intelligences Equal?
        David L. Van Rooy, Stephan Dilchert, Chockalingam
        Viswesvaran, and Deniz S. Ones

11 Business Susceptibility to Consulting Fads: 263
        The Case of Emotional Intelligence
        Robert Hogan and Louis W. Stokes

IV. Improving EI Research and Applications   281

12 The Fadification of Emotional Intelligence   283
        Kevin R. Murphy and Lori Sideman

13 The Case for an Ability-Based Model   301
        of Emotional Intelligence
        Catherine S. Daus

14 Improving the Definition, Measurement,   325
        and Application of Emotional Intelligence
        Paul E. Spector and Hazel-Anne M. Johnson

15 Four Conclusions About Emotional Intelligence   345
        Kevin R. Murphy

        Author Index   355

        Subject Index   369

Series Foreword

Jeanette N. Cleveland
Pennsylvania State University

Edwin A. Fleishman
George Mason University

A CRITIQUE OF EMOTIONAL INTELLIGENCE: WHAT ARE THE PROBLEMS AND HOW CAN THEY BE FIXED?

There is a compelling need for innovative approaches to the solution of many pressing problems involving human relationship in today's society. Such approaches are more likely to be successful when they are based on sound research and applications. This Series in Applied Psychology offers publications that emphasize state-of-the-art research and its applications to important issues of human behavior in a variety of social settings. The objective is to bridge both academic and applied interests.

Ten years ago, Goleman's best-seller *Emotional Intelligence* brought this controversial construct to the attention of a broad cross-section of researchers, business leaders, and educators. Since then, the topic of emotional intelligence (EI) has been the focus of numerous articles, presentations, and debates. Kevin Murphy has enlisted an impressive group of authors who summarize the key controversies surrounding EI. We are pleased to have what we believe is a ground-breaking examination of this construct.

This book argues that the critical issues in the debate over emotional intelligence revolve around three key concerns. First, there are many different ideas about exactly what EI really means; disagreements over the definition of EI have contributed strongly to the EI controversy. Questions about the definition of EI are made even more complex by deep disagreements about how EI should be measured. The first three chapters in this volume describe the various definitions and measures of EI, and help to make sense of the issues involved in decribing what EI really means.

Second, there are questions about whether EI is simply a new name for existing constructs. Chapters 4 through 7 of this volume examine the relationships between EI and a number of well-established constructs such as personality and ability. This section also examines a variety of explanations for the apparent popularity of the EI construct.

Third, some EI proponents have made bold claims about the importance and relevance of EI. Perhaps the most famous of these is the notion that EI might be more important than IQ in determining success in a variety of fields. There is considerable skepticism about many of these claims; chapters 8 through 11 examine the limits of EI.

The final section of this book looks at prospects for improving EI research and practice. This section notes that ability-based definitions of EI (which preceeded Goleman's best-seller) have potential validity and utility, but they also note that there are many problems that need to be solved in order to determine the overall value and applicability of the EI construct.

The set of chapters and authors represented in the book reflect expertise and scholarship across scientific and applied domains. This ground-breaking book sets a research agenda for the future that is designed to clarify this controversial construct and for improving EI research and practice.

The book is appropriate for students in industrial and organizational psychology, human resources management, organizational behavior, and leadership education and for courses dealing with selection, training and development, and performance feedback. Professionals who are engaged in the development of employees and leaders in organizational and academic settings will find this book essential to their work.

Preface

Emotional Intelligence (EI) has become one of the more hotly debated topics in the behavioral and social sciences. There are sometimes bitter disagreements about the meaning, measurement, definition, and implications of EI. There have even been suggestions in the academic literature that there is no such thing as EI. On the other hand, tests, training programs, and other interventions designed to assess, improve, or apply EI have grown at an amazing rate, suggesting that some users find the concept of EI both attractive and useful.

The controversy over EI is due, in part, to the overly optimistic claims made by some EI proponents about the definition, meaning, and importance of EI. The low regard with which some versions of EI are viewed in the scientific press is sufficiently intense that a good deal of scientifically respectable research on EI and related constructs suffers a sort of guilt by association. If you mention "emotional intelligence" at a scientific conference, it is likely that many members of the audience will roll their eyes and tune out, regardless of whether you are describing the results of well-conducted, peer-reviewed studies or the latest pronouncements from the Web site of some self-appointed EI guru.

It is especially important to understand the reasons for the EI controversy because, unlike many other concepts that have been strongly criticized by the research community, EI *should be* a useful construct that is amenable to rigorous research. The best and more useful models of EI identify several related abilities and skills that appear to hang together and that might have broad relevance. Individuals who show skills in the range of areas included in the most reasonable EI models should have significant advantages over others who show lower levels of these skills in school, in the workplace, and in most other social situations. Some of the better EI models also point toward specific things people might do to increase their effectiveness in social situations. Given the potential relevance of this construct, it is disappointing to see how little regard many mainstream researchers have for the construct "emotional intelligence."

Part of the problem is that much of the discussion about EI has occurred outside of the normal academic milieu that is familiar and comfortable to researchers. That is, some of the biggest players in the EI literature simply don't play by the same set of rules as those accepted by academic researchers. Books by Goleman (1995, 1998) helped to propel the concept of EI into public prominence, in part on the basis of sweeping claims about its importance. Discussions of EI in the popular press have helped to popularize a number of EI measures, training programs, and interventions, some of which are likely to be highly valuable and some of which are likely to be worthless. Enthusiastic discussions of EI in the popular press and in trade magazines, marketing brochures, and so on, have in turn led to a cottage industry in academia devoted to critiquing EI. In one sense, the popularity of EI has been a winning proposition for everyone—test publishers, consultants, and academic EI bashers.

You can argue that popular discussions of EI have done significant harm by making promises that are impossible to keep and by pushing EI programs that have little real value. The very popularity of EI has also been problematic for its academic critics; academic attacks on the popular-press version of EI have sometimes been superficial, in part because of the very low quality of some popular EI publications. Attacks that focus on such "low-hanging fruit" of the EI industry are of limited value, and they can unfairly tarnish serious EI research. On the whole, both sides in the EI debate are vulnerable to the criticism that their "products" (i.e., EI tests vs. articles claiming EI is worthless) are not all that useful.

You can just as easily argue, however, that the popularity of EI has had positive effects. First, popular-press discussions of EI have heightened public awareness of a range of social skills that are important for success in school, in the workplace, and in life. Second, it is hard to imagine that the distinguished set of authors included in this volume, (or more generally, the growing group of researchers doing serious work on EI) would have been drawn to EI in the absence of the controversy that the hype over this construct generated. The overselling of EI might ironically be the key to its future improvement, in the sense that an increasing number of researchers are devoting attention to EI and suggesting ways to improve its definition, measurement, and application.

Criticism of EI research and applications has taken a number of tacks, but three issues seem most important in understanding why so many researchers have strong concerns about EI. First, EI is widely regarded as a construct that is poorly defined and that is not adequately measured. Second, EI is often seen as a new name for constructs that have been studied (sometimes with limited success) for decades. Finally, and perhaps most important, sweeping claims about the importance of EI (which are largely responsible for its popularity) are, at best, hard to document; at worst, they are simply false.

The chapters that follow are organized around these themes, laying out in some detail why so many social and behavioral scientists have serious concerns about EI. Several of these chapters, however, also lay out reasons for optimism. There are some realistic prospects for developing consensus about what EI does and does not mean, for developing useful measures of the skills and abilities that underlie EI, and for finding out when, where, and why EI is likely to be an important determinant of success in school, in the workplace, and in life. By articulating criticisms of EI, as it is currently defined, it is also possible to chart a course for improving EI research and practice. The final summary chapter attempts to distill the main points raised in chapters 1–14 by arguing that these chapters provide interlocking support for a number of key conclusions about the strengths and weaknesses of research and practice in the area of emotional intelligence, and about prospects for improving this work.

REFERENCES

Goleman, D. (1995). *Emotional intelligence.* New York: Bantam Books.
Goleman, D. (1998). *Working with emotional intelligence.* New York: Bantam Books.

I

The Definition and Measurement of EI

The first major concern raised by critics of emotional intelligence is that the definition of EI is too broad and too fuzzy to be useful, and the second is that none of the available measures provides a reliable and valid assessment of EI. These two concerns are to some extent interlocking: Without an adequate definition of EI, it is hard to imagine how adequate measures can be constructed. In chapter 1, Matthews, Emo, Roberts, and Zeidner explore the range of meanings that are attached to the term *emotional intelligence* and discuss both the measures currently used in assessing this construct and the myths associated with EI.

In chapter 2, Murphy and Sideman suggest that the various definitions of EI can be grouped into two broad categories: ability-based models, which have been developed and tested largely in the context of traditional social science research, and expansive models, which have been developed and discussed in the popular literature. They discuss the clash between the cultures of scientific research and marketing, and the role of this clash of values in generating controversy and debate in the area of EI.

In chapter 3, Conte and Dean examine and critique the most common measures of emotional intelligence. Their review suggests that many popular measures are so riddled with psychometric weaknesses that they are unlikely to provide any useful information about the respondent. Even the best measures of EI are suspect; the best scales look good only in comparison to the abysmal competition.

The bottom line conclusion that emerges from reading these three chapters is that when someone says "Joe shows a higher level of emotional intelligence than Ed," it is very hard to know what that really means; it is even hard to know what it is about Joe and Ed that would lead someone to conclude that one was more emotionally intelligent than the other.

1

What Is This Thing Called Emotional Intelligence?

Gerald Matthews and Amanda K. Emo
University of Cincinnati

Richard D. Roberts
Educational Testing Service

Moshe Zeidner
University of Haifa

The subject of emotional intelligence (EI) has gained widespread public attention over the past decade. A recent search for "emotional intelligence" in a Web engine (i.e., Google, February 2005) produced nearly 900,000 results. In addition to Web sites devoted to the topic, numerous magazines and newspapers have devoted space to the discussion of EI and do-it-yourself "EQ" assessments have come into vogue. The popularity of this concept raises a stimulating question: "What is this thing called emotional intelligence"? We note from the outset that the answer to the question is by no means straightforward; contemporary scientific accounts are suggestive, but not definitive. The purpose of this chapter is therefore somewhat modest: to draw to the reader's attention to current scientific thinking and evidence supporting (or otherwise) theory, measures, and applications of emotional intelligence.

3

Rather than be entirely critical, we intersperse each section with a number of suggestions for theory-driven research. Before turning to our first scientific concern—conceptualization—we offer a brief commentary suggesting why popular accounts may misrepresent what is currently understood of the construct.

ONCE POPULAR! NOW SCIENTIFIC?

Interest in EI has spread from the popular media to the scientific community far more cautiously than some proponents might suggest. Its popular success has nonetheless spawned an unfortunate tendency for suffixing a construct with "intelligence" as a promotional device, as in "sexual intelligence," "entrepreneurial intelligence," "spiritual intelligence," and the like. Popular authors may be forgiven for this ploy, but scientists, conscious of their duty-of-care to the public, should be more wary. Indeed, the American Psychological Association's ethics code requires researchers (a) to use assessment techniques for purposes that are appropriate in the light of research evidence on the usefulness and proper application of the techniques (Standard 9.02), (b) to use appropriate psychometric procedures and current scientific or professional knowledge for test design (9.05), (c) to correct or minimize the misuse or misrepresentation of their work (1.01), and (d) avoid false or deceptive public statements (5.01). Supporting exaggerated claims for the importance of any of these new intelligences, including EI, is likely to conflict with one or more of these professional standards.

In part, EI has gained popularity because it is thought to be an intelligence that anyone can have, and have in near equal measure (Goleman, 1995). The term *EQ* is sometimes used for EI, by analogy with IQ, although a scoring metric comparable to those supporting traditional intelligence tests has yet to be developed. Unlike traditional measures of cognitive abilities, which are correlated with factors such as socioeconomic status and access to education, it is popularly believed that EI is less constrained by social (and for that matter, biological) factors. As Mayer, Salovey, and Caruso (2000a) state, EI is "suggestive of a kinder, gentler intelligence—an intelligence anyone can have" (p. 97). Indeed, proponents of EI claim that, unlike academic intelligence, EI is highly malleable, so that individuals who have generally low emotional competencies may be able to improve their overall abilities to identify, express, and regulate emotion (Goleman, 1995). (On a terminological note, we use *intelligence* to refer to a basic aptitude, defined in psychometric terms as a latent factor in a structural model of ability, and *competence* as a more loosely defined capability for performing some physical or mental activity that may be influenced by learning and context as well as aptitude.)

Regardless of the current accolades that the construct of EI is receiving, we have argued, in various reviews, for a more seasoned approach to the topic (see Matthews, Roberts, & Zeidner, 2004; Matthews, Zeidner, & Roberts, 2002). Thus, while EI is frequently referred to as being extraordinarily important for personal and career success, these claims, on the balance of available evidence, appear hollow and to lack a solid scientific basis. There are also good reasons to be concerned with the adequacy and validity of widely used EI measures. The gold standard for conventional intelligence tests is that responses to questions can be scored as "right" or "wrong," according to some explicit rationale. In the emotional domain, though, determining the "correct" answers to questions concerning how best to resolve an argument, comfort a friend, or deal with strong personal emotions is by no means straightforward, especially when there may be many viable solutions. In this context, EI carries with it the same measurement problems that have faced the assessment of social intelligence where, despite decades of research, there is still no validated and widely accepted test of social intelligence (e.g., Kihlstrom & Cantor, 2000). Moreover, measures of EI overlap with other more established and validated measures of psychological factors (particularly personality), such that the fundamental question as to whether assessments of EI provide the scientist or practitioner with anything new remains unresolved.

Another difficulty relates to finding an appropriate scientific definition of the construct. EI might be purely a personality-like trait, purely a type of ability, or some combination of the two domains (Petrides & Furnham, 2003). Determining how to operationalize EI dictates both measurement strategies and interpretation of data from test scores. From an ability perspective, tests for EI should assess performance on tasks such as identifying emotions and choosing the appropriate course of action in difficult circumstances. Personality-oriented EI scales face the problem of differentiating EI from more established trait constructs. In fact, several questionnaires for EI are substantially correlated with existing traits, including, but not limited to, the Big Five personality factors (Davies, Stankov, & Roberts, 1998; MacCann, Matthews, Zeidner, & Roberts, 2004; Matthews et al., 2002). Some proponents of EI have argued that strong relationships between EI and personality support the validity of the EI construct (e.g., Bar-On, 2000). This is a curious argument; the strength of the correlation between EI and personality implies that the EI questionnaire may simply measure the existing personality dimension. In addition, EI may be defined in terms of constructs that are more narrowly focused on emotional competence than are broad personality traits, such as self-awareness, coping strategies, positive emotional experiences, and awareness of self—psychological functions that overlap with personality (McCrae, 2000). EI might also relate to qualities that are at the crossroads of personality and ability, including openness, self-efficacy, and ego resiliency (Zeidner & Matthews, 2000).

WHAT IS EMOTIONAL INTELLIGENCE ANYWAY? DEFINITIONS AND CONCEPTUALIZATIONS

It is important to have a scientifically defensible definition of EI as the basis for devising satisfactory tests of the construct. Unfortunately, there is no one consensual definition of what EI is and what it should (and should not) encompass. Popular definitions of EI are varied and inconsistent. They include being able to intuitively "read" the emotions of others, to maintain a successful long-term relationship with an intimate partner, and to be "in touch" with one's own emotions. Indeed, definitions tend to be overinclusive, at the limit of being no more than a laundry list of positive qualities other than conventional, academic intelligence. Over-inclusiveness is a problem in both the popular literature and in some scientific writings. For example, Bar-On (1997) defines EI as "an array of non-cognitive capabilities, competencies, and skills that influence one's ability to succeed in coping with environmental demands and pressures" (p. 14), a definition that excludes very little that is "non-cognitive." Another difficulty, most evident in popular works, is a conflating of EI with desirable moral qualities. According to Goleman (1995), "there is an old-fashioned word for the body of skills that EI represents: character" (p. 34). Educators have picked up on the need for schools to build character as well as academic competence, seemingly rediscovering an opinion recorded by Spearman (1927) that "[academic] learning is apt to produce a swollen head at the expense of weak bowels" (p. 105).

Any good measure must be based on a clear conceptual definition of a construct (e.g., American Educational Research Association, American Psychological Association, & National Council on Measurement in Education [AERA/APA/NCME], 1999; Cronbach & Meehl, 1955), but even when considering only more scientific based definitions, it remains unclear how EI should be conceptualized. Although proponents argue that EI is a conceptually coherent construct (e.g., Bar-On, 2000), a review of the EI literature suggests otherwise (e.g., Matthews et al., 2004). According to Mayer, Salovey, and Caruso (2000b), EI may be defined either within an ability model, as a set of aptitudes directly supporting better performance of emotional tasks, or within a broader mixed model, that adds traits that facilitate emotional competence to basic abilities. Mayer et al.'s (2000b) four-branch model is based on one of the clearer definitions of EI, encompassing emotion identification, assimilating emotions into thought, understanding emotion, and emotion management. However, although a useful starting point for research, this definition (in common with many others) still raises several difficulties.

1. Several qualities commonly attributed to EI are excluded, such as emotional expressiveness, empathy, perspective-taking, and self-control. The point is not that the four branches are necessarily poorly chosen, but rather that there exist no explicit criteria for deciding which qualities belong to EI and which do not.

2. The definition refers to functions, not processes. Thus, emotion identification may be controlled by multiple processes ranging from low-level subcortical pattern matching to high-level cognitive evaluation of multiple cues to emotion. It is unclear that individual differences in these processes are, in fact, correlated.

3. The definition ignores the role of contextual information in emotional processing and judgment. For example, EI may reside less in accurate reading of facial emotion than in integrating multiple sources of information within a given context (e.g., judging when facial expression is a reliable cue, knowing the particular ways in which each of our friends expresses their feelings). A related point is that much of emotional competence may reside in learned skills, acquired within specific contexts, rather than to general aptitudes. Definitions of EI typically fail to distinguish learned capabilities from basic aptitudes.

4. Most definitions assume that EI is expressed through declarative knowledge. That is, it is thought that individuals are aware of their own EI and are able to report on it. However, the definition ignores the key distinction between implicit and explicit processing and knowledge. It seems plausible that a part of emotional competence resides in largely unconscious behaviors, such as nonverbal expression of emotion, and in unconscious processes, such as registering the nonverbal cues provided by others. Studies of skill have indicated that much of this type of expertise is procedural (rather than declarative) such that the individual has little conscious awareness to support or verbalize the expertise (Anderson, 1996). For example, in the social-emotional context, people may be able to detect deceit from verbal and/or nonverbal cues without being aware of how they do so. Therefore, measures assessing academic knowledge of emotion (as do ability tests of EI) may not be predictive of this behavioral skill. In short, knowing that anger can lead to aggression does not necessarily help deal with aggressive individuals or help an individual to manage his own anger.

5. There is also an assumption that EI generalizes across the qualitatively different emotions. For example, most definitions of EI imply that a person who is skilled at managing anger should be equally as skilled in situations involving happiness, fear, boredom, or contempt. By contrast, basic emotions theories commonly state that each emotion is supported by its own distinct neuropsychological system (e.g., Panksepp, 1998), which seems to directly contradict this notion. Indeed, to date, generality of EI across emotions has yet to be tested empirically.

One of the major themes of the current chapter is that the label "emotional intelligence" has been rather haphazardly used to refer to a multitude of distinct constructs that may or may not be interrelated. In a recent review, we identified examples of EI conceptualized as temperament, character, basic information processing, acquired implicit skills, acquired explicit skills, adaptiveness, insightful self-awareness, and good emotional personal–environmental fit (Matthews et al., 2004). Table 1.1 summarizes four different conceptualizations, each of which suggests different assessment techniques, developmental concomitants, and conceptual significance (Matthews et al., 2004). Some definitions of EI, corresponding to questionnaire measures, appear to overlap with those of basic temperaments or personality (e.g., optimism and cheerfulness). EI may also refer to more narrowly focused qualities of self-regulation, including confidence in handling one's own emotional state, which may be assessed by some of the more distinctive questionnaires in the field (see below). Other qualities are best assessed by objective means such as speed and accuracy of emotional information-processing, and the knowledge and skills related to emotion. Table 1.1 also suggests that existing tests may, in fact, correspond to different classes of construct.

Zeidner, Matthews, Roberts, and MacCann (2003) have suggested that the multiple constructs that might be labeled EI may be linked developmentally rather than structurally. Three such constructs correspond to different levels of emotional development: temperament, rule-based emotional skills, and emotional discourse. Present from birth, and influenced by biology and genetics, temperament may affect social interactions with caregivers and others that shape emotional development. For example, distress-prone children may elicit poorer quality parenting, especially as these children and parents share common genes for personality that may increase the likelihood of mutual frustration or withdrawal from social engagement (e.g., Kochanska & Coy, 2002). Emotion regulation relies heavily on culture-bound learned skills for experiencing appropriate feelings, displaying emotion, and coping with emotion (Denham, 1998). In this situation, lack of EI may be the result of faulty learning of the rules supporting these skills. Emotional discourse provides an individual

TABLE 1.1 **Constructs That May Contribute to Emotional Competence**

Construct	Corresponding current measure	Equivalent in ability research	Key processes assessed	Adaptive significance	Developmental influences
Temperament	Scales for Big Five Personality, EQ-i (Bar-On, 1997)	None	Neural and cognitive processes controlling arousal, attention, and reinforcement sensitivity	Temperamental factors confer a mixture of both benefits and costs to the organism	Genetic and early learning
Emotion regulation	TMMS, Subscales of SSRI and TEIQue	Self-assessed cognitive ability	Self-concept and self-regulation	Predominantly positive (but not exclusively so); presumed similar to self-esteem	Learning and socialization (e.g, mastery experiences, modeling, direct reinforcement [in emotive contexts])
Information processing	Recognition of emotion, Emotional Stroop, Emotional memory	Choice reaction time, inspection time, working memory	Specific processing modules	Mixed: Memory is likely adaptive but it is uncertain whether this is true of all processes (e.g., speed of processing)	Genetic and early learning
Emotional knowledge and skills	MSCEIT	Crystallized intelligence, domains of specialized knowledge	Multiply acquired procedural and declarative skills	Adaptive within context for learning; may be irrelevant or counter-productive in other contexts	Learning, socialization and training of specific skills and knowledge modules

Note. EQ-i = Emotional Quotient-Inventory; TMMS = Trait Meta-Mood Scale; SSRI = Schutte Self-Report Inventory; TEIQUE = Trait Emotional Intelligence Questionnaire; MSCIET = Mayer-Salovey-Caruso Emotional Intelligence Test.

with personal insight and emotional understanding that enables self-evaluation and self-reflection (Saarni, 2000). Development of more sophisticated emotional competencies may be constrained both by more primitive competencies and cognitive abilities. For example, learning skills for emotion display may be limited by temperamental factors (e.g., high irritability) and by lack of verbal ability (e.g., poor comprehension of instructions and advice about showing emotion). Thus, overall competence may depend on multiple, weakly interrelated constructs.

Another source of difficulty for the field is vagueness about the causal status of EI as a predictor of behavior. Differential psychology typically draws a sharp distinction between aptitudes as intrapersonal qualities and the outcomes (i.e., individual differences in behavior) that are predicted by these aptitudes. In research on EI, this distinction is frequently blurred. For example, Bar-On (1997) refers to positive mood as a component of EI, but mood might best be viewed as the outcome of a successful resolution to a challenging situation. There may be a place for "ecological" definitions of EI that are distributed across person and environment, similar to Snow's dynamic view of intelligence as an emergent property of person-situation interaction (Stanford Aptitude Seminar, 2001). EI might be seen as the property of a developmental trajectory that binds personal characteristics promoting competence to external environments that are shaped by, and support, competence (Zeidner et al., 2003). Beyond personal aptitude, EI may then be attributed to emotionally supportive features of the environment, including availability of social support, the absence of emotionally damaging relationships, and a positive reputation among others. In addition, EI may be viewed as the "goodness of fit" between person and social environment (Zeidner, Matthews, & Roberts, 2001). That is to say, our emotional functioning is optimal when our beliefs are congruent with those of others in our current situation (regardless of whether these beliefs are accurate or not). Of course, whether such goodness-of-fit may be described as a form of "intelligence" remains a moot point in this line of reasoning.

RULERS FOR EMOTIONAL INTELLIGENCE: TESTS AND SCALES

As stated previously, newspapers, popular magazines, and Web sites offer a multitude of EI assessments, which are typically of limited scientific worth. In response, the scientific community has developed some measures for assessing EI, although, in the absence of a coherent and consensual definition, the path toward an acceptable measure of EI becomes more problematic than would otherwise be the case. Ideally, test development should start with the creation of an accept-

able, theoretically defensible definition of the construct. This conceptualization then helps set the stage for measurement of the construct.
Updating principles for test development we have provided previously
(see e.g., Matthews, Zeidner, & Roberts, 2002, 2005) to reflect contemporary views on the nature of validity (see, especially,
AERA/APA/NCME, 1999), the following brief guidelines would appear
requisite for developing a satisfactory EI measure:

1. Provide evidence for the reliability of the measure and infor-
    mation on the standard error of measurement.
2. Demonstrate that a meaningful relationship exists between
    the test's content and the construct it is intended to mea-
    sure.
3. Provide theoretical and empirical analyses supporting (or
    disconfirming) relationships between the construct and the
    responses provided by the test taker (e.g., ensure that a re-
    sponse to a test supposedly measuring EI is not an artifact
    of extraneous factors such as social conformity, response
    bias, or faking).
4. Demonstrate that the construct's internal structure is as
    suggested by the underlying theoretical framework (i.e., ei-
    ther unidimensional or composed of disparate compo-
    nents).
5. Localize the construct within the sphere of other individual
    differences variables. This includes establishing both con-
    vergent and discriminant evidence, test-criterion relation-
    ships, and documenting how validity generalizes across
    samples and situations.

Issues of consequential validity (i.e., demonstrating that the test
will have meaningful societal consequences), fairness (i.e., showing
that items are not biased against a particular subpopulation for inappropriate reasons), and how to appropriately document test development are also critical components of developing an EI measure. All of
these various processes are ongoing and should feed back to guide
theoretical refinements and test development. Each piece of evidence
is also equally important to establish. We note at this point that the authors view "EI" as a broad umbrella term, referring to a variety of quite
distinct constructs. In turn, this implies a need for multiple, parallel
tracks of test development and validation.

In practice, Mayer et al.'s (2000b) distinction between ability and
mixed models is paralleled by two different philosophies for assessment of EI. Ability models suggest that EI should be operationalized

through tests similar to intelligence tests made up of items with right or wrong answers. The leading ability tests are the Multifactor Emotional Intelligence Scale (MEIS; Mayer, Caruso, & Salovey, 1999) and the Mayer-Salovey-Caruso Emotional Intelligence Test (MSCEIT; Mayer, Salovey, Caruso, & Sitarenios, 2003). By contrast, mixed models lend themselves to the development of inventories, each of which appear to resemble (arguably to both the expert and casual observer) existing personality questionnaires to a considerable degree. Table 1.2 summarizes some of the ability and questionnaire assessments to which we will refer throughout these passages.

Questionnaires for EI

Perhaps unfortunately, the questionnaire approach has proved to be far more popular than the ability test approach: Pérez (2003) identified over 50 questionnaires for EI, and the number continues to proliferate (see Pérez, Petrides, & Furnham, 2005). Most questionnaires provide global and subscale values of EI. A review of these measures is beyond the scope of this chapter. We will focus on two of the more widely used scales, the Emotional Quotient Inventory (EQ-i; Bar-On, 1997) and the Self-Report Inventory (SSRI; Schutte et al., 1998). Other notable questionnaires include the Emotional Competence Inventory (ECI; Sala, 2002), developed for occupational contexts, the Trait Emotional Intelligence Questionnaire (TEIque; Petrides & Furnham, 2003), and the Trait Meta-Mood Scale (TMMS; Salovey, Mayer, Goldman, Turvey, & Palfai, 1995). The TMMS differs from the other scales in focusing narrowly on mood regulation. However, it has been used quite widely in research, and, perhaps dubiously, has been reconceptualized by Salovey, Stroud, Woolery, and Epel (2002) as "perceived emotional intelligence."

We note from the outset that there are general concerns about contamination of self-reports by self-enhancing response styles. There is also a paradox inherent in expecting people with low EI to have insights into their own emotional functioning and thus rate their capabilities accurately. Studies of the related construct of alexithymia (difficulties in recognizing, verbalizing, and understanding feelings) demonstrate that some individuals have very limited capacities for reporting on their own emotional functioning (Taylor & Bagby, 2000).

The EQ-i comprises 15 scales grouped together into five higher-order composites: Intrapersonal Skills, Interpersonal Skills, Adaptation, Stress Management, and General Mood (Bar-On, 1997). Bar-On (2000) has conducted research establishing cross-cultural reliability and showing that the EQ-i predicts mental health, coping, work satisfaction, and personality traits associated with hardiness. Unfortu-

TABLE 1.2   **Sampling Domain and Scoring Methodology of Select Self-Report and Ability Measures of Emotional Intelligence**

Test	Sampling Domain	Tests	Scoring
Self-report scales			
EQ-i (Emotional Quotient Inventory) Bar-On, 1997	Intrapersonal, Interpersonal, Adaptation, Stress Management, General Mood	15 scales (132 items)	5-point scale; self-report
ECI (Emotional Competence Inventory) Boyatzis et al., 2000	Self-Awareness, Self-Management, Social Awareness, Social Skills	19 scales (63 items)	7-point scale; self, manager, direct, and peer reports
SSRI (Schutte Self-Report Index) Schutte et al., 1998	Four-branch hierarchical model	1 test: 33 items	5-point scale; self-report
TEIque (Trait Emotional Intelligence Questionnaire) Petrides & Furnham, 2003	Comprehensive domain sampling (mainly four-branch and EQ-i)	15 scales (144 items)	5-point scale: self-report
Ability scale			
MSCEIT (Mayer-Salovey-Caruso Emotional Intelligence Test Battery) Mayer et al., 2003	Four-branch hierarchical model, with Strategic and Experiential superfactors	8 subscales (2 per branch)	Rating scales & multiple choice, scored using consensus weights (general and expert)

nately, discriminant evidence supporting the scale remains uncertain. Dawda and Hart (2000) showed high correlations between the EQ-i and Big Five personality dimensions, including low Neuroticism and high Extraversion, Agreeableness, and Conscientiousness (with some of these correlations approaching .70). The (negative) correlations of the EQ-i with trait anxiety and psychiatric symptom scales are even higher (Bar-On, 1997; Newsome, Day, & Catano, 2000). The EQ-i appears also to be independent of general intelligence (Bar-On, 2000); the near zero correlations might be construed by some as problematic given it is meant to measure a form of intelligence. Equally vexing, the factor structure of the EQ-i is difficult to replicate, with considerable redundancy between scales (Matthews et al., 2002). Notwithstanding, it appears that the EQ-i correlates with various indices of well-being (e.g., Bar-On, 1997, 2000; Brackett & Mayer, 2003), establishing aspects of its validity. Similarly, Parker, Summerfeldt, Hogan, and Majeski (2004) showed that a short version of the EQ-i, given to Canadian first-year college students, predicts academic success at the end of the year. However, a more elaborately designed study shows that relations between the EQ-i and academic criteria are mediated by personality factors (Barchard, 2003).

The SSRI (Schutte et al., 1998) is based on Mayer et al.'s (2000b) conception of EI but appears somewhat similar to the EQ-i. Schutte et al. extracted four factors in their initial study. They claimed that the first represented a general factor of EI, and they discarded the remaining factors. However, confirmatory factor analyses have shown that the scale is not unidimensional; other researchers have suggested that the scale is made up of four distinct subfactors (Optimism/Mood Regulation, Appraisal of Emotions, Social Skills, and Utilization of Emotions) in addition to an overall EI factor (Austin, Saklofske, Huang, & McKenney, 2004; Petrides & Furnham, 2001). Like the EQ-i, the SSRI shows some convergent evidence, but again, at least part of this may be accounted for by its substantial overlap with personality. However, when compared with the EQ-i, the SSRI has two points in its favor: First, although still substantial, the correlations of the SSRI with the "Big Five" are smaller (i.e., the largest correlation was .51; Petrides & Furnham, 2001). Second, Saklofske, Austin, and Minsky (2003) showed that the SSRI predicted well-being even with the "Big Five" statistically controlled, although the incremental variance explained by the SSRI alone was rather small.

Ability Tests

Of the ability models, the most comprehensive is the four-branch (i.e., emotion identification, assimilating emotions into thought, under-

standing emotion, and emotion management) model, first represented in the MEIS (Mayer et al., 2000b). Other more specialized tests
include the Japanese and Caucasian Brief Affect Recognition Test
(JACBART), which involves assessment of emotion in faces
(Matsumoto et al., 2000); the Levels of Emotional Awareness Scale
(LEAS), which measures the sophistication of emotional language
(Lane, Quinlan, Schwartz, Walker, & Zeitlin, 1990); and the Emotional Accuracy Research Scale (EARS), a rating scale for the detection of emotions in stories (Geher, Warner, & Brown, 2001). The
abbreviated and refined version of the MEIS, the MSCEIT, comprises
eight subtests that collectively provide scores for the four branches, as
well as Strategic, Experiential, and overall EI. There are concerns
about the reliability of some of the subtests; however, reliability for the
higher order constructs (and especially General EI) is very good, ex-
ceeding .90 (Mayer et al., 2003). Furthermore, the MSCEIT is only
modestly correlated (typically, less than .30) with existing personality
and intelligence measures, providing evidence that it discriminates
some new construct. A recent meta-analysis estimates, for example,
that the correlation between the MEIS and general mental ability is
.30 (Van Rooy & Viswesvaran, 2004). Overall, it has a better claim to
measure some novel trait than does a questionnaire-based assessment of EI.

Although the MSCEIT appears one of the best scientifically based
measures of EI, it is far from problem free. As pointed out by several
commentators, there are difficulties with scoring the MSCEIT items;
how do we know if the answer to a test item is right or wrong (e.g.,
Brody, 2004; Matthews et al., 2002)? With a complex construct such
as EI, it is difficult to create a set of appropriate rules that specify
which responses are highly emotionally intelligent and which are not
(see Kerlinger, 1964). Mayer et al.'s (2000b, 2003) solution is to use
two scoring methods. *Expert scoring* requires that experts in the field
of emotion make the judgments of correct answers. However, experts
are fallible, there is the problem of determining what makes an expert, and experts from different fields may disagree as to the correct
answer. In contrast, the correct answer in *consensus scoring* is based
on the answer most frequently given by a normative sample. A person's EI is determined by the congruence of his or her answers with
those of the normative sample. This method raises the problem that
the popular belief about emotion may be false. Therefore, answers
may reflect social conformity rather than emotional competence. Furthermore, consensus scoring precludes the use of difficult items (i.e.,
those that might be answered correctly by a gifted minority) while simultaneously introducing a number of statistical anomalies (e.g.,
high negative skew; see MacCann, Roberts, Matthews, & Zeidner,

2004). The scoring method tends to identify a group of "majority-opinion" individuals that define a highly peaked cluster at the upper end of the distribution, together with a "tail" of individuals at the lower end, representing various degrees of nonconformity.

In support of these scoring methods, Mayer et al. (2003) showed a high degree of convergence between expert and consensus scores on the MSCEIT. Brody (2004), however, argues that MSCEIT items are qualitatively different from cognitive ability items. The latter directly assess problem-solving ability, whereas MSCEIT items relate "to knowledge of emotions but not necessarily the ability to perform tasks that are related to the knowledge that is assessed" (Brody, 2004, p. 234). Brody (2004) also points out that Mayer et al. have not addressed disagreements between experts. (One might add that it may be common cultural beliefs that generate similarities between experts, leading to the high correlation with consensus scoring.) Brody further charges that psychometric studies of the MSCEIT fail to establish the critical distinction between a latent trait of EI and the measurement model for that trait and that there is no convincing evidence for incremental predictive validity for the MSCEIT with respect to existing intelligence and personality tests (see Mayer et al., 2004, for a rejoinder).

A further source of difficulty is poor convergence between self-report and ability measures. Brackett and Mayer (2003) report weak correlations between the MSCEIT and EQ-i ® = .21) and SSRI ® = .18). With the Big Five personality traits controlled, these rs dropped to values that did not differ significantly from zero. Warwick and Nettelbeck (2004) reported a correlation of .18 between MSCEIT and TMMS total scores. Other studies have confirmed that self-report and ability-based EI scales measure essentially different constructs, suggesting convergent evidence is poor (MacCann, Matthews, et al., 2004).

Even within the domain of self-report measures, it is likely that different questionnaires measure different things. For example, Brackett and Mayer report only a moderate correlation between EQ-i and SSRI ® = .43; MacCann, Matthews, et al., 2004). Brackett and Mayer (2003) used factor analysis to discriminate one factor that combined the EQ-i with low Neuroticism, whereas a second, correlated factor had high loadings on the SSRI, extraversion, and well-being. There may be different brands of self-report EI that reflect the extent to which they pick up high positive affectivity (e.g., SSRI) versus low negative affectivity (e.g., EQ-i).

Future Prospects for Measurement and Assessment

Thus far, test developers have succeeded in producing scales that meet some basic psychometric criteria, notably reliability. Both personality and ability measures also demonstrate construct validity to the extent that they correlate with measures such as well-being and social adjustment (e.g., Brackett & Mayer, 2003), although very few studies have used objective behavioral measures, or controlled for personality and ability (cf., Brody, 2004). However, difficulties remain. The lack of convergent evidence across different measures of "emotional intelligence" is a problem for establishing the field as credible. One of the fundamental difficulties in measurement is that we are only able to measure properties of systems, not the systems themselves (Torgeson, 1958). In attempting to measure a new and fuzzily defined construct (like EI), the convergence of alternate measures becomes especially important. Currently, we do not know whether: (a) "true" EI does not exist and so is impossible to measure, (b) one of the existing tests measures "true" EI and the remainder measure existing constructs and trivia, or (c) several existing tests measure distinct facets of EI that could be interrelated in some more complex psychometric model. Discriminant evidence for validity, and especially the high degree of overlap between questionnaire measures and existing personality and well-being constructs, demonstrates the problems of self-report, although, possibly, better questionnaires may be constructed in the future. At the least, there appears to be a growing awareness among questionnaire developers of the need to develop scales that are clearly distinct from existing personality dimensions.

Also notable is the lack of any comprehensive multistratum model of constructs labeled as EI. The classic work of Carroll (1993) on intelligence provides an exemplar of good practice. He showed how primary constructs might be defined in terms of the latent factors common to specific intelligence tests. The intercorrelations of the primary factors in turn define intermediate or group level factors such as crystallized and fluid intelligence, whose intercorrelations define the general factor (g) at the apex. Somewhat less sophisticated multistratum models also exist for personality (with five top-level factors), allowing researchers to establish (at least modest) empirical linkage between personality and ability constructs (Ackerman & Heggestad, 1997; Zeidner & Matthews, 2000). By contrast, although EI researchers tend to assume that their instruments assess a top-level "EQ" analogous to a g factor, there is no evidence to support such contentions. It is entirely possible that even the best instruments assess only a specific primary ability. To put the point differently, we have no way to gauge perspective in viewing EI constructs: Are we looking at a range of towering peaks in the psychometric landscape or simply minor foothills?

Acknowledging many of the preceding limitations, we have begun to develop assessment instruments according to a taxonomic model that employs the four branches as a starting point, but further divides them in relation to the self and others, and still further by positive and negative affective dimensions (Roberts, Schulze, Matthews, & Zeidner, 2005). Using a variety of both new and established methodologies, we have created tests that are currently being given to samples of secondary school, community college, and university students at sites in the United States, Australia, Germany, and Israel. These methodologies include the situational judgment test paradigm (where participants rate a scenario for emotional relevance and/or salience), conditional reasoning approaches (where one of two correct responses to a conditional reasoning problem implies an aggressive outlook, the other a more passive set of inferences), and cloze techniques (where an emotional term completes, for example, a quote made by a famous philosopher). Many of these tests also borrow on text analysis; for example, scenarios constructed for an emotion perception measure may be evaluated for "correctness" using the "Linguistic Inquiry and Word Count" method (see Pennebaker, Francis, & Booth, 2001). It is our hope that these "next generation" measures, which were constructed using many of the principles outlined earlier in this chapter, may move the field forward. Tantamount in this process will be not only demonstration of acceptable psychometric properties but also meaningful correlations with criteria like grade point average (GPA), student attrition rates, mental health, and perceived social support.

BUILDING THEORIES: EMOTIONAL INTELLIGENCE AND VALIDATION

The aim of many of the studies reviewed thus far has been to show that the test predicts some external criterion, concurrently or in the future. As we suggested earlier, the validation process requires still further steps, including demonstrating that the correlations between test and criteria may be explained and predicted by a coherent theory of the construct. In the context of EI, Matthews and Zeidner (2000) propose two further steps. First, the test must predict intervening processes that control the criterion of interest, as predicted by a theory. Second, to the extent that EI represents an ability rather than a qualitative style of behavior, it must be shown that the criterion relates to individual differences in adaptive success or failure (i.e., that high EI leads to outcomes that are generally positive). For example, suppose that the Smith EI test correlates with the Jones well-being measure (with personality and cognitive ability controlled), that is, a demonstration that it is predictive of an important criterion. Construct validity also requires identification of intervening processes specified by some theory of EI (e.g., more positive appraisals of life events), and evidence that the Jones well-being measure relates to positive outcomes such as greater objective life success or superior health.

Current accounts of EI tend to be weak on specification of mediating processes and on validating tests as measures of individual differences in adaptive outcome. As discussed previously, a common weakness of current EI theories is that they deal with *functions* rather than *processes*. Thus, individual differences in emotion perception might be influenced by several, separate processes, including subcortical analysis of key facial features, retrieval of information in memory about the other person, focusing attention on cues to emotion, and assimilating contextual information such as knowledge of the person's motives. It is unclear if these varied processes cohere around some common construct. With respect to adaptation, it is plausible that superior emotion perception helps the individual to handle life encounters successfully, but empirical evidence on the importance and relevance of the function in real life is lacking. How often does misreading emotions make a substantial difference to social encounters? Are people that score poorly on laboratory emotion perception tests actually disadvantaged in real life? Are some misperceptions, such as overestimating the friendliness of others, sometimes beneficial? Research has not adequately addressed such questions and, in fact, raises some warning flags. For example, Ciarrochi, Dean, and Anderson (2002), found, first, that self-report and objective emotion perception measures are uncorrelated, and, second, that individuals with good objective emotion perception reported greater negative affective responses to daily hassles. Awareness of the (negative) emotions of others may carry costs as well as benefits.

These issues are pressing because our culture encourages us to believe in "myths" or propositions about emotion that may not in fact be correct. For example, it is widely believed that "working through" and expressing grief is more beneficial and "emotionally intelligent" than suppressing it. In fact, the evidence tells a different story. Focusing on and expressing negative emotions is associated with delayed recovery from bereavement; indeed, therapies that focus on working through grief can be harmful in some instances (Bonnano, 2004). Another cultural belief is that high self-esteem is intrinsically beneficial, so that parents and schools are encouraged to boost the self-esteem of children. However, high self-esteem may have a "dark side," associated with narcissism, denial of problems, and excessive self-enhancement (Baumeister, Smart, & Boden, 1996). As a third example, it is believed that women are more empathic than men, but research on person perception suggests a gender difference in interest rather than in ability (Graham & Ickes, 1997). Although women score higher than men on empathy scales, conventional intelligence is, ironically, a better predictor of empathic accuracy than is self-report empathy (Davis & Kraus, 1997).

El and Stress

We explore the problems of establishing construct validity further with reference to stress and well-being. As previously discussed, much of the evidence for the validity of EI measures comes from studies showing associations between EI and questionnaire scales for various aspects of well-being and stress. Thus, it becomes important to demonstrate that (a) EI is a causal influence on the cognitive and physiological processes that control the stress response, and (b) the processes and outcomes influenced by EI confer a genuine adaptive advantage. Many theories of EI contend that lack of emotional competence may compromise the ability to cope adaptively with changing circumstances (see Matthews & Zeidner, 2000, for a review). Bar-On (2000) places adaptability at the center of this conceptualization and includes within the EQ-i scales for measuring resilience and stress management. High EI may also be advantageous in the regulation of moods and self-referent thoughts (Ciarrochi, Chan, & Caputi, 2000; Ciarrochi et al., 2002; Salovey, Bedell, Detweiler, & Mayer, 2000). In fact, there are multiple pathways through which EI might bias the stress process described by contemporary, transactional models of stress (e.g., Lazarus, 1999). In a recent review, we list the following candidate mechanisms as follows (see Zeidner, Matthews, & Roberts, in press):

1. *Use of effective and flexible coping strategies*: Deployment of strategies that resolve challenging situations effectively and selection of strategies appropriate for the specific situation.
2. *Avoidance of stressful encounters*: Use of personal insight to avoid situations that are unduly distressing or emotionally damaging (without running away from worthy challenges).
3. *More constructive perceptions and situational appraisals*: Constructive evaluation of situations, so as to find opportunities for personal growth and to avoid maladaptive construals (Epstein, 1998).
4. *Adaptive regulation and repairing of emotions*: More effective management of emotion, entailing clarity of emotional experience, and effective repair of negative emotional states (Salovey et al., 2000).
5. *Richer coping resources*: More extensive personal and social resources for coping with adversity, such as the availability of rich social networks to provide an emotional buffer against negative life events (Salovey et al., 2000).

Research is only beginning to investigate some of these processes. Bar-On (1997, 2000) reported that the EQ-i correlates moderately with high problem-focused coping and low emotion-focused coping, a pattern that might be seen as adaptive. However, this is exactly the result to be expected based on the confounding of the EQ-i with low Neuroticism, which is similarly related to coping (Endler & Parker, 1999): for example, Bar-On (1997, 2000) failed to control for personality confounds in interpreting EI-coping correlations. More counterintuitively, Furnham, Petrides, and Spencer-Bowdage (2002) showed a positive association between the SSRI and repressive coping, that is, coping through suppressing feelings of anxiety and other negative emotions. Most experts would not judge repressive coping to be an "intelligent" response.

Experimental studies suggest that skills in mood management relate to EI as measured by both the SSRI (Ciarrochi, Chan, & Bajgar, 2001) and the MEIS (Ciarrochi et al., 2000). Comparable results were reported in a study using the TMMS (Salovey et al., 2002), an instrument that assesses self-reported mood regulation rather than EI, per se. In this study, self-reported "mood repair" (i.e., attempts to manage negative moods) was found to relate to greater active coping, less passive coping, less rumination, and a perception of laboratory stressors as being less threatening. However, Salovey et al.'s data also showed that mood repair was quite substantially correlated with self-esteem, and they did not control for the influence of this confound. This study is also one of the few to use a measure of stress response other than self-report: The attention subscale of the TMMS was found to be related to reduced cortisol reactivity.

A third line of research has been concerned with social skills and social support. Several studies using questionnaire assessments of EI have shown associations with seeking social support (e.g., Chan, 2003; Ciarrochi et al., 2001; Gohm & Clore, 2002). Chan's (2003) study used the SSRI, which includes items that aim to assess social skills, so there may be some overlap between predictor and criterion. A study using the MSCEIT (Lopes, Salovey, & Strauss, 2003) failed to find any relationship between overall EI and self-report measures of social skills and social support. However, the Managing Emotions subfactor of the MSCEIT was modestly predictive of these criteria; this is a finding we have subsequently replicated in Norway for functional social support but not structural social support (Aicher, Storladen, Zeidner, Matthews, & Roberts, in preparation).

Indeed, we take these initial findings as suggesting that scales for EI have some promise as predictors of stress processes, although we also note the heterogeneity of EI measures, frequent failure to control for personality confounds, and overreliance on self-report criteria.

The next issue is whether the styles of processing favored by high EI individuals actually confer adaptive benefits. We note from the outset that a basic tenet of transactional theory suggests that styles of appraisal and coping cannot be prejudged as being universally adaptive or maladaptive (see Lazarus, 1999). Indeed, empirical studies often fail to confirm common assumptions, for example, that problem-focused coping is universally superior to emotion-focused coping (Zeidner & Saklofske, 1996; see also Zeidner et al., in press).

For the most part, EI researchers have failed to present independent evidence for the adaptiveness of the criteria examined in studies of stress. Indeed, published studies of mood regulation suggest that the association between EI and adaptation may not be straightforward. For example, although Ciarrochi et al. (2000) found that the SSRI was related to mood-regulation strategies, EI did not moderate emotional response to negative and positive mood inductions used in the study, so it is unclear that the strategies favored by high scorers on the SSRI actually help to alter mood adaptively. By contrast, Petrides and Furnham (2003) showed that EI (assessed by the TEIque) related to stronger mood response to both positive and negative mood inductions. These data suggest that EI relates to emotional sensitivity, but there is no evidence that EI relates to skills in maintaining positive mood in unhappy circumstances. More generally, such studies highlight the fundamental problem of deciding whether changes in subjective state are adaptive (or, for that matter, "intelligent"); we cannot say it is necessarily maladaptive to experience negative moods. As Matthews et al. (2002) discuss, negative affectivity may confer a mixture of adaptive costs and benefits, the latter including anticipation of threat and awareness of potential danger.

A recent study further illustrates the difficulty in showing that tests for EI index individual differences in stress processes that confer a genuine adaptive advantage. Matthews et al. (in press) conducted an experimental study of 200 participants in which stress was induced using high workload tasks. Subjective response, situational coping, and task performance were assessed. Personality confounds were controlled using a standard measure of the Big Five personality traits. The study provided partial support for the utility of the MSCEIT as a predictor of task-induced stress states: EI was associated with lower worry and lower avoidance coping during performance, even with personality controlled. However, effect sizes were small, and EI failed to predict the task-induced stress response (i.e., changes in subjective state induced by task performance). Indeed, if anything, EI was more strongly correlated with reduced worry in a nonstressful condition than in the task stress conditions. EI was also uncorrelated with objective performance, which was better predicted by personality traits. Thus, contrary to much theorizing, high EI does not seem to provide protection against the impact of task stressors and is not adaptive to the extent of promoting better objective performance.

Thus, many questions and uncertainties concerning construct validation remain. At this early stage of test development, it has perhaps been reasonable for EI researchers to focus on convergent and discriminant evidence and test-criterion relationships. Nevertheless, it is troubling that so little is known about the basis for correlations between EI and well-being, which provide the most robust validity evidence for EI tests thus far. To reiterate points made previously: Progress in construct validation may require discrimination of multiple constructs *and* a willingness to consider these constructs as qualities other than abilities.

EMOTIONAL INTELLIGENCE ON THE LOOSE: APPLICATIONS AND UTILITY

Although research supporting the validity of EI appears modest, there remains a great deal of hype surrounding the utility of EI in a variety of settings. We focus here on organizational applications, although there is interest among educators, clinicians, and health professionals alike in the construct (Roberts et al., 2005). On the heels of his bestseller, Goleman (1998) has published a second book heralding the use of EI in successful workplace settings, in the process also advocating its use in the selection and promotion of employees. Indeed, many workplaces are making the move to become more "emotionally intelligent." Corporations are selecting managers based on their EI quotient, EI tests are being required of new hires in some employment settings, and seminars promising to increase EI have become the standard fare of staff in-service. However, one might worry that the corporate world has walked into the EI realm lulled by the bright lights and flashy claims, unaware that the scientific footing they are resting on may be less than solid. Indeed, criticisms of the conceptualization and assessment of EI have begun to appear in the management literature (e.g., Becker, 2003).

Current literature on the subject of the utility of EI in the workplace has been written from a largely managerial perspective (e.g., Ashkanasy, Zerbe, & Hartel, 2002; Lord, Klimoski, & Kanfer, 2002). There is interest in EI both as a predictor of job performance, and hence a selection tool, and as a quality that might be trained. Some qualitative studies have supported the view that EI is a valuable personal quality. Cross and Travaglione (2003) used a structured interview technique to assess EI in highly successful Australian entrepreneurs. This study found that in addition to the high general EI scores of these individuals, they all had high scores on all subscales of EI. The authors advocate EI as the missing piece of the puzzle to explain entrepreneurial success. However, there are several relevant variables that were uncontrolled in this study, and it is possible that the interview technique, structured though it may be, may have been subject to interviewer bias.

In reviewing empirical research on the validity of EI in occupational settings, Zeidner, Matthews, and Roberts (2004) concluded that the various scales for EI are, at best, weak predictors of job performance, although EI may be rather more predictive of job satisfaction (Slaski & Cartwright, 2002). On a positive note, several studies have demonstrated significant correlations between EI measures and ratings of performance (e.g., Higgs, 2004; Slaski & Cartwright, 2002), and Jordan, Ashkanasy, and Hartel (2002) reported an interesting study relating EI to team performance. Other recent studies illustrate the concerns expressed by Zeidner et al. (2004). For example, Charbonneau and Nicol (2002) investigated the SSRI and items from a scale developed by Weisinger (1998) as predictors of leadership in adolescents attending a military training camp. Both scales appeared to be contaminated by social desirability, and the SSRI failed to predict peer nominations of individuals as leaders. The Weisinger scale did correlate with peer nominations of leadership, but there was no correlation between self-rated and other-rated versions of the scale. In a study of customer service teams, Feyerherm and Rice (2002) found that, at the team level, a short version of the MEIS predicted some subjective performance criteria, including customer service but not productivity. However, contrary to expectation, several significant negative correlations were found between the EI of the team leader and team performance. The authors speculate that "emotionally intelligent" team leaders may focus on being considerate to team members at the expense of actual work activities. A recent study of 290 workers in the United Kingdom focused on well-being at work (Donaldson-Feilder & Bond, 2004). Results of the study showed that with psychological acceptance and job control statistically controlled, EI did not significantly predict any of the well-being outcomes, including job satisfaction. The authors suggest that it may be more important to accept one's thoughts and feelings, rather than to try to control and regulate them.

Van Rooy and Viswesvaran's (2004) previously discussed meta-analysis included 69 studies of EI and performance, although, importantly, many of these studies, even now, have not appeared in the peer-reviewed literature. A mean correlation of .20 (corrected to .23) was found, a validity coefficient far short of the .50 or so typical of mental ability tests. The corrected correlation for the 19 studies of work performance was .24. One concern is that occupational studies typically use supervisor ratings: Given that EI scales typically correlate with social involvement and desirable personality characteristics, such ratings may be confounded by a halo effect. Another serious problem is that studies have typically ignored the personality and ability confounds of EI tests, which might be responsible for the modest validity coefficients that have been reported. On the flip side, the criterion that EI might need to predict in work settings remains poorly operationalized and in need of urgent attention.

Goleman (1995) has argued that EI, unlike academic intelligence, is able to increase throughout the life span and individuals can be trained to have higher "EQs." Many have hoped that, if EI is truly trainable, EI will provide an intelligence measure that is unaffected by socioeconomic status, access to education, and other factors (such as adverse impact) that tend to taint traditional intelligence test scores. The benefits of training EI, however, remain to be demonstrated satisfactorily. For example, Slaski and Cartwright (2002) found that a training program improved EQ-i scores but had no effect on ratings of managerial performance. Training studies using objective measures to assess interventions would arguably be more compelling, with the interventions perhaps tailored to each of the specific dimensions provided by the four-branch model. There is an urgent need to conduct these types of studies, as well as suitably designed longitudinal studies, which would ultimately give measures of EI (if suggestive) greater impact in the occupational context.

These facts notwithstanding, EI has become increasingly prominent in educational and school psychology. The Collaborative of Academic, Social, and Emotional Learning (CASEL) has highlighted the importance of training students' social and emotional learning (SEL) skills and evaluating programs intended to improve such skills (Greenberg et al., 2003; Zins, Weissberg, Wang, Walberg, & Goleman, 2004). Measured against criteria including psychological test scores, and children's, parents', and teachers' evaluations of behavior, such programs have achieved signal success in areas such as mental health, antisocial behaviors, and academic performance and learning, as evidenced by several meta-analytic reviews (Greenberg et al., 2003). However, as we have discussed in a review of EI and education, it is unclear that such programs owe much to laboratory studies of EI, and few have sought to measure (or alter) EI directly (Zeidner, Roberts, & Matthews, 2002).

CONCLUSIONS

Despite popular enthusiasm, current research on EI raises many issues; the answer to the question "What is this thing called EI?" remains elusive. In fact, the clearest conclusion from the evidence is that the inflated claims made for the importance of EI in the popular literature are simply untrue. We see little evidence in the validation studies that would support the current use of existing EI measures for making real-life, high-stakes decisions for individuals. Such measures are not suitable for occupational selection or allocating people to training or remedial programs, for example. On a more positive note, published studies suggest that this field of inquiry may have made some modest, incremental progress in identifying new personality and (arguably) ability constructs. Regrettably, much effort has been wasted developing questionnaire measures that repackage established personality traits. There remains scope for developing questionnaires that expand the personality sphere, and self-reports of mood regulation style (e.g., Salovey et al., 1995) may be especially promising in this respect.

Our evaluation of the leading ability tests, the MEIS and MSCEIT, is mixed. There is some discriminant evidence for these instruments, especially with respect to personality and general intelligence, but more work on demonstrating convergent aspects of validity and the place of latent constructs in a multistratum psychometric model is needed. Validity coefficients for both the MEIS and MSCEIT are very modest, especially when personality and ability are controlled (Brackett & Mayer, 2003; Brody, 2004; cf. also Mayer, Salovey, & Caruso, 2004). The issue of veridical scoring for a measure of this kind remains a serious concern, given the deficiencies of both expert and consensual scoring techniques. At the same time, the development of additional objective tests is a priority for the field. As discussed above, there are various methods that may be useful, although it is currently unclear whether any will yield measures that are structurally independent of existing constructs. We are cautiously optimistic that there are indeed new ability dimensions to be discovered by these techniques; at the least, interest in EI may prove a "soupstone" that stimulates research on emotional functioning (Matthews et al., 2002). Applied programs seeking to measure and enhance emotional competence are also likely to be of value, and their utility has been demonstrated in the educational field (Zins et al., 2004). Our major concern here is whether educational programs are simply training specific skills, as opposed to enhancing general emotional intelligence.

In a recent state-of-the-art review, we identified seven common myths concerning EI, that is, beliefs widely held but not adequately substantiated (Matthews et al., 2004). Table 1.3 provides a summary of these beliefs. We were optimistic about prospects in some areas, such as improving the psychometric properties of existing instruments and relating EI constructs to stress processes and coping. Other myths, such as the view that there exists an EQ as important for emotions as IQ is to cognition are, on balance of available evidence, likely erroneous. Other issues, such as the optimum assessment

TABLE 1.3   Summary of Seven Myths Concerning EI Identified by Matthews et al., 2004

Myth	Status	Prospects for Future Progress
1. Definitions of EI are conceptually coherent.	Several different and conflicting definitions, with varying degrees of internal coherence.	Fair. Current work does not adequately address the possible roles of implicit skills and person–environment fit. Progress requires better consensus among researchers on what EI is and is not, with greater reference to theories of emotion and intelligence. However, researchers may be reluctant to abandon cherished but incorrect assumptions about the nature of EI.
2. Measures of EI may meet standard psychometric criteria.	Some progress has been made. Test reliabilities are often good. Conceptual problems lead to questions concerning match between test content and theory. Despite promising beginnings, evidence for test-criterion relationships is limited. Lack of convergence between self-report and ability-based tests is a major issue.	Good. The normal processes of test development may suffice to improve reliability and test-criterion relationships. Problems matching content to theory, establishing convergent and discriminant evidence, and other forms of validity evidence are more difficult, owing to the uncertain conceptual and theoretical bases for EI. Following historical precedent in ability testing, development of psychometrically sound measures, and a conceptually derived multistratum model may lead to theoretical progress.
3. Self-report EI is distinct from existing personality constructs.	A severe problem, with considerable overlap with Big Five, and narrower "mid-level" personality constructs (e.g., empathy, self-esteem, optimism).	Poor to fair. The lack of discriminant evidence from personality severely limits the utility of self-report. Evidence that self-reported emotional competence fails to predict objective measures of EI is discouraging. At best, questionnaire scales may add further primary or mid-level personality traits that add somewhat to current personality models.
4. Ability tests for EI meet criteria for a cognitive intelligence.	It is still unclear whether ability tests measure a form of intelligence, while difficulties establishing veridical criteria for scoring are potentially serious.	Fair. Current tests may or may not measure ability. Essential future work includes validating test scores against behavioral indices of competence and further investigating the universe of emotional competencies to identify a set of primary abilities that may jointly support a higher order EI factor.

(continued)

TABLE 1.3 (continued)

Myth	Status	Prospects for Future Progress
5. EI relates to emotion as IQ relates to cognition.	The notion of separate cognitive and emotional systems that each has its own "intelligence" is conceptually confusing and conflicts with theories of emotion and self-regulation.	Poor. Models of self-regulation and executive function that integrate cognitive, emotional, and motivational functioning appear to be more likely to explain empirical data, although linking such models to the various different psychometric abilities remains a considerable challenge, even within the intellectual domain.
6. EI predicts adaptive coping.	EI tests may correlate with coping scales and outcome measures, sometimes. However, it is simplistic to suppose such findings support a single continuum of individual differences in adaptation.	Good. As with other personal qualities that relate to the stress process, normal research should be informative about which outcomes and processes may be influenced by the various components of EI. However, such research is likely to provide a much more complex and nuanced picture of the personal advantages (and, possibly, disadvantages) of the qualities currently described as EI.
7. EI is critical for real-world success.	So far, applied studies provide little basis for supposing either that EI is strongly predictive of outcomes in real-world settings, or that interventions to increase EI will be cost-effective.	Fair. Current progress appears too limited to offer much to the practitioner, given the availability of better validated personality and ability measures. Over time, we expect tests for emotional skills and knowledge to have greater utility, although it is unclear whether such tests will resemble those in current use. It is also moot whether it will ever be preferable for interventions to target generalized EI, as opposed to more specific, context-bound skills.

strategy for measuring abilities and the practical importance of EI tests, cannot, on the balance of available evidence, be determined. We look forward to further research that will increase the ratio of "knowns" to "unknowns" in this emerging science. However, a key conceptual point for further progress is recognition that there are multiple types of constructs that contribute to emotional competence, some of which are well-known already (Matthews et al., 2004, 2005).

We conclude with the following recommendations for improving test development and measurement practice in the field (see MacCann et al., 2003):

1. A major goal of test development should be to place tests within a multistratum model of latent constructs that includes personality and conventional ability constructs. Thus, research on measuring EI cannot be performed in isolation from research on existing constructs.

2. It should be recognized that "emotional intelligence" is open to multiple definitions (and may or may not exist). Thus, we recommend a focused sweep of different types of construct including, minimally, the various conceptualizations differentiated previously. Initially, it may be preferable to direct test development toward multiple primary abilities, such as emotion perception (Davies et al., 1998), in that questions about higher level dimensional structure cannot be answered without some acceptable sampling of lower level constructs.

3. The difficulties of measuring EI through self-report should be properly acknowledged. We suggest a moratorium on the use and development of instruments that share the majority of their variance with the Big Five personality traits. As with measurement in general, we suggest that future research should be focused on identifying *new* traits that expand the range of measurable individual differences in personality.

4. Further development of objective tests is the main priority. Researchers have generally neglected the use of objective measures, such as speed and accuracy measures obtained from information-processing tasks. There also appears to be scope for using techniques such as the situational judgment test paradigm, conditional reasoning approaches, implicit learning methods, and the like, embedded within technology, including principles borrowed from linguistic analysis and affective computing (Matthews et al., in preparation). We reit-

erate that the scope and validity of latent constructs related to such tests will require further validation, a process we are involved with right now. Further work on the construct validity of the best existing test of this kind, the MSCEIT, would also be valuable. It is currently unclear whether it measures genuine abilities, declarative knowledge of emotion, or conformity with cultural values and beliefs.

5. It is also important to focus more on the validation process. If there are indeed multiple constructs under the umbrella of EI, it is important that theory sharpens the conceptual distinctions between them, by specifying the physiological, cognitive, and social processes to which they relate. It is time to move beyond simple demonstrations that EI measures correlate with well-being and related criteria to explore the underlying mechanisms. It is essential also to adopt a more contextualized perspective, which looks at how such mechanisms may be helpful (or damaging) in dealing with specific challenges and social encounters. We expect that many of the constructs labeled as EI, such as sensitivity to emotion and high self-confidence, may prove to be double-edged swords that confer both costs and benefits, depending on the context.

6. There is a marked disconnection between theory and practice, which should be addressed. For the most part, programs for improving social and emotional competence are not directly based on the emerging science of emotional competence. Instead, "emotional intelligence" is useful for publicity, a banner that highlights and energizes existing programs. It remains unclear what the practitioner can usefully take from the psychological research, but we may hope for greater communication, in both directions, between basic and applied researchers.

REFERENCES

Ackerman, P. L., & Heggestad, E. D. (1997). Intelligence, personality and interests: Evidence for overlapping traits. *Psychological Bulletin, 121,* 219–245.

Aicher, C., Storladen, M., Zeidner, M., Matthews, G., & Roberts, R. D. (in preparation). *A multivariate investigation of emotional intelligence and social support.*

American Educational Research Association, American Psychological Association, and National Council on Measurement in Education (1999). *Standards for educational and psychological testing.* Washington, DC: AERA.

Anderson, J. R. (1996). ACT: A simple theory of complex cognition. *American Psychologist, 51,* 355–365.

Ashkanasy, N. M., Zerbe, W. J., & Hartel, C. E. J. (2002). *Managing emotions in the workplace.* Armonk, NY: M. E. Sharpe.

Austin, E. J., Saklofske, D. H., Huang, S. H. S., & McKenney, D. (2004). Measurement of trait emotional intelligence: Testing and cross-validating a modified version of Schutte et al.'s (1998) measure. *Personality and Individual Differences, 36,* 555–562.

Barchard, K. A. (2003). Does emotional intelligence assist in the prediction of academic success? *Educational and Psychological Measurement, 63,* 840–858.

Bar-On, R. (1997). *The Emotional Intelligence Inventory (EQ-i): Technical manual.* Toronto, ON: Multi-Health Systems.

Bar-On, R. (2000). Emotional and social intelligence: Insights from the Emotional Quotient Inventory. In R. Bar-On & J. D. A. Parker (Eds.), *The handbook of emotional intelligence* (pp. 363–388). San Francisco: Jossey-Bass.

Baumeister, R.F., Smart, L., & Boden, J.M. (1996). Relation of threatened egotism to violence and aggression: The dark side of high self-esteem. *Psychological Review, 103,* 5–33.

Becker, T. (2003). Is emotional intelligence a viable concept? *Academy of Management Review, 28,* 192–195.

Bonanno, G. A. (2004). Loss, trauma, and human resilience: Have we underestimated the human capacity to thrive after extremely aversive events? *American Psychologist, 59,* 20–28.

Boyatzis, R. E., Goleman, D., & Rhee, K. (2000). Clustering competence in emotional intelligence: Insights from the Emotional Competence Inventory (ECI). In R. Bar-On & J. D. A. Parker (Eds.), *The handbook of emotional intelligence* (pp. 343–362). San Francisco: Jossey-Bass.

Brackett, M. A., & Mayer, J. D. (2003). Convergent, discriminant, and incremental validity of competing measures of emotional intelligence. *Personality and Social Psychology Bulletin, 29,* 1147–1158.

Brody, N. (2004).What cognitive intelligence is, and emotional intelligence is not. *Psychological Inquiry, 15,* 234–238.

Carroll, J. B. (1993). *Human cognitive abilities: A survey of factor-analytic studies.* New York: Cambridge University Press.

Chan, D. W. (2003). Dimensions of emotional intelligence and their relationships with social coping among gifted adolescents in Hong Kong. *Journal of Youth and Adolescence, 32,* 409–418.

Charbonneau, D., & Nicol, A. A. M. (2002). Emotional intelligence and prosocial behaviors in adolescents. *Psychological Reports, 90,* 361–370.

Ciarrochi, J. V., Chan, A. Y. C., & Caputi, P. (2000). A critical evaluation of the emotional intelligence construct. *Personality and Individual Differences, 28,* 539–561.

Ciarrochi, J. V., Dean, F. P., & Anderson, S. (2002). Emotional intelligence moderates the relationship between stress and mental health. *Personality and Individual Differences, 32,* 197–209.

Ciarrochi, J., Chan, A., & Bajgar, J. (2001). Measuring emotional intelligence in adolescents. *Personality and Individual Differences, 31,* 1105–1119.

Cronbach, L., & Meehl, P. (1955). Construct validity in psychological tests. *Psychological Bulletin, 52,* 281–302.

Cross, B., & Travaglione, A. (2003). The untold story: Is the entrepreneur of the 21st century defined by emotional intelligence? *International Journal of Organizational Analysis, 11*, 221– 228.

Davies, M., Stankov, L., & Roberts, R. D. (1998). Emotional intelligence: In search of an elusive construct. *Journal of Personality and Social Psychology, 75*, 989– 1015.

Davis, M. H., & Kraus, L. A. (1997). Personality and empathic accuracy. In W. Ickes (Ed.), *Empathic accuracy* (pp. 144–168). New York: Guilford Press.

Dawda, D., & Hart, S. D. (2000). Assessing emotional intelligence: Reliability and validity of the Bar-On Emotional Quotient Inventory (EQ-i) in university students. *Personality & Individual Differences, 28*, 797–812.

Denham, S. A. (1998). *Emotional development in young children.* New York: Guilford Press.

Donaldson-Feilder, E. J., & Bond, F. W. (2004). The relative importance of psychological acceptance and emotional intelligence to workplace well-being. *British Journal of Guidance and Counselling, 32*, 187–203.

Endler, N., & Parker, J. (1999). *The Coping Inventory for Stressful Situations (CISS) Manual* (2nd ed.). Toronto, ON: Multi-Health Systems.

Epstein, S. (1998). *Constructive thinking: The key to emotional intelligence.* New York: Praeger.

Feyerherm, A. E., & Rice, C. L. (2002). Emotional intelligence and team performance: The good, the bad and the ugly. *International Journal of Organizational Analysis, 10*, 343–362.

Furnham, A., Petrides, K. V., & Spencer-Bowdage, S. (2002). The effects of different types of social desirability on the identification of repressors. *Personality and Individual Differences, 33*, 119–130.

Geher, G., Warner, R. M., & Brown, A. S. (2001). Predictive validity of the Emotional Accuracy Research Scale. *Intelligence, 29*, 373–388.

Gohm, C. L., & Clore, G. L. (2002). Four latent traits of emotional experience and their involvement in well-being, coping, and attributional style. *Cognition & Emotion, 16*, 495–518.

Goleman, D. (1995). *Emotional intelligence.* New York: Bantam Books.

Goleman, D. (1998). *Working with emotional intelligence.* New York: Bantam Books.

Graham, T., & Ickes, W. (1997). When women's intuition isn't greater than men's. In W. Ickes (Ed.), *Empathic accuracy* (pp. 117–143). New York: Guilford Press.

Greenberg, M. T., Weissberg, R. P., O'Brien, M.U., Zins, J. E., Fredericks, L., Resnik, H., et al. (2003). Enhancing school-based prevention and youth development through coordinated social, emotional, and academic learning. *American Psychologist, 58*, 466–474.

Higgs, M. (2004). A study of the relationship between emotional intelligence and performance in UK call centres. *Journal of Managerial Psychology, 19*, 442–454.

Jordan, P. J., Ashkanasy, N. M., & Hartel, C. E. J. (2002). Emotional intelligence as a moderator of emotional and behavioral reactions to job insecurity. *Academy of Management Review, 27*, 361–372.

Kerlinger, F.N. (1964). *Foundations of behavioural research* (2nd ed.). New York: Holt, Rinehart & Winston.

Kihlstrom, J. F., & Cantor, N. (2000). Social intelligence. In R. J. Sternberg (Ed.), *Handbook of intelligence* (pp. 359–379). New York: Cambridge University Press.

Kochanska, G., & Coy, K. C. (2002). Child emotionality and maternal responsiveness as predictors of reunion behaviors in the Strange Situation: Links mediated and unmediated by separation distress. *Child Development, 73,* 228–240.

Lane, R. D., Quinlan, D. M., Schwartz, G. E., Walker, P. A., & Zeitlin, S. B. (1990). The Levels of Emotional Awareness Scale: A cognitive-development measure of emotion. *Journal of Personality Assessment, 55,* 124–134.

Lazarus, R. S. (1999). *Stress and emotions: A new synthesis.* New York: Springer.

Lopes, P. N., Salovey, P., & Strauss, R. (2003). Emotional intelligence, personality, and the perceived quality of social relationships. *Personality and Individual Differences, 35,* 641–658.

Lord, R. G., Klimoski, R. J., & Kanfer, R. (Eds.) (2002). *Emotions in the workplace: Understanding the structure and role of emotions in organizational behavior.* San-Francisco: Jossey-Bass.

MacCann, C., Matthews, G., Zeidner, M., & Roberts, R. D. (2003). Psychological assessment of emotional intelligence: A review of self-report and performance-based testing. *The International Journal of Organizational Analysis, 11,* 247–274.

MacCann, C., Roberts, R. D., Matthews, G., & Zeidner, M. (2004). Consensus scoring and empirical option weighting of performance-based Emotional Intelligence (EI) tests. *Personality and Individual Differences, 36,* 645–662.

Matsumoto, D., LeRoux, J., Wilson-Cohn, C., Raroque, J., Kooken, K., Ekman, P., et al. (2000). A new test to measure emotion recognition ability: Matsumoto and Ekman's Japanese and Caucasian Brief Affect Recognition Test (JACBART). *Journal of Nonverbal Behavior, 24,* 179–209.

Matthews, G., Emo, A. K, Funke, G., Zeidner, M., Roberts, R. D., Costa, P. T., et al. (in press). Emotional intelligence, personality, and task-induced stress. *Journal of Experimental Psychology: Applied.*

Matthews, G., Roberts, R. D., & Zeidner, M. (2004). Seven myths about emotional intelligence. *Psychological Inquiry, 15,* 179–196.

Matthews, G., Zeidner, M., & Roberts, R. D. (2002). *Emotional intelligence: Science and myth.* Boston: MIT Press.

Matthews, G., Zeidner, M., & Roberts, R.D. (2005). Emotional intelligence: An elusive ability? In O. Wilhelm & R. Engle (Eds.), *Handbook of understanding and measuring intelligence* (pp. 79–99). Thousand Oaks, CA: Sage.

Mayer, J. D., Caruso, D., & Salovey, P. (1999). Emotional intelligence meets traditional standards for an intelligence. *Intelligence, 27,* 267–298.

Mayer, J. D., Salovey, P. R., & Caruso, D. R. (2000a). Emotional intelligence as *Zeitgeist,* as personality, and as a mental ability. In R. Bar-On & J. D. A. Parker (Eds.), *The handbook of emotional intelligence* (pp. 92–117). San Francisco: Jossey-Bass.

Mayer, J. D., Salovey, P., & Caruso, D. R. (2000b). Models of emotional intelligence. In R. J. Sternberg (Ed.), *Handbook of human intelligence* (2nd ed., pp. 396–422). New York: Cambridge University Press.

Mayer, J. D., Salovey, P., & Caruso, D. R. (2004). Emotional intelligence: Theory, findings, and implications. *Psychological Inquiry, 15,* 197–215.

Mayer, J. D., Salovey, P., Caruso, D. R., & Sitarenios, G. (2003). Modeling and measuring emotional intelligence with the MSCEIT V2.0. *Emotion, 3,* 97–105.

McCrae, R. R. (2000). Emotional intelligence from the perspective of the Five-Factor Model of Personality. In R. Bar-On & J. D. A. Parker (Eds.), *The handbook of emotional intelligence* (pp. 263–276). San Francisco: Jossey-Bass.

Newsome, S., Day, A. L, & Catano, V. M. (2000). Assessing the predictive validity of emotional intelligence. *Personality and Individual Differences, 29,* 1005–1016.

Parker, J. D. A., Summerfeldt, L. J., Hogan, M. J., & Majeski, S. A. (2004). Emotional intelligence and academic success: examining the transition from high school to university. *Personality and Individual Differences, 36,* 163–172.

Pennebaker, J. W., Francis, M. E., & Booth, R. J. (2001). *Linguistic inquiry and word count (LIWC).* Mahwah, NJ: Lawrence Erlbaum Associates.

Pérez, J. C. (2003, July). *How can emotional intelligence be measured?* Poster presented at the 11th Biennial Meeting of the International Society for the Study of Individual Differences, Graz, Austria.

Pérez, J. C., Petrides, K., & Furnham, A. (2005). Measuring trait emotional intelligence. In R. Schulze & R. D. Roberts (Eds.), *International handbook of emotional intelligence* (pp. 181–201). Cambridge, MA: Hogrefe & Huber.

Petrides, K. V., & Furnham, A. (2001). Trait emotional intelligence: Psychometric investigation with reference to established trait taxonomies. *European Journal of Personality, 15,* 425–448.

Petrides, K. V., & Furnham, A. (2003). Trait emotional intelligence: Behavioural validation in two studies of emotion recognition and reactivity to mood induction. *European Journal of Personality, 17,* 39–57.

Roberts, R. D., Schulze, R., Matthews, G., & Zeidner, M. (2005). Understanding, measuring, and applying emotional intelligence: What have we learned? What have we missed? In R. Schulze & R. D. Roberts (Eds.), *International handbook of emotional intelligence* (pp. 311–341). Cambridge, MA: Hogrefe & Huber.

Saarni, C. (2000). Emotional competence: A developmental perspective. In R. Bar-On & J. D. A. Parker (Eds.), *The handbook of emotional intelligence* (pp. 68–91). San Francisco: Jossey-Bass.

Sala, F. (2002). *Emotional Competence Inventory: Technical manual.* Hay Group, McClelland Center for Research and Innovation. Retrieved March 31, 2003, from http://www.eiconsortium.org/research/ECI_Tech_Manual.pdf

Salovey, P., Bedell, B. T., Detweiler, J. B., & Mayer, J. D. (2000). Current directions in emotional intelligence research. In M. Lewis & J. M. Haviland-Jones (Eds.), *Handbook of emotions* (pp. 504–520). New York: Guilford Press.

Salovey, P., Mayer, J. D, Goldman, S., Turvey, C., & Palfai, T. (1995). Emotional attention, clarity, and repair: Exploring emotional intelligence using the Trait Meta-Mood Scale. In J. W. Pennebaker (Ed.), *Emotion, disclo-*

sure, and health (pp. 125–154). Washington, DC: American Psychological Association.

Salovey, P., Stroud, L. R., Woolery, A., & Epel, E. S. (2002). Perceived emotional intelligence, stress reactivity, and symptom reports: Further explorations using the trait meta-mood scale. *Psychology and Health, 17*, 611–627.

Schutte, N. S., Malouff, J. M., Hall, L. E., Haggerty, D. J., Cooper, J. T., Golden, C. J., et al. (1998). Development and validation of a measure of emotional intelligence. *Personality and Individual Differences, 25*, 167–177.

Slaski, M., & Cartwright, S. (2002). Health, performance and emotional intelligence: An exploratory study of retail managers. *Stress and Health, 18*, 63–68.

Spearman, C. (1927). *Abilities of man: Their nature and measurement.* New York: Macmillan.

Stanford Aptitude Seminar. (2001). *Remaking the concept of aptitude: Extending the legacy of Richard E. Snow.* Mahwah, NJ: Lawrence Erlbaum Associates.

Taylor, G. J., & Bagby, R. M. (2000). An overview of the alexithymia construct. In R. Bar-On and J. D. A. Parker (Eds.), *Handbook of emotional intelligence* (pp. 40–67). San Francisco: Jossey-Bass.

Torgerson, W. S. (1958). *Theory and methods of scaling.* New York: Wiley.

Van Rooy, D. L., & Viswesvaran, C. (2004). Emotional intelligence: A meta-analytic investigation of predictive validity and nomological net. *Journal of Vocational Behavior, 65*, 71–95.

Warwick, J., & Nettelbeck, T. (2004). Emotional intelligence is …? *Personality and Individual Differences, 37*, 1091–1100.

Weisinger, H. (1998). *Emotional intelligence at work: The untapped edge for success.* San Francisco: Jossey-Bass.

Zeidner, M., & Matthews, G. (2000). Personality and intelligence. In R.J. Sternberg (Ed.), *Handbook of human intelligence* (2nd ed., pp. 581–610). New York: Cambridge University Press.

Zeidner, M., Matthews, G., & Roberts, R. D. (2001). Slow down, you move too fast: Emotional intelligence remains an "elusive" intelligence. *Emotion, 1*, 265–275.

Zeidner, M., Matthews G., & Roberts, R. D. (2004). Emotional intelligence in the workplace: A critical review. *Applied Psychology: An International Review, 53*, 371–399.

Zeidner, M., Matthews G., & Roberts, R. D. (in press). Emotional intelligence, coping with stress, and adaptation. In J. Ciarrochi, J. Forgas, & J. D. Mayer (Eds.), *Emotional intelligence in everyday life: A scientific inquiry* (2nd ed.). Philadelphia: Psychology Press.

Zeidner, M., Matthews, G., Roberts, R. D., & MacCann, C. (2003). Development of emotional intelligence: Toward a multi-level investment model. *Human Development, 46*, 69–96.

Zeidner, M., Roberts, R. D., & Matthews, G. (2002). Can emotional intelligence be schooled? A critical review. *Educational Psychologist, 37*, 215–231.

Zeidner, M., & Saklofske, D. S. (1996). Adaptive and maladaptive coping. In M. Zeidner & N. S. Endler (Eds.), *Handbook of coping* (pp. 505–531). New York: John Wiley and Sons.

Zins, J. E., Weissberg, R. P., Wang, M. C., Walberg, H. J., & Goleman, D. (Eds.). (2004). *Building school success through social and emotional learning: What does the research say?* New York: Teachers College Press.

AUTHOR NOTE

The views expressed here are not necessarily those of the Educational Testing Service. Correspondence regarding this chapter should be sent to:

Dr. Gerald Matthews
Department of Psychology
University of Cincinnati
Cincinnati OH 45221
Email: matthegd@email.uc.edu

2

The Two Els

Kevin R. Murphy and Lori Sideman
Pennsylvania State University

The concept of emotional intelligence (EI) has a long history in psychology. The idea that abilities and skills related to processing, managing, and using information about one's own emotions and the emotions of others are an important part of intelligent and successful behavior was given serious consideration by Wechsler in his development of ability tests (Kaufman & Kaufman, 2001). Binet considered EI as a part of general intelligence that was crucial for adapting to one's social environment. Wechsler believed noncognitive factors such as EI were part of general intelligence, but he was not successful in identifying and measuring them. Thorndike (1920) proposed the concept of social intelligence, suggesting that some people had more ability than others to attend to and use information about factors like emotions that affected social interactions.

Some contemporary theories of intelligence and mental ability include components similar to Thorndike's social intelligence (e.g., Gardner, 1993), but until the 1990s there was relatively little scientific or popular interest in the topic of social or emotional intelligence. In 1990, Salovey, Mayer, and their colleagues published the first in a series of articles dealing with the construct "emotional intelligence"; these papers introduced EI to the mainstream of scientific research.

Five years later, Goleman's (1995) best-selling book *Emotional Intelligence* introduced this construct to a wider audience. Seen in part as a rebuttal to Herrnstein and Murray's (1994) pessimistic and elitist conclusions about the role of IQ in society, Goleman's formulation of EI caught fire, appearing on the cover of *Time* magazine in October of 1995. Since then, studies of EI and applications of EI in the workplace, in schools, in mental health, and so on have grown at an astounding rate.

DEBATE AND CONTROVERSY OVER EI

The explosion of interest in EI is viewed very differently by different audiences. There are many researchers and practitioners who see the rapid growth of EI as a very good thing, and others who see it as a disaster. EI enthusiasts argue that psychologists have, for too long, overlooked critically important abilities and skills, focusing on narrow conceptions of intelligence, and that research in EI promises to explain phenomena that are not explained by traditional intelligence measures. More important, they argue that EI can be developed and improved, and that individuals, groups, and organizations function better as the general level of EI goes up.

EI skeptics complain that EI is "old wine in new bottles," that EI is not a new or different construct, that it is poorly defined and poorly measured, and that claims about the benefits of EI and EI interventions are sometimes wildly exaggerated. (EI skeptics include researchers who dismiss the construct of EI entirely as well as those who argue for a narrow formulation of EI and question the broad popular claims about this construct.) EI skeptics also question the rapid growth of EI, suggesting that it has been fueled by unrealistic expectations about the importance and meaning of this construct rather than by the real contributions of EI to understanding and improving behavior in social settings. The intensity of the EI controversy has been noted by many authors (Daus & Ashkanasy, 2003; Davies, Stankov, & Roberts, 1998; Emmerling & Goleman, 2003; Matthews, Zeidner & Roberts, 2003); the purpose of the present chapter is to articulate the root causes of the controversy over EI and to discuss how these shed light on the discussions between EI enthusiasts and EI skeptics.

We will argue that there are three factors largely responsible for the EI controversy: questions about what EI really is, discomfort with the claims that have been made regarding EI and the applications of EI, and, most important, the clash of cultures between the most vocal EI enthusiasts and skeptics. The first two issues, questions about the meaning and nature of EI and questions about its importance and its applicability, have been discussed extensively (and are also dealt with by several authors in this volume—see especially chapters 1, 3–8). The third issue, the clash of cultures, has received less attention but is, in our view, the most important element in the EI controversy. This issue will be dealt with in more depth.

Defining the Construct

One reason for controversy over EI is that there is no clear consensus about what EI really means (Emerling & Goleman, 2003; Matthews et al., 2003; Van Rooy & Viswesvaran, 2004). The three most widely accepted models for defining EI are those described by Mayer and Salovey (1997), Bar-On (1997a, 1997b, 2000) and Goleman (1998; 2001). Mayer and Salovey (1997) described EI as a set of abilities and argued that EI shares key characteristics with cognitive and intellectual abilities, notably its relationship with performance on a range of tasks and its developmental trajectory (i.e., in their model, EI develops gradually with age and crystallizes in adulthood; Mayer, Salovey, Caruso, & Sitarenios, 2001; Mayer, Caruso, & Salovey, 1999). In the Mayer-Salovey model, a person's level of EI is likely to be somewhat difficult to change.

Bar-On coined the term *emotional quotient* (EQ); in his model, Bar-On (2000) defines EI in terms of a fairly extensive set of traits and abilities that are related to coping with and adapting to one's environmental in ways that promote psychological well-being. This model focuses on interpersonal and intrapersonal skills, adaptability, stress management, and mood (Bar-On, 1997b). Bar-On's definition of EI is relatively broad, and it spans both personality and ability domains.

Goleman (1998) defines EI largely in terms of learned competencies, that is, skills and abilities that can be acquired with practice and that are focused on successfully negotiating social interactions and on managing one's own behavior (Goleman, 2001). His theory concentrates on skills such as self-awareness, self-management, social awareness, and relationship management (Goleman, 2001), and it is arguably the most expansive version of EI and probably the version that has been most responsible for the enthusiasm shown in many quarters for EI. Recent statements of this model (e.g., Boyatzis, Goleman, & Rhee, 2000) have included 25 different competencies, clustered into five broad groups; these are summarized in Table 2.1. According to Goleman's various models, EI includes many of the dimensions of competence in social situations that are not strictly academic in nature. Most important, according to Goleman's model, EI can be learned and developed, and structured programs can be de-

TABLE 2.1   **Competencies Included in Goleman's EI Model**

Self-Awareness Cluster

   Emotional Awareness

   Accurate Self- Assessment

   Self-Confidence

Self-Regulation Cluster

   Self-Control

   Trustworthiness

   Conscientiousness

   Adaptability

   Innovation

Motivation Cluster

   Achievement Drive

   Commitment

   Initiative

   Optimism

Empathy Cluster

   Understanding Others

   Developing Others

   Service Orientation

   Leveraging Diversity

   Political Awareness

Social Skills Cluster

   Influence

   Communication

   Conflict Management

   Leadership

   Change Catalyst

   Building Bonds

   Collaboration and Cooperation

   Team Capabilities

signed that might have a relatively strong and permanent effect on raising EI.

EI Claims and the EI Bandwagon

We use the phrase "EI bandwagon" to refer to the explosive growth of books, training programs, institutes, and so forth devoted to EI. This bandwagon has emerged for two related reasons. First, EI might be relevant to a wide array of important problems, ranging from increasing the effectiveness of organizations to improving mental health. That is, learning about someone's EI might lead to predicting and understanding a wide range of outcomes that are not captured very well by more traditional measures; depending on how it is defined, EI might be relevant to success in a wide range of social situations. Second, sweeping claims have been made for the importance and the effects of individual differences in EI.

Claims about the importance and relevance of EI started on the cover of Goleman's (1995) best-seller *Emotional Intelligence: Why It Can Matter More Than IQ.* The subtitle of this book stakes a claim that is both bold and tantalizing. For example, many researchers have concluded that cognitive ability tests (a class that includes traditional IQ measures) are among the best predictors of success in school, the workplace, and other settings (Herrnstein & Murray, 1994; Schmidt & Hunter, 1998). Schmidt and Hunter (1998) reviewed 85 years of research on predicting performance in the workplace and in training and concluded that cognitive ability tests were unique in terms of their ability to explain a substantial portion of the variance of performance in virtually all jobs studied, explaining 20% to 25% of the variability in performance in most jobs. The claim that measures of EI might be more useful than the best of the traditional tests (i.e., tests of cognitive ability or IQ) is an important factor in explaining the emergence of EI in recent years. As we will note later, empirical tests of the claim that EI is as important as or even more important than IQ (e.g., Van Rooy & Viswesvaran, 2004) have not provided much support, but the lack of empirical confirmation has not led to modification or withdrawal of this claim.

The jacket cover of Goleman's (1995) book makes a second equally bold claim: that this model "… redefines what is means to be smart." Consistent with Gardner's (1993) multiple intelligence model, the idea that EI research redefines what it means to be smart might provide considerable solace to people who have performed poorly on traditional academic tests or IQ scales; if there are multiple ways to be smart, this should substantially increase the probability that each person who reads Goleman's books will turn out to be smart in one way or another.

Goleman's subsequent books emphasized the particular relevance of EI in the workplace. Goleman (1998) claimed that EI plays a significant role in career success and in the success of organizations. Goleman, McKee, and Boyatzis (2002) argued that EI is an important determinant of success as a leader. A theme running through many of these books and similar works is that traditional cognitive tests, at best, explain 20% to 25% of the variability in performance, meaning that there is another 75% to 80% not explained by these traditional tests. It is often claimed or implied that EI might account for a significant chunk of this unexplained variance.

EI models, tests, and interventions have been applied in schools, corporations, health care, parenting, and even analyses of the causes of war and peace. There are a number of centers devoted to the study of EI and related phenomena (e.g., Center for Social Emotional Education, Institute for Health and Human Potential, EI Consortium, and Centre for Applied Emotional Intelligence), as well as consulting firms devoted largely or solely to EI (e.g., Emotional Intelligence Services division of the Hay Group, TalentSmart, and Simmons Management Systems). There are Internet directories for locating research and resources connected to EI (e.g., www.eq.org/; www.eqi.org/). There are a number of self-help and EI activity books (e.g., Bradbury & Greaves, 2003; Doty, 2001; Lynn, 2002). The rapid growth of EI is hard to contest, but the question of whether this growth is a good thing is a matter of considerable controversy.

Finally, it is useful to note that disputes about the meaning and definition of EI have a direct bearing on questions about its importance and applicability. For example, Mayer and Salovey's (1997) ability-based model of EI does have several implications for understanding effectiveness in social situations, but it would not lead to the wide variety of interventions suggested by Goleman's model. Ability-based conceptions of EI suggest that this construct refers to a relatively limited set of abilities that develop slowly and that might be hard to change without concerted effort. The competencies included in Goleman's model (see Table 2.1) cover a much broader range of situations, and at least some of these might be developed through training, practice, or other short-term interventions. Given the expansive definition of EI presented by Goleman, the claim that EI might be as important as IQ (Goleman, 1995), or that it might in some cases be twice as important at IQ (Goleman, 1998), might seem quite feasible (although empirical support for these claims remains elusive; Mayer, 2001; Van Rooy & Viswesvaran, 2004). Anyone who has developed skills in all of the 25 competencies listed in Table 2.1 would stand a very good chance of success in a wide range of situations, even if he or she is not particularly smart (as measured by traditional cognitive ability tests).

TWO EIS: A CLASH OF CULTURES

Academic arguments can be intense and bitter, and it is tempting to treat the controversy over EI as just another example of the favorite indoor sport of academics, that is, disagreeing with one's peers. We suspect that the gap between parties in the EI debate is more profound than a garden-variety academic squabble. In many respects, the EI debate seems to represent a clash of cultures. That is, many of the participants in the EI controversy (e.g., proponents and opponents of EI in general, opponents and proponents of specific approaches to EI) appear to be acting on incompatible assumptions, pursuing different goals, articulating different values, and using different criteria to determine what to do and how to evaluate what they have done. At the risk of oversimplifying the EI debate, we believe that many of the most vocal participants in the EI controversy can be sorted into two broad groups, each of which represents a fundamentally different way of thinking about the links between behavioral science and the rest of the world. Some of the participants in the EI controversy can be characterized as following a science-driven culture, characterized by an emphasis on precision, empirical confirmation, and scientific caution. The science-driven approach does not necessarily lead one to oppose or question EI; Mayer, Salovey, and their colleagues have, to a large extent, emphasized the norms and values of a science-driven culture in their work on EI. Their model links EI with other abilities studied by mainstream researchers (Mayer et al., 2001). Their approach has led to the development of one of the better EI scales; all measures of EI are problematic in various ways (see Conte & Dean, chap. 3, this volume), but the MSCEIT is closest in its measurement properties to other validated ability tests. Finally, much of the research on this model has been presented in peer-reviewed journals (e.g., Mayer, Caruso, & Salovey, 1999; Mayer & Salovey, 1993; Mayer et al., 2001; Salovey & Mayer, 1990).

Other leading participants in the EI controversy (notably Goleman and his colleagues) can be characterized as following a practice-driven culture, an approach that emphasizes attempting to solve real-world problems, without necessarily waiting to work out all of the details of the underlying theory or the empirical tests. This approach usually leads one to look favorably on EI, in part because many formulations of EI appear to lead to action that will help solve pressing real-world problems. For example, Goleman's (1995, 1998) version of EI is broader than the Mayer-Solvey version (Goleman's current model includes 25 separate competencies), but this version of EI is not "intelligence" in the sense of the term that is used in the mainstream psychometric literature (his version of EI is more closely linked to Gardner's multiple intelligence model). Empirical support for key claims of Goleman's model is sometimes weak and unconvincing (e.g., Van Rooy & Viswesvaran, 2004), in part because Goleman's work on EI has rarely, if ever, appeared in peer-reviewed scientific journals. However, the Goleman formulation leads more directly to action and intervention (e.g., training programs) than does the Mayer-Solvey formulation of EI.

Most of the applications of the behavioral and social sciences in the real world (e.g., IQ testing, vocational counseling, psychotherapy) draw to some extent from both cultures, and the process of sorting participants in the EI debate into science-driven versus practice-driven cultures does not do complete justice to any of the participants. We believe, however, that this approach helps move the EI controversy from the name-calling stage (in which EI enthusiasts are often cast as hucksters and EI skeptics as narrow-minded snobs) to an analysis of why different individuals seem to have such radically different ideas of what EI means and how it might be used.

We are not the first to suggest that broad differences in outlook, values, and so forth can lead to controversies between scientists and practitioners. McIntyre (1990) used an analogy from geology to describe scientist–practitioner interactions in industrial and organizational psychology, describing university-based research versus organization-focused practice as two tectonic plates, each floating on a sea of molten lava that influence each other, that sometimes collide (producing earthquakes and upheaval), and that are each driven in particular directions by different sets of underlying forces. The focus of academic research is on the scientific method, publication in scientific journals, the incremental advancement of theories, and so on. The focus in practice settings is on solving problems that people really care about. He suggested that the biases, reward systems, and assumptions of the two camps lead to profound differences in goals and values that often hamper the successful integration of science and practice. Ashkanasy, Zerbe, and Hartel (2002) commented on the scientist–practitioner split in approaches to EI. In particular, they noted that scientists often focus on issues related to the definition and measurement of EI, whereas practitioners are more drawn to the question of whether various EI interventions work.

We believe that an analysis of specific ways that science-driven versus practice-driven cultures differ sheds considerable light on debates over EI and also suggests a variety of ways that differing perspectives on EI can be reconciled. Three dimensions of the science-driven and practice-driven cultures have a particularly important effect on the EI debate: (1) the values that dominate each culture, (2) the criteria used in each culture for evaluating its products, and (3) the audience each culture attempts to influence. Table 2.2 illustrates these three dimensions and some of their implications for the development of EI research and practice.

Values

Scientists study a wide range of phenomena, but they share a broad commitment to the same general method of working. The defining feature of a scientific approach to problems is the use of methods that emphasize formulating, testing, and revising hypotheses, sharing and criticizing work in a public forum, and a generally skeptical and cautious approach. The emphasis in scientific research is on "getting it right," that is, clearly articulating constructs and theories, measuring variables with precision, making and testing specific predictions, and revising theories and assumptions in the light of what the data show. Scientific work is most likely to be judged valuable when it (a) is solidly anchored in existing research and theory, (b) advances theory and knowledge, and (c)) withstands skeptical inquiry.

TABLE 2.2   **Values, Criteria, and Audience Emphasized by Science-Driven Versus Practice-Driven Cultures**

	Science-driven	Practice-driven
Value	Primacy of the method	Primacy of the problems
	Leads to	
	Emphasis on construct explication	Emphasis on problem-solving
	"Get it right" goals	"Get it moving" goals
Criteria	Replicability, precision	Persuasiveness, action orientation
	Leads to	
	Tight models	Expansive models
Audience	Other scientists	Potential users
	Leads to	
	Emphasis on the regard of your peers	Emphasis on market success
	Peer-reviewed publication	Popular press and Internet publication
	Slow development	Quick dissemination

Practitioners are likely to place more emphasis on the importance of the problem than on the importance of the method. Whereas scientists devote considerable time and energy to "getting it right," practitioners are likely to be more interested in "getting it moving," that is, to making a stab at solving important problems. Real-world problems do not respect disciplinary boundaries or assumptions, nor can they be put on hold until all of the details of competing theories, empirical tests, and so on are worked out, and as a result, practitioners are often called on to solve problems that the underlying science cannot fully address. Practitioners are most likely to value a particular intervention or approach when it (a) appears relevant to problems people really care about, (b) provides some guidance for solving the problem, and (c)) is accepted by end users as a reasonable and appropriate solution.

One way to appreciate the differences in values of science-driven versus practice-driven cultures is to consider the following dilemma. Suppose you had a choice to spend the next 6 months working on (a) a methodologically rigorous solution to a problem that concerned few hundred other people whose training was similar to yours, or (b) a novel approach that had weak theoretical and empirical support but that appeared to have potential for solving a problem that was of concern to thousands of managers. People who are strongly committed to science-driven versus practice-driven cultures probably don't find this much of a dilemma at all; they will, however, make completely different choices between these two alternatives.

Criteria

The criteria that define good science versus good practice are quite different. Good science is precise, replicable, and tied to tightly woven theories or models, whereas good practice involves action to solve problems that are of broad concern. Because the solution of important problems usually requires the cooperation of others who are not behavioral or social scientists (e.g., managers, parents), a critically important part of good practice is the ability to persuade others to sponsor and participate in your interventions or applications. From the perspective of good science, it is critically important to demonstrate linkages to and improvements on prior research within one's discipline. Thus, a social psychology study stands little chance of being published or reviewed favorably if it is not linked with previous research in social psychology. From the perspective of good practice, it is important to solve the problem, and it hardly matters where the solution comes from. Thus, practitioners often draw freely (and sometimes superficially) from research, theory, and applications in several disciplines, and their models are likely to feature more breadth and often less depth than the models in the scientific literature.

Audience

A key difference between scientists and practitioners is that each group is often trying to influence a completely different audience, Scientists are often most interested in influencing other scientists, whereas practitioners are often most interested in influencing potential users of their services. This difference influences the venues in which they publish and disseminate their work, the rewards that are associated with successful influence, and even the pace at which ideas are developed and implemented.

In science-driven cultures, the coin of the realm is the regard and respect of your peers. Thus, scientists often care a great deal about what other scientists working in related areas think of their work, and they sometimes ignore or even belittle the opinions of virtually everyone else. Scientists prefer to publish in peer-reviewed journals, usually written by and for specialists in their field, and care greatly about the frequency and impact of their peers' citation of their work.

In practice-driven culture, the coin of the realm is often the coin of the realm. That is, successful practice (particularly in areas such as organizational consulting) is often defined in terms of success in the market. This definition of success is not necessarily driven by a desire for financial gain: Practitioners who have a large number of influential clients have a greater opportunity to solve problems that really matter than practitioners who rarely work with clients. More to the point, the likelihood that a practitioner's advice will be listened to seems to be directly related to perceptions on the client's part that the practitioner is a "major player." One piece of advice that consultants often receive is that if they charge too little for their services, nobody will listen to their advice.

Practitioners are more likely to aim for the popular press and the Internet rather than peer-reviewed journals as outlets for disseminating their work. These outlets are much more likely to reach the desired audience than the best journal articles, and it is often possible to publish work quickly in the popular press (and instantaneously on the Internet); publication in scientific journals often takes 1 to 2 years (time from the initial submission to final publication; journals of the American Psychological Association list the date a paper was first received, the date of the final revision, and the date the paper was accepted). This difference in venues, in turn, has a dramatic effect on the pace at which ideas, innovations, and findings move in the scientific versus the popular press. Science-driven approaches often develop slowly, with each new article making an incremental contribution that has been carefully scrutinized by skeptical reviewers (high-quality journals in the social and behavioral sciences often publish only a small fraction of the papers they receive). In a practice-driven culture, there are more opportunities for quick development and dissemination of ideas, approaches, and services.

EI in the Workplace: An Illustration of the Gap Between Cultures

One of the most important claims in the EI literature is that EI might be as important as, and perhaps even more important than, IQ is many settings. This claim has been investigated in detail in the workplace, and a description of how science-driven versus practice-driven authors framed this issue and how they interpreted the same data illustrates nicely the conflicting biases, assumptions, and methods that the two cultures support.

VAN ROOY AND VISWESVARAN

Van Rooy and Viswesvaran (2004) report a meta-analysis of the relationship between EI and measures of job performance, cognitive ability, and normal personality. They estimated that the validity of EI as a predictor of job performance was .23 (this estimate includes corrections for measurement error and other psychometric adjustments). This is a respectable level of validity; their results refute the claim sometimes seen in the EI debate that measures of EI have no real value. However, their analysis also demonstrated that EI shows virtually no incremental validity over measures of general cognitive ability. That is, in Van Rooy and Viswesvaran's analysis, EI added very little to the prediction of job performance that was not already accounted for by IQ. In contrast, IQ accounted for a substantial proportion of the variance in job performance that was not explained by EI. They also showed that EI is correlated with *all* of the dimensions of normal personality that characterize the widely used five-factor model (corrected correlations with Agreeableness, Conscientiousness, Emotional Stability, Extraversion, and Openness to Experience ranged from .23 to .34), and that the correlations between EI and personality were generally higher than the correlations between EI and job performance. Their analysis was based on the results of 59 independent empirical studies, with aggregate sample sizes of up to $N = 9522$.

In contrast, Emmerling and Goleman (2003) claim that EI really is (or at least can be) more important than IQ:

> When it comes to the question of whether a person will become a "star performer" (in the top ten percent, however such performance is appropriately

assessed) within that role, or be an outstanding leader, IQ may be a less powerful predictor than emotional intelligence .... While social scientists are
mainly interested in the main predictive relationship between IQ and work
success, practitioners and those who must make decisions on hiring and promotion within organizations are understandably far more interested in assessing capabilities related to outstanding performance and leadership ....
Qualitative research, however, suggests that IQ measures fail to account for
large portions of the variance related to performance and career success, especially among top managers and senior leaders. (pp. 5–6)

Emmerling and Goleman (2003) do not openly dispute the findings
from the 59 studies summarized by Van Rooy and Viswesvaran
(2004). Rather, they dismiss them as being, if not irrelevant, at least
uninteresting and prefer to draw on qualitative reports from top managers and senior leaders to support their contention that EI is more
important than IQ. That is, Emmerling and Goleman are unlikely to
be swayed by analyses like those presented by Van Rooy and
Viswesvaran because these researchers have made a choice that is
typical of the science-driven culture: to obtain precise, well-documented, and persuasive empirical answers to relatively small questions. The big, important, and interesting questions (in the eyes of
members of a practice-driven culture) are often ones for which the
sort of data analyzed by Van Rooy and Viswesvaran simply don't exist.

BRIDGING THE TWO CULTURES

We have purposely focused on the two extremes: (a) a science-driven
culture in which psychologists and other social scientists focus on getting it right, without much regard for applying their work to solve
problems that people outside of the scientific community care about;
and (b) the practice-driven culture, in which psychologists and other
practitioners focus on solving problems in the real world, without
worrying unduly about the niceties of theory development, hypothesis
testing, and so forth. Many psychologists straddle the two cultures,
working in areas that subscribe to the scientist–practitioner model
(Frank, 1984; Murphy & Saal, 1990). The scientist–practitioner
model was originally developed in the area of clinical psychology,
where it remains a somewhat controversial topic (Frank, 1984). The
model has been embraced most successfully in areas such as indus-
trial/organizational psychology (Murphy & Saal, 1990), the area in
which the authors of this chapter were trained.

The scientist–practitioner model embraces the idea that psychologists should be concerned with both the scientific foundation of their
work and its relevance to solving problems in the real world. This
model suggests that practice is most effective when it is strongly an-

chored in solid science, but it also recognizes that the solution to real-world problems often stretches the boundaries of what we know with scientific certainty. The model suggests that scientific research is most valuable when it is relevant to solving problems nonscientists also care about. This model does not require that every decision made in practice be subject to stringent scientific tests, nor does it require that all research be devoted to immediate application. Rather, it suggests that the values driving the behavior of scientist-practitioners should reflect the need for both scientific rigor and applicability.

The recent movement to identify and disseminate information about empirically supported treatments in the area of psychotherapy is an excellent example of the scientist-practitioner model in action. The American Psychological Association's Society for Clinical Psychology (Division 12) has developed criteria for empirically supported treatments and has begun to create lists of techniques that meet these criteria (Chambless & Ollendick, 2001; see also Lilienfeld, Lynn, & Lohr, 2003). This approach increases the likelihood that the choices made by practicing clinicians will be guided by current empirical research.

Action research (Corey, 1953; Lewin, 1947) represents another approach that reflects the values of both science-driven and practice-driven cultures. Lewin (1947/1977) described action research as a process that involves (a) learning about the environment in which problems will be addressed and using scientific knowledge to help develop a plan of attack for dealing with real-world problems in that environment, (b) taking action, and (c) collecting data or information about the results of your action. The data collected in Lewin's third step might then be used to initiate another round of environmental scanning, action, and evaluation.

Both the scientist-practitioner model and the action research model encourage psychologists to pay attention to the goals of both the science-driven and the practice-driven cultures. The dilemma often faced by scientist-practitioners and by action researchers is how to balance the competing demands of these two cultures.

Balancing Goals

Both the science-driven culture and the practice-driven culture emphasize the pursuit of worthwhile goals (i.e., getting the right answer, solving real-world problems), but it is not always possible to pursue both sets of goals simultaneously. If you define EI narrowly and constrain it tightly in terms of the types of measures that might be used to tap EI and the range of behaviors that EI might relate to, you run the risk of creating a product that is both pristine and useless. That is, EI applications that are fully vetted by the scientific approach might take a very long time to produce and might turn out to be useful for solving only a relatively small set-off problems. If you define EI broadly and use it as a hammer to hit a wide variety of problems in organizations, in education systems, and the like, you run the risk of creating a mountain of fluff. EI interventions might help (or appear to help) you address many problems, but the rush to application and problem solving may impel you to create versions of EI and applications of EI that are so fuzzy as to be little more than feel-good exercises.

The task of balancing the risks and benefits of the two different approaches to EI is similar in many ways to the problems faced when testing statistical hypotheses. For example, suppose that you have the hypothesis that applying a new EI training program will help police officers respond more effectively to domestic violence calls. When testing this hypothesis, you risk facing one of two types of errors: Type I error—deciding that the training program is effective, when in fact it has no real effects on how officers respond; or Type II error—deciding that you should not use the training program, when in fact its use would have made a real difference in the way officers responded to these calls. The science-driven approach, with its emphasis on precision, replication, and the need for compelling evidence often focuses on minimizing Type I errors. The practice-driven approach, with its emphasis on solving important problems (even if you are not certain that the theory and data completely support the intervention) usually focuses largely on minimizing Type II errors. That is, the science-driven culture encourages waiting until you are certain before implementing an intervention, whereas the practice-driven culture encourages action, even in the face of considerable uncertainty.

It is often difficult to simultaneously minimize Type I *and* Type II errors (in this context, this would requiring obtaining enough information to be quite certain that the intervention works without missing any opportunities to intervene), but this does not mean that you must simply concentrate on one type of error and ignore the other. Rather, decision makers need to balance the risks inherent in both types of decision error and make decisions about whether they should be conservative or bold when implementing a new idea or technology. The problem of balancing your tolerance for Type I versus Type II errors has been addressed in the methodological literature (Cascio & Zedeck, 1983; Murphy, 2002; Murphy & Myors, 2003); these papers suggest that the decision of whether to follow a science-driven or a practice-driven approach when making a decision about this EI training program for police officers should not be made simply on the basis of the assumptions inherent in each culture about which sorts of errors should be avoided.

Applying procedures developed by Cascio and Zedeck (1983), Murphy and Myors (2003) showed that the question of whether it makes sense to be cautious (avoid the possibility that you will implement an intervention that doesn't work) or bold (implement the program, taking the risk that it might not really work) when making decisions about whether or not to implement a particular program or intervention depends substantially on one's definition of what it means for a program to work. They note, for example, that the traditional formulation of the null hypothesis leads to two possible outcomes: (1) the program has no true effect whatsoever [H_0], or (2) the program has some effect [H_1]. The null hypothesis that an EI training program will do nothing whatsoever is generally easy to reject, in part because a program that has *any* effect will be judged, according to this definition, to work. If the definition of a successful EI training program is framed in terms of the tradditional null hypothesis (i.e., a program that has any effect whatsoever is a success), it is hard to argue for scientific caution; using this definition of success, the practitioner's bias for action is the only one that makes sense (Murphy & Myors, 2003).

On the other hand, if we decide that the training program will be evaluated as successful only if it has at least a moderate or large effect on the officers' behavior when responding to domestic violence calls, there is a much stronger argument for being cautious before going ahead with implementation. If the claim that a program works implies that it has a susbtantial and meaningful effect on the officers' performance, there is a greater need for scientific caution, and a higher bar should be set.

Murphy and Myors' (2003) analysis suggests that the evidentiary standard for claims about EI depends substantially on the strength of the claims. If the claims are relatively modest (this program will probably do some good, but we cannot be all that sure), a lower standard of evidentiary support is reasonable, and less caution is needed before before implementation. If claims regarding the effects of this program are more substantial (e.g., that it will increase effectiveness in a meaningful way), higher evidentiary standards are required, and it makes senes to apply considerable scientific caution.

Ethical Issues

Practitioners face some particularly challenging ethical dilemmas. As the previous section suggests, the orientation to act now and study later can be problematic, especially if the practitioner makes substantial claims about the results that might be expected from his or her interventions. On the other hand, if the claims are sufficiently modest to allay the concerns of scientists, it is unlikely that the practitioners will be able to interest many customers. That is, a practitioner who makes only modest claims about the theory or intervention he or she is offering will win the accolades of scientists but will also go out of business. The practitioner who promises astounding results to clients will probably do quite well in the marketplace but will be branded as a huckster by scientists.

The American Psychological Association's *Ethical Principles of Psychologists and Code of Conduct* (2002) provides some sound practical guidance to practitioners that can help rein in the temptation to promise more than they can deliver. Psychologists who are members of this association have pledged to abide by this code of conduct, and practitioners in the area of EI who live up to that pledge will have met a set of standards that protect the welfare of potential users of that practitioner's services and that protect the integrity of his or her work.

The APA principles require the following:

1. Psychologists provide services only with the boundaries of their competence—Principle 1.04.
2. Psychologists rely on scientifically and professionally derived knowledge when engaging in scholarly and professional endeavors—Principle 1.06.
3. Psychologists take reasonable steps to avoid harming their clients—Principle 1.14.
4. Psychologists are alert to and guard against financial and organization factors that lead to a misuse of their influence—Principle 1.16.
5. Psychologists use scientific procedures and current professional knowledge in designing, validating, and recommending tests and assessments [these procedures are articulated in APA's (1999) *Standards for educational and psychological* testing]—Principle 2.03.
6. Psychologists provide explanations of test results in terms that are reasonably expected to be understandable to the persons being assessed—Principle 2.09.
7. Psychologists do not make public statements about their work that are false, deceptive, misleading because of what they state, convey, or omit—Principle 3.03.
8. Psychologists do not fabricate or present false results in their publications, and if they become aware of significant errors in their published data, they take reasonable steps to correct such errors—Principle 6.21.

Without close attention to this ethics code, the pressures of the marketplace push practitioners almost inexorably toward making inflated claims, disdaining evidence, putting financial success above the welfare of the client, and manifesting all the other symptoms of hucksterism. The ethics code constrains the choices of practitioners and probably makes it difficult for them to compete with others who are not bound by, or who do not observe, this code. However, it could be argued that practitoiners benefit as much from this code as do their clients. The APA ethical principles represent the first line of defense against sliding down the slippery slope toward becoming a great salesman and a lousy psychologist.

Scientists who do not apply their work outside of the laboratory do not run the same risks of violating the APA ethical principles (although the document includes principles dealing with the ethical conduct of research), and in a way, this is a shame. Practitioners run the risk of unethical behavior by their actions, whereas scientists run few risks of violating this particular code by their inaction. Suppose, for example, that you have discovered some important principle or developed a way of assessing some important construct, and it is clear that putting this into action could have real benefits for potential clients. There is no concrete ethical rule preventing you from running one more experiment, or spending another 6 months collecting additional data, or any number of other pursuits that will, in effect, withhold this advance from people who could truly benefit from it for an indefinite period. Research scientists who subscribe to the APA principles are bound by a general obligation to be mindful of the welfare of others, but it is unlikely that scientists will be bought up on ethical charges because they were too careful, whereas an overly bold practitioner always runs the risk of being branded a charleton.

CHOOSING AMONG EIS

We have focused primarily on the Mayer-Salovey model and the Goleman model, which we regard as exemplars of the science-driven and the practice-driven cultures, respectively. However, these two versions do not exhaust the EI domain; as noted earlier, Bar-On has proposed a model of EI that shares some features with the Goleman model (e.g., broad conception of the EI construct, limited empirical support) but that differs in the domains included in EI. Which approach should one follow, and why?

We believe that one key to choosing among EI models is the extent to which you take the "intelligence" part of EI seriously. The Mayer-Salovey formulation is linked with conceptions of intelligence and ability that are accepted by mainstream psychologists, whereas the Goleman model does not appear to take the concept of ability or inteligence seriously at all. This shows up most clearly by examining the tests developed by Goleman and colleagues to measure EI (ECI and ECI 360), which rely mostly on self-reports. A self-report version of the Graduate Record Examination would not be accepted as an ability measure, and the same can be said for measures proposed for the Goleman model.

The second key in choosing among EI models is the extent to which you find the sort of empirical research published in scientific journals convincing. Practitioners often complain, with considerable justification, that the journals spend too much time on devising elegant solutions for trivial problems and that the big problems that are worth studying are often either ignored or are not amenable to this sort of research. Scientists complain that without the rigor implicit in peer-reviewed publications, there is no way of knowing whether the claims of various EI enthusiasts are true.

The third and perhaps most important consideration is to ask why you are studying EI in the first place. The Goleman model is attractive largely as an antidote to the sort of fatalism and pessimism that is endemic to research on IQ (e.g., Herrnstein & Murray, 1994). Whereas low IQ seems to doom one to dreary, low-paying jobs, low EI can be fixed, and a person with high EI is equipped to go far. So, if you don't like what you have heard about IQ, ignore it and think about EI instead. On the other hand, if you are studying EI because you believe that Binet, Thorndike, Wechsler, and others were right in believing that the domain of ability extended to cover one's social interactions, you will probably be drawn to the Mayer-Salovey model.

Life would be easier, or at least less complicated, if one group or another would concede ownership of the term *emotional intelligence* and use some other term to describe their construct or family of constructs. It is unlikely that this will happen any time soon, and as a result, the question you should always ask when you see a paper, advertisement, or book that deals with EI is "Which EI ?" There are at least two distinctly different versions of this construct, each emerging from fundamentally different sets of assumptions, values, and norms, and without knowing which EI is being discussed, it is often impossible to make any sense of the EI debate.

REFERENCES

American Psychological Association. (1999). *Standards for educational and psychological testing.* Washington, DC: Author.
American Psychological Association. (2002). *Ethical principles of psychologists and code of conduct.* Washington, DC: Author.
Ashkanasy, N., Zerbe, W., & Hartel, C. (2002). Managing emotions in a changing workplace. In N. Ashkanasy, W. Zerbe, & C. Hartel (Eds.), *Managing emotions in the workplace* (pp. 3–22). London: M.E. Sharpe.

Bar-On, R. (1997a). *The Bar-On Emotional Quotient Inventory (EQ-I): A test of emotional intelligence.* Toronto, IN: Multi-Health Systems.

Bar-On, R. (1997b). *The Emotional Quotient Inventory (EQ-I): Technical manual.* Toronto, ON: Multi-Health Systems.

Bar-On, R. (2000). *Emotional and social intelligence: Insights from the Emotional Quotient Inventory (EQ-I).* In R. Bar-On & J. D. A. Parker (Eds.), *Handbook of emotional intelligence* (pp. 363–388). San Francisco: Jossey-Bass.

Boyatzis, R. E., Goleman, D., & Rhee, K. (2000). Clustering competence in emotional intelligence: Insights from the Emotional Competence Inventory (ECI). In R. Bar-On & J. Parker (Eds.), *Handbook of emotional intelligence* (pp. 343–362). San Francisco: Jossey-Bass.

Bradbury, T., & Greaves, J. (2003). *The emotional intelligence quickbook.* San Diego, CA: TalentSmart.

Cascio, W. F., & Zedeck, S. (1983). Open a new window in rational research planning: Adjust alpha to maximize statistical power. *Personnel Psychology, 36,* 517–526.

Chambless, D. L., & Ollendick, T. H. (2001). Empirically supported psychological interventions: Controversies and evidence. *Annual Review of Psychology, 52,* 685–716.

Corey, S. (1953). *Action research to improve school practice.* New York: Teachers College, Columbia University.

Daus, C. S., & Ashkanasy, N. M. (2003). On deconstructing the emotional intelligence "debate". *The Industrial-Organizational Psychologist, 41,* 16–18.

Davies, M., Stankov, L., & Roberts, R. D. (1998). Emotional intelligence: In search of an elusive construct. *Journal of Personality and Social Psychology, 75,* 989–1015.

Doty, G. (2001). *Fostering emotional intelligence in K–8 students: Simple strategies and ready to use activities.* Thousand Oaks, CA: Corwin Press.

Emerling, R. J., & Goleman, D. (2003). *Emotional intelligence: Issues and common misunderstandings.* New Brunswick, NJ: The Consortium on Research on Emotional Intelligence in Organizations

Ethical Principles of Psychologists and Code of Conduct. (2002). *American Psychologist, 57,* 1060–1073.

Frank, G. (1984). The Boulder Model: History, rationale, and critique. *Professional Psychology—Research & Practice, 15,* 417–435.

Gardner, H. (1993). *Multiple intelligences: The theory in practice.* New York: Basic Books.

Goleman, D. (1995). *Emotional intelligence.* New York: Bantam Books.

Goleman, D. (1998). *Working with emotional intelligence.* New York: Bantam Books.

Goleman, D. (2001). Emotional intelligence: Issues in paradigm building. In C. Cherniss & D. Goleman (Eds.), *The emotionally intelligent workplace* (pp. 13–26). San Francisco: Jossey-Bass.

Goleman, D., McKee, A., & Boyatzis, R.E. (2002). *Primal leadership: Realizing the power of emotional intelligence.* Boston: Harvard Business School Press.

Herrnstein, R. J., & Murray, C. (1994). *The bell curve: Intelligence and class structure in American life.* New York: Free Press.

Kaufman, A. S., & Kaufman, J. C. (2001). Emotional intelligence as an aspect of general intelligence: What would David Wechsler say? *Emotion, 1,* 258–264.

Lewin, K. (1947). *Resolving social conflicts.* Re-issued by American Psychological Association, Washington, DC, 1997.

Lilienfeld, S. O., Lynn, S. J., & Lohr, J. M. (2003). *Science and pseudoscience in clinical psychology.* New York: Guilford Press.

Lynn, A. B. (2002). *The emotional intelligence activity book: 50 activities for promoting EQ at work.* New York: AMACOM.

Matthews, G., Zeidner, M., & Roberts, R. D. (2003). *Emotional intelligence: Science and myth.* Boston: MIT Press.

Mayer, J. D. (2001). A field guide to emotional intelligence. In J. Ciarrochi, J. Forgas, & J. Mayer (Eds.), *Emotional intelligence in everyday life* (pp. 3–24). New York: Psychology Press.

Mayer, J. D., Caruso, D. R., & Salovey, P. (1999). Emotional intelligence meets traditional standards for an intelligence. *Intelligence, 27,* 267–298.

Mayer, J. D., & Salovey, P. (1993). The intelligence of emotional intelligence. *Intelligence, 17,* 433–442.

Mayer, J. D., & Salovey, P. (1997). What is emotional intelligence? In P. Salovey & D. Sluyter (Eds.), *Emotional development and emotional intelligence: Implications for educators* (pp. 3–34). New York: Basic Books.

Mayer, J. D., Salovey, P., & Caruso, D. R. (2000a). Emotional intelligence as zeitgeist, as personality and as a mental ability. In R. Bar-On & J. Parker (Eds.), *The handbook of emotional intelligence: Theory, development, assessment and application at home, school and in the workplace* (pp. 92–117). San Francisco: Jossey-Bass.

Mayer, J. D., Salovey, P., & Caruso, D. R. (2000b). Models of emotional intelligence. In R. J. Sternberg (Ed.), *Handbook of intelligence* (pp. 396–420). New York: Cambridge Press.

Mayer, J. D., Salovey, P., Caruso, D. R., & Sitarenios, G. (2001). Emotional intelligence as standard intelligence. *Emotion, 1,* 232–242.

McIntyre, R. M. (1990). Our science-practice: The ghost of industrial-organizational psychology yet to come. In K. Murphy & F. Saal (Eds.), *Psychology in organizations: Integrating science and practice* (pp. 49–68). Hillsdale, NJ: Lawrence Erlbaum Associates.

Murphy, K. (2002). Using power analysis to evaluate and improve research. In S. Rogleberg (Ed.), *Handbook of research methods in industrial and organizational psychology* (pp. 119–137). Malden, MA: Blackwell.

Murphy, K., & Myors, B. (2003). *Statistical power analysis: A simple and general model for traditional and modern hypothesis tests* (2nd ed.). Mahwah, NJ: Lawrence Erlbaum Associates.

Murphy, K. R., & Saal, F. (1990). *Psychology in organizations: Integrating science and practice.* Hillsdale, NJ: Lawrence Erlbaum Associates.

Salovey, P., & Mayer, J. D. (1990). Emotional intelligence. *Imagination, Cognition and Personality, 9,* 185–211.

Schmidt, F. L., & Hunter, J. E . (1998). The validity and utility of selection methods in personnel psychology: Practical and theoretical implications of 85 years of research findings. *Psychological Bulletin, 124,* 262–274.

Thorndike, E. L. (1920). Intelligence and its uses. *Harper's Magazine, 140,* 227–235.

Van Rooy, D. L., & Viswesvaran, C. (2004). Emotional intelligence: A meta-analytic investigation of predictive validity and nomological net. *Journal of Vocational Behavior, 65,* 71–95.

3

Can Emotional Intelligence Be Measured?

Jeffrey M. Conte and Michelle A. Dean
San Diego State University

> When you can measure what you are speaking about, and express it in numbers, you know something about it; but when you cannot measure it, when you cannot express it in numbers, your knowledge is of a meager and unsatisfactory kind; it may be the beginning of knowledge, but you have scarcely in your thoughts advanced to the stage of science.
>
> —Lord Kelvin (1883/1891, p. 80)

Lord Kelvin's often-cited quote, which has been used to highlight the importance of accurate measurement in many different fields, provides a cautious perspective with which to begin a chapter examining the measurement of a relatively new and controversial construct such as emotional intelligence. Interest in emotional intelligence (EI) has increased substantially over the last decade, but a few researchers have raised questions about the adequacy of EI measures (e.g., Matthews, Zeidner, & Roberts, 2002). Although some practitioners have been quite optimistic about the importance of EI in organizations, critical questions remain about the concept, theory, and measurement of EI (Landy, 2005; Landy & Conte, 2004; Matthews et al., 2002).

This paper reviews and critiques EI measures, which vary widely in both their content and their method of assessment. First, the measurement and psychometric properties of six prominent EI measures (Emotional Competence Inventory, Emotional Quotient Inventory, Wong and Law EI Scale, Emotional Intelligence Scale, Multifactor Emotional Intelligence Scale, Mayer-Salovey-Caruso Emotional Intelligence Test) are considered. These six measures were chosen because they have received the most attention by emotional intelligence researchers and consultants. The strategies used to measure EI can be broken down into personality-based and ability-based approaches. These approaches result in different conceptualizations of EI as well as very different measures. Personality-based EI measures are discussed first, and then ability-based EI measures are examined. Table 3.1 shows basic information about each of the measures, which are described in more detail below. Second, the EI measures are compared and examined in light of their reliability and validity evidence. Third, this chapter addresses measurement issues related to the struggle between the science and marketing of EI. Fourth, recent meta-analyses on EI are examined, and some conclusions and suggestions for future research on EI measures are provided.

EMOTIONAL COMPETENCE INVENTORY (ECI)

The Emotional Competence Inventory (ECI) is designed to assess emotional competencies and positive social behaviors (Boyatzis, Goleman, & Rhee, 2000; Sala, 2002). Boyatzis and Sala (2004) define an emotional intelligence competence as "an ability to recognize, understand, and use emotional information about oneself or others that leads to or causes effective or superior performance" (p. 149). Although the developers of the ECI describe EI as an ability, a close examination of the ECI indicates that it assesses several dispositional variables (conscientiousness, trustworthiness) that resemble personality traits (MacCann, Matthews, Zeidner, & Roberts, 2003); thus, the ECI is typically classified as a personality-based EI measure.

The ECI is organized into four dimensions or clusters: Self-Awareness, Social Awareness, Self-Management, and Social Skills. The ECI begins with a self-report questionnaire, but it also has 360-degree assessment techniques that include peer and supervisor ratings of emotional competencies. The most recent version is the ECI Version 2 (ECI-2), which has 72 items and 18 competency scales. The internal consistency reliability of ECI-2 competencies measured by self-assessment ranges from .45 to .77, whereas the internal consistency re-

TABLE 3.1   Summary of Emotional Intelligence Measures and Their Reliability/Validity Evidence

EI Measure	# of Items	# of Dimensions	Dimension Names	Response Format	Reliability Evidence	Validity Evidence
Emotional Competence Inventory (ECI; Sala, 2002)	72	4 dimensions 18 competencies	Self-Awareness Social Awareness Self-Management Social Skills	Self-report, Informant report (Peer, Supervisor)	Internal consistency reliability ranges from .45 to .77 for self-assessment, and from .54 to .90 for peer and supervisor assessment.	Little discriminant or predictive validity evidence
Emotional Quotient Inventory (EQ-i; Bar-On, 1997)	133	5 dimensions 15 subscales	Intrapersonal Interpersonal Stress Management Adaptability General Mood	Self-Report	Alpha = .76 for overall scale; has been independently confirmed outside of Bar-On's lab.	Little discriminant validity evidence; validity of .01 in predicting GPA
Wong Law Emotional Intelligence Scale (WLEIS; Law et al., 2004)	16	4	Self-Emotions Appraisal Others-Emotion Appraisal Use of Emotion Regulation of Emotion	Self-Report	Adequate internal consistency reliability for scale scores ranging from .79 to .93	MTMM analyses provide some construct validity evidence; evidence for incremental validity above Big Five personality; investigation of incremental validity above "g" needed
Emotional Intelligence Scale (EIS; Schutte et al., 1998)	33	1	Overall Emotional Intelligence	Self-Report	Internal consistency of .90; 2-week test–retest reliability of .78	Low correlation (-0.06) with SAT; low discriminant validity with Openness to Experience (r = .54)

(continued)

TABLE 3.1 (continued)

EI Measure	# of Items	# of Dimensions	Dimension Names	Response Format	Reliability Evidence	Validity Evidence
Multifactor Emotional Intelligence Scale (MEIS; Mayer, Salovey, & Caruso, 1999)	402	4	Perception Assimilation Understanding Managing Emotions	Ability scale	Test–retest overall (2 weeks): .75. Overall scale has adequate internal consistency reliability (alpha = .95), some subscales have lower than adequate reliability.	Discriminant validity, incremental validity above Big 5 personality dimensions; little incremental validity above "g"
Mayer, Salovey, Caruso Emotional Intelligence Test (MSCEIT; Mayer et al., 2003)	141	4	Perception of Emotions Emotional Facilitation Understanding Emotions Managing Emotions	Ability scale	Adequate internal consistency reliability for overall scale; Test-retest (2 weeks) = .86.	New measure, lack of studies on predictive validity

liability of ECI-2 competencies measured by others' assessment ranges from .54 to .90 (Boyatzis & Sala, 2004). In the most recent presentation of validity evidence supporting the ECI and the ECI-2, Boyatzis and Sala (2004) cite studies that use samples from many different parts of the world. Clearly, a wide sample of investigators has utilized the ECI or the ECI-2 in their work. However, all of the empirical criterion-related validity studies cited are unpublished technical reports, working papers, online articles, theses, or dissertations. No empirical, peer-reviewed journal articles are presented to support the validity of the ECI.

The developers of the ECI suggest that it is supported by validity evidence from the Self-Assessment Questionnaire (SAQ), which is the ECI's predecessor. However, for proprietary reasons, the ECI's developers have allowed few items to be evaluated by other researchers (Matthews et al., 2002). Nevertheless, investigators who have examined the content of the ECI competencies have concluded that they overlap with four of the Big Five personality dimensions (Conscientiousness, Emotional Stability, Extraversion, and Openness) and with other psychological concepts such as self-awareness and self-confidence (Matthews et al., 2002; Van Rooy & Viswesvaran, 2004). Overall, little discriminant, predictive, and incremental validity evidence for the ECI has been provided, and the ECI does not deserve serious consideration until peer-reviewed empirical studies using this measure are conducted.

BAR-ON EMOTIONAL QUOTIENT INVENTORY (EQ-i)

Bar-On (2004) proposes that "emotional and social intelligence is a cross-section of inter-related emotional and social competencies that determine how effectively we understand and express ourselves, understand others and relate with them, and cope with daily demands and pressures" (p. 117). Based on this definition, Bar-On developed the Emotional Quotient Inventory (EQ-i), which is a self-report, personality-based EI measure that has 133 items and takes approximately 30 minutes to complete (Bar-On, 2000). The measure yields an overall EQ score and scores for five composite scales: Intrapersonal, Interpersonal, Adaptability, General Mood, and 5) Stress Management. However, questions have been raised about whether the dimensional structure of the EQ-i as described by Bar-On has been adequately supported by empirical analyses. For example, in a sample of 377 participants drawn from the general population in Australia, Palmer, Manocha, Gignac, and Stough (2003) did not find support for the five-factor structure proposed by Bar-On. Instead, they found that the dimensional structure of the EQ-i comprised a general factor and six subdimensions. They concluded by highlighting the need for analyses of EI measures by independent researchers, a conclusion that we strongly support with regard to all EI measures.

The overall EQ-i has shown test–retest reliability of .79 after 3 months and an internal consistency reliability of .97 (Bar-On, 2004). In assessing convergent validity evidence for the EQ-i, Bar-On (2004) reported that the EQ-i correlated from .58 to .69 with a variety of other self-report EI measures. With respect to discriminant validity, the EQ-I correlated .12 with the Wechsler Adult Intelligence Scale (Bar-On, 2000). In a Dutch sample of 873 participants, Derksen, Kramer, and Katzko (2002) found that the EQ-i had a low correlation with a measure of fluid intelligence, providing further discriminant validity evidence for the EQ-I. However, in a study by Dawda and Hart (2000), the average correlation between the EQ-i and the Big Five personality measures was approximately .50. In addition, the EQ-I correlated –.77 with the anxiety scale from Cattell's 16PF, indicating that this EI measure overlaps substantially with a well-established measure of trait anxiety (Newsome, Day, & Catano, 2000).

Some research has investigated the criterion-related validity of the EQ-i. In a study of retail managers by Slaski and Cartwright (2002), the EQ-i was significantly correlated with morale (.55), stress (–.41), general health (–.50), and supervisor performance ratings (.22). Another important criterion that EI might predict is student grade point average (GPA). Bar-On (1997, 2004) proposed that the EQ-i assesses noncognitive aspects of personal functioning, such as students' ability to cope with environmental demands. Thus, based on unpublished studies cited in the *EQ-i Technical Manual*, Bar-On concluded that EI was an important predictor of academic success. Similarly, Goleman (1995, 1998) proposed that EI could predict success both in school and at work as well as or better than traditional intelligence measures. In terms of peer-reviewed research that has investigated this hypothesis, Newsome et al. (2000) found that the EQ-i total score had a correlation of .01 with GPA and that none of the five composite EQ-i scores was significantly associated with GPA in a sample of 160 Canadian college students. In contrast, cognitive ability (i.e., the Wonderlic Personnel Test) and some personality dimensions (e.g., self-control) were significantly correlated with GPA. In a similar study, O'Connor and Little (2003) found that the EQ-i correlated .23 with GPA in a sample of 90 introductory psychology students; based on these results, O'Connor and Little concluded that EI did not have a strong relationship with GPA. Overall, although the EQ-i demonstrates adequate reliability and some validity evidence, it lacks discriminant and criterion validity evidence. In addition, few peer-reviewed studies have examined whether the EQ-i provides incremental predictive validity above the contribution of established predictors such as the Big Five personality dimensions and general mental ability.

WONG AND LAW EMOTIONAL INTELLIGENCE SCALE (WLEIS)

In a series of recently published papers, Law and colleagues developed a self-report, personality-based EI measure, the Wong and Law EI Scale (WLEIS; Law, Wong, & Song, 2004; Wong, Law, & Wong, 2004). The WLEIS consists of 16 items that tap four EI dimensions: Self-Emotions Appraisal, Others-Emotion Appraisal, Use of Emotion, and Regulation of Emotion. Law and his colleagues examined relationships between WLEIS dimensions and both cognitive ability and Big Five personality dimensions in several studies, which provide initial validity evidence for the WLEIS in both student and field settings. These studies also include samples from Chinese and Hong Kong employees and students, samples that have not been studied much by EI researchers. In addition, in the Law et al. (2004) paper, peer ratings of the EI of Chinese employees in a cigarette factory were found to be significant predictors of supervisor job performance ratings even after controlling for Big Five personality dimensions. Thus, this relatively new EI measure holds some promise in terms of providing incremental validity evidence. Nevertheless, the WLEIS includes many of the same limitations as do other personality-based, self-report EI measures. In fact, Law et al. (2004) concluded their study by noting that because EI is traditionally defined as an ability facet, ability-based tests of EI might be more important than self-report EI measures.

EMOTIONAL INTELLIGENCE SCALE (EIS)

Schutte and colleagues (1998) proposed that EI involves the ability to adaptively understand and regulate emotions. They suggested that EI can be measured as a personality trait, and they developed a 33-item self-report Emotional Intelligence Scale (EIS) that has been used by many researchers. Unlike most other EI measures, the EIS is treated as unidimensional by its developers. Some discriminant validity evidence for the EIS was provided in terms of a low correlation ($r = -.06$) with SAT scores. However, the EIS overlapped with Big Five measures, most notably with Openness to Experience ($r = .54$). In a follow-up study, Schutte, Malouff, Simunek, McKenley, and Hollander (2002) found that the EIS was positively associated with self-esteem ($r = .57$) and positive mood ($r = .55$). Schutte and colleagues (1998) noted that this scale seems susceptible to faking good, and thus should probably not be used for selection decisions. Instead, they suggested that the scale might be used to help individuals who are at risk for performing poorly on tasks that require EI and in evaluating individuals who want a valid assessment of their EI.

Additional research on the EIS has been conducted by Saklofske, Austin, and colleagues (e.g., Austin, Saklofske, Huang, McKenney, 2004; Saklofske, Austin, Minski, 2003). This research investigated the number of dimensions in the EIS, and it has raised the possibility that the EIS might, in fact, include multiple dimensions such as Optimism/Mood Regulation, Utilization of Emotions, and Appraisal of Emotions. This easy-to-administer, self-report EI measure is likely to continue to be used widely, but questions remain about its dimensionality, discriminant validity from the Big Five personality dimensions, and incremental validity above existing individual difference measures.

ABILITY-BASED MEASURES: MEIS AND MSCEIT

Mayer, Caruso, and Salovey (2000) proposed that emotional intelligence involves the capacity or ability to reason with and about emotions. They have been critical of EI tests that use self-report measures, which Salovey has noted is like creating a traditional general intelligence test that asks test takers, "Do you think you're pretty smart?" (Paul, 1999). Accordingly, Mayer and colleagues have explicitly designed EI tests in an intelligence or ability testing tradition. First, they developed the Multifactor Emotional Intelligence Scale (MEIS), which had some subscales with low reliability and some problems with scoring procedures. Second, they developed an update of the MEIS called the Mayer-Salovey-Caruso Emotional Intelligence Test (MSCEIT). The most recent version of the MSCEIT is Version 2 (V.2), which was developed by Salovey, Mayer, Caruso, and Lopes (2003). Although the MSCEIT V.2 has improved some of the problems of the MEIS, both tests are described below because the MSCEIT V.2 is relatively new and few studies have been published using it.

The MEIS includes 402 items and has four subscales: Perception, Assimilation, Understanding, and Managing Emotions (Mayer et al., 2000). Because the MEIS is an ability test, the test developers have tried different approaches to identify the correct answers, including consensus scoring and expert scoring. Consensus scoring involves determining the correct answer to a test item by pooling the judgments of hundreds of people. This scoring approach assesses the extent to which the test taker's choice matches majority opinion. Thus, consensus scoring techniques are "in direct contrast to traditional measures of intelligence where an objective measure of truth is considered" (Matthews et al., 2002, p. 186). Expert scoring typically involves determining the correct answer by pooling the judgments of researchers who have expertise in emotions. This type of scoring is most similar to that used in traditional intelligence tests. However, Matthews et al. (2002) raised questions about how "experts" were chosen when determining the correct answers for EI tasks and questions using the expert scoring approach. On a more positive note, expert and consensus scores are highly correlated ($r = .93–.99$; Mayer, Salovey, & Caruso, 2002), indicating that experts and nonexperts tend to agree about which response is best. Nevertheless, several researchers have expressed concerns about the absence of scientific standards for determining the accuracy of consensus and expert scores for these ability-based EI tests, and thus, determining the correct type of scoring to use for ability-based EI tests remains critical and controversial (MacCann et al., 2003).

Despite concerns about scoring approaches to these ability-based EI tests, Mayer and colleagues have developed initial reliability and validity evidence for such tests. Mayer et al. (2000) reported that the internal consistency reliability of the overall MEIS was .95. Across the four branch scores, the average internal consistency reliability was .77 for consensus-scored scales, and the average internal consistency reliability was .62 for expert-scored scales (Caruso, Mayer, & Salovey, 2002). Over a 2-week period, the test–retest reliability of the overall MEIS was .75, whereas the test–retest reliability of the MEIS branch scores ranged from .60 to .68. In terms of discriminant validity evidence, correlations between the Big Five personality dimensions and the MEIS (consensus-scored) ranged from .13 for Openness and Extraversion to .24 for Agreeableness (Roberts, Zeidner, & Matthews, 2001). Data from several studies indicate that the MEIS has a correlation between .30 and .40 with traditional cognitive ability measures (Roberts et al., 2001; Van Rooy & Viswesvaran, 2004). In terms of convergent validity evidence, Mayer et al. (2000) reported that the MEIS had a correlation of .36 with the EQ-i, indicating that these EI tests share approximately 13% of their variance.

The Mayer-Salovey-Caruso Emotional Intelligence Test (MSCEIT) V.2 also assesses the four branches of Mayer and Salovey's (1993, 1997) EI ability model. The MSCEIT V.2 provides a total EI score and four branch scores: Perception of Emotion, Integration and Assimilation of Emotion, Knowledge about Emotions, and Management of Emotions. The 141-item MSCEIT V.2 is shorter and quicker to administer than the MEIS, and it provides consensus and expert scores for all branch scores. The MSCEIT V.2 includes eight subtests, two for each of the four branches of the EI ability model (Salovey et al., 2003). In a study by Mayer, Salovey, Caruso, and Sitarenios (2003), internal consistency reliabilities for the total scale and branch levels were all above .75. Averaging across all of the scales in the MSCEIT V.2, the internal consistency reliability was .68 for consensus scoring and .71 for expert scoring. By comparison, reliability coefficients for cognitive ability tests typically range from .85 to .95 (Kaplan & Saccuzzo, 2004; Murphy & Davidshofer, 2005). Given that the MSCEIT has been explicitly developed as an ability measure, the reliabilities of the subscales are far from optimal (Matthews et al., 2002).

In terms of discriminant validity, a recent study by Schulte, Ree, and Carretta (2004) found that the uncorrected correlation between the MSCEIT and a measure of "g" (Wonderlic Personnel Test [WPT]) was .45 in a sample of 102 graduate and undergraduate students. They found correlations between the MSCEIT and Big Five personality dimensions measured by the NEO Personality Inventory (NEO-PI) that ranged from –.28 for Neuroticism to .27 for both Openness and Agreeableness. After correcting for unreliability in the measures used and entering the WPT, Big Five dimensions, and gender into a regression equation predicting scores on the MSCEIT, they found that the multiple correlation was .81, indicating that the MSCEIT overlapped substantially with traditional predictors such as cognitive ability and Big Five personality dimensions. They concluded by questioning the uniqueness of EI as a construct and its potential for advancing the understanding of human performance. That is, these results indicate that the MSCEIT is likely to provide very little information that one would not already know from assessing "g" and the Big Five personality dimensions. Alternatively, MSCEIT proponents might argue that 'g' and the Big Five personality dimensions would not necessarily add much to what one could predict on the basis of the MSCEIT, but they have not provided data to support this claim. Van Rooy and Viswesvaran (2004) conducted analyses that began to examine these issues, but they used the MEIS as an ability measure rather than the more updated MSCEIT.

COMPARABILITY OF EMOTIONAL INTELLIGENCE MEASURES

In comparing the different EI measures, it is first important to reiterate that the developers of EI measures have used different definitions of EI, which has resulted in different types and numbers of dimensions for the various measures (Gowing, 2001). Also notable is the fact that EI measures use different response formats, including self-report, ability, and informant (peer, supervisor) approaches. Self-report EI measures (e.g., ECI, EQ-i, EIS, WLEIS) sample a broad range of individual differences, but nearly all self-report EI scales relate to well-established personality dimensions such as Neuroticism and Extraversion (Daus & Ashkanasy, 2003; Davies, Stankov, & Roberts, 1998). Alternatively, ability-based EI measures (i.e., MEIS,

MSCEIT), which are more distinct from the Big Five personality dimensions, have higher correlations with general mental ability (GMA) than do self-report EI measures (Van Rooy & Viswesvaran, 2004), leaving less room for such measures to provide incremental prediction of work criteria such as job performance, leader emergence, and leader effectiveness.

Some studies have examined both personality-based and ability-based EI measures to examine the extent of the overlap. Two studies examined the correlation between the MSCEIT and the EQ-i. Mayer et al. (2000) reported that the MSCEIT and the EQ-i correlated .36, whereas Brackett and Mayer (2003) found that the MSCEIT and the EQ-i correlated .21. Together, these studies indicate that these two EI measures share between 4% and 13% of their variance. In general, the weak relationship between different EI measures raises serious questions about whether they all are actually measuring the same construct (Matthews et al., 2002).

In a comprehensive analysis of a variety of different EI scales, Barchard and Hakstian (2004) found that self-report EI measures correlate with personality dimensions but not with cognitive ability. They concluded that self-report EI measures may be better understood as measures of *self-perceptions* of emotional abilities rather than as measures of EI abilities themselves. They also found that existing ability-based EI measures could be accounted for by two factors: Emotional Congruence and Social Perceptiveness. Emotional Congruence, which was defined as the similarity between the perceived affective quality of a stimulus for the participant as compared to most other people, was relatively independent of various traditional cognitive abilities and personality dimensions. Social Perceptiveness, which was defined as the understanding of interpersonal relations and the relationship between emotions and behaviors in various situations, had moderate correlations with both Verbal Ability and Inductive Reasoning, leading Barchard and Hakstian to suggest further research into the unique contribution this particular dimension can provide above the contribution of traditional intelligence measures.

THE STRUGGLE BETWEEN THE SCIENCE AND MARKETING OF EI

Measurement and psychometric issues play a large part in the struggle between the science and marketing of EI. In particular, measurement issues and considerations seem to be heavily affected by the scientific or marketing orientation of those evaluating (and marketing) EI measures. Consultants, trainers, and other business professionals most often prefer self-report EI measures that are easy to develop and administer. They are more likely to support the efficacy of such measures in predicting work performance, leadership success, and other positive organizational outcomes, often without providing any peer-reviewed evidence supporting those claims. For example, Goleman's (1995, 1998) claim that EI is more important than "g" is controversial and appears to ignore 85 years of personnel selection research (Schmidt & Hunter, 1998). Some EI researchers also claim that EI is distinct from traditional intelligence. With personality-based EI measures, it is no surprise that the empirical data support the contention that EI measures are distinct from general mental ability (GMA). However, the correlations between personality-based EI measures and traditional Big Five personality measures are higher than is preferred (e.g., some EI measures correlate as high as –.77 with Neuroticism) when researchers are attempting to develop a unique measure that can provide incremental validity above the contribution of existing reliable and valid measures (Van Rooy & Viswesvaran, 2004).

In contrast, scientists and academicians have generally been more skeptical about EI measurement, particularly self-report measures that do not appear to be assessing an "intelligence" of any kind. Even when evaluating ability-based EI measures that are much more time consuming to develop, scientists and researchers have remained critical and skeptical of the scoring and validity of such approaches (e.g., Matthews et al., 2002). These differing assessments of EI measures by consultants and scientists are not surprising; however, the large degree of disagreement about the cumulative validity evidence and usefulness of EI measures is striking. A more promising note is that the popularity of EI in the corporate world and the media attention it has received have led to a large increase in interest among academic researchers who, although they have remained skeptical, have recently poured their energy and research time into developing an empirical database on EI measures. Emotional intelligence has been a popular and controversial topic at the annual Society for Industrial and Organizational Psychology conference (e.g., Van Rooy, 2004), and it is likely to continue to be discussed and examined among industrial and organizational psychologists, management scholars, and consultants.

EI MEASURES: META-ANALYSES, CONCLUSIONS, AND FUTURE RESEARCH SUGGESTIONS

Psychological measures are most often evaluated in terms of their reliability and validity, and the same evaluation of course needs to be done with EI measures. In general, EI measures have demonstrated adequate reliability. For the most part, personality-based EI measures have acceptable internal consistency as do the overall scales for ability-based measures. However, these reliability data provide no indication about whether EI measures are simply assessing constructs already measured by other, more established psychological constructs. Furthermore, some subscales for the ability-based EI measures have marginally acceptable internal consistency and test–retest reliability.

In terms of validity evidence, much more work needs to be conducted. Existing validity evidence for EI measures ranges from weak to moderate. First, content validity evidence for EI measures is lacking because of vague theoretical development for many of the measures (e.g., ECI, EQ-i). Given that discussions of emotional intelligence have often been criticized for their lack of definitional clarity (e.g., Locke, 2005), it is no surprise that attempts to measure EI have been varied and have varied in their success. In addition, both the Standards for Educational and Psychological Testing (AERA, APA, NCME, 1999) and the American Psychological Association's Ethical Principles (APA, 2002) require that the measures psychologists use are meaningful and valid. It may not be possible to demonstrate much in the way of content and construct validity for the personality-based EI measures because it is just not clear what many of them are supposed to measure. At this point, there is certainly not the type of evidence that would lead a professional to make a well-informed judgment that these personality-based EI tests measure what they claim to measure.

Most EI measures also lack convergent and discriminant validity evidence. First, EI measures have failed to converge on a common construct (Van Rooy, Viswesvaran, & Pluta, 2005). Second, self-report EI measures seem to assess existing personality characteristics or perhaps emotional competencies, but they do not assess the construct of intelligence, despite the fact that the construct's name includes the term *intelligence* (Mayer, Caruso, & Salovey, 1999). In their meta-analysis, Van Rooy and Viswesvaran (2004) found that EI and Big Five personality dimensions had correlations (corrected for unreliability) that ranged from .23 to .34. When the analyses are broken down by a particular measure, some correlations between EI measures and Big Five personality dimensions approach .80. Thus, EI and the Big Five personality dimensions are more highly correlated than many EI researchers and consultants have acknowledged, suggesting that these EI measures are lacking in discriminant validity.

Emotional intelligence measures can also be examined in terms of criterion-related and incremental validity. Van Rooy and Viswesvaran (2004) found that EI explained 5% of the variance in performance, which is substantially lower than the claims of some EI proponents (e.g., Goleman, 1995, 1998), who have argued that EI is more important than GMA in predicting life success and work performance. By comparison, the percentage of variance in job performance that GMA typically accounts for is approximately 26% (Hunter & Hunter, 1984; Schmidt & Hunter, 1998). Accordingly, based on empirical research to date, broad claims that EI is a more important predictor than GMA are unfounded and unsubstantiated.

General mental ability typically provides incremental validity in predicting work outcomes above other measures, whereas initial research indicates that EI demonstrates little or no incremental validity above GMA in predicting performance outcomes. In their meta-analysis, Van Rooy and Viswesvaran (2004) found that EI provided incremental validity above the Big Five personality dimensions in predicting performance. However, EI measures provided minimal (.02) incremental validity above GMA in predicting performance. In contrast, GMA provided substantial incremental validity (.31) above EI. It should be noted that ability-based and personality-based EI measures were not separated in the incremental validity analyses in this meta-analysis.

In a follow-up meta-analytic study, Van Rooy et al. (2005) examined self-report and ability EI measures separately. They found that ability-based EI measures were most strongly related to GMA (.34), Agreeableness (.18), and Openness to Experience (.14). In contrast, personality-based EI measures were most highly correlated with Emotional Stability (.40), Extraversion (.36), Conscientiousness (.33), and Openness to Experience (.32). They also found that the average correlation between self-report and ability EI measures was .14, leading the authors to conclude that different constructs were being tapped by self-report and ability-based EI measures.

The potential for faking on self-report EI measures has also been raised as a concern. A study by Van Rooy, Viswesvaran, and Alonso (2004) investigated the potential for faking on Schutte et al.'s (1998) self-report EIS with a Solomon four-group research design. They found that participants completing this measure were able to fake-bad more than they were able to fake-good. This strong experimental design provides a good start to investigations of faking in emotional intelligence, but more research on the potential for applicant faking is needed, particularly because self-report EI measures are being used increasingly in applied settings.

As with any relatively new construct, another consideration is whether there are group differences in EI measures. Van Rooy, Alonso, and Viswesvaran (2005) found that females scored slightly higher than males on the EIS (Schutte et al., 1998). Differences also existed in EI scores across ethnic groups, but such differences favored ethnic groups, reducing concerns about adverse impact in personnel selection and other Human Resource decisions. Mayer et al.

(2003) found that women scored higher than men on the MSCEIT, but there were no significant ethnic group differences. Day and Carroll (2004) found that females performed significantly better than males on all four scales of the MSCEIT. For both personality-based and ability-based EI measures, it appears that group differences may not cause adverse impact against protected groups; however, additional investigations of potential adverse impact based on the use of EI measures in personnel selection are necessary. Because EI may be culturally bound, investigations of cross-cultural similarities and differences in EI are needed as well.

In conclusion, concerns remain for both personality-based and ability-based EI measures. Many researchers argue that the prospect of developing reliable and valid personality-based measures of EI is quite low. Alternatively, researchers have more enthusiasm for the ultimate success of ability-based measures, which show greater discriminant validity and greater promise for incremental validity above the contribution of more established predictors such as cognitive ability and Big Five personality dimensions. Another research and practical question has to do with the stability (or lack thereof) of a person's level of emotional intelligence. Because many applications of EI involve attempts to develop EI, additional investigations of the "trainability" of EI in individuals and teams are needed (Dulewicz & Higgs, 2004; Slaski & Cartwright, 2003). Questions about whether training can increase EI can be answered only with the use of reliable and valid EI measures as well as rigorous training designs (Goldstein & Ford, 2002; Noe, 2005). Certainly, any organizational decisions that depend on the measurement of EI should be made very cautiously given the current state of research on EI. Nevertheless, we look forward to the continuing debate on EI measurement and an increase in the empirical database on EI measures.

ACKNOWLEDGMENTS

The authors would like to thank Kevin Murphy and Frank Landy for valuable comments and suggestions on an earlier version of this chapter.

An earlier treatment of this topic appears in Conte, J. M. (2005). A review and critique of emotional intelligence measures. *Journal of Organizational Behavior, 26,* 433–440.

REFERENCES

American Educational Research Association, American Psychological Association, & National Council on Measurement in Education (Joint Committee). (1999). *Standards for educational and psychological testing.* Washington, DC: American Educational Research Association.

American Psychological Association. (2002). Ethical principles of psychologists and code of conduct. *American Psychologist, 57,* 1060–1073.

Austin, E. J., Saklofske, D. H., Huang, S. H., McKenney, D. (2004). Measurement of trait emotional intelligence: Testing and cross-validating a modified version of Schutte et al.'s (1998) measure. *Personality and Individual Differences, 36,* 555–562.

Barchard, K. A., & Hakstian, A. R. (2004). The nature and measurement of emotional intelligence abilities: Basic dimensions and their relationships with other cognitive ability and personality variables. *Educational and Psychological Measurement, 64,* 437–462.

Bar-On, R. (1997). *Bar-On Emotional Quotient Inventory: Technical manual (EQ-i).* Toronto, ON: Multi-Health Systems.

Bar-On, R. (2000). Emotional and social intelligence: Insights from the Emotional Quotient Inventory (EQ-i). In R. Bar-On & J. D. Parker (Eds.), *Handbook of emotional intelligence* (pp. 363–388). San Francisco: Jossey-Bass.

Bar-On, R. (2004). The Bar-On Emotional Quotient Inventory (EQ-i): Rationale, description, and summary of psychometric properties. In G. Geher (Ed.), *The measurement of emotional intelligence: Common ground and controversy* (pp. 115–145). Hauppauge, NY: Nova Science.

Boyatzis, R. E., Goleman, D., & Rhee, K. S. (2000). Clustering competence in emotional intelligence. In R. Bar-On & J. D. Parker (Eds.). *The handbook of emotional intelligence: Theory, development, and assessment, and application at home, school, and in the workplace* (pp. 343–362). San Francisco: Jossey-Bass.

Boyatzis, R. E., & Sala, F. (2004). Assessing emotional intelligence competencies. In G. Geher (Ed.), *The measurement of emotional intelligence: Common ground and controversy* (pp. 147–180). Hauppauge, NY: Nova Science.

Brackett, M. A., & Mayer, J. D. (2003). Convergent, discriminant, and incremental validity of competing measures of emotional intelligence. *Personality and Social Psychology Bulletin, 29,* 1147–1158.

Caruso, D. R., Mayer, J. D., & Salovey, P. (2002). Relation of an ability measure of emotional intelligence to personality. *Journal of Personality Assessment, 79,* 306–320.

Conte, J. (2005). A review and critique of emotional intelligence measures. *Journal of Organizational Behavior, 26,* 433–440.

Daus, C. S., & Ashkanasy, N. M. (2003). Will the real emotional intelligence please stand up? On deconstructing the emotional intelligence "debate". *The Industrial-Organizational Psychologist, 41*(2), 69–72.

Davies, M., Stankov, L., & Roberts, R. D. (1998). Emotional intelligence: In search of an elusive construct. *Journal of Personality and Social Psychology, 75,* 989–1015.

Dawda, D., & Hart, S. D. (2000). Assessing emotional intelligence: Reliability and validity of the Bar-On Emotional Quotient Inventory (EQ-i) in university students. *Personality and Individual Differences, 28,* 797–812.

Day, A. L., & Carroll, S. A. (2004). Using an ability-based measure of emotional intelligence to predict individual performance, group performance, and group citizenship behaviors. *Personality and Individual Differences, 36,* 1443–1458.

Derksen, J., Kramer, I., & Katzko, M. (2002). Does a self-report measure for emotional intelligence assess something different than general intelligence? *Personality & Individual Differences, 32,* 37–48.

Dulewicz, V., & Higgs, M. (2004). Can emotional intelligence be developed? *International Journal of Human Resource Management, 15,* 95–111.

Goldstein, I. L., & Ford, J. K. (2002). *Training in organizations: Needs assessment, development, and evaluation* (4th ed.). Belmont, CA: Wadsworth.

Goleman, D. (1995). *Emotional intelligence: Why it can matter more than IQ.* New York: Bantam.

Goleman, D. (1998). *Working with emotional intelligence.* New York: Bantam Books.

Gowing, M. K. (2001). Measurement of individual emotional competence. In C. Cherniss & D. Goleman (Eds.), *The emotionally intelligent workplace: How to select for, measure, and improve emotional intelligence in individuals, groups, and organizations* (pp. 83–131). San Francisco: Jossey-Bass.

Hunter, J. E., & Hunter, R. F. (1984). Validity and utility of alternative predictors of job performance. *Psychological Bulletin, 96,* 72–98.

Kaplan, R. M., & Saccuzzo, D. P. (2004). *Psychological testing: Principles, applications, and issues* (6th ed.). Belmont, CA: Thomson/Wadsworth.

Landy, F. J. (2005). Some historical and scientific issues related to research on emotional intelligence. *Journal of Organizational Behavior, 26,* 411–424.

Landy, F. J., & Conte, J. M. (2004). *Work in the 21st century: An introduction to industrial and organizational psychology.* Boston: McGraw-Hill.

Law, K. S., Wong, C. S., & Song, L. (2004). The construct and criterion validity of emotional intelligence and its potential utility for management studies. *Journal of Applied Psychology, 89,* 483–496.

Locke, E. A. (2005). Why emotional intelligence is an invalid concept. *Journal of Organizational Behavior, 26,* 425–431.

Lord Kelvin (Sir William Thomson). (1891). Lecture to the Institution of Civil Engineers (May 3, 1883). In *Popular lectures and addresses* (Vol. 1, p. 80). London: Macmillan.

MacCann, C., Matthews, G., Zeidner, M., & Roberts, R. D. (2003). Psychological assessment of emotional intelligence: A review of self-report and performance-based testing. *International Journal of Organizational Analysis, 11,* 249–276.

Matthews, G., Zeidner, M., & Roberts, R. D. (2002). *Emotional intelligence: Science and myth.* Cambridge, MA: MIT Press.

Mayer, J. D., Caruso, D. R., & Salovey, P. (1999). Emotional intelligence meets traditional standards for an intelligence. *Intelligence, 27,* 267–298.

Mayer, J. D., Caruso, D., & Salovey, P. (2000). Selecting a measure of emotional intelligence: The case for ability scales. In R. Bar-On & J. D. Parker (Eds.), *The handbook of emotional intelligence.* New York: Jossey-Bass.

Mayer, J. D., & Salovey, P. (1993). The intelligence of emotional intelligence. *Intelligence, 17,* 433–442.

Mayer, J. D., & Salovey, P. (1997). What is emotional intelligence? In P. Salovey & D. Sluyter (Eds.), *Emotional development and emotional intelligence: Implications for educators* (pp. 3–34). New York: Basic Books.

Mayer, J. D., Salovey, P., & Caruso, D. R. (2002). *Mayer-Salovey-Caruso Emotional Intelligence Test (MSCEIT) User's Manual.* Toronto, ON: Multi-Health Systems.

Mayer, J. D., Salovey, P., Caruso, D. R., & Sitarenios, G. (2003). Measuring emotional intelligence with the MSCEIT V2.0. *Emotion, 3,* 97–105.

Murphy, K. R., & Davidshofer, C. O. (2005). *Psychological testing: Principles and application* (6th ed.). Upper Saddle River, NJ: Prentice Hall.

Newsome, S., Day, A. L., & Catano, V. M. (2000). Assessing the predictive validity of emotional intelligence. *Personality & Individual Differences, 29,* 1005–1016.

Noe, R. A. (2005). *Employee training and development* (3rd ed.). Boston: McGraw Hill.

O'Connor, R. M., & Little, I. S. (2003). Revisiting the predictive validity of emotional intelligence: Self-report versus ability-based measures. *Personality & Individual Differences, 35,* 1893–1902.

Palmer, B. R., Manocha, R., Gignac, G., & Stough, C. (2003). Examining the factor structure of the Bar-On Emotional Quotient Inventory with an Australian general population sample. *Personality & Individual Differences, 35,* 1191–1210.

Paul, A. M. (1999, June 28). Promotional intelligence. Retrieved November 7, 2005, from http://www.salon.com/books/it/1999/06/28/emotional

Roberts, R. D., Zeidner, M., & Matthews, G. (2001). Does emotional intelligence meet traditional standards for an intelligence? Some new data and conclusions. *Emotion, 1,* 196–231.

Saklofske, D. H., Austin, E. J., & Minski, P. S. (2003). Factor structure and validity of a trait emotional intelligence measure. *Personality and Individual Differences, 34,* 707–721.

Sala, F. (2002). *Emotional Competence Inventory: Technical Manual.* Boston: The Hay Group.

Salovey, P., Mayer, J. D., Caruso, D., & Lopes, P. N. (2003). Measuring emotional intelligence as a set of abilities with the Mayer-Salovey-Caruso Emotional Intelligence Test. In S. J. Lopez & C. R. Snyder (Eds.), *Positive psychological assessment: A handbook of models and measures* (pp. 251–265). Washington, DC: American Psychological Association.

Schmidt, F. L., & Hunter, J. E. (1998). The validity and utility of selection methods in personnel psychology: Practical and theoretical implications of 85 years of research findings. *Psychological Bulletin, 124,* 262–274.

Schulte, M. J., Ree, M. J., & Carretta, T. R. (2004). Emotional intelligence: Not much more than g and personality. *Personality and Individual Differences, 37,* 1059–1068.

Schutte, N. S., Malouff, J. M., Hall, L. E., Haggerty, D. J., Cooper, J. T., Golden, C. J., et al. (1998). Development and validation of a measure of emotional intelligence. *Personality and Individual Differences, 25,* 167–177.

Schutte, N. S., Malouff, J. M., Simunek, M., McKenley, J., & Hollander, S. (2002). Characteristic emotional intelligence and emotional well-being. *Cognition and Emotion, 16,* 769–785.

Slaski, M., & Cartwright, S. (2002). Health, performance, and emotional intelligence: An exploratory study of retail managers. *Stress and Health, 18,* 63–68.

Slaski, M., & Cartwright, S. (2003). Emotional intelligence training and its implications for stress, health, and performance. *Stress and Health, 19,* 233–239.

Van Rooy, D. L. (2004, April). *Emotional intelligence: Practical questions for I-O psychologists.* Symposium presented at the Nineteenth Annual Conference of the Society for Industrial and Organizational Psychology, Chicago, IL.

Van Rooy, D. L., Alonso, A., & Viswesvaran, C. (2005). Group differences in emotional intelligence scores: Theoretical and practical implications. *Personality and Individual Differences, 38,* 689–700.

Van Rooy, D. L., Viswesvaran, C., & Pluta, P. (2005). An evaluation of construct validity: What is this thing called Emotional Intelligence? *Human Performance, 18,* 445–462.

Van Rooy, D. L., & Viswesvaran, C. (2004). Emotional intelligence: A meta-analytic investigation of predictive validity and nomological net. *Journal of Vocational Behavior, 65,* 71–95.

Van Rooy, D. L., Viswesvaran, C., & Alonso, A. (2004, April). *The susceptibility of a measure of emotional intelligence to faking: A Solomon 4-group design.* Paper presented at the Nineteenth Annual Conference of the Society for Industrial and Organizational Psychology, Chicago, IL.

Wong, C. S., Law, K. S., & Wong, P. M. (2004). Development and validation of a force-choice emotional intelligence measure for Chinese respondents in Hong Kong. *Asia Pacific Journal of Management, 21,* 535–559.

II

The Relationships Between EI and Other Constructs

The second important critique of emotional intelligence (EI) is that there are a number of social skills, abilities, preferences, and behaviors that have something to do with the perception, understanding, and management of emotions that don't seem to fall under the heading "emotional intelligence." First, many of these behaviors, abilities, skills, and so forth have been studied for decades under different names, and re-labeling them "emotional intelligence" does not contribute very much. In chapter 4, Landy traces the long and disappointing history of research on "social intelligence." Psychologists spent many years trying to develop adequate theories and adequate measures of social intelligence; many of the concepts discussed in this body of research seem to overlap with current conceptualizations of EI. The ultimate failure of this line of research should have clear lessons for EI researchers, but sadly, most of this work is simply ignored by EI enthusiasts.

In chapter 5, Allen and Cohen describe a variety of EI-oriented interventions currently being pursued in the schools. This chapter is valuable for a number of reasons, in particular, because it provides a very concrete description of the wide range of attitudes, beliefs, skills, and knowledge that might fall under the umbrella of EI. The breadth of topics noted in this chapter is almost certainly an indication of the fact that when educators say "emotional intelligence," they can mean a fairly wide range of things, and that emotional intelligence is more likely to be a generic label for several sometimes weakly related concepts rather than a single, well-defined construct.

In chapter 6, Furnham addresses the question of why EI is so popular. His analysis suggests that the loose, expansive definitions that are characteristic of market-oriented EI models is not a hindrance to their success but rather a key to their popular acceptance. He suggests that the combination of fuzzy definitions and sweeping claims is a common path to success in the current business environments. In other words, his analysis suggests if tighter definitions of EI had been proposed and followed, there probably would not be much of a market for EI.

In chapter 7, Brody carefully examines the definition of "intelligence," and asks whether a variety of alternative definitions of what it means to be intelligent, including being emotionally intelligent, really refer to the same phenomena. His conclusion is that "emotional intelligence" is a somewhat misleading label. We know a good deal about human intelligence, and many of the defining features of intelligence (e.g., its developmental track) do not seem to be shared by EI or by other alternative definitions of intelligence.

The bottom line of this section is that knowing that someone works intelligently with emotions is not the same thing as knowing that someone is emotionally intelligent.

4

The Long, Frustrating, and Fruitless Search for Social Intelligence: A Cautionary Tale

Frank J. Landy
Landy Litigation Support Group

In this chapter, I cover the development of the construct of social intelligence from its introduction into the scientific literature until it was replaced with the more modern term of *emotional intelligence*. From a historical viewpoint, it is not necessary to debate whether emotional and social intelligence represent identical constructs. The fact is that for 65 years, *social intelligence* was the term used to represent much of what has come to be known as emotional intelligence. The term *emotional intelligence* was introduced as part of Howard Gardner's conception of multiple intelligences. Goleman's presentation of emotional intelligence represents a variation on the theme laid out in Gardner's theory.

In my review, I cover the period from the beginning of the 20th century until the publication of Gardner's theory in 1983. My review is based on an electronic literature search (PsycINFO) of the term *social intelligence* for all archived years, ending with the year 1983. In addition, I examined several hundred basic, applied, and commercial texts published during the period 1900–1983 for coverage of terms such as *intelligence, social intelligence*, the *George Washington Test of Social Intelligence* (Moss, Hunt, Omwake, & Ronning, 1927) and references to F. A. Moss (the primary author of the George Washington Test) and E. L. Thorndike. The examination of texts printed prior to approximately 1930 was particularly challenging because of the poor, and often nonexistent, subject or author index to accompany the text. This meant examining footnotes, casual references, the body of the text in appropriate chapters, and the like. As a result, the early historical record may be somewhat less complete and accurate than the later record.

Some of the material covered in this chapter has been addressed by Matthews, Zeidner, and Roberts (2002) in Appendix A to their comprehensive text, *Emotional Intelligence: Science and Myth*. In examining that appendix, I find it less complete than the present chapter. This should not be taken as a criticism. Their main point, one with which I agree, was that the early foundation for emotional intelligence can be found in the literature on social intelligence. Similarly, a 1973 review by Walker and Foley is detailed and insightful with respect to aspects of the development of the concept of social intelligence, but it does not deal with the early conceptions of Thorndike. I have written the current chapter in a way that I hope will position it to be a comprehensive historical treatment of the construct and measurement of social intelligence.

CHAPTER OVERVIEW

Given the lengthy period of time covered in this review, and the diversity of the literature to be covered, an overview of what will follow might prove valuable to the reader.

It is clear that the construct of social intelligence has endured in spite of often disappointing empirical results and substantial theoretical criticism. It has been part of the psychological landscape for almost 100 years and has captured the time and attention of many distinguished psychometricians and theoreticians. The major impetus for this attention was clearly E. L. Thorndike, who suggested that intelligence might have three facets: abstract, mechanical, and social. The mere suggestion of this by someone as respected as Thorndike was enough to unleash an epidemic of speculation but, unfortunately, little serious or programmatic research. In the late 1920s, Moss and his colleagues (Moss et al., 1927) developed a test for measuring social intelligence, and it remained the major research and applied instrument for the study of social intelligence until the late 1960s when Guilford and his colleagues developed a competing test (O'Sullivan,

Guilford, & deMille, 1965). When Thorndike introduced the term in 1920, American psychology was at the crossroads of change. The concept of social intelligence was introduced at a time when the debate about its very existence was central to the evolution of theories of mental ability, measures of mental ability, and the application of mental measurements to work and school behavior. It was an attractive foil for some serious scientific and sociopolitical debates.

In the first section of the chapter, I place Thorndike's use of the term *social intelligence* in 1920 in historical and sociopolitical context. Some of this material is excerpted from an earlier article I prepared as part of debate regarding the status of social intelligence (Landy, 2005). In subsequent sections, I examine the literature on social intelligence both in time periods (the 1920s, the 1930s, 1940–1965, and 1965–1983) as well as from theoretical and applied perspectives. The reason for identifying 1965 as a year of demarcation is because Guilford formally introduced social intelligence into his complex "structure of the intellect" model of mental ability in that year (O'Sullivan et al., 1965) .

1909–1980s: Who "Noticed" Social Intelligence?

With respect to well-known psychologists who were active during the period 1909–1983, it is interesting to see who paid attention to the proposed construct of social intelligence, if only to dismiss it. To some extent, even rising to the level of criticism among knowledgeable psychologists says something for a construct. It might be equally interesting to list the names of eminent psychologists who did not (but worked in an area where they *could*) mention social intelligence, but attributions for a failure to mention a construct get messy. It is interesting to note that a substantial number of authors over the decades felt it necessary to place quotation marks around the term "social intelligence" as if to denote its precarious position in the hierarchy of human attributes. Such quotation marks were seldom placed around other attributes (both established and proposed) by those same authors.

Psychologists who might be easily recognized by theoreticians who studied human attributes and/or psychometricians and applied psychologists include the following (in rough chronological order): John Dewey, E. L. Thorndike, Max Freyd, Harold Burtt, A. T. Poffenberger, Charles Spearman, Harry Kitson, Truman Kelley, Lewis Terman, Clark Hull, Walter Van Dyke Bingham, Rudolph Pintner, O. K. Buros, Morris Viteles, Bruce Moore, J. P. Guilford, Ross Stagner, F. Stuart Chapin, R. L. Thorndike, Irving Lorge, Donald Super, Gardner Lindzey, Jerome Bruner, E. E. Ghiselli, David Wechsler, Anne

Anastasi, Joseph Tiffin, Lee Cronbach, Milton Blum, Henry Clay Smith, Lee Sechrest, Douglas Jackson, Samuel Osipow, Robert Guion, and Mary Tenopyr.

Even to have a distinguished group such as those listed *criticize* your work would be a mark of some distinction, and as you will see in subsequent sections, not all of these distinguished psychologists were critical. Because the construct remained at least a part of the psychological vocabulary from 1909 until 1983, one must at least grudgingly admire the attractiveness of the concept. In some respects, it might have represented the allure of the "undiscovered" or "unmeasured" human attribute to the differential psychologist. In other respects, it might have represented the opportunity to explain or predict additional variance in some valued dependent variable such as work or school performance for the applied psychologist. There is also little doubt that it represented an opportunity for consultants to add another tool to their consulting bag, thus increasing revenue potential.

THE EMERGENCE OF SOCIAL INTELLIGENCE

It appears to be generally accepted that the term *social intelligence* was first introduced by E. L. Thorndike, in an article that appeared in *Harper's Magazine* in 1920. This is incorrect. The term and concept appears much earlier in the writings of John Dewey that addressed morality and public education. In 1909, Dewey wrote

> The moral has been conceived in too goody-goody a way. Ultimate moral motives and forces are nothing more or less than social *intelligence* (italics in the original)—the power of observing and comprehending social situations—and *social power* (italics in the original)—trained capacities of control—at work in the service of social interests and aims .... The moral trinity of the school (includes) the demand for social intelligence, social power, and social interests. (p. 43)

This same theme was picked up by Herbert Lull in the *American Journal of Sociology* in 1911 in an article titled "Moral Instruction through Social Intelligence". To place the introduction of the term in context, it is clear that both Dewey and Lull were really talking about revising the school curriculum of the time to be more relevant, and thus engaging to the student, by including issues that were socially current. This was a position embraced by Thorndike as well. They were not proposing social intelligence as a human attribute as Thorndike would a few years later.

Although it is unclear if Thorndike was aware of the work of Lull because he makes no reference to Lull in his own publications, he was most certainly aware of the work of his fellow educational psychologist John Dewey and would have heard the term *social intelligence* used, and even defined, before his *Harper's* article. Thorndike cited Dewey often and credits him with guidance in his own thinking (E. L. Thorndike, 1936) about education and psychology (although *not* Dewey's 1909 book that introduced the concept and initial definition of social intelligence). It was John Dewey who first introduced and defined the term *social intelligence*—a term that would forever after be linked to his fellow educational psychologist E.L. Thorndike after the appearance of *Harper's Magazine* in 1920.

E. L. Thorndike, Social Intelligence, and Emotional Intelligence

Emotional intelligence research anchors its classical heritage in a comment made by E. L. Thorndike in *Harper's Magazine* in 1920 about the possibility of a form of intelligence that he termed "social intelligence" that was distinct from abstract or academic intelligence (e.g. Bar On, 2000; Derksen, Kramer, & Katzko, 2002; Mayer & Geher, 1996; Mayer & Salovey, 1993; Roberts, Zeidner, & Matthews, 2001). As we have seen above, the concept most likely had its roots in the thoughts of John Dewey rather than Thorndike, but it was Thorndike's use of the concept that attracted the attention of colleagues. He suggested three modes of intelligence: abstract, mechanical, and social. The definitions were simple and straightforward:

> Abstract intelligence ... .is the ability to understand and manage ideas and symbols, such as words, numbers, chemical or physical formulae, legal decisions, scientific laws and principles, and the like.
>
> Mechanical intelligence ... is the ability to learn to understand and manage things and mechanisms such as a knife, gun, mowing machine, automobile, boat, lathe, piece of land, river, or storm.
>
> Social intelligence ... is the ability to manage and understand men and women, boys and girls, to act wisely in human relations. (Thorndike, 1920, p. 228)

It was Thorndike's tripartite division—and in particular, the nomination of social intelligence as one of those divisions—that fueled interest both then, in measuring social intelligence, and now, in measuring emotional intelligence. Note that Thorndike identified social intelligence as, at least in part, a behavioral rather than simply a cognitive phenomenon. He specified that the socially intelligent person could "manage" men and women and "act" wisely in human relations. Unlike Dewey, Thorndike proposed that social intelligence included both the comprehension of social behavior and norms as well as social conduct itself. Dewey had specified that social intelligence was largely an issue of comprehension while social power represented an action or behavior. Dewey's distinction would prove to be an important one, one that would have been useful for Thorndike to maintain. Most subsequent research concentrated on the knowledge component and largely ignored the behavioral one. This was not surprising given the difficulty of operationalizing and assessing the behavioral side of the equation. Nevertheless, the subsequent research would have been enhanced had the behavioral and knowledge components been kept distinct. I will return to this point later in the chapter.

At the time of the *Harper's* article, Thorndike was certainly one of the best known theoretical and applied psychologists in America. He was a respected learning theorist and premier educational psychologist. He was also just about to join the Psychological Corporation at the request of his colleague and early mentor James McKeen Cattell and was developing a good reputation as a psychologist with an understanding of industry. It is not surprising that when he spoke, others listened. But it is important to put his comments in context.

Thorndike had published extensively on the topic of intelligence in the years preceding the *Harper's* article. He had written the defining three-volume work outlining the "new" educational psychology. He had written books and articles on animal and human intelligence. He was emerging as an authority in applied psychometrics and statistics. He had written texts in general psychology. He had used all of these outlets as opportunities to lay out his views of learning and human attributes. Yet never before the *Harper's* article had he mentioned social intelligence or the tripartite division of cognitive function. One might reasonably wonder why he chose to introduce the concept at this point.

In 1920, Thorndike's theory of intelligence was well known. Through a combination of nature (via hereditary and congenital factors) and nurture (exposure to environments and experiences), some people had more neural connections or a more elaborated neural network than others. Those with more connections were more intelligent than those with fewer connections. He had a very elaborated architecture for his theory of intelligence, including concepts of level (difficulty of a task), range (number of tasks at a given degree of difficulty), area (total number of situations to which an individual was capable of responding), and speed (the rapidity with which a response could be made; Joncich, 1962; Thorndike, 1921). By 1920, Thorndike, along with other contemporaries (e.g., Terman, Pintner, Thurstone, Yerkes), was very concerned about the narrowness of the instruments used to measure intelligence. This was closely tied to his notion of "area" as defined above. He believed that intelligence could be demonstrated in many different venues and in many different ways, constrained only by the sheer number of connections possessed by a given individual. As a result, he cautioned that the typical tests of abstract intelligence were highly loaded with verbal content and that other media of assessment might be valuable to explore. This was the foundation for his speculation regarding different "intelligences"—not that they were conceptually or fundamentally unique, but that intelligence (which he firmly believed was unitary) could and should be *measured* in many different ways and in many different venues. Nevertheless, intelligence in any venue would always be the result of the sheer number of neural connections possessed by an individual. He was pessimistic, as was his son R. L. Thorndike in a later review of social intelligence research, (R. L. Thorndike, 1936; R. L. Thorndike & Stein, 1937) that paper and pencil tests could ever capture the *use* of intelligence in social situations. In the *Harper's* article, E. L. Thorndike cautioned:

> For most of the activities of intelligence in response to the behavior of human beings, a genuine situation with real persons is essential .... It requires human beings to respond to, time to adapt its responses, and face, voice, and gesture, and mien as tools. (p. 231)

Harper's Magazine in 1920

In 1920, *Harper's Magazine* was a popular not a scientific outlet. In the same volume of *Harper's* which presented Thorndike's comment about social intelligence, we find a piece on bird intimacies, photos of the cave dwellers of the Grand Canary Islands, a story by Zane Grey about Death Valley, a short story by G. K. Chesterton called "The Man Who Knew Too Much," and a piece by Clarence Day (best known for his stories which resulted in the classic film *Life with Father*). Thorndike had another article in that volume as well, titled "Psychology of the Half-Educated Man." Outlets like the *New York Times* and *Harper's Magazine* became conduits for public discourse of a nonscientific nature about scientific concepts, much like current publications such as the *New Yorker*, *Harper's Magazine*, the *Atlantic Monthly* or the *New Republic*. Benjamin (in press) describes the context as follows:

> When the new experimental psychologists arrived on the scene in America in the last two decades of the nineteenth century, promotional activities were important. As noted above, there was an American public that knew psychology as phrenologists, physiognomists, seers, psychics, and mediums. Most of the new experimental psychologists felt that it was their obligation to get the word out about their science, and one way to do that was to write articles for popular magazines. A survey of the popular literature indicates that there were hun-

dreds of such articles published between 1890 and 1930 by Hall, James, Jastrow, Scripture, Cattell, Münsterberg, John Watson, Mary Whiton Calkins, John Dewey, Edward Thorndike, James Mark Baldwin, Robert Yerkes, and many others in such magazines as *Atlantic Monthly, Harper's, Forum, Collier's, McCall's, New World, American Magazine, Independent Woman,* and others (see Michaels, Ganong, & Viney, 1980). (Benjamin, in press)

It was in this context that Thorndike presented his comments about different "types" of intelligence. It was a commonsense caution against a narrowly based *measurement* of intelligence. It was not a *theory* of intelligence like Guilford's magnum opus, the "structure of the intellect" (Guilford, 1956, 1967); or the ETS "French kit" (French, Ekstrom, & Price, 1963); or Carroll's (1993) three strata theory. It was a simple caution. Thorndike (1920) said at one point, "Intelligence varies according to the life situations in which it works" (p. 228). At another point, he wrote,

A man has not some one amount of one kind of intelligence, but varying amounts of different intelligences. His ability to think with numbers may be great; his ability to think with words, small. He may be a successful student of history and a failure at learning physics. Compare Grant's intelligence in using an army with his intelligence as a business trader.

... A perfect description and measurement of intelligence would involve testing man's ability to think in all possible lines, just as a perfect description of mineral wealth of a state would involve adequate testing for iron, copper, gold, silver, lead, tin, zinc, antinomy, petroleum, platinum, tungsten, iridium, and the long list of rarer metals.

For ordinary practical purposes (italics added) it suffices to examine for three "intelligences" (quotation marks in the original), which we may call mechanical intelligence, social intelligence and abstract intelligence. (p. 228)

It appears that Thorndike was using the concept of social intelligence as a way of helping the nonscientific reader, the reader of *Harper's Magazine,* to understand that intelligence could manifest itself in many venues. In an illustration in the same article, he identifies the following alternative "intelligences": language, mathematics, science, philosophical questions, moral questions, tools, children, adults, business, music, and art.

Thorndike's Other Publications

Thorndike was a prolific writer; yet in only one instance other than the *Harper's* article (Thorndike, Bregman, Cobb, & Woodyard, 1926) does he even mention social intelligence. In that 1926 text on the measurement of intelligence, Thorndike and his colleagues simply note that the description of the intelligence test they are proposing does not include "any tasks involving responses to actual human beings or to material objects present to sense—tasks of what has been called social intelligence and mechanical intelligence" (p. 64).

It is worth noting that Thorndike does not cite his *Harper's* article nor any other work with respect to the mention of social intelligence in this measurement book. He does, however, use this text as an opportunity to restate his position with respect to the *method* of intelligence testing as his major concern:

> Man can use intellect and display the amount of it which he possesses in operations with any sort of material object, any living plant or animal, including himself, any quantity or relation that exists in reality or in imagination, any idea, emotion, or act. (p. 20)

Interestingly, in a book written in 1925, Thorndike proposes only *two* different types of intelligence: working with ideas and working with things (p. 87). It is notable that he does not propose any form of social intelligence (e.g., working with people). It was Thorndike's view that reasoning was reasoning, no matter where it occurred and no matter what was being reasoned *about*, for example, people, things, or ideas. A reasonable extrapolation of his position would be that there are some individuals who may not be able to display their intelligence through standard paper and pencil intelligence tests (e.g., the illiterate), and for those people, tests based on mechanical and/or social situations might better assess their intelligence. Similarly, individuals high in abstract intelligence but inexperienced in either social situations or with mechanical reasoning would best be assessed using standard paper and pencil intelligence tests. The issue was about *modes of testing* not different *types* of intelligence. It is also telling that Thorndike makes no mention of social intelligence or the tripartite division of intelligence in his autobiography (E. L. Thorndike, 1936).

So how are we to view Thorndike's suggestion of the three intelligences of abstract, mechanical, and social? We should view them as metaphors, much like McGregor's suggestion of Theory X and Y styles of management (1960) or Cronbach's and Meehl's (1955) suggestion of three "types" of validity. The suggestions were not to be taken literally. McGregor and Cronbach were not suggesting theories or constructs. They were simply suggesting a few of the many ways to approach a topic. Thorndike had something much more specific in mind, that is, disabusing researchers and the public from using only one type of intelligence *test* as a basis for making inferences about the intelligence of an individual. Perhaps Pintner (1924), a colleague of Thorndike's at Columbia during the period in question described Thorndike's position most succinctly: "This three fold division of intelligence is merely a convenient scheme for dividing numerous reactions which may be indicative of intelligence" (p. 56).

If we simply look at what Thorndike said about the measurement of mental ability, we discover that the challenges faced by psychometricians in 1920 remain the challenges of today—the challenge of assessing mental ability in ways other than simply administering multiple choice paper and pencil tests. This was a point worth noting then, just as it is now. But this falls far short of positing a special kind of intelligence called social intelligence.

1920 in Context

As I indicated earlier, 1920 was a critical time for the evolution of applied psychology in the United States. The leaders in the field were looking for any opportunity to popularize psychology to the masses (Benjamin, in press). Thus, it was not surprising that Thorndike would reach out to those masses through *Harper's Magazine*. But beyond the simple issue of making psychology more respectable and accessible to a nonscientific audience, the concept of social intelligence provided a platform for many other serious substantial and sociopolitical debates that were going on at the time. A sampling of those issues includes the following:

Structuralism Versus Functionalism. The legacy of both Titchener and European psychology (though not the psychology of Wilhelm Wundt) was one of structuralism—an examination of the elements of consciousness largely through introspection and assessments of the link of sensation/perception to consciousness. The "new" American psychology, in contrast, was founded on the notions of functionalism and was largely pragmatic.

Functionalism "entertained a host of interesting problems that affected the daily lives of people: the problems of child rearing, education, aging, the work environment, and emotional disorders" (Viney & King, 2003, p. 276).

Thorndike and his colleagues were concerned about the *function* of intelligence in everyday life. Social intelligence was a way of acknowledging that mental ability played a role in many different venues; it highlighted the fact that different environments presented different challenges. And it provided an opportunity to distinguish between the structuralist paradigm and the functionalist paradigm.

Nature Versus Nurture. The British psychometricians (e.g., Spearman, Burt, and Stephenson) emphasized abstract intelligence as the overarching mental ability. To some extent, this emphasis supported deeper sociopolitical views embracing a class system based largely on educational opportunity and attainment. Most psychometricians, both British and American, were advocates of the eugenics movement popular at the turn of the century. Galton in England and Cattell and Goddard in America were three of the best known eugenicists. This meant an emphasis on the "nature" position as opposed to the emerging "nurture" position becoming popular in America through the efforts of John B. Watson and the early behaviorists. In addition, America had evolved as a sociopolitical system that, at least in theory, was opposed to the elitism of money/power/education caste systems of Europe, systems compatible with the principles and aims of the eugenicists. In suggesting the possibility of mechanical and social intelligence, in addition to abstract intelligence, researchers and practitioners could be seen as rebutting an elitist view that emphasized only abstract intelligence and ignored the effect of experience and environment. Because Thorndike's theory of intelligence—associationism/connectionism—allowed for the possibility of an environmental influence on intelligence, one could infer that exposure to mechanical and social environments (as opposed to the abstract environments produced through formal educational systems), allowed for greater environmental influence (i.e., nurture) and the expression of cognitive ability in different venues.

The Emergence of Statistical Theories of Intelligence.   Spurred by the pioneering efforts of Francis Galton in developing methods of correlation and regression, the British psychometricians, and in particular Charles Spearman, introduced the notion of factor analysis as a way of "verifying" the structure of the intellect. The Spearman school concluded mental ability was composed of an overarching general mental ability ("g") and several small but distinct correlated mental abilities ("s"). Thorndike was of two minds regarding Spearman's view (although he eventually accepted it). On the one hand, his associationist/connectionist theory could easily tolerate a unitary dimension of intelligence—a "g" (although allowing for both nature *and* nurture as influences on the number of neural connections). On the other hand, he was unimpressed with statistical analyses of exclusively paper and pencil tests of abstract intelligence as a foundation for a "theory" of intelligence. L. L. Thurstone had also begun his work in developing the more sophisticated analytical systems that would eventually yield the seven Primary Mental Abilities. Thurstone's approach would be seen as a rebuttal to the "g"/ "s" approach of the Spearman school. For his part, Thorndike was comfortable supporting a position of an almost infinite number of avenues in which intelligence might be displayed (a position compatible with his functionalist views) and was more than willing to resist the statistical theory building of his British counterparts.

In summary, then, it would appear that there were several possible forces operating to elevate the role of social intelligence to something more than a simple psychometric squabble. In addition to psychometric issues, there were theoretical, sociopolitical, and philosophical issues in the mix. As you will see in other chapters in this book, many of these issues remain unresolved today. Thus, the attention that the concept of social intelligence received, particularly by his scientific colleagues, when introduced by Thorndike in his *Harper's* article becomes more comprehensible. He was speaking to issues broader than simply a new human attribute. How else can one account for the fact that a casual comment in a popular magazine would be so often cited in subsequent scientific and applied literature?

In the following sections, I will trace the appearance of social intelligence in literature subsequent to Thorndike's speculation in 1920.

SOCIAL INTELLIGENCE IN THE 1920S

Theoretical Treatment of Social Intelligence

One of the first researchers to address Thorndike's proposition regarding social intelligence was Max Freyd (1923) in a study of the personalities of 30 men enrolled in a sales course and 30 men enrolled in a technical course. He contrasted the expressed interests of the two groups and found that individuals enrolled in the sales course expressed greater interest in social activities, whereas those enrolled in the technical course expressed greater interests in mechanical environments. He cites Thorndike's tripartite division of intelligence as an "explanation" but cautions that abstract intelligence is needed for the expression of both mechanical and social intelligence.

Thorndike et al.'s 1926 book on the measurement of intelligence makes brief mention of social and mechanical intelligence and concentrates exclusively on the measurement of abstract intelligence. Spearman's 1927 book *The Abilities of Man* makes no mention of Thorndike's *Harper's* article nor of social intelligence. In contrast, in a broader treatment of the evolution of psychology as a science published in 1937, Spearman acknowledges the concept of social intelligence but dismisses it by saying that "g" pervades all tests of intelligence, including tests of social intelligence.

In 1927, Truman Kelley published a text on interpreting educational measurements. This might be seen as the predecessor of the Mental Measurements Yearbook series to be introduced by Buros in 1938. Kelley acknowledges the suggestion of social intelligence by Thorndike but notes that Thorndike had yet to present any "statistical evidence" supporting the suggestion. Kelley also reports some statistical analyses he had conducted on available tests and suggests that the development of a test of social intelligence would be of some value in assessing school children. He mentions the newly developed test of social intelligence prepared by Moss and his colleagues at George Washington University and describes it as a test "designed to measure one's ability to get along with others" (p. 344) but does not review the test since no technical or statistical information was available for such a review at the time. In a text written a year later (1928), Kelley cites Thorndike's *Harper's* article, but interprets Thorndike's trichotomy as describing the different *interests* of individuals rather than different intelligences.

Clark Hull, in his seminal text on aptitude testing (1928), cites Thorndike's Harper's article and even excerpts a lengthy section of the article, but concludes that Thorndike's proposition of three intelligences was "unaccompanied by evidence and was probably intended merely as shrewd conjecture or hypothesis" and further that "Thorndike's position regarding three intelligences has not found much support" (pp. 206–207).

The George Washington Test of Social Intelligence.   In 1928, the *Journal of Applied Psychology* published an article on a new test of social intelligence developed on the basis of Thorndike's suggestion (Hunt, 1928). This was a watershed event because it represented the first psychometric device intended to assess social intelligence. Although the test had been developed over a several-year period preceding this journal publication, this article made the concepts and measurement device much more widely available to researchers and practitioners. There were six parts to the test:

1. Judgment in Social Situations—a subtest of knowledge of solutions to common social relationship problems.
2. Memory for Names and Faces—a subtest of the ability to memorize names and associated faces, then recall the appropriate pairings at a later time.
3. Recognition of Mental States from Facial Expression—a subtest measuring the individual's ability to recognize mental states (emotions) from photographs.
4. Observation of Human Behavior—a true/false test of behavioral knowledge.
5. Social Information—a true/false test of social information.
6. Recognition of Mental States Behind Words—a subtest that asked the individual to identify a mental state (emotion) implied by quotations from literature and current speech.

This test has been variously known as the George Washington Test of Social Intelligence, the Moss test of social intelligence, or simply the George Washington or Moss test. This early version is described in some detail in a text by Moss (1929) as well as in an earlier text by Laird (1927). Following its introduction, the test went through several revisions, the most recent occurring in 1955.

The appearance of the George Washington Test permitted, for the first time since Thorndike's suggestion, an empirical evaluation of the extent to which social intelligence could be distinguished from abstract intelligence. Virtually every early attempt to demonstrate such independence or discriminant validity showed correlations of the magnitude of +.60 between abstract and social intelligence (Broom, 1928; Garrett, 1927; Garrett and Kellogg, 1928; Grosvenor, 1927; McClatchey, 1929; Pintner and Upshall, 1928). In several analyses, the magnitude of the corrected correlation certainly would have been higher had corrections for range restriction and unreliability been applied. The general conclusion of the authors of these articles was that there was little evidence that social intelligence differed in any important way from abstract intelligence.

A Test of Sociability.   In 1926, Gilliland and Burke described the development of a measure of social intelligence based on three subtests related to photographs and a fourth subtest represented by a questionnaire. The premise of the development of the sociability test was that more socially inclined individuals would be more likely to store and retrieve information related to faces. The questionnaire was a form of bio-data instrument asking for descriptions of social experiences. The authors reported that the reliability of the questionnaire was considerably higher than those seen in the photograph subtests and suggested that the questionnaire is most worthy of continued investigation. Since the authors make no mention of the George Washington Test, it would appear that the sociability test either preceded or was being developed at the same time as the George Washington Test.

Applied Treatment of Social Intelligence

Kitson (1925), in a text on employment psychology, references Thorndike's *Harper's* article and describes research distinguishing between abstract and mechanical intelligence but makes no further mention of social intelligence. Bingham and Freyd (1926) cite Thorndike's *Harper's* article and list social intelligence under "intellectual abilities" but make no further comment. Burtt (1926) refers to social intelligence but notes that there are no current tests available. In the 1942 edition of his text, Burtt refers to the George Washington

Test but questions the extent to which experience plays a role in assessed social intelligence and notes that tests of social intelligence are still in the "experimental" phase. In his 1948 edition, Burtt simply identifies the George Washington Test and gives some examples of test items. A. T. Poffenberger (1929) describes abstract, mechanical, and social intelligence without attribution to Thorndike but indicates agreement with Thorndike et al.'s (1926) concern for measuring intelligence with just one type of test.

In 1927, Thelma Hunt, the author of the *Journal of Applied Psychology* article yet to come describing the George Washington Test, published an article in *Industrial Psychology Monthly* extolling the virtues of the test of social intelligence. The article is nontechnical and alludes to data sets from workers and college students. In an article authored by Moss and Hunt (1927) in *Scientific American*, similar claims (without any technical data about the test) are made for the value of social intelligence in predicting vocational success. Moss, Hunt, and their colleagues had already begun to develop a test of "salesmanship" based on the George Washington Test. A perennial complaint about the George Washington Test was that the technical data, particularly data supporting the claims of validity, were inadequate. Similar claims have been leveled about current measures of emotional intelligence (Matthews et al., 2002)

SOCIAL INTELLIGENCE IN THE 1930S

Largely as the result of an available measurement instrument, there was a great deal of both psychometric and applied research on the proposed construct of social intelligence. The lion's share of this research revolved around the George Washington Test.

Theoretical Treatment of Social Intelligence

Strang (1932) conducted psychometric research on the intrinsic properties of the George Washington Test (e.g., an analysis of errors) and concluded that there were numerous and serious flaws in scoring the items that comprised the test. Her analysis consisted largely of examining incorrectly chosen alternatives in subtests for a sample of 321 female graduate students. As an example, in the subtest Recognition of the Mental State of the Speaker, the correct response to the statement "A perfect mother. No other words can do her justice" is keyed as "admiration," but the answer "love" was given equally frequently. Similarly, for the statement "This is cold news for me. Thus all my hopes are blasted," the correct answer is keyed as "disappointment" yet most people chose the term "despair" as the mental state. She also summarized (1930a, 1930b) published and unpublished studies correlating scores on the George Washington Test with scores on tests of abstract intelligence and concluded that they were of the magnitude that led to the conclusion that the George Washington Test was simply a novel form of abstract intelligence test. Nevertheless, in line with E. L. Thorndike's original conception, she was enthusiastic about the possibility of assessing sociability/social intelligence using "real" social situations rather than the easily available paper and pencil tests. She noted the low correlations between the questionnaire developed by Gilliland and Burke (1926) to measure sociability and the George Washington Test of social intelligence and used this low value to question the reliability of the construct being examined. The developers of the George Washington Test reported reliabilities in the high .80s while Gilliland and Burke reported questionnaire reliabilities in the mid .50s. She also suggested that the newly developed Strong Vocational Interest Blank might be keyed to illuminate differences in social intelligence. In the same article, she referred to the novel research of the young J. P. Guilford (1927) in the identification of emotions from photographs. Forty years later, Guilford would resurrect this research in his development of the structure of the intellect model (O"Sullivan et al., 1965). Others also suggested that the ability to assess emotions from facial expressions was an important aspect of social intelligence (Clarke, 1934; Jenness, 1932)

Several authors began to interpret social intelligence as a measure of personality rather than one of mental ability (Flemming, 1932; Oliver, 1930; Stagner, 1932, 1933a, 1933b; Wang, 1932) by correlating scores on the George Washington Test with measures of introversion and extroversion, although Guilford (1934) considered the substantial positive relationship between introversion and scores on the George Washington Test (e.g., +.53) as an indication that the latter test was really just a measure of general intelligence.

Burks (1937) questioned the validity of the George Washington Test in light of the fact that it did not have substantial correlations with ratings of sociability for college women. Broom (1928, 1930) concluded, from the high correlations between the reading scores from the Thorndike Intelligence Tests and the George Washington Test, that the latter was simply a test of reading comprehension. Similarly, Woodrow (1939) examined the interrelationships of 52 mental tests (including the George Washington Test) and concluded that most of the George Washington subtests (with the exception of the test for memory of names and faces) were simply tests of verbal ability. Chapin (1939) reviewed the relationship between the George Washington scores and social participation in university groups as reported by Hunt (1928) and concluded that the positive association she reported (approximately a correlation of +.38 estimated from contingency tables she presents) is evidence of the construct validity of social intelligence and, on the basis of a positive correlation, argued in favor of the construct validity of social intelligence. He also began a decades-long research program in developing a measure of social participation to supplement paper and pencil measures of social intelligence.

In his text on intelligence testing, Pintner (1931) described Thorndike's tripartite taxonomy as follows:

> This three-fold division of intelligence is merely a convenient scheme for dividing the numerous reactions which may be indicative of intelligence. There is no reason why other divisions should not be made, and indeed, it is quite common to speak of verbal intelligence as opposed to non-verbal intelligence .... Or we may, with Thorndike, divide abstract intelligence into as many different kinds as there are different test situations. (p. 55)

By far, the most telling blow to both the concept and the measurement of social intelligence delivered to date was the psychometric analysis of the responses of 500 George Washington University students to measures of both social and abstract intelligence, an analysis conducted by R. L. Thorndike (R. L. Thorndike, 1936; R. L. Thorndike & Stein, 1937). Interestingly, at the time of publication, R. L. Thorndike was on the faculty at George Washington, the home of the most frequently used measure of social intelligence. After factor analyzing the subtest scores of the students, Thorndike (1936) concluded that the George Washington Test "measures primarily the ability to understand and work with words which bulks so large in an abstract intelligence test" (p. 233).

The same basic analysis was repeated in R. L. Thorndike and Stein (1937) and again, the value of the George Washington test was questioned. They referred to it as "a rather poor test of general intelligence" (p. 284). Once again in line with the original observation of E. L. Thorndike, they made the following conclusion:

> It seems doubtful that any test which is predominantly verbal can measure social ability. We hope that further investigation, via situation tests, movies etc. getting closer to the actual social reaction and further from words, may throw more light on the nature of the ability to manage and understand people. (p. 284)

One might reasonably assume that this would be the death knell for at least the George Washington Test, if not to the construct of social intelligence itself. But one would be wrong.

Applied Treatment of Social Intelligence

During the 1930s, it was increasingly common to find references to the George Washington Test as well as the general topic of social intelligence. In 1931, Moore and Hartmann included an excerpt from Thorndike's 1920 *Harper's* article in a book of readings in industrial psychology. In his landmark text *Industrial Psychology* Morris Viteles (1932) cited the Thorndike 1920 article but only to argue that intelligence manifests itself somewhat differently depending on the test material presented. It is also interesting to note in passing that in the same text, Viteles dismisses the work of Spearman and the concept of "g" as of no practical value in industrial situations.

Garrett and Schneck (1933), citing the Thorndike *Harper's* article, described two different George Washington Tests: the initial test developed by Moss et al for the measurement of social intelligence and a new test designed to measure the "Ability to Sell." The ability to sell test had three of the subtests of the original test plus three new subscales: learning selling points in merchandise, following store directions, and solving selling problems. If anything, the new "Ability to Sell" test was even *more* a measure of abstract intelligence than the earlier general version.

In 1937, Walter Van Dyke Bingham published a text on aptitudes and aptitude testing. He cites Thorndike's concept of social intelligence but notes that tests for such an attribute have lagged well behind the testing of abstract intelligence. He further observes that abstract intelligence is necessary for mechanical and social environments as well as abstract problem solving. In an Appendix, he describes an extensive applied research project conducted under the direction of D. G. Paterson at the University of Minnesota to rate occupations on *four* intelligences: abstract, mechanical, social, and musical. Twenty industrial psychologists rated over 400 job titles on the levels of the four intelligences required by the 400 jobs. As an example, it was discovered that auctioneers required high levels of social intelligence in contrast to bee keepers, who needed very little. During the course of the research project, Paterson and his colleagues identified six different categories of social intelligence: persuasive (face-to-face), managerial, persuasive (indirect), business contact and service, rank and file, and asocial occupations. The study reported by Bingham is described in greater detail in an article by Lorge and Blau (1942). In 1939, in a text on psychology for business, Moore describes the Moss (George Washington) Test of selling ability but concludes that such an ability would be better measured by assessing general intelligence and using a specific situation test. Finally, in a speculative article on the causes of crime, Young (1938) proposes that one factor to be considered in criminal behavior is defective social intelligence.

Several articles in scientific journals describe attempts to use scores on a social intelligence test (most commonly the George Washington Test) to predict various outcomes. Ross Stagner (1933b) examined the value of the George Washington Test for predicting college grades. He found that social intelligence accounted for no incremental variance once general intelligence had been entered into a regression equation. Shedden and Witmer (1939) used the George Washington test to predict performance of social workers. They report that social intelligence was a significant predictor of success and should be included in a final test battery, but fail to point out that a test of general intelligence was a marginally better predictor of success, that success was defined as a high score on a job knowledge test, and that the uncorrected correlation between the George Washington Test and the test of general intelligence was +.65.

In two texts written by Laird (1936, 1937) for a nontechnical audience, anecdotal evidence is presented related to the George Washington Test, and the test itself is reproduced as a test of emotional makeup and job adjustment. In contrast, he identifies Thurstone's Primary Mental Abilities as the facets of intelligence.

SOCIAL INTELLIGENCE: 1940–1964

Theoretical Treatment of Social Intelligence

Empirical research on social intelligence, and in particular on the George Washington Test, diminished substantially after 1940. This may have been due, at least in part, to the negative review of the available measures of social intelligence by R. L. Thorndike and Stein (1937), but there was also exasperation in the psychometric community with the continued failure of Moss and his colleagues to provide basic technical information on the George Washington Test (e.g., Guion, 1965) . In 1941, R. L. Thorndike reviewed the George Washington Test for the Second Mental Measurements Yearbook and repeated his earlier criticisms of both the convergent and discriminant validity of the test. He remained "suspicious" of the test because he had seen no satisfactory validation information. In addition, the only "competing" test of social intelligence—the Gilliland questionnaire (Gilliland & Burke, 1926)—had largely disappeared from the psychometric landscape. A study by Eimecke and Fish (1948) replicates earlier findings related to the lack of discriminant validity by showing a correlation between the George Washington Test and the Army Alpha (a test of general mental ability) of +.67. Smith (1948) also reports a strong and positive association between Thurstone's tests of Primary Ability (particularly the verbal subtest) and the

George Washington Test scores, although he does not report the correlation coefficient in question.

Even though the measurement of social intelligence remained problematic, some interest in the construct remained, although the term *social intelligence* was used less frequently. Instead, terms such as *person* or *interpersonal perception, social insight,* and *social proficiency* were used more frequently to describe the ability implied by Thorndike in his description of social intelligence. Jackson (1940) developed a test of social proficiency based on the failure of the George Washington Test to demonstrate discriminant validity vis à vis general mental ability. She developed a multiple-choice test requiring the individual to choose the correct alternative for behavior in common social situations. She then developed a rating scale of "social proficiency" with which to categorize individuals based on observed social proficiency. By correlating responses to the new social proficiency test with independent ratings of the social proficiency of the respondents, she claimed to have demonstrated the validity of the new scale. Unfortunately, the new scale correlated highly with the George Washington Test scores. Nevertheless, ignoring her concerns about the George Washington Test, she takes comfort in the observed correlation, stating, "the author's social situation test measures some phase of social behavior if these other tests do" (p. 451). In a related study (Jackson, 1940) once again correlating the George Washington Test to the social situations test, she finds a much lower correlation coefficient, but the true value of the intercorrelation was likely much higher than the reported value as a result of severe range restriction on both the George Washington scores and the social situation scores. It would appear that the "new" measure of social proficiency was little more than a variation on the George Washington Test, using more practical situations, but still paper and pencil items, to elicit knowledge regarding interpersonal behavior.

As I described in the last section, Chapin (1939) had begun preliminary work on the relationship of social intelligence to sociability. This work evolved into a development of his own measure of social insight (Chapin, 1942). He used a design very much like that of Jackson (1940), asking independent observers to categorize individuals as high or low on social insight, defined as "the capacity to see into a social situation, to appreciate the implications of things said and to interpret effectively the attitudes expressed so as to appreciate the significance of past behavior, or estimate the trend of future behavior" (p. 215).

Like Jackson's social proficiency test, the test of social insight presented the respondent with a situation but instead of simply asking the respondent to describe how he or she would behave, Chapin's test also asked the respondent to identify/analyze the behavior of others. His analysis showed that the new test of social insight significantly distinguished between those rated as high on social insight and those rated as low. No comparisons were made between scores on the social insight test and scores on either a measure of general mental ability or to any other device intended to measure social intelligence; these deficits raised the continuing nagging questions of both convergent and discriminant validity.

In 1947, Wedeck published a report describing a 16-year effort, begun under the direction of Spearman, to determine if " 'psychological ability' involved simply general intelligence, or also a special ability or factor." Psychological ability was defined as "the ability to judge correctly the feelings, moods, and motivations of others" (p. 133). One can infer from this research report that Spearman had been directly concerned with the issue of social intelligence (even though it was renamed as "psychological ability") as early as 1930. It is further interesting to note that Wedeck (and Spearman) concentrated on the knowledge and reasoning aspect of social intelligence rather than including any behavioral element. Recall that in his original statement regarding social intelligence, Thorndike (1920) emphasized not only the *knowledge* aspect of the proposed construct, but also the *behavioral* (i.e., "manage" and "act") aspect. It is one thing to know what to do. It is quite another to actually do it. This was one reason why not only E. L. Thorndike but also his son R. L. Thorndike and others were pessimistic about any method of measurement that used standard psychometric approaches, such as paper and pencil multiple-choice stimulus elements. Using drawings, cartoons, or photographs as test items did not solve the fundamental problem of building behavior into the response repertoire of the test taker.

Wedeck developed a set of pictorial and verbal tests which required the respondent to choose the "correct" emotion expressed in the picture or paragraph from a number of alternatives. He also administered a number of non-"psychological" tests (i.e., verbal and general mental ability tests). A factor analysis revealed (a) a high "saturation" of general mental ability on all tests, (b) a high saturation of verbal ability on all verbal tests, and (c)) a distinct "psychological ability" factor emerging from the pictorial tests, with some nontrivial loadings on certain verbal tests. The emergence of the third (albeit small) factor—a factor that might be identified as social intelligence—is surprising given the failure of other earlier attempts to demonstrate the discriminant validity of the construct. By 1947, this study stood virtually alone in identifying a distinct factor representing social intelligence. Wedeck describes the "psychological ability" factor as an individual's "breadth in relation to the variety of psychological situations into which he can 'project' himself correctly, depth as manifested by the strength of his response indicated his selection from the verbal elements of the test" (p. 150). As we will see in a later section, Wedeck's data matrix eventually played a major role in the reinvigoration of interest in social intelligence.

In a review of the literature on the ability to judge people (most certainly an important element of any construct of social intelligence), Taft (1955) concludes that this ability is based on three elements: (1) general intelligence and specific mental ability (i.e., judgment/reasoning), (2) awareness of behavioral norms, and (3) motivation. In that review, he places the George Washington and Chapin tests into a category called "miscellaneous" or "indirect methods" of the measurement of the ability to judge people. But because these tests were used so infrequently in empirical research, he made no evaluative comments about them. Bruner and Taguiri (1954), in a review of the perception of people, agree that the ability to perceive emotional states of others is largely a function of general mental ability.

Karlin and Schwartz (1953) hypothesized that performance on the Rosenzweig Picture Frustration Test (a semi-projective personality test) would be moderated by social intelligence. In addition to the Rosenzweig and George Washington tests, the Otis test of general mental ability was administered. They found some relationship between the subscale "Recognition of the Mental State of the Speaker" of the George Washington Test and certain subscales of the Picture Frustration Test. There is no indication of the correlation between the George Washington scores and the Otis scores, thus, once again, leaving the discriminant validity question unanswered.

Kaess and Witroyl (1955) conducted some research to examine the validity of the "Memory for Names and Faces" subscale of the George Washington Test by comparing test scores with the demonstrated ability of subjects to remember names and faces of interviewees who they observed in interview situation. The resulting correlation was +.30, and the authors concluded that this represented at least modest support for the validity of that one George Washington subscale. No measures of general mental ability were obtained, so there is no way of knowing if a test of general mental ability might have done as well or better than the "Memory for Names and Faces" scale.

Finally, Sechrest and Jackson (1961) derive a complex measure of social intelligence (i.e., rated reputation for social intelligence) and conclude that social intelligence has a role in predicting interpersonal judgment skill. Nevertheless, they also report a high positive correlation between social intelligence and cognitive complexity, leading them to conclude that cognitive complexity contributes to social effectiveness.

Applied Treatment of Social Intelligence

As had been the case in earlier periods, textbook authors (both psychometric and industrial) were either equivocal or unenthusiastic about both the construct and the measurement of social intelligence. In a text on differential psychology, Anastasi (1937) had commented on the construct as follows:

> Thorndike's frequently quoted analysis of intelligence into abstract, mechanical, and social "intelligences" within each of which is found "relatively great consistency" whereas "between one and another of these three there is relatively great disparity" also appeared at this time [i.e., *Harper's* article]. It is doubtful, however, whether this analysis should be incorporated into a survey of Thorndike's basic theory since it was offered only as a practical suggestion to expedite testing. (p. 303)

In a later text on testing, Anastasi (1954) addresses the George Washington Test (still being used almost 30 years after its introduction and in spite of little scientific support and considerable psychometric criticism!):

> Efforts have been made to develop paper-and-pencil tests of "social intelligence" ... but the validity of such instruments has not been convincingly established. It is doubtful, for instance, whether the George Washington Test measures abilities not covered by tests of abstract verbal intelligence with which it correlates highly. There is no need for further research on the nature and measurement of the behavior characteristics commonly designated by such terms as "social intelligence" and "social sensitivity." (pp. 502–503)

In his first text on the measurement of intelligence (1944) as well as in the fourth edition of that text (1958), Wechsler dismisses social intelligence: "We ... do not believe in such an entity. Our point of view is that social intelligence is just general intelligence applied to social situations" (1944, pp. 88–89).

Cronbach (1960) is equally dismissive of both the construct and the instruments to measure social intelligence in his text on testing:

> After 50 years of intermittent investigation social intelligence remains undefined and unmeasured .... [The George Washington Test] measures general or verbal ability to some degree but there is no evidence that it measures any distinct ability which has practical predictive value. Enough attempts were made to establish the validity of the test for the selection of salesmen, etc. to indicate that this line of approach is fruitless. (R. L. Thorndike and Stein, 1937) (p. 319)

Super (1949) describes the George Washington Test as the "Moss Test for the Ability to Sell" (a variation on the more general test and one developed exclusively for commercial use). He is critical of the failure to provide basic psychometric and validation data: "Although it has been tried in numerous sales situations, the results have not generally been published in the journals. The prevailing opinion of it among department store personnel workers known to the writer is not favorable" (p. 351).

In the same text, Super summarizes the works of various psychometricans (e.g., Spearman, Kelley, Thurstone, Shartle, and Guilford) and makes no mention of social intelligence as an ability of any sort.

The "Ability to Sell" variation of the George Washington Test, although available since 1929, was not formally considered in the Mental Measurements Yearbook until its third edition, in a review done by Floyd Ruch (1949). Ruch is critical of the psychometric characteristics (reliability and validity) of the tests, as well as the normative data. He suggests other tests as better measures of selling ability because the "Ability to Sell" test had not "had the benefit of rigorous statistical treatment" (p. 750). In the same edition of the Mental Measurements Yearbook, the more general George Washington Test was reviewed for a second time (Cleeton, 1949; Taylor, 1949). Both of the reviews were negative. One reviewer (Taylor) repeated the earlier criticism of Thorndike and Stein (1937) that the test was simply a "disguised ... and imperfect measure of verbal intelligence." The other reviewer (Cleeton) makes the point that "the results of 'thinking over' the thing to do in hypothetical situations rarely indicates how the person would respond in actual social situations" (p. 97). The issue of knowing/comprehending versus acting and managing was identified once more as a central issue in attempts to assess social intelligence.

Texts in industrial psychology were more equivocal about both the construct and its measurement. Hepner (1941) describes scales he developed for measuring social knowledge and sociability without reference to either Thorndike or Moss. Drake (1942) takes a decidedly human factors view of the phenomenon and considers social intelligence to be an aspect of sensation/perception and not related to intelligence. He asserted that some people see imperceptible cues that others do not. Tiffin (1947) simply mentions in passing that the "Moss Social Intelligence Test" (it is not clear if he is referring to the George Washington Test or its "Ability to Sell" offspring) had been included in a battery to measure the success of social workers. Blum (1949) lists the George Washington Test in an appendix of available tests. He further comments that there is no satisfactory validity reported for the test and that reliabilities have not been reported. Blum also reports that the Moss "Ability to Sell" test had been used by the Klein Institute of New York to evaluate applicants for sales positions, but he provides no details regarding the success of that test in the prediction scheme.

Eimeke (1949) administered the Kuder Preference Record, the Army Alpha, the George Washington Test, and the Bernreuter Personality Inventory to 500 newly returned WWII veterans enrolled in a sales training program administered by City College of New York. The purpose of the exercise was to develop norms for sales trainees on the various instruments to add to the student and employed norms that were already available for the George Washington Test. Interestingly, Eimicke administered the original George Washington Test rather than what would have seemed to be the more appropriate "Ability to Sell" adaptation of the test. No intercorrelations among the various measures were reported.

Clark (1948) attempted to use the concept of social intelligence to explain why certain soldiers went AWOL before being shipped out to battle in WWII. The (apprehended) AWOL soldiers were given the Wechsler Mental Ability Scale. Results showed that the subjects were in the "dull normal" range of intelligence. Although he did not assess the social intelligence of these individuals, Clark concluded that because the comprehension subtest scores of the Wechsler were lower than other subtest scores, it was possible that the soldiers in question were deficient in social intelligence and in the ability to properly evaluate past experience. One might speculate that had a test of social intelligence been administered, the correlation between those scores and the Wechsler would have been characteristically high.

George W. Crane, a popularizer of psychological principles and practice, after identifying the George Washington Test, devoted a large section of his text (1946) to the development of social intelligence. This was consistent with his assertion that social intelligence was acquired rather than "native" or inherited. He assures the reader that social intelligence could be turned into financial success.

Martin Gross (1962) in his deconstruction and criticism of the psychological testing movement, describes a subtest of the George Washington Test as follows: "'Judgment in Social Situations' is a test that invites platitudinous answers to unimportant questions" (p. 244).

To summarize this rather lengthy period from 1940 to 1964, it appears that both the construct and the measurement of social intelligence continued to wander somewhat aimlessly across the psychometric landscape. Cronbach's (1960) characterization of the research as "intermittent" was apt. There is one noteworthy omission of any comment on either social intelligence as a construct or its measurement during this period. Volumes I and II of the *Handbook of Applied Psychology* (Fryer & Henry, 1950), which included 115 chapters authored by more than 100 contributors who were considered leaders in applied psychology at the time, makes no mention of either the construct or measurement of social intelligence.

SOCIAL INTELLIGENCE: 1965–1980

Theoretical Treatment of Social Intelligence

J. P. Guilford had been developing his "structure of the intellect" model of mental ability for many years (1956) and had been interested in the nature and role of emotions in behavior even longer (1934). By developing, testing, and administering various psychometric devices, he was gradually filling in the 120 cells of his model with data supporting various aspects of his multidimensional model of mental ability. Guilford had posited an aspect of intelligence called "behavioral intelligence," which was presumed to deal with content information characterized as feelings, motives, thoughts, intentions, attitudes, or other psychological dispositions which might affect an individual's social behavior (O'Sullivan et al., 1965). Although he agreed that social intelligence could be a viable cognitive construct, he disagreed with Thorndike's implication that it was a unitary dimension and instead suggested that there were many different ways of being socially intelligent. In fact, the structure of the intellect model suggested 30 different social intelligence factors. This multidimensionality was in no way unique to social intelligence; the structure of the intellect model posited many variations of each specific type of intelligence.

Guilford and his colleagues (O'Sullivan et al., 1965) began investigating the existence and nature of the 30 factors of social intelligence. They started with a reanalysis of the data matrix created by Wedeck in 1947. As was described in an earlier section, Wedeck was virtually alone in having established through factor analysis the existence of a factor of social intelligence (what he labeled "psychological ability"). The reanalysis, using different factor extraction and rotation criteria, confirmed the existence of the "psychological ability" but found that there were three separate factors involved in the ability, not just one as Wedeck found. This was encouraging and in keeping with Guilford's view that there were many different types of social intelligence. This finding encouraged Guilford and his colleagues to develop a series of new pictorial tests to assess social intelligence. A battery of 47 tests, including devices intended to tap social intelligence as well as other more abstract forms of intelligence, was administered to 250 eleventh-grade students. The subsequent factor analysis identified six factors related to social intelligence, defined as "the abilities to understand the thoughts, feelings, and intentions of other people. These factors correspond roughly to the domain termed person perception, empathy, or social awareness by other investigators" (O'Sullivan et al., 1965, p. 16).

One of these factors was labeled cognition of behavioral relationships (CBR) and was thought to assess an individual's understanding of dyadic relationships.

In the 1960 edition of Cronbach's book on psychological testing, he had dismissed social intelligence as unworthy of further effort. In his 1970 edition, Cronbach reversed his opinion, based largely on the new Guilford data and analyses (O'Sullivan et al., 1965). "[CBR] has a substantial degree of independence (from other tests intended to measure more abstract facets of intelligence) and is evidently worthy of further consideration; it might prove to be of great significance, practically and theoretically" (Cronbach, 1970, p. 343).

> After a decade of work along these lines, the instruments will be ready so that a start can be made toward tracing theoretical meanings and relationships to practical affairs .... The findings on the CBR tests hint that Guilford may have opened a new chapter in the study of abilities. (Cronbach, 1970, p. 345)

Cronbach was suitably realistic about the considerable amount of work that would be involved in developing and evaluating all of the tests that would be needed to confirm some or all of the other 29 factors proposed by Guilford as defining social intelligence, cautioning that because of low reliabilities of many of the tests proposed by Guilford, it would be necessary to develop a substantial number of tests for each of the 30 cells. Nevertheless, this was the first acceptance by a "luminary" (as well as by an earlier critic) of the possible theoretical and applied value of the construct of social intelligence since the construct had been proposed 50 years earlier. This was (or should have been) a major breakthrough for the construct of social intelligence. Hoepfner and O'Sullivan (1968) and O'Sullivan and Guilford (1975) further elaborated on the potential practical value of assessing CBR but presented no new data, simply repeating the results of the 1965 analysis. O'Sullivan and Guilford (1975) reported that CBR scores were positively related to performance of IBM salesmen and probation officer trainees, but the citations to both of these assertions are simply listed as "personal communications."

Other analyses of these same data led to radically different conclusions about the viability of Guilford's multifactor model of social intelligence. In a LISREL reanalysis of the O'Sullivan et al. (1965) data matrix, Romney and Pyryt (1999) argue that there really was only one social intelligence factor evident in the matrix, not the six identified in the original analysis. Shanley, Walker, and Foley (1971) reported some disturbingly high relationships between the CBR scales of O'Sullivan and Guilford (one as high as +.67) and measures of general mental ability. They implied that Guilford and his associates may have overestimated the discriminant validity of their measures of social intelligence. Snyder and Michael (1983) examined subtests of the Guilford social intelligence factor other than the CBR tests more commonly employed. They found modest relationships (ranging from +.30 to +.47) between these social intelligence measures and scores on math and reading tests for elementary school children. This represented a problem because it had been hypothesized that social intelligence was distinct from abstract intelligence.

Jackson (1972) reviewed the CBR tests for the Seventh Mental Measurements Yearbook and expressed the same admiration for the early work of Guilford and his associates as had Cronbach. But he had reservations as well. Jackson felt that the reliabilities of certain of the subscales were too low (some as low as .33) to be of any value for individual prediction. He also questioned the extent to which tests developed exclusively with high school and college students would generalize to adult nonstudent populations. He strongly urged researchers to begin gathering data that related the CBR scores to criterion variables rather than simply to other cognitive and non-cognitive tests.

Between the introduction of the CBR approach to social intelligence in 1965 and 1983, there was little serious research on developing additional tests of the other social intelligence factors suggested by Guilford's model of intelligence. The failure of the research community to follow up on the promise of the Guilford approach is disappointing but not surprising given the increasing disenchantment with the entire structure of the intellect model (Matthews et al., 2002). Finally, it appeared there might be at least an answer to the construct question after decades of failed attempts to identify social intelligence. But neither the Guilford group nor other researchers completed the hard work described by Cronbach (1970). They could have easily isolated the social intelligence construct and investigated the Guilford lead without embracing the structure of the intellect model, but they did not. For whatever reason, the promise of the approach was never realized.

References to the older conceptions of social intelligence (i.e., the Moss instruments) remained sporadic during this period. Guion (1965) repeats the concerns of earlier authors and psychometricians that there is little available psychometric information about the George Washington Tests in spite of the fact that they had been available for almost 40 years commercially.

The construct of social intelligence appears occasionally in the clinical literature (e.g., Johnson, 1969) as a correlate of introversion/extroversion. Hartman (1967) proposed that socially intelligent individuals should be easier to hypnotize and examined the relationship between scores on the George Washington Test and the Barber Suggestibility scale. The correlation was nonsignificant. Burley and McGuiness (1977) hypothesized that social intelligent subjects (as defined by scores on the George Washington Test) would be less likely to deliver electric shocks to another individual (the Milgram paradigm) than those low in social intelligence. The hypothesis was supported, but there were no companion measures of general mental ability gathered, so the role of social intelligence vis à vis general mental ability remained obscure. Clark and Neuringer (1971) proposed "sensitizers" would be more socially intelligent than "repressors" and administered the George Washington Test to a group of sensitizers and repressors. There were no differences between the groups.

Keating (1978) included Chapin's (1942) test of social insight along with two other tests intended to measure social intelligence and three tests of abstract intelligence. A factor analysis revealed no "social" factor. Nevertheless, Keating attributed this failure to find a social factor, at least in part, to the nature of the medium used to measure social intelligence:

> It may be the very format of such measures, i.e. paper and pencil format with delimited response options, activates an academic framework so constraining that relevant social skills contribute little true variance to the resulting scores. Accurate assessment of social competence may require a different approach to measurement, presumably one that capitalizes on systemic in situ observation. (p. 221)

R. L. Thorndike said as much in 1937, and his father E. L. Thorndike cautioned the same 17 years earlier (E. L. Thorndike, 1920). In a follow-up to Keating's suggestion, Ford and Tisak (1983) assessed social competence using ratings of peers, teachers, and self, as well as a self-report measure of empathy. When combined with measures of abstract/academic intelligence and factor-analyzed, Ford and Tisak were able to demonstrate a factor independent of academic measures that they interpreted to indicate social intelligence.

Although Chapin's Social Insight Test had been available since 1942, it was not reviewed in the Mental Measurements Yearbook until the seventh edition, which appeared in 1972. This lag was largely due to the fact that it was not until the late 1960s that Harrison Gough included the test in the offerings of the Consulting Psychologists Press (Chapin, 1967). Gough (1968) prepared the technical manual to accompany Chapin's test. The reviews of the test (Lanyon, 1972; Orr, 1972) were polite but not encouraging. Like the George Washington Test, Chapin's test was criticized for low reliabilities and validity, as well as possibly representing reading comprehension rather than social intelligence. The one positive aspect noted by both reviewers was the "refreshing" willingness of the technical manual to point out the serious limitations of the test in its present form. Both reviewers encouraged additional experimental research with the instrument.

In 1973, Walker and Foley published an outstanding and detailed review of various measures of social intelligence that had been developed over the preceding decades. In their conclusion, they point to a central area of confusion in much of the research on social intelligence available then, a point I mentioned earlier in this chapter:

> The focal problem seems to have been the construction of valid social intelligence instruments. A closely related issue has involved the necessary distinction, not often made, between the *understanding* (italics in the original) of others' behavior and *acting* (italics in the original) in a socially wise way. Most attempts at evaluating social intelligence in adults have appraised ability to understand others. Future progress in the social intelligence area might be enhanced by the application of some ingenuity to the development of possible measures of socially intelligent behavior. (p. 858)

It should be clear that *knowing* and *doing* (the "managing" and "acting" elements identified in E. L. Thorndike's initial definition of social intelligence) are distinct and often influenced by other variables. It is also clear that *knowing* often represents the necessary but not sufficient for *doing*. To the extent that "managing" or "acting" in (i.e., the *doing* element) interpersonal relations was considered an important part of social intelligence, it had been sorely neglected in research on the construct. Given that the *knowing* element had been so central to the measurement of social intelligence, the relentless substantial positive correlation between tests of social intelligence and tests of general mental ability should not have come as a surprise to anyone.

One final, and telling, use of the concept of social intelligence was provided by social cognitive psychologists (Aderman and Berkowitz, 1983; Kassin and Hochreich, 1977; Kuiper, 1978; Riess, Rosenfeld, Melburg, and Tedeschi, 1981). In a typical design, false feedback on an experimental task would be used to convince subjects that they were either high or low on social intelligence. Subjects were further told that "people high in social intelligence are more successful in social relationships than those low in the trait" (Riess et al., 1981, p. 226). No actual tests of social intelligence were used in the studies, nor do any of the authors cite any of the research on social intelligence. In two of the three studies (Reiss et al., 1981; Kuiper, 1978), the social intelligence "induction" was presented to all subjects. There was no manipulation check. In the third study (Kassin & Hochreich, 1977), the social intelligence induction was a manipulation, but it was no different than another induction in which subjects were simply told to do a good job to help the experimenter. I suppose one might take it as a sign of acceptance of a construct that it can be used to induce false beliefs in subjects. This might be taken as evidence of how deeply ingrained the construct was in both the scientific and the nonscientific community, in spite of few or no data confirming that the construct even existed!

Applied Treatment of Social Intelligence

Tenopyr (1967), a student of Guilford's at the University of Southern California, examined the relationship between the CBR (social intelligence) factor identified by Guilford and subject grades for ninth-grade students. As was the case with the Snyder and Michael (1983) study described earlier, it is not clear why one would even examine such a relationship other than to cite the *lack* of relationship between CBR scores and grades as evidence for its discriminant validity. She found no relationship between social intelligence and grades but found strong relationships between abstract intelligence and grades. Osipow and Walsh (1973) found modest relationships between the CBR tests and counselor trainee performance on a knowledge test of appropriate counselor responses to client statements. Reardon, Foley, and Walker (1979) found some evidence suggesting that social intelligence (as assessed by the O'Sullivan et al., 1965, tests) was related to occupation choice.

Erez (1980) examined the relationship between leadership style (employee vs task-centered) and social intelligence using one subscale (Judgment in Social Situations) of the George Washington Test as the measure of social intelligence, although she acknowledged the existence of the Guilford scales. She found no relationship between leadership style and social intelligence.

Rice (1979), in an article in the popular magazine *Psychology Today*, stated that social intelligence had attracted the attention of increasing numbers of researchers because of public and professional concern for the relevance of the intelligence tests that were commonly used at that point. He further suggested that this concern was compounded by empirical literature that showed slight relationships between "IQ scores in school and successful performance later in life" (p. 33). Even in 1979, the suggestion of "slight" relationships between measures of general mental ability and job success was hyperbole. In less than 2 years, Schmidt and Hunter (1981, 1984) would demonstrate convincingly that the empirical literature showed quite the opposite. Anticipating an argument that would be made by Daniel Goleman (his colleague at *Psychology Today* at the time) and others in support of the construct of emotional intelligence, Rice suggested,

"Because so much of life involves getting along with other people, interpersonal skills may be just as crucial for testing as spatial reasoning or analogical reasoning" (p. 37). Unlike some current advocates of emotional intelligence (e.g., Goleman, 1995, 1998), however, he stops short of saying that this new "intelligence" may be *more* important than general mental ability. The ability wing of the EI school has largely disavowed these bombastic claims (Mayer, 1999). One difference between Rice and the advocates of emotional intelligence who would repeat his misdirected charge of irrelevance leveled against measures of general mental ability is that Rice was unaware of the meta-analyses to come that would prove him wrong (Hunter & Hunter, 1984; Schmidt, 1992); those who would make the same argument 15 years later could not claim the same level of ignorance of the important role of general mental ability in life activities.

The Similarity of Social Intelligence and Emotional Intelligence Measurement

In the assessment of emotional intelligence, distinctions are made between measures of ability and measures of personality (also called "mixed" measures). As an example, the MSCEIT II has been developed as an ability measure (Mayer, Salovey, Caruso, & Sitarenios, 2003). In contrast, the EQ-I (Bar-On, 2000) and the ECI (Boyatzis, Goleman, & Rhee, 2000; Sala, 2002) would be considered mixed or personality approaches to the measurement of emotional intelligence. Not surprisingly, the MSCEIT II has its strongest correlations with measures of cognitive ability while the EQ-I and the ECI have their strongest associations with personality measures, and in particular, the Big Five factors (Van Rooy & Viswesvaran, 2004).

In the period 1909–1983, there were only been four assessment devices formally proposed and marketed as devices for the measurement of social intelligence. These include the George Washington Test, the "Ability to Sell" test that was spun off of the George Washington Test, Chapin's test of Social Insight, and the CBR tests of O'Sullivan, Guilford and deMille. Two other "tests"—the Gilliland questionnaire and the Jackson test of social proficiency—were proposed but quickly disappeared from view. In one way or another, every one of these tests could be classified as an ability test rather than a test of personality. To be sure, the taxonomy of personality attributes with which these tests might have been correlated was somewhat undisciplined (and with a strong foundation in psychopathology) during the period covered, making an examination of observed correlations between measures of social intelligence and "personality" problematic; nevertheless, we can still examine the content of the tests and classify them as such.

The George Washington Test.   Each of the six subtests required the respondent to display social knowledge/information, recognize and categorize facial expressions, or remember names and faces. There were
no subtests or items that might fall under the rubric of personality.

The Ability to Sell Test.   In addition to the recognition and social knowledge components of the original test, the George Washington Ability to
Sell Test includes operations such as learning, problem solving, and
following directions. Like its parent examination, the Ability to Sell
Test would be categorized as an ability test.

The Gilliland Measure of Sociability.   The Gilliland test had four components. The first three were pictorial and required the respondent to
store and retrieve information related to photographs of faces. These
were clearly ability subtests. The fourth component was a questionnaire related to the extensiveness of social experiences. It is not clear
whether this last component would be classified as a personality test
(since many bio-data like devices might now considered indirect measures of personality) or an indirect measure of social knowledge (as
implied by the title of the test). Thus, it might be fair to conclude that
the Gilliland test was largely, if not wholly, a test of ability. Interestingly, the questionnaire component did not correlate highly with the
George Washington Test scores (Strang, 1932), possibly supporting
an inference that it was *not* a measure of ability, but the data sets of
that era are so poorly described and incomplete that the lack of a correlation tells us very little.

The Jackson Test of Social Proficiency.   This multiple-choice format test required the respondent to choose the correct response for a series of
social situations. This was an ability-type test.

Chapin's Test of Social Insight.   Chapin's test of social insight was similar
to Jackson's test of social proficiency in so far as the respondent was
expected to choose the "correct" response to make in a variety of social
situations. In addition, some items asked the respondent to "analyze"
the behavior of another person described in the test item. Like the
Jackson test, the Chapin test would be considered an ability test.

CBR Tests of Social Intelligence.   Although social intelligence, according to
Guilford and his colleagues, was thought to involve empathy, the initial test developed and marketed as the CBR tests were ability tests involving recognizing, categorizing, and inferring emotional
information from largely pictorial test items. Like its predecessors,
the CBR test package was an ability test.

Thus, we conclude that virtually all of the tests developed to assess social intelligence can be considered to be ability tests, like the MSCEIT II, rather than "mixed" or personality tests, like the EQ-I or ECI. In addition, with the exception of the CBR tests, all of the social intelligence scoring schemes were based on "consensus" scoring, choosing as the "correct" answer the alternative most commonly chosen by a normative sample (usually of students). The CBR tests were scored using several formats, depending on the individual scale. Some subscales were constructed using simple item statistics showing which response alternatives were most closely associated with total scores. Other subscales were scored using what the researchers referred to as "consensual validation." This appears to mean that the research team developed the scoring scheme. Still other subscales were keyed by deriving "correct" responses from the writings of psychotherapists (what might today be called "expert" scoring).

SUMMARY AND CONCLUSIONS

There are many aspects of this historical review that might be seen as cautionary, if not instructive, to the current research effort directed toward emotional intelligence. The first is a theme repeated regularly by those who embraced the construct of social intelligence, beginning with E. L. Thorndike himself. Standardized tests with substantial verbal loading are unlikely to illuminate a "new" human attribute. It does not matter if the tests are ability, personality, or mixed. The pictorial subscales (e.g., recognition of emotional expression from photographs), with their written instructions and verbal response alternatives, cannot escape this confound. Even Guilford expressed resignation, and perhaps a bit of frustration, in not being able to use more expensive, but also more veridical, means of assessing social intelligence such as film.

> At first, it was hoped that motion picture tests of behavioral intelligence could be constructed, motion pictures being closer to real life than static stimuli. The activity dimension added to expressional behavior by motion pictures was also an important consideration. The rapidity and smoothness with which an expression is executed may add greatly to its communicative value. However, cost prohibited motion picture tests of behavioral cognition. (O'Sullivan et al., 1965, p. 6)

The explosion of high-fidelity, computer-generated testing, as well as the decreasing cost of DVD presentation, makes it more feasible for researchers to move away from verbal representations of emotions to a more "realistic" presentation of at least stimulus materials. The issue of stimulus modality should no longer be an issue in research design.

A second theme apparent in the cumulative research on social intelligence is that it is critical that an emotional intelligence test demonstrate *both* convergent validity and discriminant validity. It is not sufficient to simply demonstrate that a test is *not* correlated with abstract intelligence, on the one hand, or personality measures on the other. It is necessary that one demonstrate that the proposed attribute (or more correctly, scores derived from the measuring instrument for that attribute) is associated with things it should be associated with and is not associated with irrelevant things. The attempt to show discriminant validity has dominated research on social intelligence and appears to be similarly dominating research on emotional intelligence. The demonstration of convergent validity has been largely ignored. A multitrait, multimethod design could help to overcome this challenge. Thus, even if the construct is proposed as a "new" individual attribute (thus unlikely to correlate with measures representing any current attribute), one could make the convergent validity argument using several different modes for representing emotional intelligence. Thus, for example, ratings (other than self-ratings) on proposed dimensions of emotional intelligence and nonverbal, computer-based assessments of emotional intelligence directed toward those same dimensions could be two elements of a monotrait block. The resulting statistical monotrait associations could be contrasted with similar monotrait blocks for abstract intelligence or personality. Social intelligence researchers were obsessed with discriminant validity at the expense of convergent validity. Emotional intelligence researchers would be well advised to avoid a similar obsession. Recently, Law, Wong, & Song (2004) have begun research along these lines.

A third cautionary observation that emerges from the review of social intelligence research is the nature of the subject pool used for the basic psychometric research. The pool consisted largely of young people between the ages of 8 and 19. The early research on the George Washington Test, as well as later research on alternative instruments (e.g., Chapin, Guilford), used either high school or college students. Particularly with respect to any construct linked to emotions, this may be a unique population. One might expect that interpersonal awareness means something quite different when measured in an adolescent as opposed to an individual in middle or later stages of adulthood. A review of the published empirical research is instructive here. Of the 44 empirical published studies on social intelligence, 40 studies used students as subjects. The cumulative total of the respondents of these studies exceeds 3,500. Of those 40 studies, 2 used primary school students, 5 used high school students, 28 used undergradudate students, and 5 used graduate students. Interestingly, the 5 studies that used high school students included the Wedeck (1947) study and the 4 studies associated with the Guilford (O'Sullivan et al., 1965) tests. This is intriguing because those studies, using high school students, were the only studies to identify an independent factor called social intelligence. It is also worth noting that virtually all of the undergraduate and graduate samples were psychology majors. One might speculate that the social intelligence of a population who has already chosen a largely social career might be different from a similar age-cohort having chosen a career in engineering, mathematics, or finance. The 4 studies carried out with nonstudent populations included psychiatric patients, AWOL soldiers, social service workers, and managers. The cumulative total of subjects for these studies is less than 150. The vaunted "norms" for the George Washington Test, claimed to be in excess of 12,000, were largely opaque—referred to but not available for examination. Even those norms were admittedly largely constructed from undergraduate respondents (80%+). Although it is no simple matter to determine if the normative population for the study of social intelligence might have represented a restricted population (statistically) or if the subject population lacked the broader properties necessary for generalization, what we can reasonably infer is that for the study of a construct reputed to be a "new" human attribute, sample selection was inadequate.

Similarly, virtually all research conducted on social intelligence was done in the United States. Although some research done on emotional intelligence would appear to break out of this cultural constraint, it is more a matter of appearance than reality. As examples, samples assessed in the United States, Australia, Canada, the United Kingdom, countries of the European Union beyond the United Kingdom, and even South Africa share a culture that is individualistic rather than collectivist, masculine rather than feminine, and predominantly short term in time perspective rather than long term. One or all of these parameters of culture (Hofstede, 2001) would seem to have a substantial impact on the expression of emotional intelligence. Research populations should include countries such as Iran, Pakistan, China, and Sweden, countries with cultural models very different from the U.S. model. Social intelligence research is culturally parochial. Research on emotional intelligence would benefit greatly from a more culturally diverse population of research subjects.

Research following the suggestion of Thorndike about the possible value of the construct of social intelligence was not programmatic. It tended to focus on measurement at the expense of theory. It was dominated by a few, largely identical, instruments. Little or no effort was devoted to the serious business of establishing the legitimacy of the construct. There was much more enthusiasm for demonstrating the practical value of the proposed construct. There was a tendency to emphasize what such a construct *could* mean rather than what it *did* mean. It was dustbowl empiricism at its worst. Researchers grazing for interesting covariates or predictor variables would throw social intelligence into the variable pot to see if anything came out. No encouraging relationships emerged. There was little or no discipline to the efforts. With the exception of later work of Guilford and his colleagues (O'Sullivan et al., 1965), the construct never received the serious research attention that should have been afforded a possible human attribute with so much inherent interest. Sixty years of effort were largely wasted because of an unwillingness to practice the arduous exercises of the scientific enterprise. It is tempting to come to much the same conclusion regarding current research on emotional intelligence.

AUTHOR NOTE

I was assisted in revisions of this chapter by Ben Benjamin, Jeff Conte, Kylie Harper, Jack Mayer, Kevin Murphy, and Rich Roberts. I was assisted in completing the literature review for this chapter by Geoff Burcaw, Will Lambe, and Barbara Nett. Correspondence regarding this chapter can be sent to:

FRANK LANDY, P O BOX 4869
BRECKENRIDGE, CO 80424
FRANK.LANDY@LANDYLSG.COM

REFERENCES

Aderman, D., & Berkowitz, L. (1983). Self-concern and the unwillingness to be helpful. *Social Psychology Quarterly, 46*(4), 293–301.

Anastasi, A. (1937). *Differential psychology.* New York: Macmillan.

Anastasi, A. (1954) *Psychological testing.* New York: Macmillan

Bar-On, R. (2000). Emotional and social intelligence: Insights from the Emotional Quotient Inventory (EQ-I). In R. Bar-On & J.D. Parker (Eds.), *Handbook of emotional intelligence* (pp. 363–388). San Francisco: Jossey-Bass.

Benjamin, L. T. (in press). Hugo Munsterberg's attack on the application of scientific psychology. *Journal of Applied Psychology.*

Bingham, W. V. D. (1937). *Aptitudes and aptitude testing.* New York: Harper.

Bingham, W. V. D., & Freyd, M. (1926). *Procedures in employment psychology.* Chicago: A.W. Shaw.

Blum, M. L. (1949). *Industrial psychology and its social foundations.* New York: Harper.

Boyatzis, R. E., Goleman, D., & Rhee, K. S. (2000). Clustering competence in emotional intelligence. In R. Bar-On & J.D. Parker (Eds.), *The handbook of emotional intelligence: Theory, development, and assessment, and application at home, school, and in the workplace* (pp. ??–??). San Francisco: Jossey-Bass.

Broom, M. E. (1928) A note on the validity of a test of social intelligence. *Journal of Applied Psychology, 12*, 426–428.

Broom, M. E. (1930). A further study of the validity of a test of social intelligence. *Journal of Educational Research, 22*, 403–405.

Bruner, J. S. & Taguiri, R. (1954). The perception of people. In G. Lindzey (Ed.), *Handbook of social psychology* (Vol. 2, pp. 634–654). Reading, MA: Addison-Wesley.

Burks, F. W. (1937). The relation of social intelligence test scores to ratings of social traits. *Journal of Social Psychology, 8*, 146–153.

Burley, P. M., & McGuiness, J. (1977). Effects of social intelligence on the Milgram paradigm. *Psychological Reports, 40*, 767–770.

Burtt, H. E. (1926). *Employment psychology.* New York: Houghton Mifflin

Burtt, H. E. (1942). *Principles of employment psychology.* New York: Harper

Burtt, H. E. (1948). *Applied psychology.* New York: Prentice Hall.

Carroll, J. B. (1993). *Human cognitive abilities: A survey of factor analytic studies.* New York: Cambridge University Press.

Chapin, F. S. (1939). Social participation and social intelligence. *American Sociological Review, 4*, 154–166.

Chapin, F. S. (1942). Preliminary standardization of a social insight scale. *American Sociological Review, 7*, 214–225.

Chapin, F. S. (1967). *The Social Insight Test.* Palo Alto, CA: Consulting Psychologists Press.

Clark, J. H. (1948). Intelligence test results obtained from a specific type of army A.W.O.L. *Educational and Psychological Measurement, 8*(4), 677–682.

Clark, L. F., & Neuringer, C. (1971). Repressor-sensitizer personality styles and associated levels of verbal ability, social intelligence, and quantitative ability. *The Journal of Consulting and Clinical Psychology, 36*(2), 183–188.

Clarke, H. M. (1934). Recall and recognition of names and faces. *Journal of Applied Psychology, 18*(6), 757–763.

Cleeton, G. U. (1949). Social Intelligence Test. A review in O. K. Buros (Ed.), *Third Mental Measurements Yearbook* (pp. 196–197). New Brunswick, NJ: Rutgers University Press.

Crane, G. W. (1946). *Psychology applied.* Chicago: Hopkins Syndicate.

Cronbach, L. J. (1960). *Essentials of psychological testing* (2nd ed.). New York: Harper & Row.

Cronbach, L. J. (1970) *Essentials of psychological testing* (3rd ed.). New York: Harper & Row.

Cronbach, L. J., & Meehl, P. W. (1955). Construct validity in psychological tests. *Psychological Bulletin, 52*, 281–302.

Derksen, J., Kramer, I., & Katzko, M. (2002). Does a self-report measure of emotional intelligence assess something different than general intelligence? *Personality and Individual Differences, 32*, 37–48.

Dewey, J. (1909). *Moral principles in education.* New York: Houghton Mifflin.

Drake, C. A. (1942). *Personnel selection by standard job tests.* New York: McGraw-Hill.

Eimecke, V. W. (1949). Kuder Preference Record norms for sales trainees. *Occupations, 28*(1), 5–10.

Eimecke, V. W., & Fish, H. L. (1948). A preliminary study of the relationships between the Bernreuter Personaliy Inventory and performances on the

Army Alpha examination and the George Washington Social Intelligence Test. *The Journal of Psychology, 25,* 381–387.

Erez, M. (1980). Correlates of leadership style: Field-dependence and social intelligence versus social orientation. *Perceptual and Motor Skills, 50,* 231–238.

Flemming, E. G. (1932). Testing some aspects of personality. *Journal of Social Psychology, 3,* 376–385.

Ford, M. E., & Tisak, M. S. (1983). A further search for social intelligence. *Journal of Educational Psychology, 75*(2), 196–206.

Freyd, M. (1923). The personalities of socially and mechanically inclined. *Psychological Monographs, 33*(151), 1–191.

Fryer, D. H., & Henry, E. R. (1950). *Handbook of applied psychology* (Vols. I & II). New York: Rinehart.

Gardner, H. (1983). *Frames of mind: The theory of multiple intelligences.* New York: Basic Books.

Garrett, H. E. (1927). Personality as "habit organization." *Journal of Abnormal and Social Psychology, 21,* 250–255.

Garrett, H. E., & Kellogg, W. N. (1928). The relation of physical constitution to general intelligence, social intelligence, and emotional instability. *Journal of Experimental Psychology, 11,* 113–129.

Garrett, H. E., & Schneck, M. R. (1933). *Psychological tests, methods and results.* New York: Harper.

Gilliland, A. R., & Burke, R. S. (1926). A measurement of sociability. *Journal of Applied Psychology, 10,* 315–326.

Goleman, D. (1995). *Emotional intelligence.* New York: Bantam Books

Goleman, D. (1998). What makes a leader? *Harvard Business Review, 73*(November–December), 93–102.

Gough, H. G. (1968). *Manual for the Chapin Social Insight Test.* Palo Alto, CA: Consulting Psychologists Press.

Gross, M. L. (1962). *The brain watchers.* New York: New American Library.

Grosvenor, E. L. (1927). A study of social intelligence of high school pupils. *American Physical Education Review, 32*(9), 649–657.

Guilford, J. P. (1927). An experiment in learning to read facial expression. *Journal of Abnormal and Social Psychology, 24,* 191–202.

Guilford, J. P. (1934). Introversion-extroversion. *The Psychological Bulletin, 31,* 331–354.

Guilford, J. P. (1956). The structure of the intellect. *Psychological Bulletin, 53,* 267–293.

Guilford, J. P. (1967). *The nature of human intelligence.* New York: McGraw-Hill

Guion, R. M. (1965). *Personnel testing.* New York: McGraw-Hill.

Hartman, B. J. (1967). Hypnotic susceptibility and social intelligence. *The American Journal of Clinical Hypnosis, 10*(1), 37–38.

Hoepfner, R., & O'Sullivan, M. (1968). Social intelligence and IQ. *Educational and Psychological Measurement, 28,* 339–344.

Hepner, H. W. (1941). *Psychology applied to work and life.* New York: Prentice Hall.

Hofstede, G. (2001) *Culture's consequences: Comparing values, behaviors, institutions, and organizations across nations.* Thousand Oaks, CA: Sage.

Hull, C. L. (1928). *Aptitude testing.* Yonkers-on-the-Hudson, NY: World Book.

Hunt, T. (1927). What social intelligence is and where to find it. *Industrial Psychology, 2,* 605–612.

Hunt, T. (1928). The measurement of social intelligence. *Journal of Applied Psychology, 12,* 317–334.

Hunter, J. E., & Hunter, R. F. (1984). Validity and utility of alternative measures of job performance. *Psychological Bulletin, 96,* 72–98.

Jackson, D. N. (1972). Tests of social intelligence. A review in O. K. Buros (Ed.), *Seventh Mental Measurements Yearbook* (pp. 370–371). Highland Park, NJ: Gryphon Press.

Jackson, V. D. (1940). The measurement of social proficiency. *Journal of Experimental Education, 8*(4), 422–474.

Jenness, A. (1932). The recognition of facial expressions of emotion. *Psychological Bulletin, 29,* 324–350.

Johnson, D. T. (1969). Introversion, extraversion and social intelligence: A replication. *Journal of Clinical Psychology, 25,* 181–183.

Joncich, G. M. (1962). *Psychology and the science of education: Selected writings of E. L. Thorndike.* New York: Columbia Teachers College Press.

Kaess, W. A., & Witryol, S. L. (1955). Memory for names and faces: A characteristic of social intelligence? *Journal of Applied Psychology, 39*(6), 457–462.

Karlin, L., & Schwartz, M. M. (1953). Social and general intelligence and performance on the Rosenzweig Picture-Frustration Study. *Journal of Consulting Psychology, 17*(4), 293–296.

Kassin, S. M., & Hochreich, D. J. (1977). Instructional set: A neglected variable in attributional research? *Personality and Social Psychology Bulletin, 3,* 620–623.

Keating, D. P. (1978) A search for social intelligence. *Journal of Educational Psychology, 70*(2), 218–223.

Kelley, T. L. (1927). *The interpretation of educational measurements.* Yonkers-on-the-Hudson, NY: World Book.

Kelley, T. L. (1928). *Crossroads in the mind of man.* Stanford, CA: Stanford University Press.

Kitson, H. D. (1925). *The psychology of vocational adjustment.* Philadelphia: Lippincott.

Kuiper, N. A. (1978). Depression an causal attributions for success and failure. *Journal of Personality and Social Psychology, 36*(3), 236–246.

Laird, D. A. (1927). *The psychology of selecting men.* New York: McGraw-Hill.

Laird, D. A. (1936). *How to use psychology in business.* New York: McGraw-Hill.

Laird, D. A. (1937). *The psychology of selecting employees.* New York: McGraw-Hill

Landy, F. L. (2005). Some historical and scientific issues related to research on emotional intelligence. *Journal of Organizational Behavior, 26,* 411–424.

Lanyon, R. I. (1972). Chapin Social Insight Test. A review in O.K. Buros (Ed.), *Seventh Mental Measurements Yearbook* (pp. 98–99). Highland Park, NJ: Gryphon Press.

Law, K. S., Wong, C. S., & Song, L. (2004). The construct and criterion validity of emotional intelligence and its potential utility for management studies. *Journal of Applied Psychology, 89,* 483–496.

Lorge, I., & Blau, R. D. (1942). Borad occupational groupings by estimated abilities. *Occupations, 21*(4), 288–295.

Matthews, G., Zeidner, M., & Roberts, R. (2002). *Emotional intelligence: Science and myth.* Cambridge, MA: MIT Press.

Mayer, J. D. (199, September). Emotional intelligence: Popular or scientific psychology? *APA Monitor, 30,* 50. [*Shared Perspectives* column] Washington, DC: American Psychological Association.

Mayer, J. D., & Geher, G. (1996). Emotional intelligence and the identification of emotion. *Intelligence, 22,* 89–113.

Mayer, J. D., & Salovey, P. (1993). The intelligence of emotional intelligence. *Intelligence, 17,* 433–442.

Mayer, J. D., Salovey, P., Caruso, D. R., & Sitarenios, G. (2003). Modeling and measuring emotional intelligence with the MSCEIT V2.0. *Emotion, 3,* 97–105.

McClatchey, V. R. (1929). A theoretical and statistical critique of the concept of social intelligence and of attempts to measure such a process. *Journal of Abnormal and Social Psychology, 24,* 217–220.

McGregor, D. (1960). *The human side of enterprise.* New York: McGraw-Hill.

Moore, B. V., & Hartmann, G. V. (1931). *Readings in industrial psychology.* New York: Appleton.

Moore, H. (1939). *Psychology for business and industry.* New York: McGraw-Hill

Moss, F. A. (1929). *Applications of psychology.* Cambridge, MA: Riverside Press.

Moss, F. A., & Hunt, T. (1927). Are you socially intelligent? *Scientific American, 137,* 108–110.

Moss, F. A., Hunt, T., Omwake, K. T., & Ronning, M. M. (1927). *Social Intelligence Test.* Washington, DC: Center for Psychological Services.

Oliver, R. A. C. (1930). The traits of extroverts and introverts. *The Journal of Social Psychology, 1*(3), 345–366.

Orr, D. B. (1972). Chapin Social Insight Test. A review in O.K. Buros (Ed.), *Seventh Mental Measurements Yearbook* (pp. 99 –101). Highland Park, NJ: Gryphon Press.

Osipow, S. H., & Walsh, W. B. (1973). Social intelligence and the selection of counselors. *Journal of Counseling Psychology, 20*(4), 366–369.

O'Sullivan, M., & Guilford, J. P. (1975) Six factors of behavioral cognition: Understanding other people. *Journal of Educational Measurement, 12*(4), 255–271.

O'Sullivan, M., Guilford, J. P., & deMille, R. (1965). The measurement of social intelligence. *Psychological Laboratory Report, 34.* Los Angeles: University of Southern California.

Pintner, R. (1924). *Intelligence testing.* New York: Holt.

Pintner, R. (1931). *Intelligence testing: Methods and results* (2nd ed.). New York: Holt.

Pintner, R., & Upshall, C. (1928). Some results of social intelligence tests. School and Society, 27, 369–370.

Poffenberger, A. T. (1927). *Principles of applied psychology.* Madison, WI: United States Armed Forces Institute.

Poffenberger, A. T. (1929). *Applied psychology: Its principles and methods.* New York: Appleton.

Rice, B. (1979). Brave new world of intelligence testing. *Psychology Today, 12*(September), 27–41.

Reardon, R., Foley, J., & Walker, R. E. (1979). Social intelligence and vocational choice. *Psychological Reports, 44*, 853–854.

Riess, M., Rosenfeld, P., Melburg, V., & Tedeschi, J. T. (1981). Self-serving attributions: Biased private perceptions and distorted public descriptions. *Journal of Personality and Social Psychology, 41*(2), 224–231.

Roberts, R. D., Zeidner, M., & Matthews, G. (2001). Does emotional intelligence meet traditional standards for an intelligence? Some new data and conclusions. *Emotions, 1*, 196–231.

Romney, D. M., & Pyryt, M. C. (1999). Guilford's concept of social intelligence revisited. *High Ability Studies, 10*(2), 137–199.

Ruch, F. L. (1949). Test for the ability to sell: George Washington University Series. A review in O.K. Buros (Ed.), *Third Mental Measurements Yearbook* (p.197). New Brunswick, NJ: Rutgers University Press.

Sala, F. (2002). *Emotional Competence Inventory: Technical manual.* Boston: The Hay Group.

Schmidt, F. L. (1992). What do the data really mean? Research findings, meta-analysis, and cumulative knowledge in psychology. *American Psychologist, 47*, 1173–1181.

Schmidt, F. L., & Hunter, J. E. (1981). Employment testing: Old theories and new research findings. *American Psychologist, 36*, 1128–1137

Schmidt, F. L., & Hunter, J. E. (1984). A within setting empirical test of the situational specificity hypothesis of employee selection. *Personnel Psychology, 37*(2), 317–326.

Sechrest, L., & Jackson, D. N. (1961). Social intelligence an the accuracy of interpersonal predictions. *Journal of Personality, 29*(2), 167–182.

Shanley, L. A., Walker, R. E., & Foley, J. M. (1971). Social intelligence: A concept in search of data. *Psychological Reports, 29*, 1123–1132.

Sheddan, B. R., & Witmer, L. R. (1939). *Journal of Applied Psychology, 23*(1), 271–279.

Smith, H. C. (1948). Psychometric checks on hypotheses derived from Sheldon's work on physique and temperament. *Journal of Peraonality, 17*(2), 310–320.

Snyder, S. D., & Michael, W. B. (1983). The relationship between performance on standardized tests in mathematics and reading to two measures of social intelligence and one of academic self-esteem of primary school children. *Educational and Psychological Measurement, 43*, 1141–1148.

Spearman, C. (1927). *The abilities of man.* New York: Macmillan

Stagner, R. (1932). Differential factors in the testing of personality: I. Sex differences. *The Journal of Social Psychology, 3*, 477–487.

Stagner, R. (1933a). Improved norms for four personality tests. *The American Journal of Psychology, 45*, 303–307.

Stagner, R. (1933b). The relation of personality to academic aptitude and achievement. *Journal of Educational Research, 26*, 648–660.

Strang, R. (1930a). Measures of social intelligence. *American Journal of Sociology, 36*, 263–269.

Strang, R. (1930b). Relation of social intelligence to certain other factors. *School and Society, 32*, 268–272.

Strang, R. (1932). An analysis of errors made in a test of social intelligence. *Journal of Educational Sociology, 5*(5), 291–299.

Super, D. E. (1949). *Appraising vocational fitness by means of psychological tests.* New York: Harper.

Taft, R. (1955). The ability to judge people. *Psychological Bulletin, 52,* 1–23.

Taylor, H. L. (1949). Social Intelligence Test. A review in O.K. Buros (Ed.), *Third Mental Measurements Yearbook* (p. 197). New Brunswick, NJ: Rutgers University Press.

Tenopyr, M. L. (1967). Social intelligence and academic success. *Educational and Psychological Measurement, 27,* 961–965.

Thorndike, E. L. (1910). *Educational psychology* (2nd ed.). New York: Teachers College, Columbia University.

Thorndike, E. L. (1920). Intelligence and its use. *Harper's Magazine, 140,* 227–235.

Thorndike, E. L. (1921). Intelligence and its measurement: A symposium. *Journal of Educational Psychology, 12*(3), 124–127.

Thorndike, E. L. (1925). *The principles of teaching based on psychology.* New York: A.G. Selier.

Thorndike, E. L. (1936). An autobiography. In C. Murchison (Ed.), *A history of psychology in autobiography* (pp. 263–270). New York: Russell & Russell.

Thorndike, E. L., Bregman, E. O., Cobb, M. V., & Woodyard, E. (1926). *The measurement of intelligence.* New York: Teachers College, Columbia University.

Thorndike, R. L. (1936). Factor analysis of social and abstract intelligence. *Journal of Educaitonal Psychology, 27,* 231–233.

Thorndike, R. L. (1941). The social intelligence test. A review in O. K. Buros (Ed.), *The 1940 Mental Measurements Yearbook* (p. 92). Highlands Park, NJ: Gryphon Press

Thorndike, R. L., & Stein, S. (1937). An evaluation of the attempts to measure social intelligence. *Psychological Bulletin, 34,* 275–285.

Tiffin, J. (1947). *Industrial psychology* (2nd ed.). New York: Prentice Hall.

Van Rooy, D. L., & Viswesvaran, C. (2004). Emotional intelligence: A meta-analytic investigation of predictive validity and nomological net. *Journal of Vocational Behavior, 65,* 71–95.

Viney, W., & King, D. B. (2003). *A history of psychology: Ideas and context.* Boston: Allyn & Bacon.

Viteles, M. S. (1932). *Industrial psychology.* New York: Norton

Walker, R. E., & Foley, J. M. (1973). Social intelligence: Its history and measurement. *Psychological Reports, 33,* 839–864.

Wang, C. K. A. (1932). The signicance of early personal history for certain personality traits. *The American Journal of Psychology, 44,* 768–774.

Wechsler, D. (1944). *The measurement of intelligence.* Baltimore: Williams & Wilkens.

Wechsler, D. (1958). *The measurement of intelligence* (4th ed.). Baltimore: Williams & Wilkens.

Wedeck, J. (1947). The relationship between personality and "psychological ability." *British Journal of Psychology, 37,* 133–151.

Woodrow, H. (1939). The common factors in fifty-two mental tests. *Psychometrika, 4,* 99–108.

Young, P. V. (1938). Defective social intelligence as a factor in crime. *American Sociological Review, 3*(2), 213–217.

5

Emotional Intelligence in Classrooms and in Schools: What We See in the Educational Setting

Jennifer Allen
Learning Environments, Branford, CT

Jonathan Cohen
Center for Social and Emotional Education, New York, NY

Take a moment to look back to your earliest school experiences—elementary, middle, or even high school—when you were genuinely engaged in the learning process. Try to remember a time when you felt particularly connected, a successful and important part of what was happening.

When we ask educators and parents throughout the United States and beyond to recollect such instances, more often than not they share memories of teachers who took the time to know them personally, to step into and understand their individual experiences, to establish a sense of classroom community. They tell stories of deep personal connection, unparalleled empathy, and enlightened self-understanding. They talk about remarkable educators who often knew more about them than they knew themselves.

Predictably, the reflections of these veteran students lead to conversations regarding the flip side, memories of disconnections associated with humiliation, misunderstanding, and, at best, cluelessness. While these may be stories of decades past, they are clearly the narratives that adults carry with them to this day, that have and continue to define how they see themselves as learners. These are stories that have much to say about the impact of the social and emotional context of classrooms and schools of the past, the stories that can and should inform our understanding of the essential role of social and emotional education (SEE)[1] in practice today.

While Goleman (1995) catapulted the highly accessible language of emotional intelligence into the national eye, the importance of making social and emotional connections through curriculum content, classroom pedagogy, and school climate has long been evident in the educational setting and continues to be so now (Cohen, 1999). Without a doubt, Goleman's work appealed, and continues to appeal, to educators because the stories he shared about programmatic efforts are both compelling and familiar to educators. The language he used and the basic idea that social and emotional capacities were more important than grades and SAT scores resonated with people's experience and intuitive sense of what matters.

Our goal in this account is to look back at the evolution of social and emotional education and to provide a snapshot of what we are currently seeing in schools throughout the country. We will highlight what is being done in schools (a) to teach social and emotional skills and (b) to create healthy, productive learning environments—the two core dimensions that characterize effective, evidenced-based social emotional and character education efforts today, kindergarten through Grade 12 (Berkowitz & Bier, 2004; Cohen, 2001; Greenberg et al., 2003). Unlike many of the other chapters in this book, we will not focus narrowly on the measurement, definition, and research evidence related to the construct of emotional intelligence, but rather will describe the broader context in which educational institutions are attempting to incorporate the development of broad social and emotional skills (emotional intelligence is believed to be part of this broad constellation of skills) in the education of students. While emotional intelligence is not the sole focus of this chapter, the approaches described in this chapter do provide a glimpse of the interventions that are currently being used in educational settings to develop students' skills in dealing with the social and emotional content that is at the heart of emotional intelligence.

THE ROOTS OF SOCIAL AND EMOTIONAL EDUCATION

Social emotional educational work is grounded in the coordination of two processes: promoting social, emotional, ethical and cognitive competencies and creating safe, caring, participatory, and responsive environments in which children can grow. The idea that these are important dimensions of life is both old and new.

Since the beginning of formal education 3,000 years ago in Egypt, India, and Greece, schools have first and foremost focused on socializing children to become members of society (Cohen, 1999). Ancient Greek education explicitly focused on enhancing awareness of self and others as a valuable educational endeavor in and of itself. At the Oracle of Delphi, the words *Know thyself* were carved into the walls and served as an organizing principle of scholarly life. Over the centuries, the notion of "self" and who can and should be educated has evolved in dramatic ways, but the concept that teaching needs to be a learning process for students and teachers alike is as old as formal education itself.

For many centuries, only upper-class men were educated, and the pedagogic content of schools typically reflected the dominant religious teachings of the time as well as the wish to instruct students about social norms. It is only in the last century that there has been a more explicit and ongoing appreciation that we can and should teach all children (and adults) about the social and emotional dimensions of life in schools.

The notion that the environment shapes human life is also an ancient one. In the last half of the 5th century BC, Hippocrates reportedly discussed how climate and geography shape human character (Jones, 1923), and, at roughly the same time, 2500 years ago, Herodotus' history ends with the punch line, "Soft countries breed soft men," delivered by Persia's King Cyrus, who was speaking against leaving their harsh mountain terrain, having swept the world and beginning to move to the fertile valleys. It is only in recent years, however, that educators have more explicitly begun to incorporate social and emotional factors in their definition of the environment that influences their students' development.

In the past hundred years, there have been three major, overlapping forces that have created the foundation for current social emotional educational theory and practice: psychological, educational, and societal factors. (See www.csee.net/SEE/roots.aspx for a more detailed description of the educational, mental health, and larger societal precursors to current theory, research, and practice in SEE.) Psychologically, the way we have defined "intelligence" has always shaped educational goals and, as a result, teacher and student behavior. The fateful early 20th-century translation of the Parisian psychologist Binet's test, originally intended to determine the capabilities of students with special needs, into the Stanford-Binet Test of Intelligence fostered the belief that linguistic and mathematical abilities represent the essential components of intelligence. This definition of intelligence has powerfully shaped educational practice for decades. In America today, with the advent of the No Child Left Behind Act (Office of Elementary and Secondary Education, 2001), the stakes are high. Schools receive state and district report cards based on scores on measures of linguistic and mathematical performance and face potential sanctions if students fail to meet federally mandated standards. Principals and superintendents are often evaluated (and, to some extent, paid accordingly) based on students' reading and math scores.

Over the past two decades, broader conceptions of intelligence, exemplified by Howard Gardner's (1983) and Robert Sternberg's (1997) theories and programs of research have expanded educators' understanding of intellectual capacity and functioning. As a consequence, there are more and more educators and schools pursuing a wider array of educational goals and related pedagogy as a result of research and suggesting that linguistic and mathematical competencies are not the only measures that contribute to life success, satisfaction, and the ability to be a lifelong learner.

In America, the psychologist Lightner Witmer (1909) was the first to create a true partnership between educators and experimental psychologists. Believing that emotional life shapes thinking, learning, and behavior, Witmer initiated a great tradition of mental health professionals and educators learning from each other to support student learning and healthy development.

At roughly the same time in Europe, Sigmund Freud (1923/1964) began to think about the role of emotion in learning and the education of children. Literally, from the first hours of psychoanalysis, Freud and his "Wednesday night" colleagues wondered how they could apply psychoanalytic ideas to the education of children—among them their own. These meetings opened an evolving dialogue about the application of psychoanalytically informed thinking and work to the education of young children (Cohen, 2002; for discussions of current neuroscience research supporting predictions of early psychoanalysts, see Sanfey, Rilling, Aronson, Nystrom, & Cohen, 2003; Shonkoff & Phillips, 2000; Sylwester, 2000).

In education, there has been an evolving tradition, beginning with the functionalist John Dewey (1896), that has underscored the notion that education needs to be relevant to all children—not just a privileged male minority—and designed to promote the skills, knowledge, and beliefs that contribute to effective citizenry. Dewey and ensuing generations of progressive educators highlighted the fact that we need to educate the "whole child" and integrate social and emotional dimensions into teaching and learning. This is one of the many important examples of educational discovery and research that set the stage for and, to some extent, shaped current SEE theory and practice, supporting the importance of the education and development of the whole child.

WHAT WE SEE IN SCHOOLS TODAY

Decisions regarding *what* teachers teach (curriculum content) and *how* teachers teach (classroom pedagogy) reflect a school and community's belief about how students learn. There is evidence to support the premise that schools that integrate SEE into existing curricula have a higher likelihood of improving student achievement (Elias et al., 1997). The learning theory supporting this premise builds on Piaget's premise that people construct their understanding of the world on the basis of their experiences (Resnik & Hall, 1998). Schools are, by definition, social places and school-based learning is, by definition, a social process (Zins, Weissberg, Wang, & Walberg, 2004). It follows that one important function of school is to provide students with experiences that will foster the development of critical social skills.

The importance of prosocial behaviors as an essential ingredient in student learning has been well documented (DiPerna & Elliott, 1999; Feshback and Feshback, 1987; Haynes, Ben-Avie, & Ensign, 2003; Pasi, 2001, quoted in Zins et al., 2004). One of the key goals of integrating SEE into educational institutions is to use a range of approaches, among them cooperative learning, group problem solving, and curriculum infusion (Elias, 2004; Johnson & Johnson, 2004), that will give students an opportunity to develop both the skills and the motivation to engage in these prosocial behaviors.

INTEGRATING SEE INTO CLASSROOM PRACTICE

One way of conceptualizing the core social and emotional competencies that underlie SEE is to divide them into skills and abilities that influence how students feel about themselves (self-awareness), how they see others (social awareness), how they manage their feelings and their personal needs (self-management), how they interact with others (relationship management), and how they work through dilemmas (responsible decision making; Goleman, 2000). What and how teachers choose to teach is increasingly informed by the desire to integrate these explicit SEE competencies with teaching practice, which can be accomplished in a variety of ways. For example, schools are increasingly likely to incorporate activities that encourage individual and group problem solving, which may help students to develop these competencies. These methods have long been common in elementary school classrooms; skilled teachers at the secondary level also integrate these processes into the daily activities of their classrooms.

Integrating skill development into the classroom through pedagogy or instructional practice is one method of infusing social and emotional education into existing practice. A second type of infusion takes place through the integration of social and emotional concepts into the existing curriculum. The study of history, for example, can provide students with real-life examples of practical, personal, and moral dilemmas and offers both a window and a mirror for students to think about what responsible decision making entails and what can interfere with one's judgment in the face of difficult choices. Considering John F. Kennedy's days during the Cuban Missile Crisis, for example, sheds light on the potential risks one may potentially confront and the outcomes one must weigh. Ghandi's decision to face down a colonial military power through nonviolent action is another example of textbook history supplying lessons regarding strength of character and conflict resolution skills.

The infusion of SEE into the study of literature can likewise offer students the opportunity to reflect on their own social and emotional skills through the analysis of characters in both fiction and nonfiction. Reflective questions about how a character sees himself or herself and how that view impacts the individual's relationships with others are thought to offer valuable information to the student about how to analyze his or her own behaviors, skills, and abilities. Likewise, this line of study can inform the child's interactions with others. For example, rather than simply reading the text, students might be encouraged to analyze how Huckleberry Finn managed to maintain his resilience in the face of child abuse, homelessness, and discrimination. Similarly, students might use literature to understand the bases of social norms and expectations. Thus, teachers might use a book such as *Lord of the Flies* to help students understand the potential fragility of the social contract. Analyzing the relationships of the bully, the victim, and the bystander in literature can help students develop knowledge and skills they can apply to their own school and social experiences. From the perspective of SEE, literature can provide rich and varied opportunities for students to look at themselves and others and to develop both knowledge and skills that generalize to their own development as individuals.

An alternative to the integration of collaborative processes into pedagogy of teaching and the infusion of SEE into the existing curriculum is the adoption of a specific and separate program or curriculum from an outside source. There are a number of research-based SEE curricula available today, and many schools have chosen to adopt these specific programs (Zins et al., 2004; Collaborative for Academic, Social, and Emotional Learning, 2003; Osher, Dwyer, & Jackson, 2002). These programs often focus on skill development such as making effective decisions, resolving conflicts peacefully, establishing positive peer relations, practicing healthy behaviors, and developing character.

Other specific programs look at schools as systems, focusing on building school communities and establishing strong and lasting home–school partnerships, highlighting yet another way that schools are directly addressing the matter of social and emotional competency. These programs highlight the second and equally critical dimension of SEE: fostering safe, caring, participatory, and responsive environments.

CREATING A CLIMATE FOR LEARNING

How a school is run—how people interact and treat one another, the manner in which decisions are made and communicated, how classrooms and the school as a whole are managed—contributes significantly to its social and emotional ethos. A number of researchers have specifically identified aspects of school climate that can add or detract from students' and adults' sense of connection and belonging and their degree of productivity in the learning community (Blum, McNeely, & Rinehart, 2002; McNeely, Nonnemaker, & Blum, 2002; Osterman, 2000). From our work in schools, focusing specifically on SEE, we have identified five core elements that contribute to a safe and responsive school environment: (1) order and safety: physical, social, and emotional; (2) quality of instruction; (3) expectations for student achievement; (4) collaboration and communication; and (5) parent/guardian and community involvement (Allen, Sandy. Cohen, & Chang, 2005). There are a number of ways in which schools can address these core factors.

Order and Safety: Physical, Social, and Emotional

First and foremost, schools that are attuned to the needs of all stakeholders—students, faculty and staff, parents, and community members—are thought to offer an environment where learning is most likely to take place (Berkowitz & Bier, in press; Bluestein, 2001; Raider & Coleman, 1992) Individuals who feel threatened or uncertain physically, socially, or emotionally are unlikely to be able to participate fully in the learning process (Devine & Cohen, in press; Goleman, 1995). Physical needs range from having adequate and orderly spaces in which to work to feeling safe from bodily harm to knowing what to do in the event of a school or community crisis. Social and emotional needs, while often less overt, are also an important component of providing a safe and ordered environment for learning. These range from having rules clearly communicated and consistently enforced to knowing how to report verbal abuse or bullying to having enough time in the school day to attend to personal matters.

One strategy used by some educational institutions is to develop a collaboratively constructed statement that defines the rights and responsibilities of the various members of the school community as a part of an interdependent group of people (Sergiovanni, 1992). Once this belief statement becomes accepted and understood within the school community, it serves as a platform for identifying behaviors that are counter to the organizational norms of the school. Thus, rather than simply defining antisocial behaviors as violations of rules established by the formal leadership of a school, behaviors such as teasing and bullying can be brought to the forefront in the context of "what we believe as a school." If, for example, the belief statement includes the statement, "Every individual in our school is entitled to being and feeling safe," conversations about when and why people may feel unsafe can take place. Most often the discussion focuses on matters of bullying and the role and responsibility of each individual involved—the bully, the victim, and the bystander. The goal of this approach is to develop the ability of all members of the school community to understand and accept shared social norms rather than simply abiding by rules promulgated by the principal or school board.

Many schools have turned to their discipline systems as natural opportunities to develop meaningful connections with students and their families. For example, schools that have developed comprehensive disciplinary codes focus on preventing problems by creating a school culture that promotes student engagement and prosocial behavior. The goal of these programs is to encourage parents, teachers, and students to think about school discipline and school climate as integrally related concepts (Glasser, 1991; Gossen, 1992; Watson, 2003). These programs often encourage members of school communities to ask questions such as the following:

- Do we want to focus on rules or on beliefs?
- What is the role of extrinsic motivation versus intrinsic motivation in controlling individual behavior?
- Is the teacher the person who controls discipline or the individual who facilitates student self-control and self-discipline?
- Do we want a school community where mistakes are reprimanded and a source of social isolation or a place where students learn to fix their mistakes and improve their relationships?

- Should we create a sense of community or foster competition?

Conversations regarding student discipline and school climate are likely to help all members of the school community develop a more sophisticated and integrated understanding of the bases for the rules and norms that help schools provide a social context for learning.

Other activities initiated in schools to foster a sense of safety, community, and communication are morning meetings (Kriete, 1999), generally seen at the elementary and middle school levels, and advisor–advisee programs (Ayres, 1994; George & Alexander, 1993; Ziegler & Mulhall, 1994), most frequently implemented in middle and high schools. The benefit of these activities is that they increase the likelihood that each student will feel connected to at least one adult in the school. Activities vary within morning meetings and in advisories, depending on the specific goals and objectives of the individual program. Typically, these activities focus on one or more of the following goals: building community, developing skills, advising academically, advocating for students, invigorating students, and/or emphasizing academics.

Quality of Instruction

Assessing the quality of instruction in a school requires looking at the breadth of the curriculum and its relationship to students' needs and interests as well as its alignment with state and national standards. In addition to meeting standards for literacy and numeracy, a SEE-oriented curriculum should include explicit skill instruction in self-control, effective communication, cooperation, responsibility, decision making, and problem solving (Allen et al., 2005). This curriculum reflects the belief that students' success is driven not only by traditional academic achievement but also by the school's ability to help students experience success, belonging, respect, power, structure, recognition, consistency, positivity, and varied learning . In short, the definition of high-quality instruction is likely to reflect activities and experiences that develop students' emotional and social skills as well as their traditional academic skills.

Expectations for Student Achievement

As with quality of instruction, when we think in terms of SEE, expectations for student achievement go beyond traditional paper and pencil measurement. In addition to standardized test scores, teachers should hold high expectations for students' reflective capabilities, their cooperative/collaborative skills, and their decision-making abilities. In schools where these expectations are explicit, social and emotional growth is documented in addition to traditional academic achievement; personal growth is recognized to go hand in hand with high test scores.

Collaboration and Communication

Creating a community of learners where trust, openness, respect for diversity, and shared decision making are explicit goals is thought to be critical for the development of social and emotional skills. In schools with a positive school climate, teachers not only address students' academic needs but also their general welfare and affective needs. To provide adequate support to allow this to happen, professional development opportunities should be provided to teachers and staff that help them better identify the developmental needs of individual students. In addition, to assure that teachers are provided with adequate time to focus on students' affective and cognitive needs, teachers should be given common planning time to allow them the opportunity to assess and discuss individual student needs.

One way to develop critical social and emotional skills in students, teachers, and parents is to involve them in collaborative decision making. For example, in schools where comprehensive site-based management is in effect, a specific plan is often developed to delineate how different types of decisions are made and by whom, through the creation of decision-making teams. The process of shared decision making gives members of a school community opportunities to develop and practice skills in collaboration, leadership, active listening, and other important social skills and increases the likelihood that schools will develop a climate and culture that supports both academic and social/emotional learning.

Parent/guardian and Community Involvement

In a survey, 90% of new teachers agreed that involving parents in their children's education is a priority at their school, but only 25% described their experience working with parents as "very satisfying." When asked to choose the biggest challenge they face, 31% of them cited involving parents and communicating with them as their top choice. 73% of new teachers said too many parents treat schools and teachers as adversaries.

—Gibbs (2005, pp. 44–45)

When we ask parents what their immediate priorities are for their children, consistently they cite both personal happiness and school success. Not surprisingly, when teachers are asked the question, their response is the same. Why, then, are parent–teacher relations the top concern of the teachers we work with in the field? In the recent article in *Time* magazine (Gibbs, 2005), Harvard education professor Sara Lawrence-Lightfoot cites "anxiety, panic and vulnerability" (p. 43) as the underlying emotions that both parents and teachers feel at parent–teacher conferences.

In schools where parents and teachers have come to embrace the notion of collaboration, the student becomes the central focus of conversation. Ongoing discussions regarding what is best for children take place outside of, and certainly in addition to, the intense focus of the parent–teacher conference. Parents are involved in ongoing school dialogue as well as the decision-making process. Mutual respect emerges from the sharing of ideas and the realization of commonality of concern.

Teachers in schools with more diverse populations frequently face additional challenges as they try to make connections with parents who are frequently unavailable during school hours. Sociologists contend that, in many instances, what can all too easily be categorized as indifference is, in fact, a function of cultural barriers or cultural differences regarding the expectation for home–school communication (Gibbs, 2005). The most successful efforts we have observed in this respect have resulted when a school looks for ways to involve its students and staff members in community action (Hatch, 1998; Mediratta and Karp, 2003; Zachary & Olatoye, 2001). In fact, fostering a vital dialogue and partnership between the school, homes, and the community appears to be an essential ingredient for any school reform effort (Murphy & Datnow, 2003; Senge et al., 2000).

One of the most promising approaches schools are taking to involve students and staff in community action and to strengthen SEE in the process is through the creation of service learning programs. Service learning involves relating meaningful community service (e.g., working in a soup kitchen or cleaning a local pond) with traditional academic study (e.g., the social study of poverty or the biological study of ecology) (Kaye, 2004). A growing body of educational research indicates that this strategy fosters both student engagement and achievement (Billig, 2004) in addition to furthering meaningful relations between the school and the community. At the same time, it provides rich opportunities for social-emotional as well as traditional academic learning (Wilczenski, Cohen, & Berman, in preparation).

EMOTIONAL INTELLIGENCE IN SCHOOLS TODAY

How one quantifies intelligence is a thorny topic, one with which educators and parents continue to struggle in the context of schooling.

While the term *EQ* is not typically used in schools per se, Goleman's discussion of the concept of "EQ" has raised awareness for educators and parents across America regarding the importance of social and emotional education in our schools. In particular, the consideration of specific social emotional skills or competencies (i.e., self-awareness, social awareness, self-management, relationship management, and responsible decision making) has influenced parents' and teachers' conversations regarding the fundamental aims of K–12 schooling—what skills, knowledge, and dispositions we would hope our children to have, and how the climate within our schools can and should contribute to our children's educational experiences.

Current efforts to incorporate social and emotional education into primary and secondary education do not depend ultimately on the resolution of questions in the social science literature regarding the definition, measurement, and correlated of emotional intelligence. Rather, we see efforts to incorporate SEE into the definition of what we mean by primary and secondary education as a change that is likely to have a beneficial effect on a broad range of skills, abilities, and values, some of which fall within the various frameworks used to define emotional intelligence and some of which go beyond those frameworks. Emotional intelligence is a useful construct for analyzing and understanding many of the interventions that help to define SEE-oriented curricula, and it is likely that developments in the definition and understanding of emotional intelligence will have future benefits for efforts in the schools to develop the necessary social and emotional skills and abilities that are so critical to success in education and in life.

ENDNOTES

[1]Although we are using the term *social emotional education* here, evidence-based character education, social emotional learning, and, in many ways, risk prevention efforts are all grounded in the long-term coordination of promoting students' social emotional competencies and systematically intervening to created safe, caring, participatory, and responsive schools and homes.

REFERENCES

Allen, J., Sandy, S., Cohen, J., & Chang, J. (2005). *The comprehensive school climate inventory.* In preparation

Ayres. L. R. (1994). Middle school advisory programs: Findings from the field. *Middle School Journal, 25*(3), 8–14.

Berkowitz, M. W., & Bier, M.C. (2004). Research based character education. *Annals of the American Academy of Political and Social Science, 591*(January), 72–85.

Billig, S. H. (2004). Heads, hearts, hands: The research on K–12 service-learning. In J. Kielsmeier, M. Neal, & M. McKinnon (Eds.), *Growing to greatness: The state of service learning* (pp. 12–25). St. Paul, MN: National Youth Leadership Council.

Bluestein, J. (2001). *Creating emotionally safe schools: A guide for educators and parents.* Deerfield Beach, FL: Heath Communications.

Blum, R. W. McNeely, C. A., & Rinehart, P. M. (2002). *Improving the odds: The untapped power of schools to improve the health of teens.* Minneapolis: Univeristy of Minnesota, Center for Adolescent Health and Development.

Cohen, J. (1999). Social and emotional learning past and present: A psycho educational dialogue. In J. Cohen (Ed.), *Educating minds and hearts: Social emotional learning and the passage into adolescence* (pp. 3–23). New York: Teachers College Press.

Cohen, J. (2001). Social emotional education: Core principles and practices. In J. Cohen (Ed.), *Educating minds and hearts: Social emotional learning and the passage to adolescence* (pp. 3–29). New York: Teachers College Press.

Cohen, J. (2002). Psychoanalysis and the education of children. *Journal of Applied Psychoanalytic Studies, 4*(Special Issue), 1–4.

Collaborative for Academic, Social, and Emotional Learning (2003). *Safe and sound: An educational leader's guide to evidenced-based social and emotional learning* (SEL) programs. Chicago, IL: Author.

Devine, J., & Cohen, J. (in press). *Making your school safe: Physically, socially and emotionally.* New York: Teachers College Press.

Dewey, J. (1896). The reflex concept in psychology. *Psychological Review, 3,* 357–370.

DiPerna, J. C., & Elliot, S. N. (1999). Development and validation of the Academic Competence Evaluation Scales. *Journal of Psychoeducational Assessment, 17,* 207–255.

Elias, M. J. (2004). Strategies to infuse social and emotional learning into academics. In J.E. Zins, R. P. Weissberg, M. C. Wang, & H. J. Walberg (Eds.), *Building academic success on social and emotional learning* (pp. 113–134). New York: Teachers College Press.

Elias, M. J., Zins, J. E., Weissberg, R. P., Frey, K. S., Greenberg, M. T., Haynes, N. M., et al. (1997). *Promoting social and emotional learning: Guidelines for educators.* Alexandria, VA: Association for Supervision and Curriculum Development.

Feshback, N., & Feshback, S. (1987). Affective processes and academic achievement. *Child Development, 51,* 1149–1156.

Freud, S. (1964). New introductory lectures on psychoanalysis. In J. Strachey (Ed. & Trans.), *The standard edition of the complete psychological works of Sigmund Freud,* Vol. 22. London: Hogarth Press. (Original work published 1923)

Gardner, H. (1983). *Frames of mind: The theory of multiple intelligences.* New York: Basic Books.

George, P. S., & Alexander, W. (1993). *The exemplary middle school.* New York: Harcourt Brace Jovanovich.

Gibbs, N. (2005). Parents behaving badly. *Time, 165*(8), 40–49.

Glasser, W. (1991). *The quality school: Managing students without coercion.* New York: Harper & Row.

Goleman, D. (1995). *Emotional intelligence: Why it can matter more than IQ.* New York: Bantam Books.

Goleman, D. (2000). *Working with emotional intelligence.* New York: Bantam Books.

Gossen, D. (1992). *Restitution: Restructuring school discipline.* Chapel Hill, NC: New View Publications.

Greenberg, M. T., Weissberg, R. P., O'Brien, M. U., Zins, J. E., Fredericks, L., Resnik, H., et al. (2003). Enhancing school-based prevention and youth development through coordinated social, emotional, and academic learning. *American Psychologist, 58,* 466–474.

Hatch, T. (1998). How community action contributes to achievement. *Educational Leadership, 55*(8), 16–19.

Haynes, M., Ben-Avie, M., & Ensign, J. (Eds.). (2003). *How social and emotional development add up: Getting results in math and science.* New York: Teachers College Press.

Johnson, D. W., & Johnson, R. T. (2004). The three Cs of promoting social and emotional learning. In J.E. Zins,R. P. Weissberg, M.C. Wang, & H.J. Walberg (Eds.), *Building academic success on social and emotional learning* (pp. 40 – 58). New York: Teachers College Press.

Jones, W. H. S. (1923). *Hippocrates.* Cambridge, MA: Harvard University Press.

Kaye, C.B. (2004). *The complete guide to service learning.* Minneapolis, MN: Free Spirit.

Kriete, R. (1999). *The morning meeting book.* Turners Falls, MA: Northeast Foundation for Children.

McNeely, C. A., Nonnemaker, J. M., & Blum, R. W. (2002). Promoting student connectedness to school: Evidence from the National Longitudinal Study of Adolescent Health. *Journal of School Health, 72,* 138–146.

Mediratta, K., & Karp, J. (2003). *Parent poser and urban school reform: The story of mothers on the move.* New York: New York University, Institute for Education and Social Policy.

Murphy, J., & Datnow, A. (Eds.). (2003). *Leadership lessons from comprehensive school reform.* Thousand Oaks, CA: Corwin Press.

Office of Elementary and Secondary Education. (2001). *No Child Left Behind Act.* Washington, DC: U.S. Department of Education.

Osher, D., Dwyer, K., & Jackson, S. (2002). *Safe, supportive, and successful schools step by step.* Rockville, MD: U.S. Department of Health and Human Services, Substance Abuse and Mental Health Services Administration, Center for Mental Health Services.

Osterman, K. F. (2000). Students' need for belonging in the school community. *Review of Educational Research, 70,* 323–367.

Pasi, R. (2001). *Higher expectation: Promoting social emotional learning and academic achievement in your school.* New York: Teachers College Press.

Raider, E., & Coleman, S. (1992). *Conflict resolution: Strategies for collaborative problem solving.* Brooklyn, NY: Ellen Raider International and Coleman Group International.

Resnik, L. B., & Hall, M. W. (1998). Learning organizations for sustainable education reform. *Daedalus, Journal of the American Academy of Arts and Sciences, 127*(4), 89–118.

Sanfey, A. G., Rilling, J. K., Aronson, J. A., Nystrom, L. E., & Cohen, J. (2003). The neural basis of economic decision-making in the ultimate game. *Science, 13,* 1755–1758.

Senge, P., Cambron-McCabe, N., Lucas, T., Smith, B., Dutton, J., & Kleiner, A. (2000). *Schools that learn.* New York: Doubleday.

Sergiovanni, T. (1992). *Moral leadership: Getting to the heart of school improvement.* San Francisco: Jossey-Bass.

Shonkoff, J. P., & Phillips, D.A. (Eds.). (2000). *From neurons to neighborhoods: The science of early childhood development.* Washington, DC: National Academy Press.

Sternberg, R. J. (1997). The concept of intelligence and its role in lifelong learning and success. *American Psychologist, 52*(10), 1030–1037.

Sylwester, R. (2000). *A biological brain in a cultural classroom: Applying biological research to classroom management.* Thousand Oaks, CA: Corwin Press.

Watson, M. (2003). *Learning to trust: Transforming difficult elementary classrooms through developmental discipline.* San Francisco: Jossey-Bass.

Wilczenski, F. L., Cohen, J., & Berman, S. (in preparation). *Promoting purpose in youth through social, emotional education and service learning.*

Witmer, L. (1909). Clinical psychologist. *The Psychological Clinic, 1,* 1–9.

Zachary, E., & Olatoye, S. (2001). *Community organizing for school improvement in the South Bronx.* New York: New York University, Institute for Education and Social Policy.

Ziegler, S., & Mulhall, L. (1994). Establishing and evaluating a successful advisory program in a middle school. *Middle School Journal, 25*(4), 42–46.

Zins, J. E., Weissberg, R. P., Wang, M. C., & Walberg, H. J. (2004). *Building academic success on social and emotional learning.* New York: Teachers College Press.

6

Explaining the Popularity of Emotional Intelligence

Adrian Furnham
University College London

Emotional intelligence (EI): long neglected core component of mental ability or faddish and confused idea massively commercialized? Is EI a new term for an old idea? Your grandfather might have called it "charm"; your mother "social awareness"; you understood the term "social skills"; and your children call it EI. New wine in old skins or old wine in new barrels? Is the jury still out regarding this question? Perhaps this book will signal the return of the jury, as academics try to make sense over what EI is, where it fits into our periodic table of individual differences, and why it has become so popular.

Just as history is told by the victors, so the story of EI is told rather differently by different groups. Depending on your take, EI was part of the multiple intelligence movement dating back to the social intelligences of the 1920s (Petrides, Furnham & Frederickson, 2004) or the mischievous muddling of McClelland responsible for other similar concepts like competency.

Certainly there are two dates that mark the start of academic research and popular interest. It was Salovey and Mayer's (1990) paper published in a relatively obscure journal that most academics refer to

141

as the beginning of academic and conceptual research on the topic. But it was definitely Goleman's (1995) blockbuster that spurred massive popularity of the concept.

There are, it seems, three easy markers of the massive popularity of EI. Search the Web and courses and measures jump out at you. Supply and demand works. Furthermore, it seems the growth curve is still nicely "northerly." Second, the term has already bubbled into *HR speak* and competency lists. Human resource (HR) professionals speak as if they know what EI is, how to measure it, what it predicts, and so on. More dramatically, they take for granted that it can be taught relatively easily, quickly, and cheaply. The warm, uncritical, and immediate embrace of the concept by HR is part of the mystery this chapter seeks to investigate. A third index of the popularity of the concept is the fact that EI has entered the *popular language*. Teenagers, computer experts, and homemakers use the concepts to describe and explain the behavior of others. It is usually the lack of EI that is used to explain personal problems, management failure, and all sorts of relationships issues.

So from where came the popularity of the idea? With a mixture of cynicism and scepticism, I consider, in this chapter, how and why the EI concept has become so popular. I also consider management fads, how academics respond and how traits like EI eventually make it into the academic literature.

HISTORY, MUDDLE, AND ARGUMENT

Petrides, Furnham, and Frederickson (2004) have argued that the distal roots of EI are in E. L. Thorndike's (1920) concept of "social intelligence," which was broadly defined as "the ability to understand and manage men and women, boys and girls—to act wisely in human relations" (p. 228). The proximal roots of EI lie in Gardner's (1983) theory of multiple intelligence and, more specifically, in his intrapersonal and interpersonal intelligences. The former concerns the ability to understand one's own self, including one's feelings and motives, and the latter the ability to understand others, including their moods and intentions.

The term *emotional intelligence* was first used in a German paper by Leuner (1966). However, the first formal definition of EI, along with the first model appeared in Salovey and Mayer (1990), who also carried out the first empirical studies. Goleman's (1995) international best-seller propelled EI into the limelight and influenced most subsequent conceptualizations of EI. Toward the latter half of the 1990s, the first EI measures started to appear (Bar-On, 1997; Mayer, Caruso, & Salovey, 1999; Salovey, Mayer, Goldman, Turvey, & Palfai, 1995; Schutte et al., 1998).

The operationalization of individual difference constructs hinges essentially on two issues. The first concerns the *sampling domain* of the construct (or universe of items), which refers to the elements or facets that a particular construct is hypothesized to encompass. For example, give basic or primary elements that largely define the personality dimension of Neuroticism as inferiority, unhappiness, anxiety, dependence and guilt. A difficulty arises, however, with deciding exactly which are the facets or primary factors that a construct encompasses. As Petrides and Furnham (2001) put it, "Asking what precisely should be part of a construct is like asking what sports should be in the Olympics; neither question can be answered objectively" (p. 428).

The problem can be seen with many established questionnaires. Thus, the Eysenck Personality Profiles (EPP; Eysenck's Big 3 with 21 scales) and the NEO Personality Inventory-Revised (NEO-PI-R) (Costa & McCrae's long measure) both have primary factors of both extraversion and neuroticism, but they are clearly different in length and label. What is important, however, is to recognize that two super factor scores correlate very highly, suggesting there is more overlap and agreement at the item and primary factor/facet level.

The second fundamental issue in the operationalization of a construct concerns *the procedures by which it is measured*. More specifically, there is a basic distinction between measures of maximum performance (e.g., IQ tests) and measures of typical response (e.g., personality questionnaires) with far-reaching implications for construct operationalization. Self-report measurement leads to the operationalization of the construct as a personality trait (trait EI or emotional self-efficacy), whereas potential maximum-performance measurement would lead to the operationalization of the construct as a cognitive ability (ability EI or cognitive-emotional ability). It must be understood that trait EI and ability EI are two different constructs because the procedures used in their operational definitions are fundamentally different, even though their theoretical domains might overlap. The primary basis for discriminating between trait EI and ability EI is to be found in the type of measurement approach used and not in the elements of the sampling domains of the various conceptualizations.

Petrides, Furnham, and Frederickson (2004) argue that trait EI encompasses behavioral tendencies and self-perceived abilities, as opposed to actual cognitive abilities, and thus it belongs in the realm of personality. In contrast, ability EI, which encompasses actual abilities, belongs primarily in the domain of cognitive ability. While trait EI is hypothesized to be orthogonal to cognitive ability (Furnham & Petrides, 2004; Petrides, Fredrickson, & Furnham, 2004) ability EI should be related mainly to general intelligence (g), but also to specific personality dimensions that reflect basic individual differences in emotionality (especially Neuroticism).

One difficulty with the operationalization of ability EI is that emotional experiences are inherently subjective and, consequently, lack the objectivity required to make them amenable to robust, valid, and reliable maximum performance measurement. There is no simple way of applying truly veridical criteria in the objective scoring of items relating to the intrapersonal component of ability EI (e.g., "I am aware of my emotions as I experience them") simply because the application of such scoring procedures would require direct access to privileged information, such as inner feelings and private cognitions, that is available only to the individual who is being assessed. Attempts to get around this problem (e.g., Mayer et al., 1999) are predicated on scoring procedures that had been tried in the past with limited success. In addition to conceptual limitations, these procedures produce test scores with undesirable psychometric properties (for a review, see Roberts, Zeidner, & Matthews, 2001).

At the moment, two "schools" exist that are mutually hostile: ability versus trait. The two schools measure, write, and proseletize in different ways. What of the lay person? Many talk of EQ as a skill; some of it being like intuition. Lay people seem as divided on the issue as are the academics. However, commercially the trait camp has won. There are dozens of poor or nonpsychometrized instruments on the market. A Web search soon confirms this. Nearly all are questionnaires: self-report measures that have high face validity and therefore high fakability. They look like older measures of assertiveness, social skill, or interpersonal style. Ability measures are difficult to devise, time consuming to administer, and do not always have sufficient face validity demanded by people in business.

Lay people, even hard-headed business people, are surprisingly unimpressed by psychometric evidence. Either because they do not understand or care about concepts like test–retest reliability, Cronbach's alpha, predictive validity, or orthogonal dimensionality, they appear to buy questionnaire products on packaging and promise much more than on evidence. This partly explains the popularity of EI. Demand is quickly met by supply, but not by many reputable test publishers because validation is too time consuming. This does not, however, prevent others from aggressively marketing their essentially "not proven" products. The large number of instruments available may make them appear to be more popular than they actually are.

CONCEPTUAL CONFUSION

Try the following test on a group of working people. They are told that they are in the unusual and fortunate position of having a major say in the selection of their boss: upward, not downward, selection. They are told there is a very short list of two people with equal experience, qualifications, and motivation. But one has a very high IQ and low EQ and the other the reverse. Which one would they choose? Very nonscientific sampling suggests the following: Around 70% of people choose high EQ over high IQ. However there is a sex difference: The bias to high EQ is much higher in women.

Asked to justify their choice, most explain having worked for "brainy boffins" who were hopeless at the fundamental rubrics of management: setting challenging goals, giving support and feedback, and looking after the team. Curiously, one never hears the other story of the warm and fuzzy manager who "lost the plot," failed to see opportunities, lacked a strategic plan, and could not quite tumble the numbers. Emotional sensitivity, rather than analytic power, is thought of as their key management skill.

But then ask the second question. Which is easier to train/improve? EQ or IQ? Given one has this perhaps unfair and unpleasant choice of high and low EQ/IQ, it makes sense to choose the more fixed position and put money, time, and effort into training the other. In Dweck's (2000) terminology, entity versus incremental phenomena. Is it malleable, trainable, improvable, or not—and what are the consequences? Given the answers to the previous question, the answers seem rather odd. Most people (around 80%) believe EQ is trainable but IQ is not. After all, they have probably seen and been offered EQ courses. It is rare, however, to see any business course called "Raise your IQ."

Confronted with their poor judgment, many people remain adamant. They would seem to prefer a boss whose social skills at the expense of intellectual analysis may lead to poor, even disastrous, business performance.

So how did they become enchanted by the EI debate? What was it about Goleman's (1995) book that so captivated the Zeitgeist?

THE SECRETS OF SUCCESSFUL BUSINESS BOOKS

Furnham (2000) suggested, rather cynically, that authors who want their popular books to sell well, should obey various rules:

- *Simplicity*: The book should have a simple message supported with plenty of memorable anecdotes, vignettes, and stories. Goleman's book is indeed an example of anecdotal evidence overwhelming science. It is woven together story-telling by a science journalist.
- *Changeability*: It should underscore the point that human behavior is *changeable*. The major problem for all manag-

ers is that it is very difficult to change people's attitudes and/or their work-related behaviors. Perhaps this explains why there are so many books on change management. Certainly a message of EI, as opposed to IQ, is that it can be substantially improved. Anyone can get better, be happier, and be a more successful manager.

- *The individual as the unit of analysis and change*: The successful business book must be *psychological* in its focus on people and underplay organizational, economic, and political factors that self-evidently shape organizational success. EI is an individual, not a team, group, or organizational construct.
- *Managerial control*: It must stress the techniques that increase and improve a managers' control. EI supposedly is generally empowering. Managers with EI are better and lead to greater productivity, satisfaction, team morale, and on. It helps them take charge of their lives in general.
- *List of steps and principles*: It should provide a road map to management or a simple guide to how to achieve success. Although this was not clear in the book, it is certainly spelled out in later work. Goleman's (1998) second book is an obvious response to this need. Academics, however, attest to the great conceptual muddle, naiveté, and lack of evidence in this "practical tips" approach.
- *Universality*: It is important that the book must suggest that its ideas have *universal application* and appeal. The idea is that the formula works everywhere for all groups and for all time. EQ is for all people and all time. It is fundamental for health, happiness, and so forth. The idea of cultural differences is kept firmly out-of-sight.
- *Short-termism*: The book must claim or demonstrate some *short-term payoff* or *benefit* ("quick win"). The idea that one can manage better and more cost-efficiently has enormous appeal, but the immediacy of the benefits is typically exaggerated.
- *Success stories*: Ideally, the book should provide *lists of Happy Customers* and those who have successfully adopted the ideas. They are often the author's friends or clients.
- *Self-confirmation*: The book must *not be counter-intuitive*. Self-confirming approaches endorsing prior ideas and beliefs are essential. Thus, the book can't have radi-

cally new ideas if the readers already hold them. That is why so many repackage common sense and the things people already know. What is new is the terminology, not the ideas, hence, the point that EQ seems a repackaging of social skills.

- *Unitary perspective*: Boss and employee, management and union have ultimately *shared goals and mutual benefits*. Husband and wife, doctor and patient—all benefit from the training. Everyone benefits from having a higher EQ: the person him or herself, his or her staff, customers, and boss.

The dilemma for the would-be writer, then, is not a literary one but an ethical one. Best-sellers seem to have to be simple-minded if they are to sell. Honest, practical books that do not oversimplify or promise the earth make only modest earnings. So there is a paradox—best-sellers may be compulsory reading for the jargon, but these are probably less helpful than a less well-known book that is more practical and honest about the problems that arise.

It was no doubt Goleman's book that electrified the public and popularized the term *emotional intelligence*. The book argues (usually without good, direct evidence) that at work, relationship building is more important than technical skills, and further, that technical training is easy compared to teaching EQ skills. To acquire technical skills often requires considerable dedication, and opportunities to acquire social skills (EQ) are, therefore, reduced. Then the low EQ person chooses technology rather than people for fun, comfort, and as a source of ideas because they do not understand emotions.

The argument goes that failed and derailed managers tend to be rigid, with poor self-control and poor social skills and are weak at building bonds. And yet understanding and using emotions/feelings are at the heart of business and indeed being human. It is, says Goleman (1998), no accident that motive and emotion share the same Latin root meaning "to move"—great work starts with great feeling.

But the book seems to have an overinclusive view of what EQ is. There are lists of facets and features: some derivative of each other, some quite unrelated to anything about emotion. It echoes themes in the Zeitgeist—hence its popularity. The book is also easy to dip into; it consists of a summary and précis. Hence, there were, and indeed still are, a rash of magazine and newspaper articles that popularized the book and the concept. This is not "trickle down" economics but a waterfall of publicity. The sheer amount of positive publicity given to the book must be one of the factors involved in its success and the popularity of the concept at the heart of it.

MANAGEMENT FADS

Furnham (2003) suggested that all management fads have a similar natural history that has seven separate identifiable phases: One question is whether EQ will follow this trajectory and if so, where is it now?

1. Academic Discovery

Faddish ideas can often be traced to the distinctly unfaddish world of academia. A modest discovery may result in a pretty indigestible paper in a specialist journal. These papers show the causal link between two factors relevant to work situations. These papers are not only dry, complicated, and heavily statistical but also cautious and preliminary. Academics often call for replications and more research; they are hesitant and underline the complexity of all the actual and possible factors involved. Few are interested in immediate application. Their job is understanding the process, not changing the world. The early social and emotional intelligence papers are a little like this. However, it is difficult to trace the concept to one study or paper.

2. Description of the Study

This process can last a long time and usually involves a lot of elaboration and distortion in the process. Someone reads the paper and provides a summary. The summary may be verbal and, if so, may end a little like Chinese whispers. Others hear it and repeat it. But with its very repetition, the findings become stronger and the complexity weaker. Selective memory ensures that the crucial findings are recorded and embellished. At this stage, it is unlikely that the researchers would recognize the findings as theirs in the first place. This phase is difficult to document, but it is often trainers, consultants, and industrial and organizational psychologists who are primarily responsible for this phase.

3. Popularization in a Best-Seller

The next stage is a business writer/guru takes up the call, hears about the finding, gives them a catchy title, and before you know it, the fad is about to begin. That one single and simple idea/finding/process soon becomes a book. This is where the Goleman (1998) book plays such an important role. It was very widely reviewed in the media around the world. Quizzes began to appear, and the book soon entered both common consciousness and the language. The best-seller with a snappy title and publisher hype means that the average manager reads at least a few reviews of the book. He may even buy it, but many are content to hear the gist from reviewers. They are frequently envious of seemingly powerful results that occur when the great idea is followed. It is at this stage that the fad becomes a *buzzword*.

4. Consultant Hype and Universalization

It is not the academic or the author that really powers the fad but an army of management consultants trying to look as if they are at the cutting edge of management theory. Because the concepts are easy to understand and are said to have wide application, the consultants seek to apply them everywhere. Those who don't climb aboard are made to feel left out, "fuddy-duddy," even bad for their shareholders. What made the EQ phenomen different was two things. First, the Web, which now has a very big impact on the rapid and universal popularization of ideas. The second factor was the rapid development of measures of EQ. The concept not only struck home but very easily could be (supposedly) efficiently and validly measured. It was the measurement of EQ that really appealed to the management consultants.

5. Total Commitment by True Believers

At this point, the evangelists move from the consultant to the managers. For a small number of companies, the technique *seems* to have brought quick, massive benefits. They become happy and willing product-champions, which only serves to sell more books and fan the fires of faddishness. EQ champions are paraded at conferences. EQ awareness, courses, and training improve performance and make people into better managers.

With hindsight, it is sometimes difficult to explain why the concept had such an impact on the lay public or why people seem to believe it worked. This is somewhere between the Hawthorne effect or placebo effect. The former refers to the way people react positively when they are treated differently (irrespective of what the treatment consists of) while the latter refers to the sugar pill effect, where simply believing that it will do you good is enough.

In fact, years after the fad has passed, there are little outstations of believers who continue to be the faithful. In time, they are quiet reminders of the past as they cling on. The Amish of Management, they resolutely cling on to their old ways.

6.   Doubt, Scepticism, and Defection

After pride comes the fall. After a few years of heavy product selling, the appetite for the fad becomes diminished. The market is saturated. Various "new and improved" or, just as likely, "shorter and simpler" versions of the fad are introduced. But it is apparent that the enthusiasm is gone. And then the avalanche or mudslide begins. It begins with managerial doubt and then academic scepticism, followed by journalistic cynicism, and finally consultant defection. It may be that the whole process starts with people pointing out the poor cost–benefit analysis of introducing the fad. Or it may occur because someone goes back to the original finding and shows that the gap has widened so much between what was initially demonstrated and what is now done that the two are different species.

Then management journalists smell blood. It is easy to find disaffected managers happy to squeal. They point out the thousands spent for little reward and the incredible consultant rip-off the whole thing has become. A trickle becomes a stream and then a river. And the consultants who were so eager to pick up the fad are the first to drop it. What gave them both credibility and massive invoicability now makes them look like con-artists as they distance themselves from the fad. But this phase may be some time away with EQ. After all the fad, at least in the marketplace terms, is only 3 to 5 years old. No alternative is on the horizon. Many organizations are still in the early part of their infatuation with the idea. But nemesis may be not too far behind.

7. New Discoveries

The end of one fad is an ideal time for trainers, writers, and consultants to spot a gap in the market. They know there is an incurable thirst for magic bullet, fix-all solutions, so the whole process starts again. The really clever people begin to sense when the previous fad is reaching its sell-by date, so that they have just enough time to write their new best-seller to hit the market just right.

Is EI a management or educational fad? Has it passed through the above phases? And if so where is it now? Certainly the academics are only now beginning to respond with careful, considered research that attempts to unpick the concept. Suddenly the academic journals, particularly in differential psychology, are bursting with papers that take (hopefully) a disinterested scientific and measured look at EI (Austin, 2004; Chan, 2004; Roberts et al., 2001). There has also appeared a serious, thoughtful, and balanced review of work in the area to date (Matthews, Zeidner, & Roberts, 2002). Academic researchers are not immune to fad and fashion. However, the lag time is longer and thus what interests the two worlds of science and practice may easily be out-of-synchrony.

THE DEVELOPMENT OF SINGLE-TRAIT PERSONALITY THEORIES

Whether one conceives of EQ as an ability or a trait the question is where it "fits in" with all the taxonomic work done by differential psychologists. To the extent that the psychological periodic table exists, the question is where this new concept (trait/ability) is a mix of others or indeed at what level to describe it. Is it a super or primary trait? Is it essentially a manifestation of fluid or crystalized intelligence?

In a review paper, Furnham (1990) suggested that the history of single traits or single abilities in psychology goes through various recognizable phases. He used various examples like the Type A personality trait and, more recently, Just World Beliefs (Furnham, 2003). The question is whether EI could be seen to fit the same pattern. The stages are described below:

1. Identification of the Phenomenon

This may occur as a result of laboratory experimentation or observation in a clinic, at work, or through critical reading. It may occur when a researcher operationalizes that which is well-known in the literature into a psychological measure, such as was the case with the Protestant work ethic. But what is more normally the case is that a researcher observes a psychological phenomenon which she gives a name. Examples are legion; Seligman (1975) noticed learned helplessness, the behavior in dogs which later become translated into an attribution-style questionnaire to identify the same behavior in humans. The person or persons who originally make the observations need not necessarily be the ones who develop the single-trait theory or the self-report measure. The phenomenon is often only new in the sense that it has not been recorded or reported before in quite the same way or received a particular label. This stage often occurs in the laboratory as a by-product of observational studies, or occasionally from the systematic recordings of their patients. Very rarely, if ever, are the researchers intentionally engaged in developing a trait measure of theory. The social intelligences were described in the 1920s (Thorndike, 1920). Gardner (1983) talked of intra- and interpersonal intelligence. Salovey and Mayer (1990) are usually attributed with first using the term if not identifying the phenomenon. This is the start of the process.

2. Replication of the Effect

The second state is characterized by replications and considerably more experimental work on the nature of the effect observed. The idea of this phase is to test the robustness of the findings, often by a subtle, yet simple case of data gathering in an attempt to find support for observations made, whereas in others, a series of studies attempts to test the various hypotheses that make up the nascent theory. These studies are usually reported in the first paper or book to describe the behavior pattern/phenomenon. In fact, the EQ concept seems to have been in academic limbo for about a decade. Few studies emerged in the late 1990s except from the laboratory of Mayer et al. (1999), and Mayer and Solvey (1997) the academic literature has identified essentially a postmillennium concept. Many correlational and experimental studies are now appearing that seek to describe and understand various measures of EQ and the supposed processes involved.

3. The Development of a Self-Report Measure

The next stage does involve the development of a self-report measure. The still popular Bar-On (1997) measure remains among the most popular self-report measures. However, in competition was the MISCEIT ability measure (Mayer et al., 2000). The questionnaires used may be of highly variable psychometric quality and the research that goes into establishing them somewhat inadequate. This remains true of the Bar-On measure. Reliability, validity, and normative statistics may be fairly minimal to begin with, and it is unlikely that the first versions to be published are validated in a manner acceptable to psychometricians. It is precisely because the originators of the concept are not psychometricians (being clinicians or experimentalists) that they do not always know the minimum criteria required of a good self-report measure. Frequently, the self-report measure is developed some years after the concept/behaviour (Petrides, Furnham, and Frederickson, 2004).

4. Validation of the Measure

The fourth phase involves numerous experimental and correlational studies of various sorts, all aiming to validate the measure and its underlying concepts. This seemed to be occurring in the 1998–2004 period. Studies are often of the kind that lead to a Ph.D. and include a programmatic series of studies aimed to test corollaries of the theory. These studies are essentially attempts to establish the concurrent, construct, and predictive validity of the self-report scale by correlating it with other well-known measures or behaviors. The danger of this sort of approach is that correlating a new measure with an established but poorly psychometrized measure does not provide good evidence of the validity of the theory or research. It is not lack of validity that prevents research into a measure or concept, but more likely the extent to which the measure taps the Zeitgeist of (North American) psychology.

5. Factor Analysis Work and Multidimensionality

Although researchers may identify what they believe to be a single, albeit complex, dimension or phenomenon, and hence develop a unidimensional scale, subsequent multivariate statistics nearly always show the measure to be multidimensional with specific interpretable primary factors, which may be orthogonal or oblique. Factor-analytic work usually poses problems for the original author because the theory on which the measure is founded usually assumes a unidimensional concept. Three responses are common: One is to maintain that the concept, measure, and trait are unified at a higher order (i.e., super factors) and that although it may have various components, these are second order (secondary) distinctions/factors that do not threaten the theory. A second is to revise the scale, either by attempting to eradicate items that load on irrelevant factors or by building a truly multidimensional instrument. A third approach is to do a meta-analysis of factor-analytic studies, decide on the factor structure and accept the original scale as multidimensional. This phase may last many years but may help resolve equivocal findings when they can be attributed to the multidimensional structure of the trait measure. A good example of this is Petrides and Furnham's (2000) psychometric critique of the Schutte et al. (1998) measure, which was one of the first to be published in an academic journal.

6. Multiple, Multidimensional Measures

The malaise following repeated psychometric investigations into an established unit-trait measure often leads scholars to despair because, as has been noted, it is uncertain at which level analysis should proceed. A common response however, is for a team of psychometrically oriented researchers to develop a new, better scale or self-report device. This is manifest in the work of many, particularly Schutte et al. (2001) and Petrides and Furnham (2003). These new "improved" measures often have various specific features. They are nearly always multidimensional in the sense that they provide subscale scores that may or may not be combined into a single score depending on the needs of the researchers. Secondly, researchers develop sphere-specific scales to measure the trait, belief, or behavior system within a very restricted range of behaviors, as this has been shown to improve the predictive validity. There are problems with this proliferation of measures because studies using different measures are not strictly comparable. Thirdly, it is possible that a person may score highly on one measure but low on another. Some authors have attempted to produce not so much a multidimensional measure but sphere-specific measures that set out to measure the same beliefs in different contexts. There can also be long measures (with full multidimensional analysis) and short measure for quick snapshot scores.

7. Doubts about the Original Concept

It is not infrequent that after a decade or so of intensive psychometric work on a measure/concept, authors begin to cast doubts about its conceptual and psychometric status. The complexity of measurement and the equivocal nature of the findings leads researchers to conclude that the original concept/phenomenon/behavior pattern is not worth measuring, and all questionnaires that attempt to measure it should be abandoned either in favor of a new concept, usually a subscale of the former, or else that the original behavior pattern is too unstable to be considered as a trait. This stage is characterized, not by increased empirical work but by theoretical reconceptualization. Naturally the commitment of researchers to a particular concept or scale means that they are loath to relinquish it but happy to make further attempts to refine it.

8. Acceptance and "Text-Bookisation"

Having gone through the preceding seven stages and having survived the last one, the concept and its measures are usually accepted into the canon of the established literature. A sure sign of this process is the inclusion into the textbooks on personality, social psychology, or measurement. By this stage, there is probably a sizable literature on the concept and the measure, as citation counts show. However, one should not assume that because a test and concept have won through a baptismal and confirmatory process, that it is therefore necessarily a psychometrically valid, theoretically important or diagnostically useful measure. Small bands of zealots wedded to the original ideas in the scale can propel a measure of dubious theoretical and psychometrical validity into the textbooks and research consciousness. Equally, extremely good measures based on sound theory and careful psychometric work can get "lost" and never make it to the laboratories of the world.

As in all stage-wise theories, the preceding sequence has its limitations and unanswered questions. Do theories measures have to go through all the stages sequentially? Can some stages be skipped? Does development have to be linear, or can it be cyclical? What prompts movement from one stage to another? Despite these unresolved questions, it may be useful to adapt this stage-wise model to evaluate the progress of a trait-like measure or indeed to predict further developments.

CONCLUSION

This chapter sought to try to explain the dramatic rise of popularity in the concept of EQ. The question is why some concepts and measures receive so much public acclaim compared to others. Some concepts receive massive interest, like EQ; others receive modest interest, like sensation seeking; and others, like rumination, appear to get completely ignored. Scientists are often puzzled by public reaction. There are, in Britain, Professors in the Public Understanding of Science, but none in the Scientific Understanding of the Public.

Scientists are often bewildered, even angered, by the lay public's clear flirtation with patently unscientific ideas like astrology, graphology, and the paranormal (Frazier, 1991). There has, for instance, been a flurry of interest in why people seek out and pay for complementary and alternative medicine when there is often little or no evidence that it works other than by placebo effect. Thus, Furnham and Vincent (2000) explore various explanations from a sociological, psychological, and medical perspective that attempts to explain the growth in this multimillion-dollar business.

The popularity of EQ is equally problematic for the academic. The idea and packaging seem to have various components that make it attractive. First it is a good repackaging of an old idea that does back to Dale Carnegie's *How to Win Friends and Influence People*. It is in the long line of the social, interpersonal skills tradition. Next, it is positive and optimistic. These skills are important, and they can (quite easily) be learned.

Third and perhaps paradoxically, the EQ enthusiasm may reflect a popular scepticism of the IQ approach. It may reflect a popular rejection of the IQ approach. It may be ironic to use the term *intelligence* while simultaneously rejecting the literature on intelligence. Sex, race, and other differences in IQ have caused great controversy over the years and there is a concerted effort to eliminate IQ testing and those that research it. It may then seem attractive to various people to support a concept and measure that believes itself superior to IQ in the sense that it has better predictive validity.

Fourth, and this may be a dangerous line to follow, EQ is a more feminine than a masculine concept. For instance, while there are over two dozen studies that show men give higher self-estimates for IQ than women, the opposite is true of EQ. Thus, Furnham and Petrides (2004) found males gave *higher* estimates of their general IQ than did women (as well as their Analytic and Practical IQ), and they gave *lower* estimates of their emotional intelligence than did women. Similarly Petrides, Furnham, and Martin (2004) hypothesized and found that lay people perceive psychometric (academic) intelligence as a primary masculine attribute in contrast with emotional intelligence, which they perceive as a primary feminine attribute. This may explain the popularity of the concept in certain sectors like human resources and training where, at least in certain countries, women outnumber men.

It is difficult to predict the popularity of EQ. There are already other signs of many other "intelligences" being discovered, like spiritual intelligence, business intelligence, sexual intelligence, and naturalistic intelligence. Indeed, Furnham (2005) lists 14 different intelligences before exploring work on six business intelligences, including network and intuitive intelligence. Although purists would no doubt be outraged by the overuse and abuse of the term *intelligence*, it seems a popular way of introducing new individual by different variables rather than in terms of skills or (fixed) traits.

It may well be that as the academic literature grows, the popular interest declines. Yet it is also true that, at least in academic psychology, there has always been more interest in cognition than affect. Emotional intelligence is about affect. Perhaps this comes as a salutary warning to academics that it is we who have to explain our relative neglect of affect in the first place!

REFERENCES

Austin, E. (2004). An investigation of the relationship between trait emotional intelligence and emotional task performance. *Personality and Individual Differences, 36*, 1855–1864.

Bar-On, R. (1997). *Bar-On Emotional Quotient Inventory: Technical manual.* Toronto: Multi-Health Systems.

Chan, D. (2004). Perceived emotional intelligence and self-efficacy among Chinese secondary school teachers in Hong Kong. *Personality and Individual Differences, 36*, 1781–1795.

Dweck, C. S. (2000). *Self theories.* New York: Psychologist Press.

Frazier, K. (1991). *The hundredth monkey.* Buffalo, NY: Prometheus.

Furnham, A. (1990). The development of single trait personality theories. *Personality and Individual Differences, 11*, 923–929.

Furnham, A. (2000). Secrets of success from the Heathrow School of Management. *Business Strategy Review, 11,* 61–67.

Furnham, A. (2003). Measuring the beliefs in a just world. In L. Montada & M. Lerner (Eds.), *Responses to victimizations and beliefs in a just world* (pp. 141–162). New York: Plenum.

Furnham, A. (2005) Gender and personality differences in self- and other ratings of business intelligence. *British Journal of Management, 16,* 91–103.

Furnham, A., & Petrides, K. V. (2004). Parental estimates of five types of intelligence. *Australian Journal of Psychology, 56,* 10–17.

Furnham, A., & Vincent, C. (2000). Reasons for using CAM. In M. Kellner, D. Wellman, B. Pescosolido, & M. Saks (2000). *Complementary and alternative medicine: Challenge and change* (pp. 61–78).

Gardner, H. (1983). *Frames of mind: The theory of multiple intelligences.* New York: Basic Books.

Goleman, D. (1995). *Emotional intelligence.* New York: Bantam Books.

Goleman, D. (1998). *Working with emotional intelligence.* New York: Bantam Books.

Leuner, B. (1966). Emotionale intelligenz und emanzipation (Emotional intelligence and emancipation). *Praxis der Kinderpsychologie und Kinderpsychiatry, 15,* 196–203.

Matthews, G., Zeidner, M., & Roberts, R. (2002). *Emotional intelligence: Science and myth.* Cambridge, MA: Bradford.

Mayer, J. D., Caruso, D. R., & Salovey, P. (1999). Emotional intelligence meets traditional standards for an intelligence. *Intelligence, 27,* 267–298.

Mayer, J. D., & Salovey, P. (1997). What is emotional intelligence? In P. Salovey & D. Sluyter (Eds.), *Emotional development and emotional intelligence: Educational implications.* New York: Basic Books.

Mayer, J. D. Salovey, R., & Caruso, D. R. (2000). Competing models of emotional intelligence. In R. J. Sternberg (Ed.), *Handbook of human intelligence.* New York: Cambridge University Press.

Petrides, K. V., Frederickson, N., & Furnham, A. (2004). The role of trait emotional intelligence in academic performance and deviant behaviour at school. *Personality and Individual Differences, 36,* 277–293.

Petrides, K. V. & Furnham, A. (2000). On the dimensional structure of emotional intelligence. *Personality and Individual Differences, 27,* 45–53.

Petrides, K. V. & Furnham, A. (2001). Trait emotional intelligence: Psychometric investigation with reference to established trait taxonomies. *European Journal of Personality, 15,* 425–448.

Petrides, K. V., Furnham A., & Frederickson, N. (2004). Emotional intelligence. *The Psychologist, 17*(10), 574–577.

Petrides, K. V., Furnham, A., & Martin, G. (2004). Estimates of emotional and psychometric intelligence. *Journal of Social Psychology, 144,* 149–162.

Petrides, K. V., Perez, J. C., & Furnham, A. (2003, July). The Trait Emotional Intelligence Questionnaire (TEIQue): A measure of emotional self-efficacy. In E. J. Austin & D. H. Saklofske (Chairs), *Emotional intelligence.* Symposium conducted at the 11th Biennial Meeting of the International Society for the Study of the Individual Differences, Graz, Austria.

Roberts, R., Zeidner, M., & Matthews, G. (2001). Does emotional intelligence meet traditional standards for an intelligence? Some new data and conclusions. *Emotion, 1,* 196–201.

Salovey, P. & Mayer, J. D. (1990). Emotional intelligence. *Imagination, Cognition and Personality, 9,* 185–211.

Salovey, P., Mayer, J. D., Goldman, S., Turvey, C., & Palfai, T. (1995). Emotional attention, clarity and repair: Exploring emotional intelligence using the Trait Meta-Mood scale. In J. W. Pennebaker (Ed), *Emotion, disclosure and health* (pp. 125–154). Washington, DC: American Psychological Association.

Schutte, N., Matouffi, J., Hall, L., Haggerty, D., Cooper, J., Golden, C., et al. (1998). Development and validation of a measure of emotional intelligence. *Personality and Individual Differences, 25,* 167–177.

Schutte, N. S., Malouff, J. M., Bobik, C., Coston, T. D., Greeson, C., Jedlicka, C., et al. (2001). Emotional intelligence and interpersonal relations. *Journal of Social Psychology, 141,* 523–536.

Seligman, M. (1975). *Helplessness: On depression, development and death.* San Francisco: Freeman.

Thorndike, E. L. (1920). Intelligence examinations for college entrance. *Journal of Educational Research, 1,* 329–337.

7

Beyond *g*

Nathan Brody
Wesleyan University

Is emotional intelligence a unique type of intelligence? How is it related to more traditional definitions of intelligence? Is EQ as important as IQ? All of these are important questions that are being actively debated in emotional intelligence research, but it is difficult to answer any of these without a clear understanding of what "intelligence" means. In this chapter, I will present an outline of a traditional concept of intelligence based on the notion of general intelligence (*g*). I will consider emotional intelligence as one of three recent attempts to develop new approaches to intelligence that supplement traditional notions based on *g*.

Spearman (1904) developed the concept of *g* 100 years ago. The concept is still the most important theoretical construct in contemporary research on individual differences in intelligence. It is also a concept that is controversial. The furor surrounding the publication of Herrnstein and Murray's book, *The Bell Curve*, provides abundant testimony to the controversial nature of contemporary research based on the theory of *g* (Herrnstein & Murray, 1994). Gardner's theory of multiple intelligences, Sternberg's triarchic theory of intelligence and several different versions of emotional intelligence theory share in common an attempt to deemphasize *g* and undermine its position as the theoretically preeminent construct relevant to an understanding of individual differences in intelligence (Gardner, 1983, 1993; Sternberg et al., 2000; for an analysis of theories of emotional intelligence, see Matthews, Zeidner, & Roberts, 2002).

This chapter deals with four topics: (1) a review of findings relevant to g theory, (2) a discussion of why these findings are controversial, (3) a review of the three theoretical approaches described above and an indication of the ways in which they seek to provide alternatives to g theory as well as the limitations inherent in these approaches, and (4) a discussion of implications of research on g.

WHAT IS KNOWN ABOUT g

g and Positive Manifolds

Since the development of the first test of intelligence by Binet and Simon, psychologists have devised thousands of tasks designed to measure some aspect of individual differences in cognitive functioning (Binet & Simon, 1905). Thousands of studies exist in which diverse intellectual tasks are provided to a group of individuals. It is possible to measure the relationship between all possible pairs of measures in the test battery by computing correlations and forming a correlation matrix. A remarkable finding in this huge body of research is that virtually all of the correlations in the matrix will be positive. This implies that performance on any one test of cognitive ability is positively related to performance on any other test of ability. A person may excel on tests of verbal ability more than on tests of spatial reasoning ability, but if he or she excels in verbal ability, then it is probable that his or her score on a test of spatial ability is above average. The existence of this positive manifold provides an empirical foundation for the g construct. g may be defined as the common element present in all tests of cognitive ability.

Contemporary researchers believe that g does not explain all of the relationships among different abilities (for a comprehensive analysis of the structure of human abilities, see Carroll, 1993), but many theorists believe that g has a special status as the most general and comprehensive human ability. Other theorists, such as Cattell and Horn, believe that g is an unstable construct whose composition varies with the items in a test battery. Their map of the structure of human abilities omits g and replaces the g construct with several broad intellectual abilities, the most important of which are (a) fluid intelligence, a basic capacity to reason relatively uninfluenced by educational exposures; and (b) crystallized ability, which is the result of the investment of fluid ability in the acquisition of knowledge and skills related to educational exposures (Cattell, 1971; Horn, 1989). Crystallized ability and fluid ability are positively correlated; hierarchical models of cognitive ability (e.g., Carroll, 1993) account for this positive correlation by suggesting that both crystallized and fluid intelligence are related to the more general factor *g*.

Although there are technical disagreements about the meaning of *g* and its place in the map of human abilities, it should be realized that the existence of a positive manifold implies that any test of intelligence that samples diverse abilities will yield a score that is positively related to any other test of intelligence although the tests do not share any common measure. Spearman's principle of the indifference of the indicator implies that the exact composition of tests used to sample human ability is not important, as long as the test is reasonably long and diverse. All samples of the indefinitely large set of all possible tests of abilities will yield roughly equivalent results.

The Continuity of Intelligence

Individual differences in *g* and scores on tests of intelligence that may be construed as measures of *g* are relatively invariant over the life span of individuals. It is possible to predict scores on tests of adult intelligence from characteristics of persons that are present prior to conception, at the moment of conception, and during the first year of life.

Prior to Birth.   The IQ of a child is predictable from knowledge of the IQ of his or her parents. Because parental IQ is measurable prior to the birth of a child, it is reasonable to argue that the IQ of a person is partially determined prior to his or her birth. The correlation between the average IQ test scores of the biological parents of a person and his or her adult IQ is approximately .6 (Bennett, Fulker, & DeFries, 1985). This implies (taking the square of the correlation) that approximately 36% of the adult variability in IQ is predictable from characteristics of persons knowable prior to conception. The predictability attainable from parental IQ is not trivial. It is informative to contrast it with the predictability attainable from knowledge of parental social class. The correlation between the IQ of a person and his or her parent's social class based on White's (1982) meta-analysis of studies of this relationship is .33; this implies that parental social class predicts 11% of the variance in scores on an IQ test.

From Conception to Adult IQ.   A person's genotype is formed at the moment of conception. Heritability is a statistical estimate of the extent to which variations in genotypes in a particular population are predictive of variations in a phenotype (i.e., outward characteristics and behavior exhibited by individuals). Recent studies of the heritability of IQ provide estimates for adult intelligence that are as high as .8. Consider the findings obtained in the Swedish study of older monozygotic (MZ) and dizygotic (DZ) twins reared apart and together (Pedersen, Plomin, Nesselroade, & McClearn, 1992). Pedersen and her colleagues obtained correlations of .78 for MZ twins reared apart, .80 for MZ twins reared together, .32 for DZ twins reared apart, and .22 for DZ twins reared together on measures of g for a systematic sample of older Swedish twins. The estimated heritability based on a model-fitting procedure for these data was .8.

Plomin, Fulker, Corley, and DeFries (1997) repeatedly administered intelligence tests to adopted children for the first 16 years of life in a longitudinal study. Their study also included a control sample of children reared by their natural parents. They obtained correlations between the IQs of the biological parents and the IQs of their adopted-away children at different ages. These correlations were compared to correlations between the IQs of the adoptive parents of these children and the IQs of their adopted children. In addition, correlations were obtained between the IQs of the biological parents in the control families who were rearing their natural children and the IQs of their children at comparable ages. The correlations between biological parents and children are quite similar for the biological parents who are rearing their children and for the biological parents whose children have been adopted-away and who have limited postnatal contact with their biological parents. Plomin et al. found that the correlations between the IQs of adopted parents and their children were close to zero. The correlation between the IQs of the adopted children's biological parents and their children at age 16 who were adopted shortly after birth exceeded, by a small margin, the correlation between the IQs of natural parents in the control group and the IQs of their biological children at age 16. These results imply that the relationship between parental IQ and the IQ of their biological children is primarily attributable to genetic influences. Variations in socialization practices and the characteristics of the home in which a child is reared do not appear to exert a measurable influence on adult intelligence. This generalization may not be valid for individuals reared in extreme poverty or by parents with relatively limited educational backgrounds (see Rowe, 2003). Model-fitting analysis for the Plomin et al. data indicates that the heritability of intelligence is .56.

From the First Year of Life to Adult IQ. Columbo (1993) reviewed longitudinal research in which measures of infant information processing abilities are related to childhood IQ. Several different researchers measured fixation times in a habituation paradigm in which infants under age 1 and in some instances younger than 1 month are repeatedly presented with the same stimulus. Fixation time measures are predictive of performance on measures of IQ obtained in the first several years of life. Columbo estimated that the relationship between infant information processing measures and childhood IQ accounts for over 65% of the variance in childhood IQ. Rose and Feldman (1995) obtained a correlation of .5 between a measure of information processing obtained prior to age 1 and a measure of general intelligence obtained at age 11. Given the relatively high continuity between measures of intelligence obtained at age 11 and adult intelligence, it is plausible to assume that infant information processing abilities are predictive of adult intelligence.

DiLalla et al. (1990) and Benson, Cherny, Haith, and Fulker (1993) compared the correlation between parental IQ and the IQ of their adult children to the correlation between parental IQ and infant information processing measures as a way of estimating the relationship between infant information processing measures and adult IQ. The parent-to-adult child IQ correlation of .6 sets an upper bound for the correlation between infant measures and adult intelligence. If infant measures are perfect indexes of adult intelligence, then the correlation between an infant measure and the IQs of their parents would be the same as the correlation between the IQs of parents and their adult children. Benson et al. obtained correlations ranging from .18 to .32 for various indices of childhood auditory habituation and the intelligence of the children's parents. These values suggest that there is considerable continuity between infant information processing measures and adult IQ. Because adult IQ has a substantial genetic influence, a substantial portion of the hypothetical relationship between infant measures and measures of adult intelligence is probably attributable to common genetic influences on both measures (see Thompson, 1989).

This brief review suggests that a person's adult intelligence is predictable from influences that are present prior to conception and at conception, and that are manifest by characteristics of persons measurable in the first year of life. These influences are not independent of one another. Parental influences on IQ, genetic influences on IQ, and the predictability derived from infant measures may all reflect to some degree a common genetic influence on IQ.

From Childhood to Adult IQ.   Intelligence is a highly stable trait of individuals. The most dramatic evidence for the continuity of intellectual dispositions derives from the analyses of a population of Scottish children who took a group intelligence test at the same time (The

Moray House test) at age 11. Deary, Whalley, Lemmon, Crawford, and Starr (2000) obtained correlations between the performance of 11-year-olds and the performance on the same tests for this population 66 years later. They obtained a test–retest correlation of .73 (corrected for restrictions in range of talent) for the Moray House test. They found that the time-lagged correlation between the Moray House test administered at age 11 and performance on the Ravens test of intelligence administered at age 77 was .48. This correlation may be compared to a correlation of .57 between the Ravens and Moray House tests administered to the same subjects when they were 77. The relatively small differences between concurrent and time-lagged correlations indicates that the latent disposition of general intelligence imperfectly assessed by both of these tests remains relatively invariant from age 11 to age 77.

The Malleability of Intelligence

Evidence for the continuity of intelligence implies that it is not highly responsive to many environmental variations that individuals are likely to encounter over their life spans. For example, there is evidence indicating that variations in educational exposures are not likely to have a large enduring influence on intelligence. I believe that research on preschool interventions, educational deprivation, and the intelligence of deaf individuals provides evidence for this assertion.

The Abecedarian Project randomly assigned children reared in extreme poverty to an experimental intervention in which they were provided with intensive early childhood education beginning shortly after birth and extending through the preschool period or a control group. Children assigned to the experimental group had higher scores on tests of intelligence than children in the control group. The effect sizes for the intervention on measures of intelligence declined from .38 at age 6.5, to .31 at age 12, to .19 at age 21 (the most recent follow-up data were obtained 16 years after the end of the early childhood intervention: Campbell, in press). The effect size measure used here is the difference between the means of the experimental group and the control group expressed in standard deviation units. As the standard deviation of IQ is approximately 15, the effect size of .19 implies that IQ was increased about 3 points in the experimental group at age 21. Campbell reported the results for a regression analysis in which childhood verbal ability scores were controlled for. The effect sizes for intelligence in this analysis declined from .10 at age 6.5, to –.21 at age 12, to –.38 at age 21. The negative effect sizes for the experimental intervention may be interpreted by assuming that childhood verbal ability is influenced by two components of variance: a component indicative of a core intellectual disposition and a component reflecting the effects of early intervention. This latter component declines over the adult life span of an individual. Predictions of adult intelligence that include the latter component are likely to err by overpredicting adult performance. The trends of declining effect sizes for the intervention and increasingly negative effect sizes for the intervention when it is considered after the effects of childhood verbal ability in a regression are compatible with the assumption that early intellectual stimulation does not increase intelligence, or, at the most, has only a marginal influence on intelligence. The Abecedarian Project represents the best documented, most intensive attempt to increase the intellectual ability of children reared in extreme poverty. The data presented here suggest that this project does not provide convincing evidence of an increase in general intelligence as a result of intensive early intervention.

DeGroot (1951) studied the intelligence of Dutch adolescents who had been deprived of one or more years of formal education owing to the German occupation of Holland during World War II. DeGroot's study is often cited as providing evidence for the influence of education on intelligence. DeGroot found that adolescents who had been deprived of one or more years of formal education had lower IQs than did comparable groups of adolescents from the same community who had not experienced educational deprivations. DeGroot also found that the effects of educational deprivation on IQ declined over time. The oldest group in his study, who had experienced educational deprivations several years earlier, did not exhibit intellectual declines. DeGroot's analysis thus provides simultaneous evidence of the effects of educational deprivation on intelligence and the resilience of intelligence in response to educational deprivations. The effects of the educational deprivation might appear important in the short run, but they do not seem to be long-lived.

Braden (1994) comprehensively reviewed the performance of deaf individuals on various tests of intelligence. Deaf individuals exhibit cumulative deficits on various measures of verbal ability and verbal achievement relative to hearing individuals over the course of their educational career. Despite the difficulties they exhibit in acquiring verbal skills, deaf individuals do not exhibit deficits on nonverbal measures of abstract reasoning (that are usually good measures of general intelligence). These results indicate that deaf individuals do not exhibit declines in *g* despite the apparent difficulties they have in benefiting from tuition requiring verbal skills.

There are many studies documenting changes in intelligence as a result of intervention. Few of these studies include long-term follow-ups. And, those that do, fail to demonstrate that the changes that occur as a result of intervention are long-lived. Thus, the evidence on interventions to increase intelligence is compatible with the evidence obtained from studies of the longitudinal consistency of intelligence over the life span.

On the whole, studies of interventions designed to increase intelligence suggest that g remains relatively consistent over the life span and is not easily changed by currently available technologies. Whether it is modifiable by methods other than those that have been studied to date is, obviously, not known.

The Social Relevance of Intelligence

It is possible to measure intelligence in diverse ways and obtain roughly comparable scores. The latent trait assessed by diverse measures of intelligence is highly heritable, remains relatively invariant over the life span of individuals, and is not easily modifiable. These assertions (or, arguably, empirically supported generalizations about g) would be of little significance if intelligence were not an important socially relevant trait. Much of the controversy over g stems from the fact that is seems to be important in such a wide range of contexts.

Intelligence is a socially important characteristic. There is a large and definitive literature that indicates that intelligence test scores are related to academic achievement at all educational levels, including graduate education, and to occupational success and performance on tests designed to measure job-related skills. This literature is sufficiently extensive now that it has been subject to multiple meta-analyses (see Ones, Viswesvaran, & Dilchert, 2004). The generalization that measures of g are correlated with measures of academic achievement is beyond dispute. The generalization appears to be valid for any academic setting in which students are expected to acquire academic knowledge. Cronbach and Snow (1977) reviewed all of the studies they could find dealing with interactions between pupil characteristics and variations in methods of instruction. Their review indicated that measures of g were invariably related to the outcomes of instruction and that this relationship held across a wide variety of instructional methods.

Intelligence is not only related to educational achievement but also to the amount of education that individuals obtain (Jencks, 1972, 1979). Longitudinal studies of intelligence and educational attainment indicate that intelligence scores obtained prior to adolescence are related to the number of years of education completed. The number of years of education attained is related to the prestige or status of a person's occupation. High-status occupations in our society are usually held by individuals who have completed college. As a result, intelligence is related to occupational status. The network of relationships between intelligence and educational achievement, attainment, and occupational success is mirrored by a related network of relationships between social class background and educational achievement, attainment, and occupational success. That is, social class background and intelligence are both related to educational achievement and attainment and occupational success. The relationship between intelligence and these outcome variables is not, however, substantially mediated by the relationship of social class to intelligence. That is, intelligence has a relationship to these variables that is independent of any influence of social class on intelligence. Murray (1998) provided convincing evidence of the independent contribution of intelligence by using a sibling control design. He analyzed sibling data from the National Longitudinal Survey of Youth, a 15-year longitudinal study of a representative sample of over 12,000 subjects. In this analysis, he compared outcome data for biologically related siblings who were reared in the same family but who differed in intelligence. This methodology controls for social class influences as well as for the effects of being reared in a particular family. There were 1,009 siblings in his sample whose IQs were between the 25th and 75th percentile. Of these, 19.6% received a bachelor's degree. There were 590 siblings of this group whose IQs were below the 25th percentile. Of these, 2.6% received a bachelor's degree. There were 419 siblings whose IQ was at or above the 75th percentile and whose sibling had an IQ between the 25th and 74th percentile; 56.8% of these siblings received a bachelor's degree. The data on the IQs of these siblings were obtained prior to the age of college entry. These data indicate that biologically related siblings reared in the same family who differ in IQ also differ in the probability of obtaining a bachelor's degree. Differences between siblings who differ in intelligence and in the amount of education obtained are also mirrored in corresponding differences in occupational prestige and in earned income. These data clearly indicate that intelligence is a characteristic that influences socially relevant outcome variables among individuals with comparable social backgrounds and even among individuals reared in the same family.

Intelligence is also related to a number of other significant social outcomes. Among these is an influence on mortality. Deary and his colleagues (Deary et al., 2004; Whalley & Deary, 2001) obtained a relationship between mortality at age 76 and IQ at age 11. A 1 standard deviation decrease in IQ was associated with 21% decrease in the probability of surviving to age 76; a 2 standard deviation decrease in IQ was associated with a 37% decrease in the probability of surviving to age 76. It is plausible to assume that the effects of childhood IQ on mortality are mediated by the influence of IQ on education and occupational status. Individuals with high IQ are likely to hold better jobs, work in safer occupational settings, and have better access to medical care. Although this explanation for the relationship between childhood IQ and mortality is plausible, it is not correct. Deary and Der (2005) obtained IQ scores for a representative sample of Scottish adults in 1988 when they were 56 years old. They obtained mortality data for these subjects in 2002 when they were 70 years old. They found the relationship between IQ and mortality was comparable to that obtained in their earlier studies using age 11 IQ as a predictor of mortality. They also analyzed the effects of IQ on mortality after controlling for occupational status, smoking behavior, and number of years of education attained. The relationship between IQ and mortality was not appreciably diminished after controlling for these variables. Variations in educational background and occupational status do not explain the relationship between IQ and mortality. There are two plausible possible explanations for the relationship between IQ and mortality: (1) IQ is related to health-related knowledge. Beier and Ackerman (2003) developed a comprehensive measure of health knowledge. They obtained a correlation between their health knowledge questionnaire and their measure of general intelligence of .88. Superior knowledge of health may be associated with a tendency to live a healthier lifestyle (see Gottfredson, 2004). (2) The genes that influence IQ may be related to the genes that influence mortality. Whatever the reason for the relationship between g and mortality, the relationship provides further evidence for an important social outcome related to intelligence that is relatively independent of the influence of the relationship between social class and intelligence.

WHY DO WE HATE g?

g is one of the most controversial constructs in psychology. Indeed, it is one of the few psychological constructs that has been the focus of a sustained public debate. It is useful, therefore, to understand why so much attention is devoted to g, why passions run so high in relation to this construct, and why the search for alternatives to g has attracted so many researchers.

Idiographic Complexity

People often reject the notion that a single number (e.g., a score on a cognitive ability test, often expressed as IQ) can tell much about a person and his or her prospects. We value the uniqueness of each person and the multiple ways in which we differ from one another. And, if human beings differ on an indefinitely large number of characteristics, then comparisons among them on a single or limited number of dimensions seem likely to do an injustice to the uniqueness of each individual. An attempt to reduce the complexity of human variation to a single score on a single trait appears as a grotesque oversimplification. The evidence briefly reviewed earlier in this chapter indicating that this single score is, arguably, the best single predictor of important socially relevant outcomes only adds to the sense of unease about *g*.

Heritability

There are at least three reasons why evidence for the heritability of intelligence is rejected by many commentators. First, many individuals wrongly conflate heritability and mutability. Heritability is a statistical concept that refers to the extent to which genotypes influence phenotypes in a particular population who have encountered a particular environment. Thus, heritability estimates apply to a specific set of environmental encounters. The heritability of a trait can be quite different if individuals encounter a different environment. Evidence indicating that the heritability of intelligence is low among individuals whose parents have limited formal education provides support for this principle (see Rowe, 2003). Nevertheless, many individuals believe that evidence for the heritability of a trait implies that the trait is immutable. The evidence reviewed here suggests that it is difficult to raise levels of *g*. This does not imply that it is impossible to raise a person's general intelligence.

Second, evidence for the heritability of a trait leads to a sense of defeatism. If variations in phenotypes are determined at conception, then variations in the environment that parents provide for a child may not have a dramatic influence on a phenotype. Thus, evidence for heritability may lead parents and others who seek to influence children to feel that they are powerless.

Third, the study of genetic influences on traits has a long and nefarious history of involvement with social practices that many find reprehensible. Among these are eugenic beliefs leading to forced sterilizations and attempts to limit immigration based on erroneous theories of ethnic and racial distinctions in intelligence (for a contemporary discussion of the reprehensible history of behavioral genetic research, see Joseph, 2003).

Social Policy

Research on intelligence locates differences in social outcomes in characteristics of persons rather than in the characteristics of institutions. Many individuals who are committed to social change believe that changing institutions will change the behavior of individuals. Consider, for example, the discussion of variations in educational outcomes associated with the school that an individual attends. The No Child Left Behind law assumes that variations in educational outcomes are attributable to variations in the characteristics of schools that individuals attend. Schools that exhibit chronic under achievement or fail to close gaps in achievement associated with race and class are subject to a variety of sanctions. There is evidence that most of the aggregated school variation in educational outcomes is determined by the characteristics of pupils who attend a particular school rather than by variations in the educational practices of the school (Jencks,1972, 1979; Brody, 1992, pp. 252–272).

Jencks (1972) studied a large sample of public schools in the United States. For each school, he obtained the mean social class background of all the students in the school. He also obtained a mean score for the academic achievement of all of the pupils in a school. The correlation between these two mean scores exceeded .9, implying that pupil characteristics account for most of the variation in academic achievement of different schools. Some of the remaining variance among schools that was independent of the social class background of students in the school was probably attributable to random effects. Jencks noted that many schools that performed better than expected (given the composition of their student body) in one year did not excel in the following year. Schools that did well on a measure of achievement in one subject did not necessarily do well in another subject.

Why is the social class background of pupils in a particular school such an important influence on the academic achievement of students in that school? Social class is related to IQ. If IQ is statistically controlled, social class has very little relationship to academic achievement. If social class is statistically controlled, IQ continues to have a substantial relationship to academic achievement (see Rehberg & Rosenthal, 1978, for a review of this literature). IQ is a more important influence on academic achievement than social class. Jencks' analysis of the influence of pupil characteristics on variations in what children learn in different schools is interpretable as evidence for the influence of IQ on variations in academic achievement among schools. Schools that enroll high-IQ students will have high academic achievement, and schools that enroll low-IQ students will have low academic achievement. This analysis implies that the focus of the No Child Left Behind Act is incorrect. It targets characteristics of schools as a critical variable determining variations in educational achievement for different classes of individuals rather than the characteristics of individuals who attend the schools. Head Start had a different focus. It aimed to remediate individual differences in intelligence as a way of decreasing differences in educational achievement. Unfortunately, there is little evidence that early educational interventions have enduring influence on intelligence.

Race and Class

Both race and class are related to scores on tests of intelligence. The Black–White difference in scores on tests of intelligence is approximately one standard deviation, and this difference has remained relatively constant for several decades. As a result, the use of intelligence tests as a basis for selection of individuals will contribute to racial inequality.

There is an additional source of controversy that fuels the dislike of intelligence tests. Prominent supporters of the *g* construct, such as Arthur Jensen, have argued that the Black–White difference in scores on tests of intelligence is attributable to genetic differences. Jensen's (1998) book, *The g Factor*, reviews the research evidence relating to the *g* construct. One hundred eighty pages of the 648 pages in the book are devoted to a discussion of racial differences in intelligence and defense of a genetic hypothesis as an explanation of racial differences in test scores (Jensen, 1998; see Brody, 2003b, for a critique of Jensen's views on race and intelligence). The association between intelligence research and beliefs about a genetic basis for racial differences in intelligence extends from Galton, who was the most important 19th-century theorist dealing with intelligence, to contemporary researchers. One result of this association is that any research that links race or ethnicity and intelligence is likely to be labeled as racist, in part because of the undeniable racism of earlier generations of ability researchers. The racially charged nature of the debate over intelligence testing stands in the way of serious research on the extent, origins, and implications of racial and ethnic differences in scores on measures of cognitive ability

IQ tests may be viewed as an instrument of oppression that reinforces social privilege, but in some cases they can have the opposite effect, undermining social privileges. Although it is often assumed that social class is strongly linked to scores on intelligence tests, in fact, the relationship between social class background and intelligence is weak. In his book, *Hereditary Genius,* Galton (1869) noted that genius was often related to family background. Galton knew that the relationship between family background and eminence could be explained by either a genetic hypothesis or a hypothesis that attributed the relationship to socialization practices and social privilege. He opted for a genetic explanation because he noted that many men of genius had modest family backgrounds.

The belief in the use of tests as a basis for reducing social privilege is a somewhat neglected aspect of Herrnstein and Murray's (1994) controversial book. They argued that the use of the SAT as a basis for selection of undergraduates has played a large role in changing the characteristics of Harvard undergraduates from a socially elite group to an intellectually elite group. Ironically, tests are sometimes disliked by privileged parents because they serve as a barrier to the perpetuation of social privilege. The use of multifaceted admissions criteria serves to diminish the importance of tests of cognitive ability and often results in an opaque admissions process that is more easily influenced by individuals who are socially privileged. Affluent parents can hire skilled admissions counselors to assist in the preparation of admissions material and to edit and even write personal statements for high school students. Socially privileged parents can provide lessons to their children that assist them in the development of artistic skills and talents that contribute to a personal portfolio of accomplishment, enhancing their appeal to admissions officers. Affluent parents can arrange travel opportunities and can provide financial support for children for uncompensated charitable activities that also serve to enhance credentials. Opaque admissions criteria are more subject to socially privileged manipulation than are criteria defined by objective tests. The dislike of tests is democratic; underprivileged test users dislike these tests, in part because of a belief that these tests enforce social privileges, whereas socially privileged parents sometimes dislike the same tests because they are not so easily influenced by the status of one's family, by the quality of the schools their children attend, or by the advantages that wealth and connections can provide.

One final objection to tests of general intelligence is that they often provide disappointing results. Most parents want their children to be above average in ability. The probability of attaining above-average performance on a test of ability is increased as the number of abilities that are assessed increases. Assessment on a single ability that is not easily manipulated and that is only weakly related to social privilege decreases the opportunity for parents to transfer their social status to their children.

ALTERNATIVES TO g

Three Theoretical Approaches

Gardner, Sternberg, and advocates of emotional intelligence are committed to an attempt to assess abilities that are designed to supplement traditional measurement of intelligence and, as a result, to decrease the importance of g and to minimize its allegedly pernicious influence.

Gardner. Gardner (1983, 1993) argued that standard tests of intelligence focus extensively on tasks that are not relevant to real-life accomplishments. He wanted to replace standard measures of intelligence with assessments based on portfolios and achievements in several different domains. He replaced *g* by a theory that initially postulated six different and independent intelligences: linguistic intelligence, logical-mathematical intelligence, spatial intelligence, bodily-kinesthetic intelligence, and two forms of personal intelligence—intrapersonal and interpersonal intelligence. Gardner is interested in educational reforms and in encouraging schools to identify individual abilities that provide a basis for the development of skills. His theory represents a complete repudiation of the theory of *g*.

Sternberg. Sternberg accepts the evidence for the importance of *g*. He has one major criticism of this research. He believes that the standard methods of assessing intelligence that give rise to the positive manifold are, in part, derived from the use of tests that fail to sample the entire range of human abilities. He argues that standard test batteries fail to assess practical knowledge that he defines as "the ability to adapt to, shape, and select everyday environments" (Sternberg et al., 2000, xi). This book contains a comprehensive statement of his current attempt to provide an alternative to *g* theory.) Sternberg has also developed a triarchic theory of intelligence that assumes that there are three fundamental abilities: analytical ability, which is analogous to the ability measured by conventional tests and is best defined as *g*, practical intelligence; and creative intelligence. The latter two intelligences are believed to be relatively independent of *g*. Sternberg believes that standard assessment may be supplemented by measures of creative and practical intelligence that are as predictive as *g* of educational and occupational achievement. Sternberg also believes that the use of expanded measurement of abilities will reduce racial and class disparities in selection.

Emotional Intelligence. Goleman (1995) argued that individual differences in emotional intelligence were as important as individual differences in cognitive intelligence in determining success in our society. He emphasized the malleability of emotional intelligence leading to the development of many programs designed to increase emotional intelligence. Academic researchers who have developed tests of emotional intelligence have not endorsed Goleman's claims about the importance of emotional intelligence (see Mayer, Salovey, & Caruso, 2000). These researchers believe that their tests assess an important dimension of intelligence that has a modest correlation with *g*. Tests such as the Mayer-Salovey-Caruso Emotional Intelligence Test

(MSCEIT) are assumed to measure abilities that are largely independent of g but nevertheless are related to important socially relevant outcomes. Thus, the use of the MSCEIT is assumed to provide incremental predictive validity to predictions of various social outcomes when used in conjunction with measures of g. These researchers do not believe, however, that the predictive relationship between emotional intelligence and various outcomes is as strong as the predictive relationship of g and social outcomes.

A Critique of g Alternatives

There are two fundamental claims common to each of the three alternatives to g described in the previous section. First, each assumes that it is possible to assess important dimensions of individual differences that are independent of g. Second, each assumes that these independent dimensions are predictive of socially relevant outcomes. It is obviously beyond the scope of this brief chapter to comprehensively assess these assertions, but I do want to indicate why it is reasonable to believe that these assumptions are problematic and are contradicted by relevant research.

   Gardner.   Carroll's (1993) comprehensive review of research dealing with positive manifolds among measures of linguistic abilities, spatial abilities, and logical and mathematical abilities provides overwhelming evidence that these allegedly independent abilities are substantially correlated with each other. Gardner (1983) attributes the correlations among these allegedly independent abilities to the use of language and verbal methods of assessment that lead, in effect, to method-specific contamination of measures of these abilities and create spurious correlations among them. This assertion is refutable. General intelligence can be assessed by techniques that do not require complex reasoning skills or the use of verbal intelligence. For example, Deary, Der, and Ford (2001) obtained a correlation of −.49 between a choice reaction time measure and IQ in a large representative sample of middle-aged adults. Some of the other intelligences postulated by Gardner are also related to g. Musical ability is correlated with measures of g (see Carroll, 1993, chap. 9; Shuter-Dyson & Gabriel, 1981). The MSCEIT assesses interpersonal and intrapersonal components of emotional intelligence that are at least conceptually related to Gardner's concepts, and subtests on the MSCEIT measuring these abilities are positively correlated with each other (see Matthews et al., 2002, for a comprehensive review of these studies). And, as we shall see, MSCEIT scores are positively correlated with g. It is easy to postulate the existence of independent intelligences, but Gardner has not developed tests of these intelligences that are demonstrably independent of *g*. Sackett et al. (2001) note that portfolio assessments (a method advocated by Gardner) are correlated with *g* and that predictive validities of assessments based on them are attributable to their relationship with *g*. Thus, there is little or no evidence for the belief that it is possible to obtain measures of the abilities postulated by Gardner that are independent of *g* and that have incremental predictive validities. It should be noted that Gardner has never been interested in developing psychometric tests of the intelligences he postulates. Without adequate measures of the abilities that underlie Gardner's model, however, it is impossible to demonstrate, or even evaluate, the potential contributions of Gardner's multiple-intelligence theory.

Sternberg.   Sternberg developed the Triarchic Abilities Test to assess the three independent abilities he postulates. I reviewed the studies he cites and concluded that the Sternberg Triarchic Abilities Test (STAT) is primarily a measure of *g* (Brody, 2003a, 2003c). Each of the abilities measured by STAT is correlated with scores on the Cattell Culture Fair Test of ability, a standard measure of *g*. Sternberg and Clinkenbeard (1995) obtained disattenuated correlations (i.e, correlations corrected for measurement error) between the three abilities measured by STAT and the Cattell test of .68 for analytical ability, .78 for creative ability, and .51 for practical ability. Contrary to the triarchic theory, the correlation between *g* and these abilities was not limited to analytical ability. Not only are these abilities related to a measure of *g*, they are also related to each other. The disattenuated correlations among these abilities ranged from .62 to .75. The sample used in this study was one that was restricted in range of talent. Corrections for this would have increased the correlations. These data indicate that STAT does not measure abilities that are substantially independent of *g*.

Sternberg has developed a new test of triarchic abilites that includes a wider range of items and formats. Relatively little research using this test has been published. In one of the few published studies, Henry, Sternberg, and Grigorenko (2004) used the expanded test to predict school grades. They found that the best single predictor in their battery was a score on a briefly administered multiple-choice test of creative ability used in the original version of STAT. It accounted for 14.4% of the variance. Note that this subtest was substantially related to *g*. The entire expanded battery of measures designed to more fully assess triarchic abilities accounted for 16.3% of the variance in grades. These data suggest that the new assessment of triarchic abilities has limited incremental predictive validity for academic achievement over and above the predictability obtained by measures of general intelligence.

Sternberg and his colleagues have also developed various measures of tacit knowledge that are analogous to situational judgment tests in which individuals are asked to evaluate various job-related scenarios and indicate their preferences for courses of action (Sternberg et al., 2000). Tacit knowledge tests are assumed to measure practical intelligence. Gottfredson (2003) has critically analyzed the corpus of research cited by Sternberg and his colleagues in support of the validity of these tests. She notes that the validity data deal with two different kinds of criteria: careerist, referring to such characteristics as job prestige and salary level, and noncareerist, referring to ratings of performance or objective data relevant to performance such as sales volumes. Her analysis indicates that the mean validity coefficient (weighted by sample size) for careerist indices is .28 and the comparable correlation for noncareerist indices is .12. These data are consistent with a meta-analysis of situational judgment tests performed by McDaniel, Hartman, and Grubb (2003). They obtained a meta-analytic correlation of .27 for measures of tacit knowledge and work-related indices based on studies in which both measures are obtained concurrently. They found when situational judgment tests were used to predict subsequent work related performance, the validity coefficient was .14. McDaniel et al. (2001) obtained a correlation of .46 in a meta-analysis of the relationship between g and performance on situational judgment tests. These data indicate that tacit knowledge measures of practical intelligence are correlated with g. The data that were reviewed above are compatible with the assertion that tacit knowledge tests, particularly when used as predictors of subsequent performance in occupational settings, may have only a small incremental validity over g.

Emotional Intelligence.   The MSCEIT test is assumed to correlate modestly with g. Schulte, Ree, and Caretta (2004) note that the evidence for the relationship between g and the MSCEIT is derived from studies using verbal intelligence measures. They used the Wonderlic Test, a brief measure of g that correlates .92 with the full-scale Wechsler test score to assess g. They obtained a correlation between the Wonderlic and the MSCEIT of .45 (disattenuated $r = .50$). This correlation suggests that ability-based definitions of emotional intelligence are likely to show the same sort of positive manifold as is shown by all other cognitive abilities, meaning that emotional intelligence should be positively correlated with other cognitive abilities and with g. Thus, for example, it is reasonable to believe that people who are good at spatial visualization tasks will also tend to be good at working with emotional information (much in the same way that people good at spatial visualization also tend to be good at paragraph comprehension). *g* is the factor that ultimately ties all other cognitive abilities together, and it is very likely that *g* will play the same role in abilities that are part of emotional intelligence. Emotional intelligence is likely to be one component of *g*, not a substitute for *g*.

Schulte et al. (2004) also noted that scores on the MSCEIT correlated with scores on a measure of five basic personality traits (Costa & McCrae, 1992). They obtained a disattenuated multiple correlation between the Wonderlic, personality measures and sex of participants, and the MSCEIT of .81; this implies that the MSCEIT was primarily a measure of *g* and of standard personality traits.

Mayer et al. (2004) recently summarized the evidence for the validity of the MSCEIT in a target article published in *Psychological Inquiry*. I wrote a commentary on this article (Brody, 2004), in which I noted that some of the studies control for intelligence, some control for personality, and some control for neither of these traits. Few of these studies control for both personality and intelligence. Some of these studies, including those indicating that the MSCEIT is related to occupational performance, are not published in peer-reviewed journals that are easily accessible for review. The MSCEIT yields five scores: a general factor score and a score for each of four branches of emotional intelligence. Validity correlations are sometimes reported for a general score and sometimes for one of the branch scores. The use of five measures with selective reporting of a single measure inflates the probability of wrongly obtaining a significant result. This is compounded by the use of multiple dependent variables in some of the studies and a tendency to selectively report significant results without noting that most of the correlations obtained between the MSCEIT and the dependent variables were nonsignificant. Most of the significant correlations between the MSCEIT and dependent variables were relatively low. I concluded my review of Mayer et al.'s review of validity studies as follows: "There is not a single study reported that indicates that EI has nontrivial incremental validity for a socially important outcome variable after controlling for intelligence and personality" (Brody, 2004, p. 237).

Conclusion

The three approaches to the assessment of individual differences briefly reviewed here constitute what are, arguably, the three most prominent attempts to develop assessments of individual differences that will supplement *g* or circumvent *g*. There is evidence indicating that the characteristics they assess are substantially related to *g*. Also, there is very little evidence that they measure characteristics of persons that will provide substantial incremental predictive validity to measures of g.

IMPLICATIONS

Where Do We Go From Here?

In this section, I want to briefly discuss some implications of research on intelligence that are suggested by what is known about g.

Malleability. Much of the effort to increase intelligence is focused on early interventions. We know from behavioral genetic research that the influence of early socialization practices diminishes over time. For example, Spinath and Plomin (2003) analyzed the heritability of intelligence in a large cohort of English twins using a longitudinal design in which the twins were assessed at ages 2, 3, 4, and 7. They found that the heritability of intelligence increased from .22 at ages 2, 3, and 4 to .56 at age 7. The influence of shared family environment for these ages decreased from .75 at the earlier ages to .31. The decrease in family influence and the increase in genetic influence with age are likely to continue after age 7. This implies that the attempt to change the early intellectual socialization of children as a way of increasing intelligence is misguided by virtue of the fact that it targets an influence that is likely to be of decreasing importance over the life span of individuals (see Brody, in press).

We know from the discovery of long-term, population-wide changes in g that intelligence is malleable in principle (see Flynn, 1998; his analyses show that levels of cognitive ability have been rising steadily over time). Because we do not know why intelligence is increasing, it is difficult to design interventions based on this finding. It is theoretically possible that biological interventions (e.g., changes in diet) or interventions based on findings indicating that basic information processing skills are related to intelligence might, in the future, be used to increase intelligence. For the immediate future such interventions are purely hypothetical. Therefore, a discussion of the implications of what is known about g ought to proceed on the assumption that g is relatively invariant over the life span.

Education and g. In this section, I want to briefly describe four implications of conventional psychometric research for understanding the effects of g on educational outcomes.

First, g scores do not constrain the average level of educational achievement. Asian elementary school children score approximately

1.5 standard deviations higher on tests of mathematical achievement than American elementary school children (see Stevenson & Stigler, 1992). There is little or no difference in IQ between Asian children and American children. These data indicate that children with comparable IQs can exhibit dramatically different academic achievement if exposed to different educational experiences. Thus, our knowledge of the importance of *g* in determining educational experiences does not indicate that attempts at educational reform are doomed to failure.

Second, the relationship between *g* and academic achievement measures depends somewhat on educational practices (see Cronbach & Snow, 1977). An awareness of research on *g* may provide a basis for the selection of educational practices that assist low *g* individuals to acquire educational skills without having a dramatic impact on the achievement of high *g* individuals.

Third, owing to the relatively low correlation between *g* and social class background, standard tests of ability can be used to identify intellectually talented students with disadvantaged backgrounds who would likely benefit from enriched educational opportunities. This type of tracking is controversial, but objections to this early identification of talent are often ideologically rather than scientifically driven. Thus, the debate over tracking on the basis of scores on ability tests is not an issue of whether to track or not but rather an issue of who and when to track. Although intelligence tests are often thought of as barriers to equal opportunity, tracking and selection using *g*-related measures is, in fact, one way of increasing the socioeconomic diversity of students attending selective colleges.

Finally, there are many intellectual abilities that can be assessed in addition to *g*. Spatial abilities (which are not assessed in standard batteries used for the selection of college students) are of particular relevance. Shea, Lubinski, and Benbow (2001) indicate that individuals with comparable *g* levels who differ in spatial abilities are likely to differ in educationally relevant interests. Individuals with high spatial ability tend to like laboratory courses and courses that have manipulative, as opposed to abstract, verbal dimensions. They often underperform in educational settings. Shea et al. suggested that expanded assessments of spatial and mechanical abilities and efforts to adjust the curriculum or assign students who excel in these abilities to appropriate educational experiences would enable such students to be more successful in school. There may be a number of additional abilities assessed by standard psychometric tests that can be used to assign students to appropriate educational experiences. Note that the attempt to measure such abilities does not require the development of new tests or the attempt to reanalyze the corpus of studies supporting the existence of a positive manifold supporting the *g* construct.

CONCLUSION

In this chapter, I have reviewed research relating to the g construct, and I have argued that what we know about g provides a better foundation for thinking about public policy issues than the attempt to develop alternatives to g, including emotional intelligence. I view the attempt to overcome geocentricity shared by theorists of emotional intelligence, Gardner and Sternberg, as misguided owing largely to the fact that these alternatives to g lack an adequate empirical foundation. Public policy based on empirically derived knowledge, however imperfect, is likely to be superior to public policy derived from theories that lack an empirical foundation. While we might wish that measures of emotional intelligence would provide an adequate substitute for measures of g, the data do not support this conclusion. None of the alternatives described in this chapter has been shown to be as useful and as relevant as measures of g.

REFERENCES

Beier, M. E., & Ackerman, P. L. (2003). Determinants of health knowledge: An investigation of age, gender, abilities, personality, and interests. *Journal of Personality and Social Psychology, 84,* 439–447.

Bennett, B., Fulker, D. W., & DeFries, J. C. (1985). Familial resemblance for general cognitive ability in the Hawaii Family Study of Cognition. *Behavior Genetics, 15,* 401–406.

Benson, J. B., Cherny, S. S., Haith, M. M., & Fulker, D. W. (1993). Rapid assessment of infant predictors of adult IQ: Mid-twin mid-parent analyses. *Developmental Psychology, 29,* 434–447.

Binet, A., & Simon, T. (1905). Methodes nouvelles pour le diagnostic du niveau intellectual des anormaux. *L'Annee Psychologique, 11,* 191–244.

Braden, J. P. (1994). *Deafness, deprivation, and IQ.* New York: Plenum.

Brody, N. (1992). *Intelligence* (2nd ed.). San Diego, CA: Academic Press.

Brody, N. (2003a). Construct validation of the Sternberg Triarchic Abilities Test (STAT): Comment and reanalysis. *Intelligence, 31,* 319–329.

Brody, N. (2003b). Jensen's genetic interpretation of racial differences in intelligence: Critical evaluation. In H. Nyborg (Ed.), *The scientific study of general intelligence: Tribute to Arthur R. Jensen* (pp. 397–410). Amsterdam: Pergamon.

Brody, N. (2003c). What Sternberg should have concluded. *Intelligence, 31,* 339–342.

Brody, N. (2004). What cognitive intelligence is and what emotional intelligence is not. *Psychological Inquiry, 15,* 234–238.

Brody, N. (in press). Interventions to increase intelligence. In P. Kyllonen, R. Roberts, L. Stankov (Eds.), *Extending intelligence: Enhancement and new constructs.* Mahwah, NJ: Lawrence Erlbaum Associates.

Campbell, F. A. (in press). Outcomes for the Abecedarian Project. In P. Kyllonen, R. Roberts, & L. Stankov (Eds.), *Extending intelligence: Enhancement and new constructs.* Mahwah, NJ: Lawrence Erlbaum Associates.

Carroll, J. B. (1993). *Human cognitive abilities*. Cambridge, UK: Cambridge University Press.

Cattell, R. B. (1971). *Abilities, their structure, growth, and action*. Boston: Houghton-Mifflin.

Columbo, J. (1993). *Infant cognition: Predicting later intellectual functioning*. Newbury Park, CA: Sage.

Costa, P. T., & McCrae, R. R. (1992). NEO PI-R: Professional manual revised NEO Personality Inventory (NEO PI-R) and NEO Five-Factor Inventory (NEO-FFI). Lutz, FL: Psychological Assessment Resources.

Cronbach, L. J., & Snow, R. (1977). *Aptitudes and instructional methods: A handbook for research on interactions*. New York: Irvington.

Deary, I. J., & Der, G. (2005). Reaction time explains the IQ association with mortality. *Psychological Science, 16*(1), 64–69.

Deary, I. J., Der, G., & Ford, G. (2001). Reaction time and intelligence differences: A population based cohort study. *Intelligence, 29*, 389–399.

Deary, I. J., Whalley, L. J., Lemmon, H., Crawford, J. R., & Starr, J. M. (2000). The stability of mental ability from childhood to old age: Follow-up of the 1932 Scottish Mental Survey. *Intelligence, 28*, 49–55.

Deary, I. J., Whiteman, M. C., Starr, J. M., Whalley, L. J., & Fox, H. C. (2004). The impact of childhood intelligence on later life: Following up the Scottish Mental Surveys of 1932 and 1947. *Journal of Personality and Social Psychology, 86*, 130–147.

DeGroot, A.D. (1951). War and the intelligence of youth. *Journal of Abnormal and Social Psychology, 46*, 596–597.

DiLalla, L. F., Thompson, L. A., Plomin, R., Phillips, K., Fagan, J. F., Haith, M. M., et al. (1990). Infant predictors of preschool and adult IQ: A study of infant twins and their parents. *Developmental Psychology, 26*, 759–769.

Flynn, J. R. (1998). IQ gains over time. Toward finding the causes. In U. Neisser (Ed.), *The rising curve* (pp. 25–66). Washington, DC: American Psychological Association.

Galton, F. (1869). *Hereditary genius: An enquiry into its laws and consequences*. London: Macmillan.

Gardner, H. (1983). *Frames of mind*. New York: Basic Books.

Gardner, H. (1993). *Frames of mind* (10th anniversary ed.). New York: Basic Books.

Goleman, D. (1995). *Emotional intelligence*. New York: Bantam.

Gottfredson, L.S. (2003). Dissecting practical intelligence theory: Its claims and evidence. *Intelligence, 31*, 343–397.

Gottfredson, L. S. (2004). Intelligence: Is it the epidemiologists' elusive "fundamental cause" of social class inequalities in health? *Journal of Personality and Social Psychology, 86*, 174–199.

Henry, P. J., Sternberg, R. J., & Grigorenko, E. (2004). Capturing successful intelligence through measures of analytic, creative, and practical skills. In O. Wilhelm & R. Engle (Eds.), *Understanding and measuring intelligence* (pp. 295–311). London: Sage.

Herrnstein, R. J., & Murray, C. (1994). *The bell curve: Intelligence and class structure in American life*. New York: Free Press.

Horn, J. (1989). Models of intelligence. In R. L. Linn (Ed.), *Intelligence: Measurement, theory, and public policy* (pp. 29–73). Urbana: University of Illinois Press.

Jencks, C. (1972). *Inequality: A reassessment of the effect of family and schooling in America.* New York: Basic Books.

Jencks, C. (1979). *Who gets ahead? The determinants of economic success in America.* New York: Basic Books.

Jensen, A. R. (1998). *The g factor: The science of mental ability.* Westport, CT: Praeger.

Joseph, J. (2003). *The gene illusion: Genetic research in psychiatry and psychology under the microscope.* Ross-on-Wye, UK: PCCS Books.

Matthews, G., Zeidner, M., & Roberts, R. A. (2002). *Emotional intelligence: Science and myth.* Cambridge, MA: MIT Press.

Mayer J. D., Salovey, P., & Caruso, D. (2000). Models of emotional intelligence. In R. Sternberg (Ed.), *Handbook of intelligence* (pp. 396–422). Cambridge, UK: Cambridge University Press.

McDaniel, M. A., Hartman, N. S., & Grubb, W. L., III. (April, 2003). *Situational judgment tests, knowledge, behavioral tendency, and validity: A meta-analysis.* Paper presented at the 18th Annual Conference of the Society for Industrial and Organizational Psychology, Orlando, FL.

McDaniel, M. A., Morgeson, F. P., Finnegan, E. B., Campion, M. A., & Braverman, E. P. (2001). Use of situational judgment tasks to predict job performance: A clarification of the literature. *Journal of Applied Psychology, 86,* 730–740.

Murray, C. (1998). *Income, inequality and IQ.* Washington, DC: American Enterprise Institute.

Ones, D. S, Viswesvaran, C., & Dilchert, S. (2004). Cognitive ability in selection decisions. In O. Wilhelm, & R. Engle (Eds.), *Understanding and measuring intelligence* (pp. 431–468). London: Sage.

Pedersen, N. L., Plomin, R., Nesselroade, J. R., & McClearn, G. E. (1992). A quantitative genetic analysis of cognitive abilities during the second half of the life-span. *Psychological Science, 3,* 346–352.

Plomin, R., Fulker, D. W., Corley, R., & DeFries, J. C. (1997). Nature, nurture and cognitive development from 1 to 16 years: A parent-offspring adoption study. *Psychological Science, 8,* 442–447.

Rehberg, R. A., & Rosenthal, R E. R. (1978). *Class and merit in the American high school: An assessment of the revisionist and meritocratic arguments.* New York: Longman.

Rose, S., & Feldman, J. (1995). Prediction of IQ and specific cognitive abilities at age 11 from infancy measures. *Developmental Psychology, 31,* 685–696.

Rowe, D. C. (2003). Assessing genotype-environment interactions in the postgenomic era. In R. Plomin, J.C. DeFries, I.W. Craig, & P. McGuffin (Eds.), *Behavioral genetics in the postgenomic era* (pp. 71–86). Washington, DC: American Psychological Association.

Sackett, P. R., Schmitt, N., Kalin, M., & Ellingson, J. E. (2001). High stakes testing in employment, credentialing and higher education: Prospects in a post-affirmative action world. *American Psychologist, 56,* 302–318.

Schulte, M. J., Ree, M. J., & Carretta, T. R. (2004). Emotional intelligence: Not much more than *g* and personality. *Personality and Individual Differences, 37,* 1059–1068.

Shea, D. L., Lubinski, D., & Benbow, C. P. (2001). Importance of assessing spatial ability in intellectually talented adolescents: A 20-year longitudinal study. *Journal of Educational Psychology, 93,* 603–614.

Shuter-Dyson, R., & Gabriel, C. (1981). *The psychology of musical ability* (2nd ed.). London: Methuen.

Spearman, C. (1904). General intelligence, objectively determined and measured. *American Journal of Psychology, 15*, 201–292.

Spinath, F. M., & Plomin, R. (December, 2003). *The amplification of genetic influences on g from early childhood to the early school years.* Paper presented at the International Society for the Study of Intelligence Meetings, Irvine, CA.

Sternberg, R. J., & Clinkenbeard, P. R. (1995). The triarchic model applied to identifying and teaching gifted children. *Roeper Review, 17*, 255–260.

Sternberg, R. J., Forsyth, G. B., Hedlund, J., Horvath, J. A., Wagner, R. K., Williams, W. M., et al. (2000). *Practical intelligence in everyday life.* Cambridge, UK: Cambridge University Press.

Stevenson, H. W., & Stigler, J. W. (1992). *The learning gap.* New York: Summit.

Thompson, L.A. (1989). Developmental behavior genetic research on infant information processing: Detection of continuity and change. In S. Doxiades and S. Stewart (Eds.), *Early influences shaping the individual* (pp. 67–83). New York: Plenum.

Whalley, L. J., & Deary, I. J. (2001). Longitudinal cohort study of childhood IQ and survival up to age 76. *British Medical Journal, 322*, 819–822.

White, K.R. (1982). The relation between socioeconomic status and academic achievement. *Psychological Bulletin, 81*, 461–481.

III

The Limits of EI

One of the key factors in the controversy over emotional intelligence (EI) is the lack of evidence to support sweeping claims about the importance of EI and the effectiveness of EI interventions. In chapter 8, Jordan, Ashton-James, and Ashkanasy examine some of the claims that have been made regarding the links between EI and performance and effectiveness in the workplace. Their analysis suggests that there is, at best, mixed evidence to support many of these claims. They argue in particular that all-encompassing popular definitions of emotional intelligence may have eroded any incremental validity that the construct can provide and that researchers in future should focus their efforts on scientifically validated measures of emotional intelligence.

In chapter 9, Schmit takes the analysis presented by Jordan, Ashton-James, and Ashkanasy a step further by drawing specific hypotheses that are either stated or implied in the EI literature and showing that hypotheses that clearly flow from various models of EI have not been supported in the literature. The combined message of chapters 8 and 9 is that many of the claims that help to account for the popularity of EI are either undocumented or untrue.

In chapter 10, Van Rooy, Dilchert, Viswesvaran, and Ones examine research comparing the empirically documented effects of general intelligence, practical intelligence, and emotional intelligence. Their analysis bolsters the conclusion that claims about the value of alternative definitions of "intelligence" are not supported by the evidence. In particular, the claim that emotional intelligence is more important that general intelligence in determining success in the workplace is almost certainly wrong.

In chapter 11, Hogan and Stokes ask why businesses are so often drawn to fads, including EI. They present arguments and evidence that suggests that many of the attributes that make people successful in the business world also make them suckers for the latest fad and that enthusiasm for EI may be a reflection of the personalities of business leaders rather than a reflection of the value and importance of this construct.

The bottom line of Part III is that claims about the importance and value of EI in the popular press are badly inflated. EI might have some value (a topic pursued in Part IV), but it is not the panacea, as some of its most enthusiastic supports might suggest.

8

Evaluating the Claims:
Emotional Intelligence in the Workplace

Peter J. Jordan
Griffith University

Claire E. Ashton-James
University of New South Wales

Neal M. Ashkanasy
University of Queensland

As the title of this book suggests, the construct of emotional intelligence has become fractured in the struggle between the scientists trying to develop a valid psychological construct on the one hand, and marketers attempting to develop a commercially viable psychological framework on the other. Given this fracturing, the importance of objective, critical evaluation of both the research and the practical application of emotional intelligence is paramount. Other chapters in this book have considered issues pertaining to the measurement of emotional intelligence (Conte & Dean, chap. 3), its definition (Matthews, Emo, Roberts, & Zeidner, chap. 1), and validity (Daus, chap. 13). In this chapter, we assess the utility of emotional intelligence measures and interventions in practice by evaluating those claims that underpin the commercial viability of this construct.

The range of claims regarding emotional intelligence is incredibly wide. These include claims that emotional intelligence

- Accounts for 80% of work performance and life success (Goleman, 1995).
- Is directly linked to career progression (Goleman, 1998).
- Results in individuals who are more altruistic (Cherniss & Adler, 2001).
- Results in individuals who make better leaders (Goleman, 1998).
- Contributes to better teamwork (Druskat & Wolff, 2001).
- Leads to better decisions (Jordan, Ashkanasy, & Hartel, 2002).
- Leads to people being self-starters and self-motivated (Goleman, 1998).
- Results in better coping with stress (Ashkanasy, Ashton-James, & Jordan, 2004).
- Is a useful construct for addressing a broad array of behavioral problems (Gillis, 2004).
- Results in individuals who have morally superior values (Cooper & Sawaf, 1997).

Clearly, it is beyond the scope of a single chapter to evaluate all of these claims. We have chosen three that we feel are significant, and have attracted a good deal of attention. These are that emotional intelligence contributes to (1) workplace performance, (2) career success, and (3) leadership.

In preparing this chapter, we were immediately stuck by two key aspects of the literature dealing with emotional intelligence. First was the number of differing definitions and models of emotional intelligence in existing research, and the second was the paucity of independent research (i.e., research not conducted by test developers). We soon came to the conclusion we would not be able to assess claims about the relevance of emotional intelligence merely by reviewing the empirical data. Rather, we considered three key criteria in evaluating claims regarding emotional intelligence: (1) empirical support, (2) theoretical justification, and (3) the availability of alternative research not specifically in the emotional intelligence field that might support or refute the proposed relationships. We also chose to limit our review of empirical support primarily to studies of emotional intelligence based on the Mayer and Salovey (1997) model of this construct. As has been noted in several other chapters in this book, this model of emotional intelligence has been most clearly articulated and enjoys the strongest theoretical and empirical support among the competing definitions of emotional intelligence. Critics of emotional intelligence often argue, with some justification, that claims about the usefulness and relevance of this construct often stretch the definition or scope of emotional intelligence in ways that make it difficult to tell what constructs are actually being measured or what processes might be affecting outcome variables of interest (see Ashkanasy & Daus, 2005; Daus & Ashkanasy, 2005). In assessing claims about the effects of emotional intelligence, therefore, we have chosen to ignore research that does not adhere to the Mayer and Salovey (1997) definition of this construct.

The first criterion we used to assess the validity of claims regarding emotional intelligence is the extent to which empirical data exist to support these claims. We concede that many of the claims will not have been extensively tested by empirical data due to the infancy of emotional intelligence research (see Jordan, Ashkanasy, & Hartel, 2003). Furthermore, in many cases, the model of emotional intelligence used to collect empirical data is inconsistent with the construct of emotional intelligence described by Mayer and Salovey (1997) and/or incorporates personality variables that expand the definition of the construct (Mayer, Salovey, & Caruso, 2000). Nevertheless, there are studies that provide relevant data and assessments of the empirical support for major claims about the relevance and utility of emotional intelligence.

The absence of empirical data to support a claim does not prevent that claim from being valid, however. Our second criterion, therefore, is the existence of a prima facie theoretical argument that links the claim to the emotional intelligence construct. Once again, we draw on Mayer and Salovey's (1997) theoretical model of emotional intelligence as a framework for conceptualizing emotional intelligence as a construct that is distinguishable from existing individual difference variables (Jordan et al., 2003). Using this framework, we ask whether sound inferences from the Mayer and Salovey (1997) model might provide support for specific claims.

Third, we evaluate each claim in light of other related research that might support or refute the claim. We justify this on the basis that studies that do not examine emotional intelligence directly might nevertheless provide relevant data about the claims and enable us to draw conclusions as to the likelihood that the claim is valid or not. For example, we draw on the extensive research on career success to determine if there are factors, other than emotional intelligence, that might contribute to career success. In sum, the validity of each claim is evaluated according to whether or not it can be logically deduced from data, theory, and relevant research findings.

The aim of this chapter is not to devalue emotional intelligence research, nor to denigrate the use of emotional intelligence assessment tools in organizational settings. To the contrary, by providing an uncompromising, objective, and criterion-driven evaluation of these claims, we hope to bring attention to the essence of emotional intelligence, highlighting that which is valid and represents a unique contribution to our understanding of individual differences in human functioning in the workplace. To this end, we first lay out the theoretical foundations of emotional intelligence as it has been conceptualized by Mayer and Salovey (1997). This model provides a framework to evaluate claims regarding the predictive utility of emotional intelligence. Following this, we address each of the three claims identified above and evaluate whether they meet each of the criteria described previously. In conclusion, we discuss those claims that are sustainable and evaluate the utility of emotional intelligence as a construct that can be applied in workplace settings.

A MODEL OF EMOTIONAL INTELLIGENCE

As discussed in the Matthews, Zeidner, and Roberts chapter of this book (chap. 1), the various definitions and models of emotional intelligence diverge on several factors. Indeed, some of the claims of the superior ability of individuals with high emotional intelligence are premised on expansive and fuzzy definitions of the emotional intelligence construct. For example, Goleman (1995) defines emotional intelligence in terms of a broad set of social and emotional competencies and at one stage even uses the term *character* interchangeably with emotional intelligence. The problem with this definition and other similar broad definitions of emotional intelligence is that they describe an "ideal" set of personality characteristics rather than a unique construct linking emotions and cognition. Although poor construct definition is grist for the mill for academics analyzing this construct (e.g., see Landy, 2005; Locke, 2005), in the popular literature this expansive definition of the construct contributes to the allure of emotional intelligence potential and, therefore, makes the claims more attractive.

The model developed by Mayer and Salovey (1997) defines emotional intelligence as a set of abilities that are separate and distinct from personality. This model does not, however, suggest the existence of a completely new or previously undiscovered set of abilities. Rather, this model recognizes the relatedness of several aspects of emotion processing that together contribute to social psychological functioning. The four related emotion processing abilities are emotion perception, emotion facilitation, emotion understanding, and emotion management.

In the following, we discuss each of the four components of Mayer and Salovey's (1997) model of emotional intelligence, highlighting research validating the existence of each of these processes and the way that individual differences in the functioning of the emotion processing mechanisms contribute to individual differences in social and workplace behavior.

Emotion Perception

Mayer and Salovey (1997) describe this component of emotional intelligence as the ability to perceive one's own and others' emotions. This is not a newly discovered ability. For example, a person's ability to perceive his or her own and others' emotions extends back to research into Chimeric faces (i.e., facial images in which the left and right half of a face are different; Indersmitten & Gur, 2003) and Ekman's research into nonverbal (facial) expression and communication of emotion (e.g., Ekman & Friesen, 1984). Also, we note that extreme examples from abnormal psychology, such as alexithymia (i.e., a condition in which individuals are unable to describe emotions in words) and autism, demonstrate that there are indeed individual differences in the ability to perceive and display emotion. This highlights the point that individual differences in emotion perception are not just a product of socialization or a developed skill. Instead, they represent a set of abilities or capacities that are restricted by individual differences in the structure and function of neurobiological mechanisms (Ashkanasy, 2003).

Emotion Facilitation

Emotional facilitation refers to an individual's ability to use emotions to prioritize thinking by focusing on important information to explain experienced feelings. This factor also includes the ability to adopt multiple perspectives to assess a problem, including pessimistic and optimistic perspectives (Mayer & Salovey, 1997) and the ability to determine emotion that is conducive to completing tasks (e.g., being enthusiastic during a brainstorming session). Examining research that mirrors the concept of emotional facilitation, we see there has been substantial research into the emotional aspects of motivation (Hamilton, Bower, & Frijda, 1988), commitment (Allen & Meyer, 1990), and emotional contagion (Barsade, 2002). On the other hand, research into emotional labor (Hochschild, 1979) acknowledges that emotional facilitation has consequences in the workplace, such as producing emotional and cognitive dissonance that might lead to increased stress (Morris & Feldman, 1996).

Emotion Understanding

Emotional knowledge is the third component of emotional intelligence and refers to an individual's ability to understand emotional cycles and complex emotions, such as simultaneous feelings of frustration and anger. This factor also refers to an ability to recognize the likely transitions between emotions, for example, moving from feelings of betrayal to feelings of anger and grief (Mayer & Salovey, 1997). In fact, this is not a new idea at all; understanding emotional progressions and cycles has been a central concept in cognitive behavior therapy (McMullin & Giles, 1981) and psychological counseling (Bordin, 1968) for decades.

Emotion Management

Finally, emotional regulation revolves around the management of emotions, that is, an individual's ability to connect or disconnect from an emotion, depending on its usefulness, in any given situation (Mayer & Salovey, 1997). Again, this is an area of significant research interest, particularly in relation to stress and coping (see Ashkanasy et al., 2004).

This brief outline of links between existing areas of research and emotional intelligence demonstrates that each of Mayer and Salovey's (1997) branches has a foundation in broadly accepted research. In this respect, we note that Mayer and Salovey have not introduced this concept "out of the blue." Instead, their model is built on a foundation of decades of research on intelligence and emotional functioning.

Following this introduction to the Mayer and Salovey (1997) four-branch model of emotional intelligence, we now move on to examine the three key claims that we identified earlier.

EVALUATING THE CLAIMS

Claim 1: Workplace Performance

IQ contributes about 20 percent to the factors that determine life success, which leaves 80 percent to other forces.

—Goleman (1995, p. 34)

Goleman further suggested that the "other forces" he referred to constitute "EQ." Indeed, this is one of the pervasive and often quoted claims regarding emotional intelligence. This statement was first made by Goleman (1995), and, while subsequently shying away from this overstatement of the emotional intelligence contribution to performance in later books, Goleman (1998) still claimed that emotional intelligence was "twice as important as IQ" in producing outstanding performance.

The way that Goleman seemed to have arrived at this claim is instructive. In the first instance, he expanded his definition of emotional intelligence to make it essentially all-encompassing; in other words, it became, by definition, the "other forces" mentioned in this section's opening quotation. Indeed, he did this specifically, when he referred to emotional intelligence as another way of describing character. A second tactic adopted by Goleman (1995, 1998) and others is to examine successful people and their behavior and then to make post hoc attributions to emotional intelligence of whatever their successful behaviors are. Cooper and Sawaf (1997) used this approach when they profiled the lives of successful business people. As one reads their book however, it becomes apparent that Cooper and Sawaf never actually measured these individuals' emotional intelligence or any other individual difference variable.

Empirical Evidence. Turning now to examination of the empirical studies that consider the relationship between performance and emotional intelligence, we find that there are two branches of research that apply: (1) studies of emotional intelligence and individual workplace performance, and (2) studies of emotional intelligence and teamwork or group performance.

At the individual level, early research on emotional intelligence and its relationships with performance focused on achievement in scholastic examinations (Pons, 1997; Schutte et al., 1998); these authors suggested that emotional intelligence could contribute to exam performance. This research has, however, been refuted by O'Connor and Little (2003), who showed that emotional intelligence was not a strong predictor of academic achievement, even when using several different methods of measuring emotional intelligence. In research specifically looking at cognitive-related workplace performance, Day and Carroll (2004) found that an individual's ability to perceive emotions (the first component of emotional intelligence) predicted performance on a cognitive decision-making task (deciding the order in which employees should be laid off in a fictitious company). Day and Carroll concluded, however, that none of the other components of emotional intelligence were related to task performance.

Research at the team level of analysis, however, have been more encouraging. In two recent studies comparing individual and team performance on a cognitive task, Jordan and Troth (2004) and Offermann, Bailey, Vasilopoulos, Seal, and Sass (2004) found that emotional intelligence was a predictor of team performance in a decision-based task, but it was not a predictor of individual performance on the same task. Jordan and Troth (2004), in particular, found links between emotional management skills (the fourth component of emotional intelligence) and team performance. That is, teams with members who were able to regulate their experience and expression of emotions achieved a higher performance than those teams whose members were not able to control their emotions. Examining the low-performing teams, Jordan and Troth (2004) noted that a lack of emotional control resulted in higher levels of conflict and therefore reduced the performance of team members who focused on their conflict rather than arriving at a decision.

Jordan, Ashkanasy, Hartel, and Hooper (2002) also identified emotional intelligence as a predictor of performance in workgroups. In a longitudinal study involving team performance, they found a significant difference between the *initial* performance of teams with high-average emotional intelligence and those with low-average emotional intelligence, in terms of goal achievement and the effectiveness of the processes they used to achieve those goals. Over the 9-week duration of the study, however, the differences between the performance of these two groups diminished to a point where, at the end of the study, the low emotional intelligence teams improved their performance to the extent that they became indistinguishable from the high emotional intelligence teams. It is not clear from this study whether this change in the performance of low-average emotional intelligence teams was due to the training or general group development over time. Based on the measures used in this study, however, it was concluded that teams with high emotional intelligence were more adaptive to group processes than teams with low emotional intelligence; emotionally intelligent teams were able to come together and share strengths and compensate for weaknesses in the team more quickly to produce higher performance.

The picture that emerges from the foregoing is that the claim that emotional intelligence is a predictor of *individual* performance does not seem to hold up, although there is accumulating evidence that emotional intelligence can play a significant role in promoting *team* performance. In the next section, we examine whether higher individual and team performance is a logical consequence of emotional intelligence as theorized by Mayer and Salovey (1997).

Theoretical Considerations.   With regard to individual task performance, Mayer and his colleagues (2000) argued specifically that emotional intelligence is distinct from, and unrelated to, academic or cognitive intelligence. Hence, being emotionally intelligent does not necessarily correlate with individual cognitive performance at work. In theory, however, emotional intelligence should enhance an individual's ability to cope with time pressures, performance anxiety, and other distracters that can limit task performance (Ashkanasy et al., 2004). If emotionally intelligent individuals are better equipped to handle factors that often interfere with successful task performance, emotional intelligence will make an indirect contribution to performance and effectiveness at work.

The arguments presented previously suggest that emotional intelligence may be linked to an ability to perform consistently under stressful or emotional workplace conditions. For example, Schutte, Schuettpelz, and Malouff (2000) found, controlling for baseline performance on a moderately difficult cognitive task, that individuals with high emotional intelligence were able to solve more problems after encountering a very difficult or frustrating set of problems than people with low emotional intelligence, who were less likely to persist. Thus, consistent with Mayer and Salovey's (1997) model of emotional intelligence, people with the ability to understand and manage their emotional reactions during the performance of cognitive tasks may be more productive at work than those who allow their emotions to interfere with task performance. Emotional intelligence alone does not predict task performance, however; it is merely a moderator of task performance under certain workplace conditions (see also Ashkanasy et al., 2004; Jordan et al., 2002).

In contrast to individual performance, Mayer and Salovey's (1997) model of emotional intelligence postulates a direct impact on team performance. First, teams of individuals who, collectively, have a high emotional intelligence, are thought to be better able to adapt to and to utilize diversity in group-member skills and work styles than groups of individuals with low collective emotional intelligence (Jordan & Troth, 2004; Offermann et al., 2004). Second, emotional intelligence might also influence group members' ability to deal with each other's emotions. Barsade (2002), Kelly and Barsade (2001), and George (2000) demonstrated that individual group members' affective states have a powerful influence on other members' affective states, consequently affecting group performance. In accordance with Mayer and Salovey's (1997) conceptual model, it follows that a group of individuals with high emotional intelligence may be better able to regulate group affect first, by regulating the experience and expression of their own emotions and hence not influencing others' moods, and second, by regulating their affective response to the emotional expressions of other group members.

Alternative Predictors of Workplace Performance. Several decades of research have demonstrated that both personality traits and intelligence are reliable predictors of performance and behavior at work. Schmidt and Hunter (1998) review of 85 years of research shows that measures of cognitive ability are among the most valid predictors of job performance. Intelligence is probably a better predictor of individual performance than team performance, because the competencies required to achieve team performance are not reflected in intelligence measures (Druskat & Kayes, 1999). Nevertheless, whereas there is a substantial body of evidence showing that intelligence is related to performance in a wide range of jobs, there is no comparable body of evidence showing that emotional intelligence is a valid predictor of individual performance.

In the past 15 to 20 years, a steady stream of research has also shown that personality inventories have potential as predictors of job performance and effectiveness. For instance, researchers have documented a consistent link between conscientiousness and performance (Barrick, Mount, & Judge, 2001); self-efficacy and work-related performance (Stajkovic & Luthans, 1998); and self-monitoring and workplace performance (Mehra, Kilduff, & Brass, 2001). In other research, Furnham, Jackson, and Miller (1999) found that extraversion and neuroticism predicted performance but pointed out that these only accounted for a small amount of variance in performance. Finally, in a meta-analysis of the relationship between personality and performance of work requiring interpersonal skills, Mount, Barrick, and Stewart (1998) found that conscientiousness, agreeableness, and emotional stability were positively related to work performance.

Claim 1 Conclusions. Based on these three sets of evidence, it is clear that emotional intelligence does not account for 80% of personal performance—or anything like this. Although links have been established between work performance and emotional intelligence, these links have been demonstrated almost exclusively in areas where strong interpersonal and communication skills have been required or where emotions were a moderator of work performance (e.g., highly stressful jobs). The evidence supports the idea that emotional intelligence can predict performance, but only in limited circumstances and not with the level of precision or accuracy suggested by some emotional intelligence proponents.

Claim 2: Career Success

A strong IQ score will often get you in the door ... but those who are successful tend to have high emotional intelligence.

—Brown (2001, p. 25)

Another marketing claim regarding emotional intelligence is that it is a predictor of career success (Goleman, 1998; Thorlakson, 2002). The general form of this argument is that cognitive intelligence improves people's chances of getting hired, but emotional intelligence is required to get promoted. For example, Thorlakson (2002) used a case study of Harry the "intelligent failure" to demonstrate the importance of emotional intelligence (and, in particular, emotional intelligence training) in the workplace over and above cognitive intelligence.

Empirical Evidence. Although there are no empirical data that directly test the relationship between emotional intelligence and career success, research by Fox and Spector (2000) provides indirect support for the claim that emotional intelligence may be important in recruitment and selection processes. Fox and Spector note that the employment interview is a complex interaction between employer and employee in which emotional management, a component of emotional intelligence, plays a central role. Although they acknowledge that the employment decision to hire is strongly affected by intelligence, their data also reveal that the positive affectivity of the interviewee also plays a major role in influencing this decision. Fox and Spector argue that emotional management skills associated with emotional intelligence contribute to interviewees' ability to regulate their affective state during interviews and to display positive affect. As such, Fox and Spector concluded that emotionally intelligent individuals, who are able to regulate their affective state during the interview process, are more successful in securing a job than other less emotionally intelligent individuals. These findings mirror the work of Isen and Baron (1991), who found that employees who were able to regulate mood in an organization were at a significant advantage in job interviews and in getting promotions.

There has also been research demonstrating that individuals with high emotional intelligence have better social skills leading to better quality social interactions. Lopes et al. (2004) found that this was so in general social interactions, and Sue-Chan and Latham (2004) reported that emotional intelligence fully mediated the relationship between situational interview scores and subsequent team-playing behavior. Further, in view of findings by Forret and Dougherty (2004) that networking ability is a predictor of career advancement, it seems reasonable to conclude that the quality of social interactions with coworkers and superiors, which serves to enhance networking potential, may therefore lead to career advancement. Plainly, however, more direct testing of this hypothesis is required before this relationship can be confirmed.

Theoretical Considerations. While there are no other empirical studies that examine the link between emotional intelligence and careers explicitly, Emmerling and Cherniss (2003) have developed the theoretical case for a link between these two variables. They argue that the

rational decision-making models that have been applied to career decision-making are deficient. Emmerling and Cherniss point to the research on the role of emotional expression in job interviews but take
the argument a step further by noting that people with high emotional
intelligence would have better access to emotional memories that
would facilitate the integration of the overt and suppressed emotional
information that informs their career decisions. In essence, these authors argue that current methods of career counseling, such as
self-assessment measures and tests, will be more useful to individuals with high emotional intelligence as they have the ability to access
the information that counts. This argument is, however, predicated on
the untested assumption that enhanced access to, and use of, emotional information would help people make better career decisions.
Clearly, research to test this assumption should be a priority.

Alternative Predictors of Career Success.   There are several predictors of career success, including interpersonal support networks (Simonton,
1992), person–organization fit (Bretz & Judge, 1994), sponsorship
(Judge, Kammeyer-Mueller, & Bretz, 2004), mentoring efficacy (Gibson, 2004), willingness to relocate (Eddleston, Baldridge, & Veiga,
2004), job satisfaction (Markiewicz, Devine, & Kausilas, 2000) and
self-efficacy (Creed, Patton, & Bartrum, 2004). The best demonstrated and most reliable predictor of career success (both in terms of
level of promotion and salary) is education (Cox & Harquail, 1991;
Judge, Cable, Boudreau, & Bretz, 1995; Melamed, 1996). Judge et al.
(1995) and Whitely, Dougherty, and Dreher (1991) indicate that the returns from educational attainment in terms of compensation level are
significant. Education is also expected to underlie one's self-efficacy
and beliefs about one's marketability (Wayne, Liden, Kraimer, & Graf,
1999).

Claim 2 Conclusions.   In summary, although Fox and Spector (2000)
demonstrated a link between emotional intelligence and interview
success, there is no evidence to support the broader claim that emotional intelligence can help individuals to achieve promotion once
they "get a foot is in the door." Theoretically, there is no reason why
emotional intelligence should be an important determinant of success
in careers that are not people oriented. Hence, it is not clear how emotional intelligence would help someone in such a career to achieve
promotion over and above their task performance. Of course, if one's
workplace performance is contingent solely or largely on social skills,
it may be that emotion perception and emotion management (two
components of emotional intelligence) can contribute to higher levels
of performance and thus to career success. From the evidence pre-

sented in this section, however, it is clear that in such jobs, emotional intelligence would only be one of many predictors of career success. Given the proven track record of these alternate predictors, it is unlikely that emotional intelligence will play the sort of preeminent role in career success predicted by Goleman (1998), Brown (2001), and others.

Claim 3: Leadership

Outstanding leaders' emotional competencies make up to 85% to 100% of the competencies crucial for success.

—Goleman (1998, p. 187)

Again, this is an important marketing claim. Those aspiring to leadership positions look for the "magic bullet" that will allow them to lead effectively, and those who are in leadership roles look for ways of improving their performance. Clearly, there is a link between an individual's ability to manage and generate emotions and leadership (Bass, 2002). Indeed, Avolio and Bass (1988) discussed the importance of individualized consideration as an aspect of transformational leadership and identify charisma as an aspect of leadership. Both individualized consideration and charisma have obvious links to emotions and emotional management.

Within some of the emotional intelligence literature, however, emotional intelligence has been described as a major determinant of effective leadership. For instance, Goleman, Boyatzis, and McKee (2001) claimed that leaders who lack emotional intelligence must rely on luck to maintain the appearance of effective leadership.

Empirical Evidence.   Although there are a number of research studies that seek to link emotional intelligence to leadership and, in particular, transformational leadership, many of these studies confound the model of emotional intelligence by adding factors to the model of emotional intelligence that include personality traits that are only weakly related to emotional intelligence (e.g., Dulewicz, Higgs, & Slaksi, 2003; Goleman et al., 2001). For example, Kobe, Reiter-Palmon, and Rickers (2001) demonstrated that emotional intelligence was correlated with self-reported leadership experiences, although they noted in their discussion that emotional intelligence did not provide unique variance over a measure of social intelligence employed in their study.

Some of the more recent work, however, appears to meet, at least in part, the standards we set in the introduction to this chapter. Sosik and Megerian (1999), for example, focused on self-awareness as an indicator of transformational leadership perceptions of followers (see also Megerian & Sosik, 1996). Although this study did not use a measure of emotional intelligence per se, and relied on proxy measures of emotional awareness and emotional management, Sosik and Megerian were able to show that self–other agreement was a predictor of leader behavior and leader performance. Rubin, Munz, and Bommer (2005), in a field study involving 145 managers, found that emotion recognition ability and positive affect predicted transformational leadership ability. In another field study, Lopes, Salovey, Côté, and Beers (2005) found that emotional intelligence was a predictor of both peer and supervisor estimates of leadership potential, even after controlling for personality and demographic influences. These results are encouraging, although more research into the specific role played by emotional intelligence factors as leadership determinants is clearly warranted.

In this respect, it is instructive that the study by Jordan et al. (2002) also demonstrated a link between self-monitoring and emotional intelligence. Specifically, Jordan and his colleagues identified a link between acquisitive self-monitoring (i.e., the propensity of individuals in social interactions to get ahead and lead the interaction; Lennox & Wolfe, 1984) and emotional intelligence. Although this is not leadership per se, it does point to a propensity for individuals with high emotional intelligence to control social interactions. By examining the theoretical links between leadership and emotional intelligence, a way to obtain further empirical evidence may be established.

Finally, and consistent with the concept of self-monitoring, Newcombe and Ashkanasy (2002) demonstrated that followers' impressions of the leader in a performance feedback situation were determined by the leader's display of positive affect and by the leader's ability to display positive or negative affect consistent with the (positive or negative) feedback being expressed. This result can be interpreted in terms of the fourth branch of the Mayer and Salovey (1997) model of emotional intelligence—management of emotion—and suggests that an important skill of leader impression management is emotional intelligence.

Theoretical Considerations.   Ashkanasy and Tse (2000) and George (2000) have linked the abilities referred to as emotional intelligence to a model of transformational leadership. These authors note that emotional awareness and emotional management skills play a major role in the development of relationships with followers. Prati, Douglas, Ferris, Ammeter, and Buckley (2003) have taken this idea a step further, suggesting that emotional intelligence plays a critical role in linking leadership to team outcomes. Indeed, considering the aspects of transformational leadership (Avolio & Bass, 1988), a leader's ability to provide inspired charismatic/idealized influence and inspirational motivation, while at the same time articulating a vision of the future that can be shared, can be aligned to the emotional intelligence ability of emotional facilitation. Moreover, individualized consideration, a transformational leadership characteristic that involves the leader paying attention to individual needs, is likely to be enhanced by the leader's ability to be aware of and manage others' emotions.

Ashkanasy and Tse (2000) also noted that this ability could lead to emotional manipulation. Connelly, Gaddis, and Helton-Fauth (2002) proposed similarly that transformational leaders who display the appropriate positive and negative emotions influence followers and generate follower commitment to the leader's vision. Dasborough and Ashkanasy (2002) took this a step further and posited that an emotionally intelligent leader is able to manipulate follower's emotions for evil and/or self-serving ends, although they characterize this as "pseudo-transformational leadership" (Bass, Avolio, & Atwater, 1996).

The argument for a link between emotional intelligence and transformational leadership has been contested by Antonakis (2003), however, who cautioned against the use of broad definitions of emotional intelligence and calls for assessment of the broad spectrum of research into leadership and its correlates before determining the relationship between emotional intelligence and transformational leadership.

Alternative Predictors of Leadership Ability. Leadership is an area in which a substantial amount of theoretical and empirical work has been carried out. For instance Neubert and Taggar (2004) found that informal leadership emergence was predicted by a combination of conscientiousness, emotional stability, and centrality to the group. Using meta-analytic techniques, Judge, Bono, Ilies, and Werner (2002) found that leadership is positively linked to extraversion, conscientiousness, and openness to experience and negatively linked to neuroticism.

Although the evidence for a link between cognitive intelligence and leadership has been shown to be relatively weak (Judge, Colbert, & Ilies, 2004), cognitive abilities are still correlated with objective measures of leadership and followers' perceptions of leaders.

Claim 3 Conclusions. Examining the relevant research on leadership, one thing becomes clear. There exist a vast array of different models of effective leadership, including Avolio and Bass' (1988) conceptualization of transformational and transactional leaders to models of charismatic leadership (House, 1977; Conger & Kanungo, 1998), situational leadership (Hersey & Blanchard, 1969), contingent leadership (e.g., Fiedler, 1967), and the path-goal theory of leadership (House, 1971). Each of these models of leadership presents a different perspective of leadership, making it exceedingly difficult to assert, as Goleman et al. (2001) do, that emotional intelligence will inevitably be an essential ingredient of effective leadership.

On the other hand, the extant research demonstrates that there is an emotional element to leadership (Humphrey, 2002). Indeed, Ashkanasy and Tse (2000) may be right that emotional intelligence moderates a specific type of leadership such as transformational leadership; recent research (e.g., Lopes et al., 2005) appears to back this up. This argument, however, still needs to be developed more thoroughly as a theoretical model and then tested to establish the veracity of the claim.

DISCUSSION AND CONCLUSIONS

Although there have been substantial claims made about the importance of the emotional intelligence construct, it is clear from this review that these can only be sustained to a very limited extent. Nonetheless, it is also clear from our review that emotional intelligence does provide additional explanatory power in industrial and organizational psychology research. To advance our knowledge of this construct and its correlates, however, well-crafted research needs to be conducted to confirm the theoretical basis for these assertions. Moreover, it is important that empirical evidence using measures based on the Mayer and Salovey (1997) model of emotional intelligence must be collected. Unless researchers stick to an established model of emotional intelligence that has some level of scientific credibility, at least in the short-to-medium future, it is going to be difficult to establish a prima facie case for the role emotional intelligence plays in predicting workplace performance outcomes.

Extravagant claims have been made in the popular press about the importance and relevance of emotional intelligence (e.g., Goleman, 1995, 1998). These claims have received considerable attention in organizations, in part because emotional intelligence appears to provide a fresh approach for solving long-standing problems, such as how to find and develop the best employees. The most sweeping claims about emotional intelligence have little empirical or theoretical support and are often based on fuzzy, all-encompassing definitions of emotional intelligence. We would argue that these claims have done considerable harm to the field, because they lead many people to regard emotional intelligence as a fad and a confidence game. The evidence reviewed here supports the notion that emotional intelligence, as defined by the Mayer and Salovey (1997) model, can be an important construct. Unfortunately, the inflated claims made in some quarters have made the whole field of emotional intelligence suspect in the eyes of many. Mud that is thrown at commercial promoters of emotional intelligence is likely also to splatter the legitimate scientists working in this field. A critical, evidence-based examination of these claims can help us sort the useful and valid work in the area of emotional intelligence from the unfounded marketing hype.

Future Directions for Research

The implications of our discussion in this chapter are fairly clear. In terms of research, there is a paucity of studies that have examined the emotional intelligence construct in work settings that has been based on the recognized definition of emotional intelligence. In particular, by introducing elements of personality into definitions of emotional intelligence, writers such as Goleman have confounded our understanding of the area. While the use of broad models and measures of emotional intelligence increases the likelihood that the construct will predict human behavior, it does not contribute the incremental validity that researchers of emotional intelligence seek. The way forward is to use models of emotional intelligence that are less contaminated by personality constructs, such as the Mayer and Salovey (1997) model.

Practical Implications

It is in the area of management practice that the advocates of emotional intelligence have had their greatest effects, with Goleman's (1995) book topping the New York Times best-seller list for weeks on end, and even getting a cover story in Time Magazine (Gibbs, 1995). It is here that the bandwagon has been rolling. Our review suggests that management practitioners need to take care that they do not overemphasize the predictive value of emotional intelligence in workplace settings. The evidence for the dramatic claims of advocates in the areas that we have canvassed—performance, career advancement, and leadership—simply does not hold up. Although there is emerging evidence that emotional intelligence has some beneficial effects, the broad and sensational claims of the commercial advocates of the construct need to be set aside by thoughtful managers. This is not to say, however, that research in emotional intelligence should not continue. Indeed, future research may well lead to useful advances in our knowledge of emotional intelligence and its effects. At the same time, we note that it is essential that claims in future be carefully assessed, first, to ascertain the level of theoretical and empirical support for the claims, and second, to discount alternative explanations for the effects claimed.

REFERENCES

Allen, N. J., & Meyer, J. P. (1990). The measurement and antecedents of affective, continuance and normative commitment to the organization. *Journal of Occupational Psychology, 63,* 1–18.

Antonakis, J. (2003). Why "emotional intelligence" does not predict leadership effectiveness: A comment on Prati, Douglas, Ferris, Ammeter, and Buckley (2003). *International Journal of Organizational Analysis, 11,* 355–361.

Ashkanasy, N. M. (2003). Emotions in organizations: A multilevel perspective. In F. Dansereau & F. J. Yammarino (Eds.), *Research in multi-level issues: Vol. 2. Multi-level issues in organizational behavior and strategy* (pp. 9–54). Oxford, UK: Elsevier Science.

Ashkanasy, N. M., Ashton-James, C. & Jordan, P. J. (2004). Performance impacts of appraisal and coping with stress in workplace settings: The role of affect and emotional intelligence. In P. Perrewe & D. Ganster (Eds.), *Research in occupational stress and well being* (pp. 1–43). Oxford, UK: Elsevier Science.

Ashkanasy, N. M., & Daus, C. S. (2005). Rumors of the death of emotional intelligence in organizational behavior are vastly exaggerated. *Journal of Organizational Behavior, 26,* 441–452

Ashkanasy, N. M., & Tse, B. (2000). Transformational leadership as management of emotion: A conceptual review. In N. M. Ashkanasy, C. E. J. Härtel, & W. Zerbe (Eds.), *Emotions in the workplace: Research, theory, and practice* (pp. 221–236). Westport, CT: Quorum Books.

Avolio, B. J., & Bass, B. M. (1988). Transformational leadership, charisma, and beyond. In J. G. Hunt & B. R. Baliga (Eds.), *Emerging leadership vistas* (pp. 29–49). Lexington, MA: Lexington Books.

Barrick, M. R., Mount, M. K., & Judge, T. A. (2001). Personality and performance at the beginning of the new millennium: What do we know and where do we go next? *International Journal of Selection & Assessment, 9,* 9–30.

Barsade, S. G. (2002). The ripple effects: Emotional contagion and its influence on group behavior. *Administrative Science Quarterly, 47,* 644–675.

Bass, B. M. (2002). Cognitive, social, and emotional intelligence of transformational leaders. In R. E. Riggio, S. E. Murphy, & F. J. Pirozzolo (Eds.), *Multiple intelligences and leadership* (pp. 105–118). Mahwah, NJ: Lawrence Erlbaum Associates.

Bass, B. M., Avolio, B. J., & Atwater, L. (1996). The transformational and transactional leadership of men and women. *Applied Psychology. An International Review, 45,* 5–34.

Bordin, E. S. (1968). *Psychological counseling.* New York : Appleton-Century-Crofts.

Bretz, R. D., & Judge, T. A. (1994). Person-organization fit and the theory of work adjustment: Implications for satisfaction, tenure, and career success. *Journal of Vocational Behavior, 44,* 32–54.

Brown, J. (2001). Emotional intelligence. *Computing Canada, 27*(2), 25.

Cherniss, C., & Adler, M. (2001). *Promoting emotional intelligence in organizations.* Alexandria, VA: American Society for Training & Development (ASTD).

Conger, J. A., & Kanungo, R. N. (1998). *Charismatic leadership in organizations.* Thousand Oaks, CA: Sage.

Connelly, S., Gaddis, B., & Helton-Fauth, W. (2002). A closer look at the role of emotions in transformational and charismatic leadership. In B. J. Avolio & F. J. Yammarino (Eds.), *Transformational and charismatic leadership: The road ahead* (pp.225–286). New York: Elsevier Science.

Cooper, R. K., & Sawaf, A. (1997). *Executive EQ: Emotional intelligence in leadership and organizations.* New York: Grossett/Putnam.

Cox, T. H., & Harquail, C. V. (1991). Career paths and career success in the early career stages of male and female MBAs. *Journal of Vocational Behavior, 39,* 54–75.

Creed, P. A., Patton, W., & Bartrum, D. (2002). Multidimensional properties of the LOT-R: Effects of optimism and pessimism on career and well-being related variables in adolescents. *Journal of Career Assessment, 10,* 42–61.

Dasborough, M. T., & Ashkanasy, N. M. (2002). Emotion and attribution of intentionality in leader-member relationships. *Leadership Quarterly, 13,* 615–634.

Daus, C. S., & Ashkanasy, N. M. (2005). The case for an ability-based model of emotional intelligence in organizational behavior. *Journal of Organizational Behavior, 26,* 453–466.

Day, A. L., & Carroll, S. A. (2004). Using an ability-based measure of emotional intelligence to predict individual performance, group performance, and group citizenship behaviors. *Personality Individual Differences, 36,* 1443–1458.

Druskat, V. U., & Wolff, S. B. (2001). Building the emotional intelligence of groups. *Harvard Business Review, 79*(3), 80–90.

Druskat, V. U., & Kayes, D. C. (1999). The antecedents of team competence: Toward a fine-grained model of self-managing team effectiveness. In R. Wageman (Ed.), *Research on managing groups and teams: Groups in context* (Vol. 2, pp. 201–231). Stamford, CT: JAI Press, Inc.

Dulewicz, V., Higgs, M. , & Slaski, M. (2003). Measuring emotional intelligence: content, construct and criterion-related validity. *Journal of Managerial Psychology, 18,* 405–421.

Eddleston, K. A, Baldridge, D. C., & Veiga, J, F. (2004). Toward modeling the predictors of managerial career success: Does gender matter? *Journal of Managerial Psychology, 19,* 360–385.

Ekman, P., & Friesen, W. V. (1984). *Unmasking the face: A guide to recognizing emotions from facial clues.* Palo Alto, CA: Consulting Psychologists Press.

Emmerling, R. J., & Cherniss, C. (2003). Emotional intelligence and the career choice process. *Journal of Career Assessment, 11,* 153–167.

Fiedler, F. E. (1967). *A theory of leadership effectiveness.* New York: McGraw-Hill.

Forret, M. L., & Dougherty, T. W. (2004). Networking behaviors and career outcomes: Differences for men and women? *Journal of Organizational Behavior, 25,* 419–437

Fox, S., & Spector, P. E. (2000). Relations of emotional intelligence, practical intelligence, general intelligence, and trait affectivity with interview outcomes: It's not all just "G". *Journal of Organizational Behavior, 21,* 203–220.

Furnham, A., Jackson, C. J., & Miller, T. (1999). Personality, learning style and work performance. *Personality & Individual Differences, 27,* 1113–1122.

George, J. M. (2000). Emotions and leadership: The role of emotional intelligence. *Human Relations, 53,* 1027–1055.

Gibbs, N. (1995, October 2). The EQ factor. *Time Magazine, 146,* 60–68.

Gibson, D. E. (2004). Role models in career development: New directions for theory and research. *Journal of Vocational Behavior, 65,* 134–156.

Gillis, C. (2004). Rude awakening. *Maclean's, 117*(14), 28–32.

Goleman, D. (1995). *Emotional intelligence: Why it can matter more than IQ.* New York: Bantam Books.

Goleman, D. (1998). *Working with emotional intelligence.* New York: Bantam Books.

Goleman, D., Boyatzis, R., & McKee, A. (2001). Primal leadership: The hidden driver of great performance. *Harvard Business Review, 79*(11), 42–48.

Hamilton, V., Bower, G. H., & Frijda, N. H. (Eds). (1988). *Cognitive perspectives on emotion and motivation.* Dordrecht, Netherlands: Kluwer Academic.

Hersey, P., & Blanchard, K. H. (1969). Life cycle theory of leadership. *Training and Development Journal, 23,* 26–34.

Hochschild, A. (1979). Emotion work, feeling rule, and social structure. *American Journal of Sociology, 85,* 551–575.

House, R. J. (1971). A path-goal theory of leader effectiveness. *Administrative Science Quarterly, 16,* 321–339.

House, R. J. (1977). A 1976 theory of charismatic leadership. In J. G. Hunt & L. L. Larson (Eds.), *Leadership: The cutting edge* (pp. 189–207). Carbondale: Southern Illinois University Press.

Humphrey, R. H. (2002). The many faces of emotional leadership. *Leadership Quarterly, 13*(5), 493–504

Indersmitten, T., & Gur, R. C. (2003). Emotion processing in chimeric faces: Hemispheric asymmetries in expression and recognition of emotions. *The Journal of Neuroscience, 23,* 3820–3825.

Isen, A. M., & Baron, R. A. (1991). Positive affect as a factor in organizational behavior. *Research in Organizational Behavior, 13,* 1–54.

Jordan, P. J., Ashkanasy, N. M., & Hartel, C. E. J. (2002). Emotional intelligence as a moderator of emotional and behavioral reactions to job insecurity. *Academy of Management Review, 27,* 1–12.

Jordan, P. J., Ashkanasy, N. M., & Hartel, C. E. J. (2003). The case for emotional intelligence in organizational research. *Academy of Management Review, 28,* 195–197.

Jordan, P. J., Ashkanasy, N. M., Hartel, C. E. J., & Hooper, G. S. (2002). Workgroup emotional intelligence: Scale development and relationship to team process effectiveness and goal focus. *Human Resource Management Review, 12,* 195–214.

Jordan, P. J., & Troth, A. C. (2004). Managing emotions during team problem solving: Emotional intelligence and conflict resolution. *Human Performance, 17,* 195–218.

Judge, T. A., Bono, J. E., Ilies, R., & Werner, M. W. (2002). Personality and leadership: A qualitative and quantitative review. *Journal of Applied Psychology, 87,* 765–780.

Judge, T. A., Cable, D. M., Boudreau, J. W., & Bretz, R. D. (1995). An empirical investigation of the predictors of executive career success. *Personnel Psychology, 48,* 485–519.

Judge, T. A., Colbert, A. E., & Ilies, R. (2004). Intelligence and leadership: A quantitative review and test of theoretical propositions. *Journal of Applied Psychology, 89,* 542–552.

Judge, T. A., Kammeyer-Mueller, J., & Bretz, R. D. (2004). A longitudinal model of sponsorship and career success: A study of industrial-organizational psychologists. *Personnel Psychology, 57,* 271–303.

Kelly, J. R., & Barsade, S. (2001). Mood and emotions in small groups and work teams. *Organizational Behavior and Human Decision Processes, 86,* 99–130.

Kobe, L. M., Reiter-Palmon, R., & Rickers, J. D. (2001). Self-reported leadership experiences in relation to inventoried social and emotional intelligence. *Current Psychology, 20,* 154–163.

Landy, F. J. (2005). Some historical and scientific issues related to research on emotional intelligence. *Journal of Organizational Behavior, 26,* 411–424.

Lennox, R. D., & Wolfe, R. N. (1984). Revision of the self-monitoring scale. *Journal of Personality and Social Psychology, 46,* 1349–1364.

Locke, E. A. (2005). Why emotional intelligence is an invalid concept. *Journal of Organizational Behavior, 26,* 425–431.

Lopes, P. N., Brackett, M. A., Nezlek, J. B., Schütz, A., Sellin, I., & Salovey, P. (2004). Emotional intelligence and social interaction. *Personality and Social Psychology Bulletin, 30,* 1018–1034.

Lopes, P. N., Salovey, P., Côté, S., & Beers, M. (2005). Emotion regulation ability and the quality of social interaction. *Emotion, 5,* 113–118.

Markiewicz, D., Devine, I., & Kausilas, D. (2000). Friendships of women and men at work: Job satisfaction and resource implications. *Journal of Managerial Psychology, 15,* 161–184.

Mayer, J., & Salovey, P. (1997). What is emotional intelligence? In P. Salovey & D. Sluyter (Eds.), *Emotional development and emotional intelligence: Implications for educators* (pp. 3–31). New York: Basic Books.

Mayer, J. D., Salovey, P., & Caruso, D. R. (2000). Competing models of emotional intelligence. In R. Sternberg (Ed.), *Handbook of intelligence* (pp. 396–420). New York: Cambridge University Press.

McMullin, R. E., & Giles, T. R. (1981). *Cognitive-behavior therapy: A restructuring approach.* New York: Grune & Stratton.

Megerian, L. E., & Sosik, J. J. (1996). An affair of the heart: Emotional intelligence and transformational leadership. *Journal of Leadership Studies, 3,* 31–48.

Mehra, A., Kilduff, M., & Brass, D. J. (2001). The social networks of high and low self-monitors: Implications for workplace performance. *Administrative Science Quarterly, 46,* 121–146.

Melamed, T. (1995). Career success: The moderating effect of gender. *Journal of Vocational Behavior, 47,* 35–60.

Morris, J. A., & Feldman, D. C. (1996). The dimensions, antecedents, and consequences of emotional labor. *Academy of Management Review, 21,* 986–1011.

Mount, M. K., Barrick, M. R., & Stewart, G. L. (1998). Five-factor model of personality and performance in jobs involving interpersonal interactions. *Human Performance, 11,* 145–165

Neubert, M. J., & Taggar, S. (2004). Pathways to informal leadership: The moderating role of gender on the relationship of individual differences and team member network centrality to informal leadership emergence. *Leadership Quarterly, 15,* 175–194.

Newcombe, M. J., & Ashkanasy, N. M. (2002). The role of affect and affective congruence in perceptions of leaders: An experimental study. *Leadership Quarterly, 13,* 601–614.

O'Connor, R. M., Jr., & Little, I. S. (2003). Revisiting the predictive validity of emotional intelligence: Self-report versus ability-based measures. *Personality & Individual Differences, 35,* 1893–1902.

Offermann, L. R., Bailey, J. R., Vasilopoulos, N. L., Seal, C., & Sass, M. (2004). The relative contribution of emotional competence and cognitive ability to individual and team performance. *Human Performance, 17,* 219–243.

Pons, M. M. (1997). The relation of emotional intelligence with selected areas of personal functioning. *Imagination, Cognition and Personality, 17,* 3–13.

Prati, L., Douglas, C., Ferris, G. R., Ammeter, A. P., & Buckley, M. R. (2003). Emotional intelligence, leadership effectiveness, and team outcomes. *International Journal of Organizational Analysis, 11,* 21–40.

Rubin, R. S., Munz, D. C., & Bommer, W. H. (2005). Leading from within: The effects of emotion recognition and personality on transformational leadership behavior. *Academy of Management Journal, 48,* 845–858.

Schmidt, F. L., & Hunter, J. E . (1998). The validity and utility of selection methods in personnel psychology: Practical and theoretical implications of 85 years of research findings. *Psychological Bulletin, 124,* 262–274.

Schutte, N. S., Malouff, J. M., Hall, L. E., Haggerty, D. J., Cooper, J. T., Golden, C. J., et al. (1998). Development and validation of a measure of emotional intelligence. *Personality and Individual Differences, 25,* 167–177.

Schutte, N. S., Schuettpelz, E., & Malouff, J. M. (2000). Emotional intelligence and task performance. *Imagination, Cognition, and Personality, 20,* 347–354.

Simonton, D. K. (1992). The social context of career success and course for 2,026 scientists and inventors. *Personality and Social Psychology Bulletin, 18,* 452.

Sosik, J. J., & Megerian, L. E. (1999). Understanding leader emotional intelligence and performance: The role of self-other agreement on transformational leadership perceptions. *Group & Organization Management, 24,* 367–391.

Stajkovic, A. D., & Luthans, F. (1998). Self-efficacy and work-related performance: A meta-analysis. *Psychological Bulletin, 124,* 240–261.

Sue-Chan, C., & Latham, G. P. (2004). The situational interview as a predictor of academic and team performance: A study of the mediating effects of cognitive ability and emotional intelligence. *International Journal of Selection and Assessment, 12,* 312–320.

Thorlakson, A. J. H. (2002). Have you heard about Harry? *The Canadian Manager, 27*(2), 28.

Wayne, S. J., Liden, R. C., Kraimer, M. L., & Graf, I. K. (1999). The role of human capital, motivation, and supervisor sponsorship in predicting career success. *Journal of Organizational Behavior, 20,* 577–595.

Whitely, W., Dougherty, T. W., & Dreher, G. F. (1991). Relationship of career mentoring and socioeconomic origin to managers' and professionals' early career progress. *Journal of Applied Psychology, 34,* 331–351.

9

EI in the Business World

Mark J. Schmit
Applied Psychological Techniques, Erie, CO

In the quest for organizational and personal success in the business world, managers are often driven to find ways to improve organizational outcomes while cutting costs, thereby improving the profitability of the company and maximizing personal rewards. There is typically a large emotional component tied to achieving these goals, as they carry with them strong consequences. Achieving managerial goals can lead to valued rewards, whereas failure to achieve them can be embarrassing and perhaps career threatening; either success or failure is likely to lead to strong emotional reactions. Consulting, publishing, and product fads play on these very emotions to help boost sales. It seems quite ironic that emotional intelligence (EI) has become one of these fads; in fact, it may be that those managers who are unable to separate emotional motivations from rational decision making are the most likely to become swept up in this latest management fad.

With most management fads, there are kernels of truth and sound research support for elements of the proposition that the perception and management of emotions have a bearing on success at work. Through various communication mediums and the motivations of commercial enterprises (e.g., consultants, test publishers), these ker-

211

nels of truth can get exaggerated and distorted until they are barely recognizable to social scientists who originally generated the supporting research. While other chapters in this volume evaluate different definitions of EI and document the tested and untested elements of the various EI constructs, this chapter is devoted to identifying how EI has been, or might be, used in the business world.

There are important barriers to conducting a comprehensive evaluation of applications of EI and related concepts in organizations. First, there is very little sound empirical research on the impact that EI products or related services can have in business organizations. In the absence of rigorous research, it is certainly a challenge to describe how EI should be used in companies. Looking at the continuum of firms engaged in selling EI products and services to managers and their organizations does not help much. At one end of the continuum are consulting, publishing, and product firms who suggest EI as a general solution for the wide range of management problems. This group has integrated EI into nearly every human resource (HR) product or service they offer to clients, and they sometimes make sweeping claims about the value of EI in the business world. Firms that are strongly committed to EI have little incentive to carry out thorough, unbiased studies of the value of this construct or of their products. At the other end of the continuum are much more conservative, research-oriented firms who are reluctant to move away from time-honored constructs and research methodologies. This group often gives little credence to the construct of EI and, therefore, also has little incentive to carry out the sort of research that would allow for a thorough evaluation of the construct.

It would be convenient and less of a challenge to describe and evaluate the uses of EI in the business world if there were representation in the middle ground of this continuum (i.e., firms willing to engage in basic research to evaluate the promise and the problems of the EI construct). One result of this polarization of the EI research and practice community is that the research related to the definition and the usefulness (e.g., reliability, validity, accuracy, utility) of EI interventions in the business world is in a very preliminary and premature stage.

Given the state of the current research support for EI, I take a more visionary approach to describing possible uses of EI in the business world where I refrain from describing how EI *should be* used in business organizations, but rather speculate on how EI *might be* useful in the business world. The framework for this chapter builds on the theoretical elements of EI from which I generate hypotheses about what may be useful in the business world.

I provide some examples of applications of EI that have been reported elsewhere throughout the remainder of this chapter. Unfortunately, few of these examples come from peer-reviewed journal articles. Most have been reported in other book chapters, popular press, and in technical/marketing materials of consulting firms (many of which are heavy on the marketing and very light on the technical aspects). A close examination of the many EI technical reports, books, and chapters reveals only a small number of unique example cases. There are very few primary citations to be found in this literature; most authors cite someone else, who in turn has relied on someone else's citation, none of which contains much more than anecdotal accounts of the use of EI in organizations. Further, each iterative description of an intervention seems to get more expansive in terms of the outcomes experienced. All this suggests that these few example cases have probably grown to the magnitude of "urban/corporate legends" that contain some elements of truth but are just as likely to contain important exaggerations.

An example of a popular EI corporate legend is provided by the widely cited case of American Express. There are many stories in books (e.g., Goleman, 1998) and popular press articles (e.g., Schwartz, 2000) regarding the successes achieved by American Express with regard to EI interventions. In particular, EI training interventions have been touted as having led to great improvements in business growth among financial advisors within the American Express Financial Advisors organization. Given the lack of strong empirical support for general claims about the success of EI training and similar interventions (Cherniss, 2000; Dulewicz & Higgs, 2004; O'Connor & Little, 2003), case examples such as this might be very important in evaluating the claim that these interventions have beneficial effects. However, it is difficult to verify even the details of this highly publicized case.

In an effort to determine the current status of EI interventions at American Express, I interviewed two of their HR professionals (one was employed in corporate HR for American Express, and the other was an HR professional in American Express Financial Advisors). These interviews suggest emotional competence is indeed an important component of this organization's culture and that skills related to emotional competence are part of several training and development programs. However, these HR professionals did not regard EI alone as highly central to the organization's mission. More to the point, there is no evidence that can be used to determine what role, if any, EI interventions have had in the success of this particular organization. Like most other organizations, American Express has not designed the sorts of studies or collected the sorts of data that would make it possible to evaluate the effectiveness of specific training programs or interventions. Because EI is interwoven into several different programs (all of which have effects that are difficult to evaluate), it is impossible to isolate the specific effects of EI intervention or to estimate how effective this organization would have been without these interventions.

Given the current state of EI research and organizational applications, I am reluctant to directly cite any specific case studies as convincing support for EI interventions in this chapter. I also refrain from endorsing any specific consulting firms and their products and services, as little direct outcome evidence or comparison studies have been published in peer-reviewed outlets. Instead, I broadly describe some interventions that have been reported, as well as propose possible interventions for further research, and how they fit with hypotheses that are generated from EI theory. As such, citations to specific cases or tools in this chapter should not be taken as supporting evidence or endorsements but merely as examples of what *might* be supported by both continuing and future research.

This chapter covers applications of EI in the world of business, focusing on personnel selection, development, and organizational development.

GENERATING HYPOTHESES ABOUT EFFECTIVE HR PRACTICES

In the HR practice domain, constructs such as EI can be used in conjunction with other constructs on which individuals differ, including competencies, or specific knowledge, skills, abilities, or other personal characteristics, to build models of successful performance. Job analysis techniques are typically used to rationally and empirically tie these constructs to job tasks, general work behaviors, positions, jobs, groups of jobs, or even organization-wide to all jobs. Through this process, models of individual, group, and organizational performance can be identified. These models explicitly identify individual difference constructs (e.g., computer programming knowledge, typing skill, cognitive ability, EI) that are hypothesized to be related to successful performance. With constructs identified, HR practices such as personnel selection, promotion, employee development, performance appraisal, and organizational development can be developed to move these models of successful performance from theory to applied research (Binning & Barrett, 1989). HR tools and systems are then built to measure the construct, cause individual change on the construct, manage performance affected by the construct, or change the organization to better support the construct. Each step of this process involves the development and testing of hypotheses (Guion, 1998).

Many times a manager will decide that a particular construct, such as EI, might be a useful construct for use in HR practices. Whatever the source of the decision (e.g., shrewd marketing, popular publications, peer referral, academic journal), the proposition should be supported by research that tests the specific hypotheses the manager has about the construct. Making decisions based on no data or faulty data can lead to costly decisions (Cascio, 2000). A particular construct may sound good to a manager but in reality have no relationship to job performance. So, using the construct in a HR practice is a waste of resources in the best scenario. A worse case scenario might include a relationship between the construct and ethnic group membership that causes adverse impact, when, for example, the construct is used in a pre-employment selection test (Hunter & Hunter, 1984). Another unsatisfactory outcome might be that the construct is actually related to job performance in the opposite direction to that expected by the manager. In other words, individuals who possess more of the construct perform more poorly on the job than those with less. Thus, arbitrary decisions by managers may lead to unwanted outcomes.

It will be in the decision maker's best interest to think more like a scientist when choosing organizational interventions related to EI. The scientific method suggests that a scientist should begin with a hypothesis to be tested regarding the causes of an observed phenomenon, such as job performance. Then, several of the most plausible explanations for the observed phenomenon should be examined such that the unique contributions of a variable, such as EI, in explaining variability in a phenomenon, such as job performance, can be isolated (Campbell & Stanley, 1963; Klahr & Simon, 1999). In other words, systematic efforts should be taken to understand the unique contributions of EI in affecting job and organizational performance before making large investments in tools or practices that use the EI construct as a foundation. Further, scientists understand that cumulative research that allows for generalizability to multiple contexts should inform practice, as opposed to limited, single studies or specific case studies (Kehoe, 2000). Although many management decisions can be effectively made on limited data and decision-making experience, there are times when a decision maker should think more like a scientist, such as when considering investments in psychological products or services.

The generation of hypotheses is facilitated by theory. Theory provides a systematic organization of informed ideas that lead to predictive hypotheses about the conditional relationship between two or more things (Dubin, 1969). Hypotheses are tested by building measurements of these things in the business world to see if their values predicted by the theory can be confirmed in the business environment. In the next section, I briefly outline one theory of EI that has been proposed. From this theory, I propose a limited set of hypotheses that might be tested and eventually lead to scientifically justified implementations of EI-related interventions in the business world.

A THEORY OF EI

The roots of EI theory are complex and often confused by various authors on the topic, particularly in the popular press. However, most agree that the work of Salovey and Mayer (e.g., Mayer, DiPaolo, & Salovey, 1990; Mayer & Salovey, 1997; Mayer, Salovey, & Caruso, 2000; Salovey & Mayer, 1990) has been among the most influential, particularly in the academic literature. Here I briefly describe the theory of EI these authors have proposed. Tenets from this theory are then used to organize the remainder of this chapter.

The Mayer and Salovey (1997) theory of EI is a four-branch model. They do not treat EI as a unitary construct, but as a construct that can be subdivided into four branches. The four branches of EI include emotional perception and expression, emotional facilitation of thought, emotional understanding, and emotional management. These four theoretical constructs are possible EI constructs that would first need to be operationalized with measures to be used in the business world in translating theory to hypotheses, testing hypotheses through research, and finally implementing interventions based on the research results.

The four branches of EI have been defined by Mayer & Salovey (1997) as sets of abilities that are defined as follows:

Emotional Perception and Expression: The ability to recognize emotion in self and others, focusing both on physical and psychological states. This construct also involves the ability to communicate emotions and feelings accurately and express needs related to emotions.

Emotional Facilitation of Thought: This ability is also referred to as "using EI." The construct includes the ability to appreciate multiple perspectives based on mood changes and to use emotional states to aid in problem solving and creativity. The ability to use EI in redirecting and prioritizing thinking or facilitating judgment and memory is also included in this construct.

Emotional Understanding: The ability to cognitively process emotional information from oneself and others. This includes understanding the complex relationships and transitions among emotions and perceiving causes and effects of emotions.

Emotional Management: This is the ability to control emotions in oneself and others. This includes the ability to be open to all types of feelings and to be able to engage, prolong, or detach an emotional state in oneself or others.

In simpler terms, the four branches of EI might be thought of as emotional communication (input and output), understanding emotion, controlling emotion, and using emotion. Thus, they are not independent constructs but facets of EI that operate in a relatively sequential pattern. Defined as such, emotion can be thought of as just a special type of information (note that one can simply substitute the word *information* for *emotion* and not lose the concept) that is common to the human experience. EI then, has to do with the effective or ineffective intake, processing, output, and use of this information. Mayer, Caruso, and Salovey (1999) have argued that this is how and why EI meets standards for a traditional intelligence. It is also how their definition of EI differs from others that tend to associate EI with a cluster of personality traits (e.g., Bar-On, 1997; Goleman, 1998).

HYPOTHESES ABOUT EI AND JOB PERFORMANCE

Given this theoretical definition of EI, how might EI be related to performance in the business world? Below I provide some possible hypotheses (H_a), though not to be confused with research outcomes, for how these constructs might be useful in the business world.

H_1: *EI is positively related to successful performance in jobs or positions that include negative, emotionally charged situations that must be successfully resolved by the incumbent.*

All jobs that involve people interacting with other people (i.e., most jobs) will, at least occasionally, include emotionally charged situations where negative emotions (e.g., anger, fear, sadness, hurt, frustration) are displayed or involved in some way. However, there will be jobs in which strong emotionally charged situations involving negative emotions will have greater impacts on job performance. These jobs will likely require high levels of at least three of the four branches of EI: perception/expression, understanding, and managing. Job families that might be more likely to include negative emotionally charged situations with consequences for performance include public safety, customer relations, health care, social services, human resources, legal services, negotiators, clergy, and many others where facets of the jobs might reasonably lead to negative emotions. These job facets would include working in situations that involve threat (both to self or others) or goal impediment, danger, or conflict. Incumbents in jobs with roles that include working with individuals who are faced with real or perceived social or psychological problems also would be faced with many negatively charged emotional situations. Incumbents in jobs with boundary spanning roles, such as a mediator in labor negotiations, are also likely to face many negatively charged situations. It is in these types of situations where EI might be positively related to job performance.

There are likely moderators to this hypothesized relationship. There are jobs where emotionally charged situations occur frequently. There are other jobs where these types of situations are encountered infrequently but have important performance implications. For example, a person working in a call center as a customer relations representative for a firm that sells relatively inexpensive and equally ineffective products might involve frequent emotional-laden complaints from customers that must be handled effectively. An employee in a similar position in a high-end manufacturing firm representing very expensive and high quality products might seldom be faced with emotionally charged calls of this type, but when one does occur, there may be very high dollar implications if it is not handled well. Still, there may be other customer relations jobs where emotionally charged situations are infrequent and do not have significant performance consequences. This example suggests that the relationship of EI with job performance may be moderated by the degree, frequency, and/or consequences of emotionally charged situations.

The frequency and degree of emotionally charged situations, if not considered fully in EI research and application, may have dramatic implications for an organization (see Zapf, 2002, for a review). For example, if a researcher attempts to validate an EI predictor for use in employee selection, yet the base rate of negatively charged situations within a particular job is low (i.e., negatively charged situations are infrequently encountered), it is unlikely that the researcher will be able to show evidence of criterion-related validity. One might then suggest training for these infrequent events as an alternative. However, in the assessment of training needs in organizations, infrequent tasks and the related skills and abilities are often ignored in favor of more general and cross-job needs where training efficiency can be optimized. In an organization where these infrequent, negatively charged situations can have a major financial impact, careful consideration of EI interventions and related research seems warranted.

The duration of emotionally charged situations encountered on the job may also be a potential moderator of the relationship between EI and job performance. Consider the situations faced by a social worker. Social workers are often faced with long-term family assignments where emotionally charged situations are multiple and are likely to extend over long periods of time (e.g., working a case of domestic abuse) and this long term-interaction with clients has been found to be correlated with high levels of burnout (Cordes & Dougherty, 1993). In this situation, EI might have a stronger relationship with job performance than in the case of a customer service representative who deals with short-term, possibly single-episode, emotional situations for each customer.

Indeed, research has identified a hierarchy of emotional labor expectations, where human service professionals report the highest levels of frequency, intensity, and duration of emotional display and expectations for control over emotional expressions (Brotheridge & Grandey, 2002). Customer service workers are lower down in this hierarchy. Thus, frequency, duration, and strength of emotionally charged situations encountered on the job are highly likely to impact the relationship between EI and job performance. Jobs highest in emotional labor expectations are likely to show higher relationships between EI and job performance versus those at the bottom of the hierarchy. Research providing evidence that the level of emotional labor expectation moderates the relationship between EI and job performance would be a significant advancement in understanding how EI might be useful in the business world.

It could be asserted that most managers of people will also be faced with negatively charged emotional situations, at least, on occasion, and there would be associated performance consequences. However, in the hierarchy of emotional labor expectations, managers were found not to be higher than most "people work" jobs (Brotheridge & Grandey, 2002), suggesting that across managers, emotional demands may not be consistently high. Again, this is an area ripe for research as it is quite possible that there is a complex set of conditions under which EI might be more highly related to performance. For example, research would need to determine if the level of employee (e.g., entry-level, hourly labor, professional, managerial) being managed makes a difference in this relationship. Emotional labor expectations are likely to differ by level, as are other factors that may be related to EI, including age, education, and social class. These factors must be accounted for in understanding the relationship between EI and managerial effectiveness. Context-driven motivators of employees will also likely make a difference. For example, employees on a competitive commission pay plan may be more likely to find themselves in situations charged with negative emotions. Managing other employees who themselves are faced with many negatively charged situations may also require the manager to have higher levels of EI than managers managing employees who are not frequently faced with these situations. Managing groups where people problems persist (e.g., interpersonal conflict) may also require higher levels of EI than managing more harmonious groups. So, although it might be tempting to suggest that all managers would be better off with high levels of EI, this broad generalization may not necessarily reap the greatest benefits for organizations. Theoretical models of how and when EI is beneficial to leaders need to be developed and tested through empirical research (e.g., George, 2000).

H₂: EI is positively related to successful performance in jobs or positions that include situations where the generation of positive emotions has substantial performance consequences.

Jobs that involve the generation of positive emotions (e.g., happiness, comfort, optimism, fascination, satisfaction) as a means of reaching positive outcomes for the organization are likely to demonstrate a positive relationship between EI and successful job performance. These jobs will also likely require high levels of at least three of the four branches of EI: perception/expression, understanding, and managing. Job families that might be more likely to include opportunities to stimulate positive emotions with consequences for performance include customer service, sales, recruiters, entertainers, and many others where there is a high degree of contact between people engaged in situations where the generation of positive emotions is related to positive outcomes for the organization. It is in these types of jobs where EI might be positively related to job performance.

It is important to point out that this group of jobs may have a substantial overlap with jobs where negatively charged situations might be frequently encountered. For example, a nurse may encounter many negatively charged situations (e.g., life and death decisions, situations involving pain and suffering) but may also encounter many situations where personal attention in a neutral situation may generate positive attitudes and patient satisfaction, a beneficial outcome for the individual and organization. In other jobs, the primary function of the incumbent may be to generate positive emotions, and he or she may seldom or never encounter negatively charged situations. An entertainer might be one example. Research should be focused on identifying how these job differences affect the relationship between EI and successful job performance.

Sales, recruitment, and marketing jobs are good examples of where the abilities to manipulate and use emotions to the benefit of the organization are a core part of the job. Incumbents in these jobs may be more effective in their attempts to persuade others by playing on their emotions. That is, a sales person may be more effective in pitching a product or service if he or she can tailor the pitch to meet the emotional need of the potential buyer. For example, American Express financial advisors are taught to identify emotions that might best be met with conservative versus aggressive financial products. Once the emotional state is identified (e.g., investment anxiety), a sales approach and set of products is fit to the emotion.

Service-oriented jobs are also likely to include many situations where improving positive emotions can have substantial performance implications for the organization as customer satisfaction improves. For example, the delivery of personal services such as hairstyling might certainly be enhanced if the stylist understands and uses the emotional information presented by the customer (e.g., what occasion is precipitating the need and what emotions are tied to that need). The ability to positively affect emotions in this type of situation is likely to generate repeat business (a benefit for the organization) and improve tipping behavior (a benefit for the individual).

It is important to point out that it is possible that both H_1 and H_2 could be rejected, depending on the criterion of interest. For example, in the retail and fast-food industries, speed of transaction processing is often an important criterion. EI might be strongly related to some aspects of performance (e.g., quality of service) and unrelated to others (e.g., speed of processing). In fact, it is possible that a negative correlation between EI and speed of transaction could be found, as individuals high on EI may take substantially more time in working with customers. This proposition points out the necessity to explicitly consider the criterion of interest in forming hypotheses related to the importance of EI in the business world (Guion, 1998).

H_1 and H_2 together suggest that EI will be important in jobs that involve intense emotions, positive or negative. In both cases, at least three of the four facets of EI described earlier will be important. One must be able to perceive and communicate the emotions, one must be able to understand the emotion, and one must be able to control the emotions. However, the conceptualization and operationalization of HR interventions may need to differ in the testing of the two hypotheses. For example, distinctions would need to be made between recognizing and understanding the causes and impacts of negative emotions versus positive emotions. Likewise, in the case of negative emotions, the goal of a job incumbent might be to simply control emotions in such a way as to restore a neutral state of emotion, whereas an alternative goal might be to increase and maintain positive emotions over a period of time. This has considerable implications for the appropriate behaviors and communication styles required in each case. Accordingly, training programs, for example, designed for jobs with frequent exposure to intense, negative emotional situations may need to differ substantially in content from those aimed at jobs where positive emotions are a more central feature, even though the core facets of EI might be equally important in both cases.

A useful advancement in EI theory that would aid in the testing of workplace hypotheses would be the development of dual taxonomies of skills and behaviors associated with each of the facets of EI. One set of skills and behaviors would be associated with the range of negative emotions likely to be experienced across work settings, whereas a second set would be associated with positive emotions. These taxonomies might then be generated for specific industries, common job elements, or roles.

H_3: EI is positively related to successful performance in jobs or positions that require creative problem solving.

One of the branches of EI, emotional facilitation of thought, includes the ability to appreciate multiple perspectives based on mood changes and the ability to use emotional states to aid in problem solving and creativity and to facilitate judgment and memory. These abilities are likely to lead to successful performance in jobs and roles that require high levels of problem solving and creativity, particularly where the use of multiple perspectives would be beneficial. Job families where these abilities may be related to success might include engineering, architecture, artist, designers, and many others that require unique problem solving and creativity, particularly where the end product generated by using these skills could be seen as more valuable because it generates a desired emotional response. Although little research has been done with this facet of EI, efforts to generate several alternative hypotheses have been undertaken (Zhou & George, 2003).

H_4: EI is positively related to successful performance in organizations/units experiencing high levels of change or in organizations experiencing performance difficulties that may require change to improve performance.

This hypothesis is based at an aggregated level (e.g., organization, unit, function, office, or team) rather than the individual or job level, as was the case with the previous hypotheses. Here the proposition is based on the fact that organizations experiencing a need for change, or are in the process of change, are more likely to generate situations in which employees are faced with negatively charged emotional situations and are more likely to be experiencing high levels of stress and anxiety (Mack, Nelson, & Quick, 1998). Example cases might include a dysfunctional team, an underperforming business unit, an office moving to a new location, or an organization in the midst of a major change in strategy. All of these cases are likely to involve change and uncertainty with associated high levels of stress for the majority, or a large subset, of individuals that may lead to a large number of negatively charged emotional situations.

With the previous hypotheses (H_1, H_2, H_3), the focus of interventions (e.g., selection, development, performance management) would be at the level of the individual. This hypothesis is focused at an aggregated level, where organizational development interventions might be most appropriate. Here, the key will be identifying group-level needs and possible solutions that may, at least in part, employ EI.

Accessing emotions at a group level and understanding, using, and controlling emotions will be the role of change agents and leaders in an organizational development project with large-scale change as the primary objective. Forces of uncertainty and defensiveness that drive emotions will need to be the focus of these efforts (Vince & Broussine, 1996). Clearly, change agents and leaders may benefit from high EI as they fulfill this type of role. Similarly, those employees directly impacted by the changes may be more likely to accept and implement changes if they are already high on EI, as they would be better equipped to deal with their own and others' emotions during times of change.

It is often tempting for managers to use untested solutions in these types of group/organization-level interventions, even when they may never consider doing so for individual-level methods or solutions. However, the effectiveness of solutions at aggregated levels must also be tested through empirical research to ensure that large investments of time and money are not wasted.

I have generated a sample of possible hypotheses using a particular theory of EI. Just this small sample of hypotheses has raised many possible avenues of research that will need to be pursued before success can be ensured in EI implementations. More hypotheses can and should be generated with additional theories of EI and relationships with individual and aggregated organizational outcomes. These hypotheses will then need to be tested with empirical research.

Given these hypotheses, what methods might be used to test them? Theoretical constructs must be measured with operational methods in order to test the hypotheses. To date, this has been a challenge for EI researchers (Davies, Stankov, & Roberts, 1998). In the next section, I discuss possible operationalizations of the EI constructs and how they might be tested and used in the business world. Still, the challenge will remain to validate these methods. The methods I will present have been used, and in most cases validated, for other constructs, but research will still be needed to show the efficacy of these methods with EI as the construct from which inferences will be made about performance or other valued organizational outcomes.

OPERATIONALIZING EI IN THE BUSINESS WORLD

Job Analysis

As noted earlier, any implementation of an EI-related tool in the business world must be preceded by a job analysis to identify the specific job task, duties, or work behaviors that require EI in order to be successfully completed. Methods for identifying emotional components of jobs as they impact tasks, duties, and work behaviors have not yet been adequately tested or implemented widely in organizations, though some approaches have been recommended. Ashforth and Saks (2002) suggested that many traditional approaches to job analysis might be adapted to identify emotional demands. These might include the critical incidents approach, observation, structured interviews, or structured surveys (Gatewood & Field, 2001) that serve to identify elements of the job that place emotional demands on the incumbent.

Another job analysis approach that has been suggested is to identify tasks and work events that trigger emotional reactions that have implications for performance (Arvey, Renz, & Watson, 1998). This might be operationalized by providing subject matter experts (SMEs), such as incumbents or supervisors, with lists of positive and negative emotions that may have implications for successful job performance. Then, the SMEs would describe critical incidents and associated tasks that have led them to feel each of the listed emotions. In addition, these SMEs might be asked to identify how the emotional demands could positively or negatively impact performance. A broader survey might then be developed to validate these emotion–task and emotion–performance links with a larger sample of SMEs.

Recruitment

There are existing methods and tools that may well lend themselves to operationalizing EI constructs in a recruitment context. Realistic job previews (Phillips, 1998; Wanous, 1989) would be a good starting place. It has been shown that at least initial levels of job satisfaction can be increased and turnover reduced when employees are given realistic job previews (Phillips, 1998), which may take the form of printed or electronic publications or video. For jobs that involve frequent and/or strong emotionally charged situations, whether positive or negative, it may be useful to highlight those situations in realistic job previews. This would allow individuals an opportunity to preview, anticipate, and consider the emotional components of the job that they may or may not be able to handle. Given this information, individuals would then have the opportunity to self-select either into or out of the process. Still, this will require individuals to have self-insight regarding their level of EI so as to judge their own ability to deal with the emotional components of the job. Alternatively, a high level of EI might be needed to actually learn something about the job from a realistic job preview and appreciate what it means for one's future. Therefore, specific elements of the situations and the skills and abilities required to handle them may need to be drawn to the attention of the potential applicant viewing the realistic job preview materials. In addition, there may need to be specific descriptions of the emotional elements of the job and how they have affected different individuals, both positively and negatively, over a period of time.

Building on the realistic job preview and self-selection process, another useful recruitment tool might include a self-assessment tool that would allow the candidate to obtain a realistic job preview at the same time that the individual is being provided questions to help him evaluate his own EI (cf., Dineen, Ash, & Noe, 2002). This self-assessment could be followed by feedback to the applicant suggesting how someone with his level of EI might handle the situation. This feedback might also include a probability of success that the applicant might have in dealing with the strong emotional components of the job. This would provide the applicant with additional information for making a self-selection decision before entering the organization's formal selection process and the associated evaluations.

Culture fit tools have received some research support in the past couple of years as potential recruitment tools (Van Vianen, 2000). As noted earlier, some organizations or subunits of organizations may be more likely to produce emotionally charged situations than others. A series of questions might be designed to help a candidate assess his ability to function in and deal with the types of situations that may come up in such an organization. This might include questions regarding the applicant's ability to (a) perceive the start of an emotionally charged situation, (b) communicate her own feelings in that situation, ©) manage emotions in that situation, or (d) manipulate emotions to overcome the situation. Again, feedback would be designed to help the applicant self-select in or out of the selection process during the recruitment phase, a process that is likely to benefit both the individual and the organization.

Selection and Promotion

There are several selection methods that might be considered in operationalizing EI. These methods include job tryout, simulations, situational judgment tests, situational and behavioral interviews, or paper and pencil assessments. These methods can range from having very high fidelity with the tasks and emotional demands of the job to having a low direct relationship to specific job tasks but having a high level of congruence with the definition of the theoretical construct. The primary objective of operationalizing EI would be the conversion of the EI theoretical constructs hypothesized to be related to the emotional demands of the job, which have performance implications, into selection tests (Binning & Barrett, 1989).

High fidelity selection devices are those that very closely match the content of the job. In this case, the high fidelity device would also have to closely resemble the emotional demands of the job. Putting an applicant into the role of an incumbent in a simulation involving actual job tasks and emotionally charged situations and then scoring the applicant's performance is an example of a high fidelity measure.

A scoring system could be developed for this high fidelity device in order to predict future performance of applicants. A possible scoring system might be a series of rating scales anchored by poor through exemplar behaviors that an applicant might demonstrate related to (a) perception and communication of emotions, (b) understanding the emotions of the situation, and (c) managing the emotions (own and others) of the situation. This last step would operationalize the theoretical constructs of EI. Other job-related constructs might also be rated during the simulation (e.g., personality constructs such as extroversion and conscientiousness). Research would then need to be conducted to show that the EI constructs add to the prediction of successful performance on the job above and beyond the other construct measures.

Lower fidelity measures might include situational and behavioral interviews or situational judgment tests used to predict future performance. With these types of measures, applicants are not put into actual situations, but job-related situations might be described to the applicant in verbal form in an interview or in printed form in a situational judgment test (Motowidlo, Dunnette, & Carter, 1990). The applicant would then have to describe what they might do in the situation in an interview format or select from a number of possible responses in a situational judgment test. In the interview format, questions could be developed that elicit responses related to how the applicant would perceive or communicate feelings, or how well the applicant understands emotions possible from all involved in the situations, or how to manage emotions of self and others in the situations. Behavioral anchored scoring scales (Bernardin & Smith, 1981) could be developed to assess the quality of the responses, which, in turn, would need to be shown to predict future performance.

The decision to choose one selection device over another should be based on research. Whether the measure chosen is high or low fidelity depends on a number of factors, including available resources for research and development of the tool, personnel available to administer the tools, and size of applicant pool. However, the ultimate decision on what measures to use in a selection system should include the consideration of the validity of the measure in terms of its representation of the content of the job, the adequacy of the representation of the theoretical EI constructs being measured, the ability to predict future job performance, and the incremental predictive usefulness of the EI measure above and beyond other constructs measured (Guion, 1998). A challenge that will face researchers is isolating the exact role, if any, of EI in either high or low fidelity simulations. That is, simulation outcomes are likely to be affected by a range of variables, and it may be difficult to show that EI had a significant role in determining performance in a particular simulation. Finally, a consideration of group differences (e.g., sex, race, age) on the measure should be considered in order to avoid legal challenges. All of these issues can and should be supported by research before a particular EI selection tool is used in a selection system.

Selection tools appear to be the major target of many of the consulting and product firms promoting EI-related products. Consistent with hypotheses I outlined earlier, most of the EI selection tools focus on sales, customer service, recruiters, and similar jobs. In addition, many of these firms emphasize the importance of EI in distinguishing top leaders from average to poor leaders. While the published research for selection tools used for these types of jobs is scarce, and the types of EI constructs cover a spectrum from personality-related clusters to ability-based constructs, the emerging uses and claims of success are concentrated in a few areas. Reports of EI being related to job performance are described for military recruiters, collections agents, consulting firm partners, insurance sales, cosmetics sales, computer sales representatives, and financial advisors. The examples of leadership benefits of EI cut across several industries. The general message is that leaders high on EI or related constructs perform better than those that score lower. Because most of these reports are not supported by published data, they should be considered as good initial input for forming and testing hypotheses through empirical research.

There are three major EI tests that appear to capture the largest part of the EI selection test market. These include the Mayer-Salovey-Caruso Emotional Intelligence Test (MSCEIT; Mayer, Salovey, Caruso, & Sitarenios, 2003), the Bar-On Emotional Quotient Inventory (EQ-I; Bar-On, 1997), and the Emotional Competence Inventory (ECI; Boyatzis, Goleman, & Hay/McBer, 1999). While each of the instruments has received research attention, each differs significantly in the test methods used, underlying theory and constructs, and the associated test scales. Organizations interested in using these tests should carefully examine the supporting research evidence that would support selection decisions for specific jobs and conduct internal research to test predictor-criterion hypotheses whenever possible.

Training and Development

Training and development interventions and outcomes associated with them can be divided into three categories: cognitive (e.g., knowledge of rules, facts, and principles), skill-based (technical, motor, customer relations), and affective (attitudes, beliefs, predispositions; Kraiger, Ford, & Salas, 1993). Each of these categories offers possibilities for training and development on the construct of EI.

A cognitive-based approach to training might include teaching specific rules to aid in development of, for example, the emotional understanding construct of EI. To better process information cognitively about emotions, a set of rules might be taught to individuals that describe the complex relationships and transitions among emotions and the causes and effects of emotions. Once trainees have an understanding of these rules, principles, and guidelines about emotions, they will need to practice applying them. Work-related practice simulations could be developed in which trainees practice and learn to decipher the emotions of self and others, thereby helping to ensure transfer of learning to situations in the workplace.

A skill-based training program might be developed for the emotional management construct. This type of training might be facilitated by a behavior-modeling approach (Baldwin, 1992; May & Kahnwieler, 2000; Pesuric & Byham, 1996). With this technique, the skills to be learned would be introduced, followed by a "model" performing various emotional management techniques that are appropriate in a variety of workplace contexts. This might include, for example, encounters with customers displaying a number of different behaviors commonly encountered on the job. The trainees then discuss how the learning points were displayed by the model. A series of practice and feedback sessions would then be held among the trainees, with each having multiple opportunities to be engaged in situations and both give and receive feedback related to the learning points.

An affective-based training program has the goal of changing attitudes, beliefs, and predispositions. A new employee socialization program might be an example of where EI-based interventions could aid in the socialization of employees to a particular organization, unit, or team in which job incumbents must perform. This might include an orientation to the variety of emotions and the situations in which they are likely to be experienced by the incumbents, both in working with other internal employees and with external stakeholders. The EI constructs would need to be operationalized in this type of training to aid the new employees in their understanding of the emotional environment in which they will be working.

This type of socialization process might be facilitated by an EI coaching or mentoring program (Greenberg, 2002). That is, new employees would be assigned an internal coach or mentor who has been trained to assist others in changing their levels of EI on each of the four branches. This person might purposefully expose the incumbent to several different emotionally charged situations and assist him in navigating his way through it. These situations would be followed by coaching sessions including discussion on how to perceive and communicate emotions successfully in the situation, use emotions to successfully resolve the situation, and control emotions to keep the situation in control. The objective of the socialization program would be to both raise the level of EI for new employees and provide a safety net in a mentor or coach to steer the newcomer through some emotionally rough terrain.

There are many reports of the success of EI training programs used in organizations. Again, the vast majority of these are anecdotal, and the definitions and operationalizations of EI vary widely. On the other hand, many of the EI training programs appear to be fairly traditional interpersonal training sessions, including stress management, anger management, conflict resolution, interpersonal skills, creative thinking, diversity, and human relations. In general, interpersonal training has been shown to be successful in organizations when evaluated against several outcome criteria (Arthur, Bennett, Edens, & Bell, 2003). Many of the EI training programs appear to be traditional interpersonal training programs with a different promotional spin. As such, one might expect these re-packaged programs to be generally successful.

Perhaps the most frequently reported training success using EI constructs is from the American Express financial advisor case described earlier. They implemented an EI training program with financial advisors and managers of financial advisors. This training focused on recognition and control of emotions in the consulting and sales of financial products. EI training has also been reported by various consulting firms to have been delivered in organizations such as AT&T, Pfizer, Deluxe, Franklin Templeton Investments, the U.S. Army and Navy, Nextel, Oracle, Johnson & Johnson, United Auto Workers, and Xerox PARC. EI training programs promoted by various firms tend to focus most on building awareness of emotions and how to manage them more effectively. However, there is a large need for further research in this area to identify effective operationalizations of EI, optimal delivery methods, and the utility of such efforts. To date, there is little research to support large-scale implementations of EI training programs unless they can be linked to more traditional interpersonal training programs where research evidence has been generated in support of the effectiveness of the program.

Organizational Development

Organizational change focuses on organizational characteristics rather than individual-level variables, as discussed up to this point (Lawson & Shen, 1998). In determining how to use EI in the context of organizational change, a review of organizational variables that might be changed to affect the emotional demands faced by individuals in the organization is required. Accordingly, organizational analysis of emotional demands would be the required starting point for organizational change, just as job analysis is the starting point for the implementation of individual-level interventions. However, there are no established practices for identifying organizational characteristics associated with emotional demands, leaving an area overripe for immediate method development and research.

There are at least two dimensions on which organization-level emotional demands can be considered. The first is a structural dimension, whereas the second is a transitory dimension. The structural elements of an organization that may contain emotional demands include job, team, group, and function. Also included in the structural dimension are elements such as work processes, market space occupied, customer base, and other relatively fixed characteristics of an organization. The transitory dimension considers elements of an organization that are more fluid in nature. Nearly all organizations have elements that are in a relatively constant state of change. A good example involves the technology components of an organization, where updates to technology such as computers and software involve a nearly never-ending race to stay up to date. Other transitory elements include any change effort, such as the introduction of new strategies, objectives, markets, products, or strategic alliances. Changes in leadership or key talent are also included in this dimension. The structural and transitory dimensions are but two rather obvious organizational characteristics for classifying and identifying emotional demands—certainly extended theory and research in this area will create more.

The structural and transitory components of the organization might next be considered in forming hypotheses about how organizational change interventions might affect the emotional demands of the organization. In the structural domain, jobs or work processes that are highly likely to evoke emotionally charged situations may need to be restructured to either reduce the emotional demands or provide safety nets for those incumbents frequently exposed to them. Similarly, in the transitory domain, changes to the products or market to be served by an organization may result in a substantial change to the emotional demands in an organization. There may be both internal situations to consider, such as how work teams will function together to service the new product or market, and external situations to consider, such as how the new customer base will change the emotional context of the sales or service situations. Organizational development interventions, just like individual-based interventions, require the theory, generation of hypotheses, and research to support the hypotheses.

THE STATE OF EI IN THE BUSINESS WORLD

EI appears to have a strong following in the business world. Judging from firms present at professional conferences and/or advertising on the Internet, it appears that there are hundreds of companies selling EI products and services to hundreds of organizations, big and small. For example, a Google search of "emotional intelligence training" turns up close to one million hits. Many of the providers of these products and services boast impressive lists of clients. However, some of this bandwagon jumping may be illusory. First, many of the firms selling EI are distributors of others' products. So, the absolute number of unique offerings is more limited than it first appears. Second, client lists typically don't distinguish as to whether the client is using an EI product or service or some other product or service offered by the firm. Third, firms who boast about relationships with huge clients often have highly limited engagements with very small parts of the much larger organization. This can make any Internet company with a couple of employees look like a major player in the market. Fourth, it is unclear how many of the EI products and services are simply repackaged offerings that may have little fidelity with current EI theory. Finally, as noted earlier, corporate legends are easily promulgated today through efficient electronic media. So, it is clear that EI has a strong presence in the HR products and services market, but it unclear as to the true size of the EI community though it at least *appears* to be large.

This situation could have unknown consequences for organizations quick to adopt EI interventions, because of the lack of research support for the sometimes substantial claims about EI products and services that are offered to organizations. Part of the problem in the dissemination of solid EI research is the fact that most of the research being conducted is done by consulting firms for corporate clients. These firms do not have strong incentives to carry out studies that might lead to questions about the value of their services, nor do they have incentives to share research that they believe provides them with competitive advantage. This means that organizations may need to produce their own research in supporting the use of EI rather than generalizing from research done in other organizations. The inclusion of academic partners in these efforts is likely to benefit the organization, as these partners can provide an unbiased, scientific perspective. Academics also have the incentives to move the research beyond single organizations and to disseminate results in ways that protect organizations from disclosing competitive secrets. This is also how the state of EI can mature beyond its infancy.

REFERENCES

Arthur, W., Jr., Bennett, W., Jr., Edens, P. S., & Bell, S. T. (2003). Effectiveness of training in organizations: A meta-analysis of design and evaluation features. *Journal of Applied Psychology, 88*, 234–245.

Arvey, R. D., Renz, G. L., & Watson, W. W. (1998). Emotionality and job performance: Implications for personnel selection. *Research in Personnel and Human Resource Management, 16*, 103–147.

Ashforth, B. E., & Saks, A. M. (2002). Feeling your way: Emotions and organizational entry. In R. G. Lord, R. J. Klimoski, & R. Kanfer (Eds.), *Emotions in the workplace* (pp. 331–369). San Francisco: Jossey-Bass.

Baldwin, T. T. (1992). Effects of alternative modeling strategies on outcomes of interpersonal-skills training. *Journal of Applied Psychology, 77*, 147–154.

Bar-On, R. (1997). *Bar-On Emotional Quotient Inventory: A measure of emotional intelligence.* Toronto, ON: Multi-Health Systems.

Bernardin, H. J., & Smith, P. C. (1981). A clarification of some issues regarding the development and use of behaviorally anchored rating scales (BARS). *Journal of Applied Psychology, 66*, 458–463.

Binning, J. F., & Barrett, G. V. (1989). Validity of personnel decisions: A conceptual analysis of the inferential and evidential bases. *Journal of Applied Psychology, 74*, 478–494.

Boyatzis, R. E., Goleman, D., & Hay/McBer. (1999). *Emotional Competence Inventory.* Boston: Hay/McBer Group.

Brotheridge, C. M., & Grandey, A. A. (2002). Emotional labor and burnout: Comparing two perspectives of "people work." *Journal of Vocational Behavior, 60*, 17–39.

Campbell, D. T., & Stanley, J. C. (1963). *Experimental and quasi-experimental designs for research.* Chicago: Rand McNally.

Cascio, W. F. (2000). *Costing human resources: The financial impact of behavior in organizations* (4th ed). Cincinnati, OH: Southwestern.

Cherniss, C. (2000). Social and emotional competence in the workplace. In R. Bar-On & J. Parker (Eds.). *The handbook of emotional intelligence: Theory, development, assessment, and application at home, school, and in the workplace* (pp. 433–458). San Francisco: Jossey-Bass.

Cordes, C. L., & Dougherty, T. W. (1993). A review and integration of research on job burnout. *Academy of Management Review, 18*, 621–656.

Davies, M., Stankov, L., & Roberts, R. D. (1998). Emotional intelligence: In search of an elusive construct. *Journal of Personality and Social Psychology, 75*, 989–1015.

Dineen, B. R., Ash, S. R., & Noe, R. A. (2002). A web of applicant attraction: Person-organization fit in the context of web-based recruitment. *Journal of Applied Psychology. 87*, 723–734.

Dubin, R. (1969). *Theory building.* New York: The Free Press.

Dulewicz, V., & Higgs, M. (2004). Can emotional intelligence be developed? *International Journal of Human Resource Management, 15*, 95–111.

Gatewood, R. D., & Field, H. S. (2001). *Human resource selection* (5th ed.). New York: Harcourt.

George, J. M. (2000). Emotions and leadership: The role of emotional intelligence. *Human Relations, 53*, 1027–1055.

Goleman, D. (1998). *Working with emotional intelligence*. New York: Bantam Books.

Greenberg, J. (2002). *Managing behavior in organizations* (3rd ed.). Upper Saddle River, NJ: Prentice Hall.

Guion, R. M. (1998). *Assessment, measurement, and prediction for personnel decisions*. Mahwah, NJ: Lawrence Erlbaum Associates.

Hunter, J. E., & Hunter, R. F. (1984). Validity and utility of alternative predictors of job performance. *Psychological Bulletin, 96*, 72–98.

Kehoe, J. F. (2000). Research and practice in selection. In J. F. Kehoe (Ed.), *Managing selection in changing organizations* (pp. 397–437). San Francisco: Jossey-Bass.

Klahr, D., & Simon, H. A. (1999). Studies of scientific discovery: Complementary approaches and convergent findings. *Psychological Bulletin, 125*, 524–543.

Kraiger, K., Ford, J. K., & Salas, E. (1993). Application of cognitive, skill-based, and affective theories of learning outcomes to new methods of training evaluation. *Journal of Applied Psychology, 78*, 311–328.

Lawson, R. B., & Shen, Z. (1998). *Organizational psychology*. New York: Oxford University Press.

Mack, D. A., Nelson, D. L., Quick, J. C. (1998). The stress of organisational change: A dynamic process model. *Applied Psychology: An International Review, 47*, 219–232.

May, G. L., & Kahnwieler, W. M. (2000). The effect of mastery practice design on learning and transfer behavior in behavior modeling training. *Personnel Psychology, 53*, 353–374.

Mayer, J. D., Caruso, D. R., & Salovey, P. (1999). Emotional intelligence meets standards for a traditional intelligence. *Intelligence, 27*, 267–298.

Mayer, J. D., DiPaolo, M. T., & Salovey, P. (1990). Perceiving affective content in ambiguous visual stimuli: A component of emotional intelligence. *Journal of Personality Assessment, 54*, 772–781.

Mayer, J. D., & Salovey, P. (1997). What is emotional intelligence? In P. Salovey & D. Sluyter (Eds.), *Emotional development and emotional intelligence: Implications for educators* (pp. 3–31). New York: Basic Books.

Mayer, J. D., Salovey, P., & Caruso, D. (2000). Models of emotional intelligence. In R. J. Sternberg (Ed.), *The handbook of intelligence* (2nd ed., pp. 396–420). New York: Cambridge University Press.

Mayer, J. D., Salovey, P., Caruso, D. R., & Sitarenios, G. (2003). Measuring emotional intelligence with the MSCEIT V2.0. *Emotion, 3*, 97–105.

Motowidlo, S. J., Dunnette, M. D., & Carter, G. W. (1990). An alternative selection procedure: The low-fidelity simulation. *Journal of Applied Psychology, 75*, 640–647.

O'Connor, R. M. & Little, I. S. (2003). Revisiting the predictive validity of emotional intelligence: Self-report versus ability-based measures. *Personality and Individual Differences, 35*, 1893–1902.

Pesuric, A., & Byham, W. (1996, July). The new look in behavioral modeling. *Training and Development*, 25–33.

Phillips, J. M. (1998). Effects of realistic job previews on multiple organizational outcomes: A meta-analysis. *Academy of Management Journal, 41*, 673–690.

Salovey, P., & Mayer, J. D. (1990). Emotional intelligence. *Imagination, Cognition, and Personality, 9*, 185–211.

Schwartz, T. (2000, June). How do you feel? *Fast Company, 35*, 296–300.

Van Vianen, A. E. M. (2000). Person-organization fit: The match between new-comers' and recruiters' preferences for organizational cultures. *Personnel Psychology, 53,* 113–149.

Vince, R., & Broussine, M. (1996). Paradox, defense and attachment: Assessing and working with emotions and relations underlying organizational change. *Organizational Studies, 17,* 1–21.

Wanous, J. P. (1989). Installing a realistic job preview: Ten tough choices. *Personnel Psychology, 42,* 117–134.

Zapf, D. (2002). Emotion work and psychological well-being: A review of the literature and some conceptual considerations. *Human Resource Management Review, 12,* 237–268.

Zhou, J., & George, J. M. (2003). Awakening employee creativity: The role of leader emotional intelligence. *Leadership Quarterly, 14,* 545–568.

10

Multiplying Intelligences: Are General, Emotional, and Practical Intelligences Equal?

David L. Van Rooy
Burger King Corporation, Miami, FL

Stephan Dilchert
University of Minnesota

Chockalingam Viswesvaran
Florida International University

Deniz S. Ones
University of Minnesota

A wide range of measures have been used to help make decisions in personnel selection, and an extensive research base exists on the criterion-related validity of these measures (Guion, 1998; Schmidt & Hunter, 1998). Across different jobs, general mental ability (GMA) has been found to be the best predictor of overall performance and task performance (Hunter & Hunter, 1984; Schmidt & Hunter, 1998). Even if organizations value additional criteria, the prediction of task performance is central to personnel selection. In a fast-changing competitive environment, organizations will generally strive to select individuals high on intelligence in an attempt to maximize performance.

On the downside, selecting individuals based on GMA often results in adverse impact for minority groups (Hartigan & Wigdor, 1989) and can lead to costly litigation for organizations in the United States. Furthermore, there is the competing demand for a diverse workforce as an advantage in a multicultural society and global economy. These two conflicting demands (the need to hire individuals high on general cognitive ability and to obtain a diverse workforce) have contributed to interest in the development of measures of alternate or multiple intelligences (see Viswesvaran, Ones, & Dilchert, 2005). In this chapter, we discuss the three intelligences that have received the most attention in the personnel selection arena. The "Big 3" intelligences consist of general, emotional, and practical intelligence. In this chapter, we provide an overview of each of these and discuss the main merits of each. We conclude by relating the three intelligences together and discuss if there is a "best" intelligence to rely on in personnel selection.

GENERAL MENTAL ABILITY

Definition and History

Cognitive abilities have been researched for over 150 years (Wilhelm & Engle, 2004). *Cognitive ability, intelligence, GMA,* and *g,* are some of the terms used to refer to the general information processing ability on which individuals differ (see Viswesvaran & Ones, 2002). Jensen (1980) provides a tour de force describing the use of GMA in selection settings and summarizes several definitions of GMA. GMA has been defined as the power of combination, the power to think abstractly, the ability to adapt to one's environment, and so forth. Early researchers such as Galton equated intelligence with sensory acuteness (see Murphy & Davidshofer, 1998) and several studies used measures of reaction time to assess GMA. With the advent of the 20th century, and starting with the works of Binet and Wechsler, GMA has been assessed to a greater extent with holistic tasks differing in difficulty and the extent of information processing required.

The early focus of the research on GMA was more structural and descriptive in that researchers attempted to clarify the content domain of GMA. Spearman (1904, 1927) argued for the primacy of a general factor based on the positive manifold of correlations across several postulated factors. Thurstone (1938) and Guilford (1956) argued for several distinct intelligences but were unable to explain the positive manifold of correlations across the "distinct" intelligences. Carroll (1993), in an encyclopedic accumulation of factor-analytic studies, surmised the presence of a general factor with several other distinct subfactors subsumed under it. This general factor is the focus of this section of our chapter.

GMA has been related to several important life outcomes (Brand, 1987). The general factor has been positively related to health, fitness, occupational income, and creativity, and negatively related to accidents, delinquency, and racial prejudice. The predictive power of this general factor has been demonstrated in so many empirical studies, and for such a broad range of criteria, that it will not be possible to summarize all of them in just one chapter. In fact, several meta-analyses have been published on the different criteria that GMA predicts, and it would be a formidable task to even summarize all of these meta-analyses. As such, in this chapter we will focus on the meta-analyses that have emphasized the predictive validity of GMA in academic and occupational settings (even here, our review will necessarily be selective, though hopefully representative).

Predictive Validity of GMA

Ghiselli (1966, 1973) was perhaps the first researcher to cumulate the validity coefficients for GMA tests, although he did not account for the biasing effects of unreliability and range restriction in the measures, which resulted in a downward bias in the estimated validities. Starting in the mid-1970s, researchers made amends for this oversight when cumulating validities. Schmidt, Hunter, Pearlman, and Shane (1979) found validities ranging from .43 to .78 for several jobs, including supervisors, clerks, and mechanics. Lilienthal and Pearlman (1980) reported substantial validities for health aid workers. Hunter and Hunter (1984), cumulating results from over 400 studies, found GMA to be the single best predictor across several jobs. Hunter (1986), based on data from over 82,000 military personnel, found GMA to be the best predictor of several criteria, a finding corroborated in subsequent large-scale studies using military samples (Project A; Campbell, McHenry, & Wise, 1990). Others have also reported similar findings with military samples (e.g., Ree, Earles, & Teachout, 1994).

Additional notable meta-analyses that have found strong evidence for the predictive power of GMA include Schmidt, Gast-Rosenberg, and Hunter (1980), Callendar and Osburn (1981), Hartigan and Wigdor (1989), and Levine, Spector, Menon, Narayanan, and Cannon-Bowers (1996). For example, Levine et al. meta-analyzed the criterion-related validities of GMA for craft jobs in a utility industry and found an operational validity of .47 for job performance ratings (after corrections) and a validity of .62 for training success. Operational va-

lidity refers to the power of a test to predict a perfectly reliable criterion. Schmidt et al. (1980) found operational validities of .43 to .73
for computer programmers (operational validity refers to the criterion-related validity of a test to predict a perfectly reliable criterion).
Hirsh, Northrop, and Schmidt (1986) found substantial validities for
GMA for predicting police performance. The predictive power of GMA
has been replicated in samples from different cultures as well. For example, Salgado et al. (2003) found substantial support for the validity
of GMA in European samples. Thus, the evidence for the predictive validity of GMA in organizational settings is so overwhelming that Reeve
and Hakel (2002) aptly summarized the conclusion that if there is one
piece of information that organizations need to know about
employees, it should be their level of GMA.

GMA has also been found to be predictive of performance in academic settings. Linn (1982) report a validity of .49 for GMA measures
in predicting success in law schools. Similar positive results are reported in Linn's (1982) meta-analysis for university students, based
on a sample of more than 1,400,000 people. Kuncel, Hezzlett, and
Ones (2001), in a comprehensive meta-analysis of different criteria of
academic success, found that several thousand validities of GMA
measures have been reported and that cumulating across these studies reveals a robust relationship between GMA and academic performance. In fact, Brand (1987) stated "GMA is to psychology what
carbon is to chemistry" (p. 257). In the 21st century, GMA continues
to be the holy grail of prediction (Ree & Carretta, 2002).

Group Differences and Malleability to Interventions

Although GMA has been found to be the best predictor of job performance in many jobs, exclusive reliance on GMA scores for personnel
selection can result in adverse impact for minority groups. Adverse
impact is legally established in the United States when the selection
rate for the minority group is less than four fifths of the selection ratio
for the majority group. Adverse impact is likely to happen (although
not necessarily; see Sackett & Roth, 1996, for factors other than
group differences that could affect adverse impact) when there are
substantial group mean differences in the predictor scores. Cumulative research has shown substantial differences in GMA test scores
between ethnic groups (Jensen, 1980; Roth, Bevier, Bobko, Switzer, &
Tyler, 2001). This results in a situation where members of low scoring
groups have less of a chance of being selected for jobs or admitted to
their educational program of choice if GMA is used in selection decisions. When this situation becomes pervasive, complaints about bias
and unfairness are likely to be raised.

Bias is a statistical concept denoting systematic over- or under-prediction of scores based on group membership. Bias in predicting a criterion with test scores can be assessed with the Cleary Regression Model (Cleary, 1968), and biased tests can subsequently be adjusted (although the Civil Rights Act of 1991 forbids the use of several types of score adjustments) or removed from use in selection decisions. Similarly, expert panels can be used to judge items for cultural fairness (i.e., the correct response to the item does not depend on experiences unique to a particular cultural group), although this type of expert judgment does not necessarily lead to reductions in test score differences. The issue becomes more intractable when the tests are not biased or culturally loaded but group differences are still sufficiently large to lead to adverse impact, as in the case of GMA predicting job and academic performance. In this scenario, the use of GMA for making selection decisions becomes unpalatable to some. Murphy (2002) describes the previously described situation as a trade-off between equity and efficiency with equity calling for the deemphasis of GMA test scores and efficiency warranting the use of GMA test scores in selection decisions (note, however, that the focus here is on *group, not individual*, equity, where groups are based on race and ethnicity).

The problem with group differences becomes more complicated when the issue of heritability is considered. Like most abilities and personality characteristics, GMA has been found to have a strong heritability component; adult heritability estimates for GMA are typically in the range of .50 to .70. There is also the implication that interventions to change GMA are less fruitful (Jensen, 1980) than interventions to develop specific skills. To some (e.g., Herrenstein & Murray, 1994; see also Matthews, Zeidner, & Roberts, 2002) this signals a society stratified by GMA that is substantially determined at birth—a view that apparently denies the indomitable spirit of humans to strive for continuous improvement and be successful in any endeavor.

Thus, although GMA has been found to be the best predictor in academic and organizational settings (Schmidt & Hunter, 1998), it has also generated controversy in its use. One potential issue is the group differences found in mean scores on GMA, especially across different ethnic groups. Although knowing that there are group differences does not mean that we know the cause of the differences (Reeve & Hakel, 2002), these differences typically lead to adverse impact against the low scoring groups when selection decisions are made based on GMA scores. This adverse impact, coupled with large estimates of heritability for GMA, has led some researchers to search for alternate intelligences such as emotional intelligence and practical intelligence. We review the literature on these two proposed constructs next.

EMOTIONAL INTELLIGENCE

Emotional intelligence (EI; Bar-On, 1997; Goleman, 1995; Salovey & Mayer, 1990) has gained both prominence and notoriety because of claims regarding its potential utility in organizational settings. It has received a great deal of attention and has frequently been touted as an emerging construct with great predictive power (e.g., Bar-On, 2000; Brackett, Mayer, & Warner, 2004; Goleman, 1998). Others have not been as supportive of the emotional intelligence construct (e.g., Conte, 2004; Davies, Stankov, & Roberts, 1998; Landy, 2004; Locke, 2004; Petrides & Furnham, 2000, 2001) and have asserted that it adds little incremental validity over existing constructs. Most notably, opponents argue that EI consists entirely of a combination of established personality factors and general intelligence (Schulte, Ree, & Carretta, 2004), which accounts for nearly all of the variance in emotional intelligence across individuals, suggesting that EI is not a new or distinct construct. Disagreement about the viability and utility of EI has been further compounded by the fact that multiple models of EI have been proposed.

Ability Versus Trait Models of EI

Emotional intelligence is typically bifurcated into distinct conceptualizations of the construct. The first of these conceptualizations, which is classified as the ability-based model, was popularized by Salovey and Mayer (1990; Mayer, Caruso, & Salovey, 1999). The ability-based model postulates that EI should be considered a type of intelligence and as such, it should be moderately related to cognitive ability. Meta-analytic findings report a correlation of .33 between the two constructs to indicate support for this requirement (Van Rooy & Viswesvaran, 2004). Mayer and his colleagues (1999) assert that two other conditions must be met in order for a construct to be classified as a type of intelligence: It should be capable of being operationalized as a set of abilities, and it should show developmental effects with age. It should also be noted that another criterion, relative independence from personality traits (see Ackerman & Heggestad, 1997), is often stated as an additional requirement (Matthews, Zeidner, & Roberts, 2002). Mayer et al. (1999) claim to have found evidence that EI conforms to these criteria, but there is disagreement regarding these findings (e.g., Matthews et al., 2002; Roberts, Zeidner, & Matthews, 2001). For instance, inferences on the development of EI have been predominantly based on comparisons of cross-sectional age cohorts, which only suggest age differences and not necessarily development differences. The scoring methods of ability-based EI measures have also been recognized as a key concern. These measures can be scored using multiple formats including expert and consensus derived response keys (see chap. 3, this volume, for a review).

The second main model of EI has been commonly referred to as a mixed model. More recently, measures based on the mixed model have been classified as trait-based (Petrides & Furnham, 2001). In addition to incorporating components of the ability model, trait-based models include other noncognitive aspects such as personality, motivation, empathy, and well-being. The trait model is broad enough that it could be described as a conglomeration of various constructs and has even been said to measure everything but GMA (Matthews et al., 2002). Nonetheless, the distinctiveness of the mixed-model EI to cognitive ability was demonstrated in the meta-analysis by Van Rooy and Viswesvaran (2004), who reported a correlation of only .09 between the two constructs. An updated meta-analysis incorporating nearly three times as many studies found a slightly higher correlation of .13 (Van Rooy, Viswesvaran, & Pluta, 2005). The chief concern with trait-based measures is the significant overlap with personality, indicating a lack of uniqueness for the construct.

Both models of EI could prove useful in selection settings. On the one hand, because of the moderate correlation between measures of EI and GMA, ability-based EI measures might have value in selection settings if no group differences are found. On the other hand, trait models, which exhibit very little overlap with traditional intelligence, may have a broad appeal in selection contexts in the search for alternate predictors that could potentially supplement cognitive ability as an assessment tool (Schmidt & Hunter, 1998). If trait-based measures continue to show high intercorrelations with the Big Five personality factors, EI could be given consideration as a compound personality variable, some of which have been shown to have respectable predictive validities (e.g., integrity; Ones, Viswesvaran, & Schmidt, 1993). Given that both models have differential relationships with personality and GMA, it is important to examine if similar performance outcomes are predicted by measures of the two EI models. Even if predictive validities are equivalent, the same individuals will not necessarily be selected. In other words, alternate predictors with equal validity may be considered, but equal validity does not necessarily result in the same workforce characteristics (Kehoe, 2002). It is important to keep this in mind as we discuss the predictive power of the two models of EI.

Predictive Validity of EI in Academic Settings

In academic settings, EI has not consistently emerged as a valid predictor of success. Parker et al. (2004) administered the trait-based

Bar-On EQ-I: YV to high school students and measured year-end grade point average (GPA). Across 667 students, the total EQ-I score correlated .33 with GPA. In a similar study with 372 students, EI significantly predicted first-year college GPA but was negatively related to cumulative high school GPA (Parker, Summerfeldt, Hogan, & Majeski, 2004). Newsome, Day, and Catano (2000) also administered the EQ-I and measured GPA. Newsome and colleagues had intended to control for GMA (which did significantly predict GPA) and personality, but determined that those analyses were unwarranted based on the trivial correlation between EI and academic performance. This is unfortunate, as the correlation between predictors is only one factor that influences the incremental validity of a measure.

Petrides, Frederickson, and Furnham (2004) found that trait-based EI was differentially related to academic performance, which could help explain the lack of an effect in the previously described studies for overall GPA. More specifically, EI was related to verbal, but not to math and science, performance. This indicates that EI may be important for more specific academic outcomes and not overall performance (e.g., GPA). In a direct comparison, O'Connor and Little (2003) administered a trait (EQ-I) and an ability measure (MSCEIT) of EI to students and also assessed GMA, personality, and academic performance. Interestingly, despite the fact that the EI measures displayed the expected correlations with personality (i.e., higher correlation of trait-based measures) and GMA (i.e., higher correlation of ability-based measures), it was the trait measure that was more predictive of academic performance (.23 vs. .08). Still, GMA was more predictive of academic performance than either of the EI measures. Unfortunately, analyses were not conducted to see if EI provided incremental validity over GMA and personality. Brackett and Mayer (2003) found conflicting results in a similar study where EI was again assessed using measures based on each model. In their study, results were reversed, and the ability-based MSCEIT measure emerged as a better predictor than either of the trait measures. However, the correlation was only .16 for the ability measure, and GMA again emerged as the best predictor of academic performance. No measure significantly predicted academic performance once GMA was partialled out. This parallels the findings of Barchard (2003) who found that multiple measures of EI (trait- and ability-based) did not show incremental validity over GMA and personality in the prediction of academic success.

Based on the nonsignificant (especially in terms of incremental validity) and inconsistent results to date, the best available estimate of the relationship between EI and academic success is probably the .10 true validity reported in a recent meta-analysis (Van Rooy &

Viswesvaran, 2004). With only 11 studies, however, the authors were unable to distinguish between ability and trait measures of EI in the prediction of academic success. Similar to O'Connor and Little (2003) and Brackett and Mayer (2003), future studies need to administer measures based on each of the models to the same sample to see if differences emerge. We suspect that EI will not hold as a strong predictor of academic success. Of all the performance domains, academic success could be the one where EI has the least potential for incremental validity over GMA. A student low on empathy would probably score low on measures of EI, but that would not unduly limit the likelihood of success given that GMA and motivation are present. This assertion should hold to a greater extent for below-college populations. At the college and graduate level, more personal interactions may be required and EI could add value.

If EI does prove useful in predicting academic success, it may occur because of an indirect effect. Findings from Petrides and colleagues (2004), who found that students with higher EI partook in less deviant behavior (e.g., truancy), support this possibility. Thus, it may be that EI leads to behaviors that contribute to success in academic settings, though potentially not to learning per se.

Predictive Power of EI in Organizational Settings

It has also been hypothesized that EI could have great value in predicting a broader set of personal outcomes. In particular, EI has been touted as being predictive of outcomes such as powerlessness (Wong & Law, 2002), life space (Brackett et al., 2004), and the quality of social relationships (Lopes, Salovey, & Straus, 2003). Not surprisingly, these outcomes are often difficult to operationalize and measure. Moreover, findings from this area have been used to show that EI predicts performance. These same findings have been used to generalize to organizational settings. If EI is to be operationalized as an intelligence, the theoretical rationale for why it should be predictive of such a broad range of criteria needs to be more fully delineated (Matthews et al., 2002). A broadside approach should not be taken where EI is used to try to predict any possible outcome without specifying how and why. For instance, it would seem that EI should be a better predictor of reduced occupational stress than of production in assembly line settings, where arguably little EI would be needed.

There can be little argument that GMA is the best overall predictor of task performance, and EI may not add much incremental validity here. EI is instead more likely to find greater utility and incremental validity in predicting less traditional outcomes such as organizational citizenship or contextual behavior. If individuals have high EI, they should better understand and empathize with the needs of others. It has been hypothesized that personality is a more valid predictor of outcomes such as contextual behavior, whereas GMA is better for predicting task performance (Borman & Motowidlo, 1997). To the extent that a trait-based measure of EI taps into personality traits, it should be predictive in this area, whereas ability EI should be less so because of its greater overlap with GMA. Results in this area have been equivocal. For instance, Wong and Law (2002) found a moderate .15 correlation between EI and contextual behavior using a trait-based measure. Using an ability-based measure of EI, Day and Carroll (2004) found no significant relationship with ratings of individual contextual performance. At the group level, however, a more promising relationship emerged, and EI displayed an average correlation of approximately .15 with ratings of group contextual performance. The latter finding is intriguing and suggests that it is possible that EI is more important in group settings where greater interpersonal interactions are required.

Leadership is another criterion that should be given more consideration as an important outcome that could be influenced by individuals' levels of EI (Goleman, McKee, & Boyatzis, 2002). Leadership requires understanding the needs and motivations of others. It also requires understanding the complex interactions present in group dynamics. Initial studies in this area have been encouraging. Wolff, Pescosolido, and Druskat (2002) found that an aspect of trait EI (i.e., empathy) was partially predictive of who emerged as leaders in self-managing teams. Mandell and Pherwani (2003) found that trait EI was predictive of self-reported transformational leadership style in a small sample of managers. In another study, on self-reported transformational leadership, EI was again found to be a strong predictor (Hartsfield, 2003). In a third study, subordinates and supervisors rated managers in a U.S.-based information technology firm on transformational leadership (Sosik & Megerian, 1999). The managers had also completed a conglomeration of short measures that were described as EI. Interestingly, subordinates' ratings of aspects of supervisor leadership were positively related to the manager's EI, but a small negative relationship was found with performance ratings given by the supervisor, who had completed these EI measures.

In both studies where transformational leadership was self-reported, a particularly strong relationship was found with EI. This is encouraging, but it should be noted that Hartsfield (2003) also found a significant link between EI and social desirability scale scores, which suggests that it is possible that correlations with personality traits assessed by social desirability scales, and possibly common method variance, are in part attributable for the findings. These are still promising findings, but results are inconclusive after considering the discrepant results reported when transformational leadership behavior was not self-reported. Research should continue to probe leadership and EI. This will require comparing self- and other-reported leadership behaviors to examine the similarity of the ratings. Studies also need to be conducted using ability-based measures, and all results need to be reported after controlling for personality and cognitive ability.

At one point, it was boldly proclaimed that EI could be more important than GMA for predicting success in the workforce (Goleman, 1995). Since that time, it has been suggested that it is only at the upper levels where those with high EI truly distinguish themselves (Goleman, 1998). There can be little disagreement that the former claim does not hold; on average, GMA is a better predictor across levels and occupations. At upper levels, it is argued, all individuals have already met a certain minimum GMA threshold (i.e., the range is restricted) necessary for success, and it is at this point that other predictors become more important. This is an intriguing hypothesis for sure, but to date, very little research has empirically explored this possibility. Even conceptually, there are problems with this hypothesis. For one, no reason has been given why the same range restriction that affects GMA does not affect EI at these levels. Indeed, claims regarding this hypothesis are often based on conjecture and measures that are not designed to assess EI (Matthews et al., 2002).

We have yet to find research that measures EI with an established inventory and that measures performance above the management level. Slaski and Cartwright (2002) administered a trait-based EI measure to a sample of 224 retail managers and found a significant relationship with supervisor ratings of job performance. In an unpublished study of 358 managers, those identified as "high performing leaders" were found to score higher on a measure of EI (Cavallo & Brienza, 2000). If the claim that EI is most important at upper levels is to hold, considerably more research is needed. In the two previously mentioned studies, GMA was not measured or controlled for. Future studies need to control for GMA to determine if the results still hold. Although provocative, at this point, it is still premature to state that EI becomes most important at upper levels.

Group Differences in EI

EI has also been touted as a supplement or alternative to GMA, based on the proposition that group differences will not be found across demographic groups. As noted earlier, GMA has been found to be predictive in many selection settings, but one of the reasons for its controversial status is the large group differences found in measures of GMA that frequently result in adverse impact for the low scoring groups. When personnel selection decisions are made in the United States, differences based on race, gender, and age are of particular interest. The popularity of EI (and other claimed alternate intelligences) is typically due to claims that (a) these intelligences enhance our predictive accuracy, and (b) group differences are smaller on these intelligences, thus providing hope for a more egalitarian society. We saw in the previous section that the empirical evidence for the enhanced predictive accuracy of EI measures over GMA is largely unsubstantiated. In this section, we summarize the empirical data on group differences in EI measures.

Roberts and colleagues (2001) conducted one of the few studies that directly evaluated ethnic group differences in EI and found conflicting results when comparing White and ethnic minority scores. More specifically, no differences were found when a consensus-based scoring format was used, but Whites scored significantly higher under the expert scoring method. The results obtained under the expert-derived scoring method, where the "correct" responses were predominantly decided on by White males, underscore the difficulty in using this format when a diverse group is not sampled. In a study using a trait-based measure, the minority groups (i.e., Blacks and Hispanics) actually scored better than the majority group; Hispanics scored the highest of the three groups (Van Rooy, Alonso, & Viswesvaran, 2005). The differential findings based on the two models of EI indicate that the more cognitively loaded ability measure is most at risk for concerns of adverse impact.

There is an increasing acceptance that women score better on tests of EI than men, and empirical results have largely supported this assertion (e.g., Day & Carroll, 2004; Mayer, Caruso, & Salovey, 1999; Schutte et al., 1998). For example, an unpublished meta-analysis with 36 studies reporting EI and gender found a mean correlation of .17, favoring females (Van Rooy & Viswesvaran, 2003). Not all studies, however, have found gender differences, and more studies are needed in this area. Bar-On (1997), for instance, found no significant gender differences on the overall trait EI score, and the effect explained less than 1% of the variance. Females did score slightly better than males for the overall average, and also for many of the EQ-I subscales, but it should be noted that males scored higher on other subscales. With an ability-based test, females were found to score higher under a consensus format, whereas males fared better under an expert format (Roberts et al., 2001). These differences are most likely a direct reflection of the composition of the populations used to derive the scoring keys.

Bar-On (1997) reported age differences in trait EI on the basis of five categories. Van Rooy and colleagues (2005) also found that trait EI scores increased with age. Mayer et al. (1999) took yet a different approach, using an ability measure, and compared the EI scores of a youth sample to that of an adult sample. In this study, scores from an adult group were found to be significantly higher than those of a comparison adolescent group. Roberts et al. (2001) found no significant age differences with an ability measure but speculated that the finding might have been attributable to range restriction in the sample. Across studies, even with the range-restricted samples, results generally indicate that EI scores tend to increase with age.

PRACTICAL INTELLIGENCE

Another relatively new construct on the market of new intelligences is that of practical intelligence. While the two research streams supporting practical and emotional intelligence can be traced back to one common source, they have evolved quite independently, developing in different directions. However, considerable confusion over the distinction between the two persists, which we illustrate and try to clarify in this section.

There has always been a choir of voices claiming that there must be more to success in life than just "book smarts." The choir resonated strongly enough with behavioral scientists that they embarked on a quest to discover new traits and constructs capable of explaining variance in human behavior that remained unexplained after taking "book smarts" into account. In modern psychological research, this resulted in an attempt to split the abilities domain to distinguish between general intelligence and its specific facets, in the hope of finding additional valid predictors of success in various specific life domains.

Link Between Emotional Intelligence and Practical Intelligence

The essence of the belief that led to the search for new ability constructs is captured by Thorndike , who pointed out, "No man is equally intelligent for all sorts of problems" (p. 228). Thorndike divided intelligence into three components: abstract, mechanical, and social intelligence (Roberts et al., 2001). He defined social intelligence as "the ability to understand and manage men and women, boys and girls—to act wisely in human relations" (p. 228). *Social* intelligence is often regarded as being the construct origin of *emotional* as well as *practical* intelligence (Roberts et al., 2001).

This is where the confusion begins: Hedlund and Sternberg (2000) pointed out that although practical intelligence is sometimes conceptualized as the same as social intelligence, practical intelligence "is not limited to use in solving problems of a social nature" (p. 149). Thus, while Salovey and Mayer defined the *subset* of social intelligence that is involved in monitoring of, discriminating among, and utilizing of emotions as emotional intelligence, Sternberg and his colleagues operationalized these skills as practical intelligence applied to the social domain (e.g., Grigorenko & Sternberg, 2001; Hedlund & Sternberg, 2000). Furthermore, there is considerable confusion over the distinction between the two constructs in the empirical literature. For example, Fox and Spector (2000) stated that emotional intelligence "may be considered a subset of practical intelligence" (p. 205). Correlations between measures of emotional intelligence and practical intelligence employed in their study ranged from .13 to .38 (observed, $N = 116$). The magnitude of these correlations indicate some small to moderate overlap and represent the only published estimate of the relationship between the two constructs that we are aware of.

Despite the muddle of scientific constructs and popular labels, there are clear distinctions between the constructs of emotional and practical intelligence as they are currently conceived of by their primary proponents and as reflected in the mainstream scientific literature. We argue that the two can be well differentiated along a number of dimensions: (a) nomological net as proposed by the proponents of the constructs, especially with regard to their relationship to GMA; (b) claims surrounding their predictive utility in applied settings; (c) degree of scientific rigor put forth to empirically validate these claims. We discuss each of these in turn.

Practical Intelligence: An Evaluation of the Construct and Its Measurement

Practical intelligence, often also called common sense, is the ability to solve problems of an everyday nature that require a certain amount of practical (as opposed to "academic" or "scholastic") skills. The proponents of the theory claim that it is the "ability to adapt to, shape, and select everyday environments" (Sternberg et al., 2000, p. xi). It is purported to predict the ability to acquire procedural knowledge underlying success in a variety of settings independent of the knowledge that has been explicitly taught and acquired. The core component of the construct is called *tacit knowledge*. One can differentiate between two primary approaches in assessing practical intelligence: assessing practical ability and skills or assessing tacit knowledge. These two have obvious parallels to the trait and ability models of EI that we discussed earlier.

Attempts to measure abilities and skills predictive of success in everyday life using more concrete and applied tasks than those commonly encountered on paper and pencil measures have been plentiful.

For example, Willis and Schaie (1986) used a variant of the Educational Testing Service (ETS) basic skills test to assess everyday intelligence and its relationship to fluid and crystallized ability. The test, which assesses the ability to perform everyday tasks such as cooking, managing finances, and fixing things around the house, was found to be highly correlated with fluid and crystallized abilities in a sample of 87 older adults (average correlation of .81 with two batteries of ability measures administered). A study by Diehl, Willis, and Schaie (1995), employing a different measure of everyday problem solving ability, also found substantial correlations between objectively scored tasks of everyday problem-solving and cognitive abilities. Attempts to measure "functional literacy," even though not directly related to practical intelligence, can also be viewed in this light (see Gottfredson, 2003b, for an extensive discussion of these measures and their relationship with general intelligence). In these tests, test takers are presented with test items resembling problems commonly encountered in everyday life, such as using a bus schedule or figuring out prescription medication instructions. Tasks on these tests are often of the type that can be objectively scored (i.e., did the participant pick the right bus to get to the target location), commensurate with the idea that there is an ability that underlies the practical skills needed to perform well on the test as well as in everyday life. However, measures of "everyday intelligence" and "practical" problem-solving skills, as opposed to "academic intelligence" and "abstract" reasoning, were also developed using a situational judgment approach (e.g., Cornelius & Caspi, 1987).

Recent conceptualizations of practical intelligence, however, are mainly concerned with measuring the (tacit) knowledge component underlying practical skills that may or may not be social in nature. Tacit knowledge is commonly defined as "the procedural knowledge one learns in everyday life that usually is not taught and often is not yet even verbalized" (Sternberg et al., 2000, p. xi). It is "knowing *how* rather than knowing *that*" (Sternberg et al., 2000, p. 107). As it represents *knowledge* and requires intimate acquaintance of the processes underlying success at a given task, job, or in a specific setting (e.g., academia, management, military), it is context dependent. It has been reasoned that tacit knowledge should not only differentiate successful and unsuccessful people on the job but also show substantial mean differences between novices and experts in a given domain (Wagner & Sternberg, 1985). The tacit knowledge approach is distinct from the ability approach, in the way that it is often assumed that "there are, of course, no 'correct' answers," a fact that is even reflected in the response instructions of tacit knowledge inventories (Wagner & Sternberg, 1991, p. 1). This fact poses problems for objectively scoring such tests, as we illustrate later.

Over the last two decades, a number of measures have been developed attempting to measure the tacit knowledge component that is purported to predict success in a variety of settings and jobs (e.g., academic psychology, military leadership, management, nursing, sales, emergency dispatch). The format commonly encountered in the assessment of tacit knowledge is that of situational judgment tests. Typically, situational judgment tests present the test taker with a scenario as well as multiple different response options. Depending on the instructions, the test taker either chooses one response option that he or she would endorse in such a scenario/situation, rates one of the response options as the most effective/most likely to be successful, or rates *all* response options for effectiveness/perceived probability of success with regard to the scenario presented. In the case of tacit knowledge assessment, all three approaches are encountered in the literature, yet the third option seems to be the most commonly used, presenting the advantage of higher item-numbers per test (each rated response option constituting one item), increasing reliability. However, the response instructions play another crucial role. Consider the following sample item:

In a team meeting, one of your employees voices the concern that the current negative atmosphere in the team is in part due to your authoritarian leadership style. How do you react?

- Tell the employee you can talk about this issue one-on-one, once the meeting is over.
- Ask all team members present how they perceive the situation.
- State that you are willing to analyze your current leadership style, but wait until the issue is brought up again to actually do something about it.
- State that you are dedicated to the team and encourage team members to give you individual feedback.
- Indicate that, as the leader, you will continue leading the team exactly as you have done in the past.

While everyone might know immediately which *one* of these response options he or she would endorse when presented with the scenario, it seems more difficult to rate *each* of the options for effectiveness in a given situation. The latter approach also poses the question of how answers on these tests are best scored. The tacit knowledge inventories most researched (e.g., the Tacit Knowledge Inventory for Managers, Tacit Knowledge Inventory for Military Leaders, Tacit Knowledge Inventory for Sales; see Sternberg et al., 2000) are scored comparing an individual's responses to the responses of an expert group, reasoning that if tacit knowledge is predictive of success in a given domain, those who are experts in this domain should also be higher in tacit knowledge. Thus, the degree of concurrence of an individual's answers with those of the expert group used to create the scoring key is taken as an indication of tacit knowledge in the domain tested and thus of practical intelligence (Sternberg, 2004).

Proponents of the theory of practical intelligence have put forth a number of quite drastic claims surrounding tacit knowledge. In their book *Practical Intelligence in Everyday Life*, Sternberg and colleagues summarize two decades of research on the topic. Their primary claims can be summarized as follows: (a) Practical intelligence "is a construct that is distinct from academic intelligence" (p. xi), (b) tacit knowledge reliably differentiates between experts and novices in a given domain (p. 156), yet it is more than just job knowledge (p. 111); and (c)) "practical intelligence is a better predictor of success than is the academic form of intelligence" (p. xii).

Evaluating the Claim That Practical Intelligence Is Distinct From GMA

The first claim (practical intelligence as an entity distinct from general intelligence, or "uncorrelated with academic intelligence," Sternberg et al., 2000, p. 10) is mainly supported by highly readable yet unsubstantiated anecdotal evidence. Everyone can probably think of a case of a relative, friend, or acquaintance who has the reputation of being incredibly smart (or even better, the test scores to back this up) but is extremely inept at the most basic, everyday tasks and activities (e.g., boiling eggs, reading maps). Also, all of us have heard of cases where individuals who were classified as "slow learners" or just below average in intelligence, as measured by standardized tests of so-called academic intelligence, still went on to have incredible success in their work and private life.

The truth is that practical intelligence and GMA (alternate labels include "academic intelligence," or "book smarts") are *not* two distinct and independent entities. The two constructs are far from being uncorrelated, as the proponents of practical intelligence often assert. In a meta-analysis summarizing the published and unpublished literature on the topic, Dilchert and Ones (2004) showed the true score correlation between the two constructs to be .58 ($N = 3,090$). The implication of this considerable construct overlap is that practical intelligence is unlikely to explain a substantial amount of additional variance in valued life outcomes over and above that explained by GMA. To quantify the incremental validity of one construct over another, their relative criterion-related validities have to be taken into account.

As is the case with any type of knowledge, individuals who have had more opportunity to acquire knowledge in a given context can be expected to show higher levels of such knowledge. Also, common wisdom suggests that individuals who acquired an expert status in a given domain are likely to possess higher levels of knowledge in their respective domain than are nonexperts or novices. In occupational settings, we know that the amount of job knowledge that individuals acquire over the span of their career is determined not only by their opportunity to do so (i.e., number of years on the job), but also by their ability to learn (i.e., GMA). In fact, after individuals spend some time on the job, the effects of job experience on job knowledge becomes less important, whereas the influence of ability remains strong (Schmidt, Hunter, & Outerbridge, 1986; Schmidt, Hunter, Outerbridge, & Goff, 1988). With regard to tacit knowledge, research has shown that samples of experts and novices differ in mean levels of tacit knowledge (Wagner & Sternberg, 1985). Even though these results have been replicated, there have been inconsistencies in findings (Wagner, 1987). Of additional concern are the often limited sample sizes of the groups under investigation (with groups containing as few as 13 subjects). Also, more research comparing expert and novice groups in tacit knowledge across different domains is desirable. All in all, it is safe to say that people who have acquired an expert status in a given domain are likely to score considerably higher than undergraduate students and inexperienced novices.

Is Practical Intelligence a Better Predictor of Outcomes Than GMA?

It has repeatedly been stated that practical intelligence is a better predictor of success in life than is the so-called academic form of intelligence. Ones, Viswesvaran, and Dilchert have summarized the meta-analytic evidence for the criterion-related validity of GMA and specific abilities for predicting various criteria in educational and job training settings, as well as for job performance and its facets. Results indicate that GMA is a strong predictor of success across domains and that validities generalize across job, settings, industries, countries, and cultures (see earlier section on General Mental Ability in this chapter). In comparison, the meta-analytic evidence for practical intelligence (Dilchert & Ones, 2004) suggests that, even though practical intelligence shows validity in the prediction of job and academic performance (.39 and .41, respectively), these levels do not favorably compare to those of GMA or that of most specific abilities (e.g., quantitative).

An important additional issue to take into consideration when evaluating the utility of practical intelligence is its incremental validity over existing constructs currently used in the prediction of valued outcomes. Based on the meta-analytic evidence, Dilchert and Ones (2004) estimated the incremental validity of practical intelligence measures over measures of GMA to be .02 and .03 for the prediction of job performance and academic success, respectively. Thus, the utility gained by adding a measure of practical intelligence to a measure of cognitive ability in the prediction of job performance is considerably lower than that gained from measures of integrity, job knowledge tests, or even unstructured interviews (Schmidt & Hunter, 1998). When it comes to incremental validity over tests of GMA, practical intelligence seems to fare just a little better than measures of biographical data, interests, and years of education.

In summary, the imbalance between the scientific evidence for the utility of practical intelligence and anecdotal accounts of its importance in real-world pursuits is astonishing. Accounts illustrating the importance of practical intelligence in the prediction of these valued outcomes are numerous but often lacking in scientific rigor. Books with titles such as *Successful Intelligence* (Sternberg, 1996) or *Why Smart People Can Be So Stupid* (Sternberg, 2002) might grab our attention, but they do not improve our understanding unless they present empirical and original data collected on samples adequate to draw inferences on the validity of the claims put forth.

MULTIPLYING INTELLIGENCES: IS THERE A BEST?

So is there a best intelligence for personnel selection? At an individual level, there is no substitute for general intelligence, and it is the best single predictor of performance (Murphy, 2002; Schmidt, 2002). At an organizational level, the answer is less clear. No organization would decide to forego selection to increase task performance (Gottfredson, 2002; Kehoe, 2002). Instead, the choice is to pick among the best available predictors. Absent any legal restrictions and diversity considerations, there can be little doubt that all organizations would implement a measure of general intelligence as the sole predictor if only one could be used. In reality, however, other intelligences become more appealing to the extent that they retain a certain level of predictive validity and are not constrained by group differences. In this sense, emotional and practical intelligence have been touted as alternatives to general intelligence.

We believe that emotional and practical intelligence can be important in personnel selection, but not based on their predictive potential. It would not be prudent to discontinue the hunt for alternate constructs and selection techniques, as it is well documented that GMA leaves in excess of 50% of the performance variance unexplained (e.g., Hunter & Hunter, 1984; Jensen, 1998). Again, this is not to suggest that either of these predictors will surpass GMA. As a starting point, measures of these alternative constructs may prove useful to the extent that they are not encumbered by problems (namely, group differences) found with tests of GMA.

To provide even greater value, incremental validity must be shown over GMA. Integrity tests have demonstrated the greatest incremental validity over GMA, whereas other predictors (e.g., unstructured interviews) have not faired as well (Ones, Viswesvaran, & Schmidt, 1993; Schmidt & Hunter, 1998). To see where EI falls, considerably more research is needed in this area. Although some studies have shown incremental validity (e.g., Wong & Law, 2002), overall results have not been conclusive, and EI has been shown to lose predictive power after accounting for GMA and personality (e.g., Janovics & Christiansen, 2004). Studies using an ability measure have often only controlled for personality, whereas those with a trait measure instead only control for GMA. The best research will assess the predictive validity of EI after controlling for GMA and personality and not just one of the constructs. Given results suggesting comparable predictive validities for trait and ability measures of EI (Van Rooy & Viswesvaran, 2004), in all likelihood, results will remain similar after controlling for these constructs. Similar bleak estimates of incremental validity have been found for measures of practical intelligence. In fact, the correlation between measures of GMA and practical intelligence is so high (.58) that prospects for incremental validity appear remote.

Emotional (e.g., Van Rooy & Viswesvaran, 2004) and practical intelligence (see Dilchert & Ones, 2004; Sternberg & Hedlund, 2002, for a summary) have demonstrated some evidence of predictive validity but should, at best, only be considered as supplements to general intelligence. The nomological nets of both still need to be more clearly defined. This will require the development of more measures. Although progress has been made, there is still a great deal of work to be done before researchers can speak with greater certainty in this area. In particular, the field of EI has been greatly limited by the lack of psychometrically acceptable measures. There have been proposals to limit discussions of EI to studies using one ability-based measure (i.e., the MSCEIT) and its refinements. Science progresses by examining constructs, not idiosyncratic measures. For example, it is not clear whether the results obtained for ability-based EI are idiosyncratic to the specific variance of the MSCEIT or are representative of the construct. With trait-based EI, inferences are often made based on instruments generally viewed as inferior measures of EI (see Matthews et al., 2002).

Similarly, conceptual clarification for practical intelligence will emerge when it is acknowledged that practical intelligence best represents the degree of investment of general cognitive ability in a specific (tacit) knowledge domain. Given the empirical data (e.g., Brody, 2003; Dilchert & Ones, 2004; Gottfredson, 2003a), intellectual honesty requires this. Zeidner, Matthews, Roberts, and MacCann (2003) have proposed an investment model for EI in children, where the child's proficiency at one level facilitates the acquisition of skills at a higher level. The authors point out that individual differences in emotional learning seem to be strongly linked to individual differences in verbal ability. While the proponents of the ability model of EI place the construct in the domain of cognitive abilities, explicitly acknowledging a correlation with GMA (Mayer, Salovey, Caruso, & Sitarenios, 2001), the proponents of practical intelligence have yet to acknowledge the fact that there is no escape from the positive manifold.

To date, there is limited longitudinal data on EI (or Practical Intelligence) and job performance and most published research is based on cross-sectional data. Research is now needed that follows a group of individuals, measuring performance at multiple time periods (e.g., Gerits, Derksen, Verbruggen, & Katzko, 2005). This could open a new line of possibilities. For instance, it would be interesting if individuals with high EI (or PI) responded better to performance feedback and subsequently had a larger performance improvement than those with lower EI (or PI). In short, the alternate intelligences may not surpass GMA as a predictor, but they could still represent intriguing and useful constructs. As research continues to lead to construct clarification, we will begin to be able to understand the performance domains to which these alternate intelligences might best be applied. We believe that the alternate intelligences may be useful for predicting a broader range of variables, such as leadership (e.g., Wolff et al., 2002), contextual behavior (e.g., Day & Carroll, 2004; Wong & Law, 2002) and satisfaction (e.g., Bar-On, 1997), that are not explicit task performance. The utility could be even greater at the group level where interpersonal skills are a necessity for maximal performance. However, even if criterion-related validity of these alternate criteria is shown, the independence of the newly proposed intelligences from already existing predictors must be established in order to substantiate claims of their unique utility.

Proponents of the alternate intelligences almost invariably imply (especially in their popular writings) that (a) the alternate intelligence is more important than GMA; (b) the alternate intelligence is more egalitarian, that is, there is no bias or adverse impact; and (c)) the alternate intelligences are not fixed, that is, they could be developed by anyone. The evidence reviewed in this chapter suggests that the evidence of incremental validity for these alternate intelligences is very weak. Few studies have investigated group differences, and no firm conclusion can be drawn regarding bias, differential validity, and so forth. No studies have systematically assessed the heritability or malleability of these alternate intelligences. GMA and other constructs, such as the Big Five factors, are more established, and the alternate intelligences have miles to go before they can be ensconced along with the more traditional individual differences variables as basic factors descriptive of humans.

Gottfredson (2003a) fittingly described the attractiveness of constructs such as practical and emotional intelligence as "tapping the popular preference for an egalitarian plurality of intelligences (everyone can be smart in some way) and a distaste for being assessed, labeled, and sorted by inscrutable mental tests" (p. 392). The popularity of both emotional and practical intelligence grew from the common root of discontent with the assertion that most valued life outcomes (success at school, work, and interpersonal relationships) could be predicted by GMA, a quantifiable trait on which people differ. Even though proponents of the universal utility of GMA never asserted that all variance in behavior is attributable to individual differences in general intelligence, many of them assert that GMA is the most powerful predictor known in the behavioral sciences (Ree & Carretta, 2002; Ree & Earles, 1991; Ree et al., 1994; Reeve & Hakel, 2002). While the proponents of these alternate intelligences do not negate the fact that GMA is of prime importance in a large number of real-life domains, and also acknowledge the fact that it is a powerful predictor of all sorts of valued outcomes in occupational settings, their popular writings seem to imply something else: (a) that general intelligence and the newly proposed intelligences are relatively independent, and (b) that the alternate intelligences are more important than GMA. However, the amassed empirical evidence indicates that this is not the case.

REFERENCES

Ackerman, P. L., & Heggestad, E. D. (1997). Intelligence, personality and interests: Evidence for overlapping traits. *Psychological Bulletin, 121,* 219–245

Barchard, K. A. (2003). Does emotional intelligence assist in the prediction of academic success? *Educational & Psychological Measurement, 65,* 840.

Bar-On, R. (1997). *Bar-On emotional quotient inventory: Technical manual.* Toronto, ON: Multihealth Systems.

Bar-On, R. (2000). Emotional and social intelligence: Insights from the Emotional Quotient Inventory. In R. Bar-On & J. D. A. Parker (Eds.), *The handbook of emotional intelligence* (pp. 363–388). San Francisco: Jossey-Bass.

Borman, W. C., & Motowidlo, S. J. (1997). Task performance and contextual performance: The meaning for personnel selection research. *Human Performance, 10,* 99–109.

Brackett, M. A., & Mayer, J. D. (2003). Convergent, discriminant, and incremental validity of competing measures of emotional intelligence. *Personality and Social Psychology Bulletin, 29,* 1147–1158.

Brackett, M. A., Mayer, J. D., & Warner, R. M. (2004). Emotional intelligence and its relation to everyday behavior. *Personality and Individual Differences, 36,* 1387–1402.

Brand, C. (1987). The importance of general intelligence. In S. Modgil & C. Modgil (Eds.), *Arthur Jensen: Consensus and controversy* (pp. 251–265). New York: Falmer.

Callender, J. C., & Osburn, H. G. (1981). Testing the constancy of validity with computer generated sampling distributions of the multiplicative model variance estimate: Results the petroleum industry validation research. *Journal of Applied Psychology, 66,* 274–281.

Campbell, J. P., McHenry, J. J., & Wise, L. L. (1990). Modeling job performance in a population of jobs. *Personnel Psychology, 43,* 313–333.

Carroll, J. B. (1993). *Human cognitive abilities: A survey of factor-analytic studies.* New York: Cambridge University Press.

Cavallo, K., & Brienza, D. (2000). *Emotional competence and leadership excellence at Johnson & Johnson: The emotional intelligence and leadership study.* Consortium for Research on Emotional Intelligence in Organizations, New York.

Cleary, T. A. (1968). Test bias: Prediction of grades of Negro and White students in integrated colleges. *Journal of Educational Measurement, 5,* 115–124.

Conte, J. M. (2004). A review and critique of emotional intelligence measures. *Journal of Organizational Behavior, 25,* 433–440.

Cornelius, S. W., & Caspi, A. (1987). Everyday problem solving in adulthood and old age. *Psychology & Aging, 2,* 144–153.

Davies, M., Stankov, L., & Roberts, R. D. (1998). Emotional intelligence: In search of an illusive construct. *Journal of Personality and Social Psychology, 75,* 989–1015.

Day, A. L., & Carroll, S. A. (2004). Using an ability-based measure of emotional intelligence to predict individual performance, group performance, and group citizenship behaviours. *Personality and Individual Differences, 36,* 1443–1458.

Diehl, M., Willis, S. L., & Schaie, K. W. (1995). Everyday problem solving in older adults: Observational assessment and cognitive correlates. *Psychology & Aging, 10,* 478–491.

Dilchert, S., & Ones, D. S. (2004, April). *Meta-analysis of practical intelligence: Contender to the throne of g?* Poster session presented at the annual conference of the Society for Industrial and Organizational Psychology, Chicago, IL.

Fox, S., & Spector, P. E. (2000). Relations of emotional intelligence, practical intelligence, general intelligence, and trait affectivity with interview outcomes: It's not all just "G". *Journal of Organizational Behavior, 21,* 203–220.

Gerits, L., Derksen, J. L., Verbruggen, A. B., & Katzko, M. (2005). Emotional intelligence profiles of nurses caring for people with severe behaviour problems. *Personality and Individual Differences, 38,* 33–43.

Ghiselli, E. E. (1973). The validity of aptitude tests in personnel selection. *Personnel Psychology, 26,* 461–477.

Goleman, D. (1995). *Emotional intelligence: Why it can matter more than IQ.* New York: Bantam Books.

Goleman, D. (1998). *Working with emotional intelligence.* New York: Bantam.

Goleman, D., McKee, A., & Boyatzis, R. E. (2002). *Primal Leadership: Realizing the power of emotional intelligence.* Harvard Business School Press.

Gottfredson, L. S. (2002). Where and why g matters: Not a mystery. *Human Performance, 15,* 25–46.

Gottfredson, L. S. (2003a). Dissecting practical intelligence theory: Its claims and evidence. *Intelligence, 31,* 343–397.

Gottfredson, L. S. (2003b). g, jobs and life. In H. Nyborg (Ed.), *The scientific study of general intelligence: A tribute to Arthur R. Jensen* (pp. 293–342). Oxford, UK: Pergamon.

Grigorenko, E. L., & Sternberg, R. J. (2001). Analytical, creative, and practical intelligence as predictors of self-reported adaptive functioning: A case study in Russia. *Intelligence, 29,* 57–73.

Guilford, J. P. (1956). The structure of intellect. *Psychological Bulletin, 53,* 267–293.

Guion, R. M. (1998). *Assessment, measurement, and prediction for personnel decisions.* Mahwah, NJ: Lawrence Erlbaum Associates.

Hartigan, J. A., & Wigdor, A. K. (1989). *Fairness in employment testing: Validity generalization, minority issues, and the General Aptitude Test Battery.* Washington, DC: National Academy Press.

Hartsfield, M. K. (2003). *The internal dynamics of transformational leadership: Effects of spirituality, emotional intelligence, and self-efficacy.* Unpublished doctoral dissertation, Regent University, Virginia Beach, VA.

Hedlund, J., & Sternberg, R. J. (2000). Too many intelligences? Integrating social, emotional, and practical intelligence. In R. Bar-On & J. D. A. Parker (Eds.), *The handbook of emotional intelligence: Theory, development, assessment, and application at home, school, and in the workplace* (pp. 136–167). San Francisco, CA: Jossey-Bass.

Herrnstein, R., & Murray, C. (1994). *The bell curve: Intelligence and class structure in American life.* New York: Free Press.

Hirsh, H. R., Northrop, L. C., & Schmidt, F. L. (1986). Validity generalization results for law enforcement occupations. *Personnel Psychology, 39,* 399–420.

Hunter, J. E. (1986). Cognitive abilities, cognitive aptitudes, job knowledge, and job performance. *Journal of Vocational Behavior, 29,* 340–362.

Hunter, J. E., & Hunter, R. F. (1984). Validity and utility of alternate predictors of job performance. *Psychological Bulletin, 96*(1), 72–98.

Janovics, J., & Christiansen, N. D. (2004). Emotional intelligence in a selection context: Criterion related validity and vulnerability to response distortion. In K. E. Fox & R. P. Tett (Eds.), *19th Annual Conference for the Society for Industrial and Organizational Psychology.* Chicago, IL.

Jensen, A. R. (1980). *Bias in mental testing.* New York: Free Press.

Jensen, J. B. (1998). *The g factor: The science of mental ability.* Westport, CT: Praeger.

Kehoe, J. F. (2002). General mental ability and selection in private sector organizations: A commentary. *Human Performance, 15,* 97–106.

Kuncel, N. R., Hezlett, S. A., & Ones, D. S. (2001). A comprehensive meta-analysis of the predictive validity of the Graduate Records Examinations: Implications for graduate student selection and performance. *Psychological Bulletin, 127,* 162–181.

Landy, F. J. (2004). Some historical and scientific issues related to research on emotional intelligence. *Journal of Organizational Behavior, 25,* 411–424.

Levine, E. L., Spector, P. E., Menon, P. E., Narayanan, L., & Cannon-Bowers, J. (1996). Validity generalization for cognitive psychomotor, and perceptual tests for craft jobs in the utility industry. *Human Performance, 9,* 1–22.

Lilienthal, R. A., & Pearlman, K. (1980). *The validity of federal selection tests for aid/technician in the health, science and engineering fields.* Washington, DC: U.S. Office of Personnel Management.

Linn, R. (1982). Ability testing: Individual differences, prediction, and differential prediction. In A.K. Wigdor & W. R. Garner (Eds.), *Ability testing: Uses, consequences, and controversies* (pp. 335–388). Washington, DC: National Academy Press.

Locke, E. A. (2004). Why emotional intelligence is an invalid concept. *Journal of Organizational Behavior, 25,* 425–431.

Lopes, P. N., Salovey, P., & Straus, R. (2003). Emotional intelligence, personality, and the perceived quality of social relationships. *Personality and Individual Differences, 35,* 641–658.

Mandell, B., & Pherwani, S. (2003). Relationship between emotional intelligence and transformational leadership style: A gender comparison. *Journal of Business and Psychology, 17,* 387–404.

Matthews, G., Zeidner, M., & Roberts, R. D. (2002). *Emotional intelligence: Science and myth.* Cambridge, MA: MIT Press.

Matthews, G., Zeidner, M., & Roberts, R. D. (2002). *Emotional intelligence: Science and myth.* (Paperback edition) Cambridge, MA: MIT Press.

Mayer, J. D., Caruso, D. R., & Salovey, P. (1999). Emotional intelligence meets traditional standards for an intelligence. *Intelligence, 27,* 267–298.

Mayer, J. D., Salovey, P., Caruso, D. R., & Sitarenios, G. (2001). Emotional intelligence as a standard intelligence. *Emotion, 1,* 232–242.

Murphy, K. R. (2002). Can conflicting perspectives on the role of g in personnel selection be resolved? *Human Performance, 15,* 173–186.

Murphy, K. R., & Davidshofer, C. O. (1998). *Psychological testing: Principles and applications* (4th ed.). Upper Saddle River, NJ: Prentice-Hall.

Newsome, S., Day, A. L., & Catano, V. M. (2000). Assessing the predictive validity of emotional intelligence. *Personality and Individual Differences, 29,* 1005–1016.

O'Connor, R. M., Jr., & Little, I. S. (2003). Revisiting the predictive validity of emotional intelligence: Self-report versus ability-based measures. *Personality and Individual Differences, 35,* 1893–1902.

Ones, D. S., Viswesvaran, C., & Dilchert, S. (2005). Intelligence testing in applied settings: Issues and opportunities. In O. Wilhelm & R. Engle (Eds.), *Handbook of understanding and measuring intelligence* (pp. 431–468). London: Sage.

Ones, D. S., Viswesvaran, C., & Schmidt, F. L. (1993). Comprehensive meta-analysis of integrity test validities: Findings and implications for personnel selection and theories of job performance. *Journal of Applied Psychology, 78*(4), 679–703.

Parker, J. D. A., Creque, Sr., R. E., Barnhart, D. L., Harris, J. I., Majeski, S. A., Wood, L. M., et al. (2004). Academic achievement in high school: Does emotional intelligence matter? *Personality and Individual Differences, 37,* 1321–1330.

Parker, J. D. A., Summerfeldt, L. J., Hogan, M. J., & Majeski, S. A. (2004). Emotional intelligence and academic success: Examining the transition from high school to university. *Personality and Individual Differences, 36,* 163–172.

Petrides, K. V., Frederickson, N., & Furnham, A. (2004). The role of trait emotional intelligence in academic performance and deviant behavior at school. *Personality and Individual Differences, 36,* 277–293.

Petrides, K. V., & Furnham, A. (2000). On the dimensional structure of emotional intelligence. *Personality and Individual Differences, 29,* 313–320.

Petrides, K. V., & Furnham, A. (2001). Trait emotional intelligence: Psychometric investigation with reference to established trait taxonomies. *European Journal of Personality, 15,* 425–448.

Ree, M. J., & Carretta, T. R. (2002). g2K. *Human Performance, 15,* 3–24.

Ree, M. J., & Earles, J. A. (1991). Predicting training success: Not much more than *g. Personnel Psychology, 44,* 321–332.

Ree, M. J., Earles, J. A., & Teachout, M. S. (1994). Predicting job performance: Not much more than *g. Journal of Applied Psychology, 79,* 518–524.

Reeve, C. L., & Hakel, M. D. (2002). Asking the right questions about *g. Human Performance, 15,* 47–74.

Roberts, R. D., Zeidner, M., & Matthews, G. (2001). Does emotional intelligence meet traditional standards for an intelligence? Some new data and conclusions. *Emotion, 1,* 196–231.

Roth, P. L., Bevier, C. A., Bobko, P. L., Switzer, F. S., & Tyler, P. (2001). Ethnic group differences in cognitive ability in employment and educational settings: A meta-analysis. *Personnel Psychology, 54,* 297–330.

Sackett, P. R., & Roth, L. (1996). Multi-stage selection strategies: A Monte Carlo investigation of effects on performance and minority hiring. *Personnel Psychology, 49,* 787–830.

Salgado, J. F., Anderson, N., Moscoso, S., Bertua, C., De Fruyt, F., & Rolland, J. P. (2003). International validity generalization of GMA and cognitive abilities: A European community meta-analysis. *Personnel Psychology, 56,* 573–605.

Salovey, P., & Mayer, J. D. (1990). Emotional intelligence. *Imagination, Cognition, and Intelligence, 9,* 185–211.

Schmidt, F. L. (2002). The role of general cognitive ability and job performance: Why there cannot be a debate. *Human Performance, 15,* 187–210.

Schmidt, F. L., Gast-Rosenberg, I. F., & Hunter, J. E. (1980). Validity generalization results for computer programmers. *Journal of Applied Psychology, 65,* 643–661.

Schmidt, F. L., & Hunter, J. E. (1998). The validity and utility of selection methods in personnel psychology: Practical and theoretical implications of 85 years of research findings. *Psychological Bulletin, 124*(2), 262–274.

Schmidt, F. L., Hunter, J. E., & Outerbridge, A. N. (1986). Impact of job experience and ability on job knowledge, work sample performance, and supervisory ratings of job performance. *Journal of Applied Psychology, 71,* 432–439.

Schmidt, F. L., Hunter, J. E., Outerbridge, A. N., & Goff, S. (1988). Joint relation of experience and ability with job performance: Test of three hypotheses. *Journal of Applied Psychology, 73,* 46–57.

Schmidt, F. L., Hunter, J. E., Pearlman, K., & Shane, G. S. (1979). Further tests of the Schmidt-Hunter Bayesian validity generalization model. *Personnel Psychology, 32,* 257–281.

Schulte, M. J., Ree, M. J., & Carretta, T. R. (2004). Emotional intelligence: Not much more than *g* and personality. *Personality and Individual Differences, 37,* 1059–1068.

Schutte, N. S., Malouff, J. M., Hall, L. E., Haggerty, D. J., Cooper, J. T., Golden, C. J., et al. (1998). Development and validation of a measure of emotional intelligence. *Personality and Individual Differences, 25,* 167–177.

Slaski, M., & Cartwright, S. (2002). Health, performance and emotional intelligence: An exploratory study of retail managers. *Stress and Health, 18,* 63–68.

Sosik, J. J., & Megerian, L. E. (1999). Understanding leader emotional intelligence and performance: The role of self-other agreement on transformational leadership perceptions. *Group & Organization Management, 24,* 367–390.

Spearman, C. (1904). General intelligence, objectively determined and measured. *American Journal of Psychology, 15,* 201–293.

Spearman, C. (1927). *The abilities of man: Their nature and measurement.* New York: Macmillan

Sternberg, R. J. (1996). *Successful intelligence: How practical and creative intelligence determine success in life.* New York: Simon & Schuster.

Sternberg, R. J. (Ed.). (2002). *Why smart people can be so stupid.* New Haven, CT: Yale University Press.

Sternberg, R. J. (2004). Why smart people can be so foolish. *European Psychologist, 9,* 145–150.

Sternberg, R. J., Forsythe, G. B., Hedlund, J., Horvath, J. A., Wagner, R. K., Williams, W. M., et al. (2000). *Practical intelligence in everyday life.* New York: Cambridge University Press.

Sternberg, R. J., & Hedlund, J. (2002). Practical intelligence, *g,* and work psychology. *Human Performance, 15,* 143–160.

Thorndike, E. L. (1920). Intelligence and its uses. *Harper's Magazine, 140,* 227–235.

Thurstone, L. L. (1938). Primary mental abilities. *Psychometric Monograph, 1.*

Van Rooy, D. L., Alonso, A., & Viswesvaran, C. (2005). Group differences in emotional intelligence test scores: Theoretical and practical implications. *Personality and Individual Differences, 38,* 689–700.

Van Rooy, D. L., & Viswesvaran, C. (2003). *The emotionally intelligent female: A meta-analysis of gender differences.* Unpublished manuscript, Florida International University.

Van Rooy, D. L., & Viswesvaran, C. (2004). Emotional intelligence: A meta-analytic investigation of predictive validity and nomological net. *Journal of Vocational Behavior, 65,* 71–95.

Van Rooy, D. L., Viswesvaran, C., & Pluta, P. (2005). An evaluation of construct validity: What is this thing called emotional intelligence? *Human Performance, 18,* 445–462.

Viswesvaran, C., Ones, D. S., Dilchert, S. (2003, May). Using cognitive ability measures in selection: Cumulative knowledge from the United States. In J. Salgado & N. Anderson (Chairs), *International advances in cognitive ability testing,* Eleventh European Congress on Work and Organizational Psychology, Lisbon, Portugal.

Viswesvaran, C., & Ones, D. S. (2002). Agreements and disagreements on the role of general mental ability (GMA) in industrial, work and organizational psychology. *Human Performance, 15,* 211–231.

Wagner, R. K. (1987). Tacit knowledge in everyday intelligent behavior. *Journal of Personality & Social Psychology, 52*, 1236–1247.

Wagner, R. K., & Sternberg, R. J. (1985). Practical intelligence in real-world pursuits: The role of tacit knowledge. *Journal of Personality and Social Psychology, 49*, 436–458.

Wagner, R. K., & Sternberg, R. J. (1991). *Tacit Knowledge Inventory for Managers*. San Antonio, TX: Psychological Corporation.

Willis, S. L., & Schaie, K. W. (1986). Practical intelligence in later adulthood. In R. J. Sternberg & R. K. Wagner (Eds.), *Practical intelligence* (pp. 236–270). New York: Cambridge University Press.

Wolff, S. B., Pescosolido, A. T., & Druskat, V. U. (2002). Emotional intelligence as the basis of leadership in self-managing teams. *The Leadership Quarterly, 13*, 505–522.

Wong, C. S., & Law, K. S. (2002). The effect of leader and follower emotional intelligence on performance and attitudes: An exploratory study. *The Leadership Quarterly, 13*, 243–274.

Zeidner, M., Matthews, G., Roberts, R. D., & MacCann, C. (2003). Development of emotional intelligence: Towards a multi-level investment model. *Human Development, 46*, 69–96.

Business Susceptibility to Consulting Fads: The Case of Emotional Intelligence

Robert Hogan and Louis W. Stokes
Hogan Assessment Systems and Boyden Leadership Institute

The concept of emotional intelligence (EI; Goleman, 1995), and the assessment and training processes that are associated with it, have enjoyed an astonishing degree of acceptance in the business community. Indeed, EI training programs have become a flourishing business serving other businesses. All of this has occurred without the support or endorsement of academic psychology in general or industrial and organizational (I/O) psychology in particular. In fact, as this book demonstrates, academic psychologists are highly critical of many aspects of the EI movement; they regard EI interventions as part of a seemingly endless series of fads perpetrated on a gullible business community by shameless purveyors of psychobabble. This chapter concerns the question of why business people seem so susceptible to fads, using the current enthusiasm for EI as a special case. We also examine why EI seems to have particular resonance for business.

That the business community appears to lurch from one fad to the next is, we believe, beyond dispute. There was Theory X, then Theory Y, then Theory Z leadership, there was the t-group movement, ropes courses, TQM, the competency movement, the coaching movement, ethics training, and a host of other interventions intended to alleviate or solve performance problems in business. Although each of these fads has been questioned and challenged by the academic community while it was (or is) running its course, each was nonetheless embraced enthusiastically by the business community. In addition, it is important to note that all of these fads concern training, so the real question in this chapter is, why are business people so susceptible to training fads?

THE ROLE OF PERSONALITY IN EXPLAINING BUSINESS FADS

There are at least four reasons why business people, as contrasted with psychologists, are such eager consumers of training programs. The first reason has to do with their personalities—business people are different from academic psychologists in ways that are easy to specify and measure. Consider the well-known and extraordinarily well-validated Holland (1997) hexagonal model of occupational types, shown in Fig. 11.1. In the Holland model, business people are usually enterprising/social (ES) types (cf. Holland, 1997). Such people are extraverted, outgoing, impulsive, stimulus seeking, and enjoy working with others as part of a team. In contrast, academic psychologists are investigative/realistic (IR) types. Such people are introverted, obsessive, and prefer to work alone, typically with data. ES and IR types are, in many ways, the psychological antitheses of one another, and they often don't understand (or even like) one another very much.

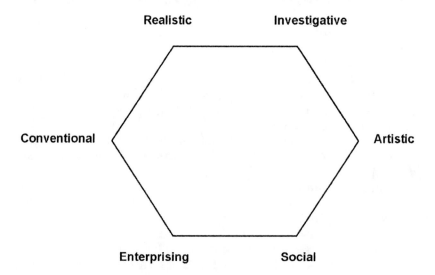

FIG. 11.1.   Hexagonal model of occupational types.

Stimulated by the Holland model, Hogan and Hogan (1996) developed the Motives, Values, Preferences Inventory (MVPI) to measure the 10 core values around which most individual identities are organized. The MVPI Science scale is pertinent to this discussion. High scores on the Science scale reflect a deep interest in research and problem solving and a preference for making decisions based on data. Low scores on the scale reflect little interest in science or data analysis and a preference for quick decisions based on intuition and personal experience. Academic psychologists usually receive high scores on this scale, and business people tend to receive low scores. Academics enjoy research and prefer to make data-based decisions that are as correct as possible (i.e., they prefer to take the time to gather and analyze the data needed to make what they perceive as high-quality decisions, at the expense of making decisions quickly); business executives typically do not enjoy research and prefer to make rapid decisions that are "good enough." Clearly, these two kinds of people will think about the benefits and utility of training in very different ways; in addition, they will find the preferred decision-making style of their opposite number to be almost unintelligible. For business people, training programs are most attractive if they seem to offer quick and face-valid solutions to recurring business problems, and they have no desire to follow the chain of evidence that would support the adoption of any single training program.

A second reason why business people seem attracted to training fads concerns the extraversion–introversion dimension that distinguishes ES types (business people) from IR types (academic psychologists). Extraverts enjoy group functions and interaction, dislike working alone, spend their days moving from one interaction to the next, and experience a training course as another form of interaction. Moreover, the work load in large organizations is not always heavy—we have spent considerable time as observers in big organizations where it is not uncommon to see large numbers of people sitting idly for extended periods of time. The point here is that training courses have significant entertainment value for underoccupied extraverts, many of whom become training junkies and eager consumers of the most recent fad.

A third reason for the popularity of training programs is that extraverts are prone to equating activity with productivity. As a result, they are attracted to meetings of any sort as a way of keeping busy. Attending training courses makes them feel as if they are accomplishing something.

The fourth reason business people seem so prone to adopting training fads concerns what we call "the secret life of organizations." Freud scandalized the Victorians by suggesting that all human activity is motivated by sexual and aggressive instincts and that most social behavior is a fusion of both impulses. We have made an alternative, but perhaps equally scandalous, proposal: namely, that the principal dynamic in every organization is the individual search for power. Striving for power is an individual differences variable, like all human characteristics. This means that a small number of people in every organization compete furiously for power, most people just do their jobs and watch the power plays unfold, and a small number of people are essentially oblivious to the meaning of the events unfolding around them. Most of the significant activity and, particularly, most of the new initiatives in any organization come from those players who are trying to advance themselves. From the perspective of managers whose most important goal is to acquire and exercise power, training interventions can be very attractive. Training purports to shape the behavior and outlook of the recipients, thereby building new skills that might be useful to the manager in his or her quest for increased power and influence.

We have been consulting with organizations for over 30 years; in our experience, clients typically do not ask for our help solely or even principally because they think our interventions will make their organizations function better. They engage us because they think that our "programs" will make them look good. As a result, there is a near-total mismatch between what we are trying to do and their reason for being interested in it. Our intentions as psychologists are to enhance and refine internal processes and generally make organizations work better. The clients, on the other hand, typically have a political, not an intellectual or scientific, agenda—they are trying to outperform their colleagues and advance their careers. In a real sense, then, our clients adopt management interventions (including training programs) for perfectly rational reasons—career advancement. This also explains why, when our client gets the eagerly sought promotion, the consulting relationship often ends; this is because the new person in the job wants to find a way to differentiate herself though the choice of a new consulting intervention.

It might be useful to consider briefly the question of whether business people are actually more irrational than academic psychologists. Some people might interpret this chapter as supporting such an assumption, but in fact we don't endorse it. What do the following topics have in common: cognitive dissonance (Festinger, 1957), the fundamental attribution error (Ross, 1977), learned helplessness (Seligman, 1975), self-monitoring (Snyder, 1987), and Zimbardo's Stanford prison experiment? On the one hand, these descriptions of social behavior are regarded by many psychologists as solid empirical milestones in the development of social psychology; they are perceived as little nuggets of truth that are passed on as reality to each generation of graduate students. On the other hand, the evidence in support of these milestones will not stand any sort of close scrutiny (Briggs, Cheek, & Buss, 1980; Chapanis & Chapanis, 1964). The evidence is clear that academic psychologists subscribe to a large number of unfounded beliefs that they are very willing to defend in public.

Stanovich and West (2000) distinguish between what they call System 1 and System 2 thinking. System 1 thinking is closely tied to the perceptual system; both perception and System 1 thinking are spontaneously drawn to motivationally relevant and emotionally arousing stimuli, and they function by generating impressions of stimuli. Kahneman (2003) describes System 1 thinking as intuitive, as "typically fast, automatic, effortless, associative, implicit...and often emotionally charged" (p. 698), and its conclusions are difficult to control or modify. System 2 thinking (or reasoning) is characterized as slow, controlled, effortful, rule-governed, and flexible. System 2 thinking serves to monitor the quality of the impressions generated by System 1 thinking. But people find careful thinking or reasoning to be effortful; they tire easily and then draw conclusions based on whatever plausible impressions come quickly to mind.

Both business people and academic psychologists share an equal propensity to engage in System 1 thinking—it is a universal human attribute. Business people and academic psychologists differ quite strongly in terms of their personalities and decision-making preferences, but they do not differ in terms of fundamental rationality—or fundamental irrationality. However, they do differ in their preferred strategies for making decisions and in their approaches to ambiguous information. Business people (predominantly ES types) prefer fast intuitive decisions, whereas academic psychologists (predominantly IR types) prefer certitude over speed. One result is that psychologists find the behavior of business people irrational. At the same time, however, business people find the ideas of psychologist unhelpful. Both are probably right. Business people define success in terms of managing commercial enterprises in a financially profitable manner. Academics define success overtly in terms of peer respect and academic honors, and covertly in terms of salary. Business people are preoccupied to a significant degree with people problems—a very smart businessman once said, "I spend 80% of my time worrying about such issues as who will get the corner office and 20% of my time thinking about my clients." In contrast, academics are primarily preoccupied with technical issues—are the data credible, were the analyses conducted correctly, have the results been reported accurately—and they spend relatively less time thinking about people problems.

STRUCTURAL EXPLANATIONS FOR THE PREVALENCE OF FADS

So far we have argued that the differences between the attitudes of business people and I/O psychologists toward EI are rooted in personality. However, some sociologically inclined writers (Logan & Stokes, 2004) believe that the interest in EI also reflects a cultural shift related to the transition from the industrial era to a knowledge economy driven by the Internet. They argue that the Internet, as a new medium of communication, is changing society and organizations in ways that are comparable to, but even more dramatic than, the invention of the printing press. A new medium shapes the scale and form of human association and action; it imposes a new environment and a new set of sensibilities on its users. Independent of the content it mediates, a medium of communication has its own intrinsic effects on our perceptions which are its unique messages. The unique set of five properties, or messages, of the Internet are (1) two-way flow of information; (2) ease and speed of access to information; (3) continuous learning; (4) alignment and integration of vision and objectives; and, based on these four properties; (5) creation of a unique community (Logan & Stokes, 2004).

The communication and networking power of the Internet has both created *and* enabled the explosive growth of the knowledge era that is transforming our organizations and institutions, and societies, on a global scale. The hierarchical structure of industrial era organizations, based on impersonal role-based functional relationships, is being supplanted by the democratic, collaborative networking structure of the knowledge era. The quality of relationships between individuals in the work environment, which was generally not considered a crucial issue in the industrial era management mindset, now has become fundamental to a team's ability to successfully collaborate. To the degree that the economy becomes knowledge based, the key assets of organizations increasingly become the creativity and innovation of their members, both management and employees—that is, its human capital. Enhancing "emotionally intelligent" behaviors, which help build trust between team members, becomes *the* critical success competency for knowledge-based enterprises. Corporate wealth now becomes increasingly defined in terms of employees' collaborative knowledge-producing behaviors—a temperamental and transient capital asset that collectively leaves the company premises every evening and hopefully returns the next morning.

Employee loyalty has always been important—but it is now becoming a sine qua non of an organization's success. However, it is not the pensioner-prison loyalty of the command-and-control industrial economy. Rather, building and maintaining employee loyalty in a modern organization requires a set of managerial and leadership skills that looks very much like EI. Loyalty cannot be so easily coerced from today's knowledge workers—they have seen too much and know too much. The mergers and acquisitions of the past two decades, coupled with the surge of business process reengineering (BPR), based on Hammer and Champy's 1993 book *Reengineering the Corporation*, led to waves of down-sizing, right-sizing and de-hiring as managers tried to reduce overhead and increase profits. Those who were fired were not the only ones who lost their trust in the corporate organization; those who remained understood that they too were expendable and could be let go in the next round of cutbacks—and over time, many were. The promise of lifetime employment in exchange for organizational loyalty came to an end.

Employees soon shifted their trust and loyalty from their employers to their own careers and professional colleagues. As better information and communication make them increasingly more strategic about their career options and development, knowledge workers today are much less willing to put up with the bad management practices to which previous generations were subjected. Research from the Gallup Organization (Buckingham & Coffman, 1999) shows that the primary reason employees leave a company is poor management—people don't quit organizations, they quit managers. Poor management results from poor interpersonal skills; interpersonal skills have been given myriad competency names by different writers, but in the human resources (HR) community, they currently fall under the general rubric of emotional intelligence. The bottom-line implication is that organizations need to develop managers who are more interpersonally aware, not out of social benevolence, but because it is essential if they want to attract and retain the quality of "human capital" that is essential for their success.

Collaboration between knowledge workers drives the development of new and innovative knowledge. Successful collaboration depends on three factors: (1) cognitive and technical skills ("IQ"), (2) social interaction skills or emotional competencies (called "EI" in the HR industry), and (3) self-motivation to collaborate with others ("MQ"; conventional I/O psychology calls this, somewhat infelicitously, organizational citizenship behavior). Each of these factors is necessary but not sufficient—successful collaboration depends on individuals being well balanced across all three skill sets. If they lack the requisite cognitive and technical IQ skills, they will have little intellectual capital to bring to the group; if they lack the requisite EI skills (i.e., their EQ), they will not be effective team players; and if they do not have the motivation (MQ) to work with others, they won't participate, focusing instead only on personal gain. Logan & Stokes (2004) expressed this point metaphorically in an equation that business people can readily understand, that is, the collaboration quotient: $CQ = IQ \times EQ \times MQ$. Assessing EI becomes a critical success factor for business leaders as they strive to optimize their organization's human resources, which is their only sustainable competitive advantage in the burgeoning knowledge economy.

Business executives must rely on other people in order to get their organization's work done, and they must achieve results quickly. Each quarter, their financial results are reviewed by analysts; poor results over as little as a year can lead to perceptions of failure and even dismissal. Lucier, Schuyt, and Handa (2004) reported, "Overall, 9.5% of the world's 2,500 largest public companies changed chief executives in 2003, compared to 10.7% in 2002. Still, the rate of CEO dismissals has increased by 170% from 1995 to 2003." No wonder executives are on the alert for new management techniques that might improve their financial results. As a CEO of a U.S. Fortune 500 national retail company said about his business strategy, "You can *never* do things fast enough!"

In contrast, academics are significantly more self-reliant and less impacted by performance time pressures. The performance capabilities of other people have a higher valence for business people than for academics, and as a result, business leaders are more likely to be aware of how differences in attitude, temperament, interpersonal style, and values (i.e., personality) affect the performance of individuals. For business people, personality has a significant pragmatic payoff; for academics, personality is usually only a matter of academic interest. Thus, for the business manager, the critical question is how to find effective measures of those variables that are practically useful for making HR decisions that drive business results.

Imagine for a moment that you are a business executive and that you think the personality characteristics of new employees are important predictors of their subsequent performance. You decide to begin using a measure of personality to screen potential employees for fit with various jobs and with the organization. Where do you go for help? The advice that you are most likely to get from the academic community is to forget about it, because they believe that personality measures are, at best, only weak predictors of job performance.

ACADEMIC SKEPTICISM REGARDING PERSONALITY

Why are academic psychologists so critical of personality? There are some good reasons to be critical, and we can summarize them in terms of three points. First, based on the membership list of the Association for Research in Personality (ARP), there are only about 200 personality psychologists in academic positions in the United States, and at most, only 40 or 50 of them are active researchers. Among the active researchers, there is virtually no agreement regarding an agenda for their discipline. One group studies the sources of psychopathology (Hare, 1985). A second group tries to identify the basic structure of personality, with little concern for practical applications (Digman, 1990). A third group evaluates the neuropsychological foundations of personality and the heritability of the major dimensions (Loehlin, 1992). A fourth and very tiny group is concerned with predicting important practical outcomes—competence, effectiveness, leadership, creativity, integrity (Hogan, 2004). Overall, however, there is no consensus about an intellectual agenda for the field, which means that the cumulative impact of the few existing researchers is minimized. In our view, the field only stays alive because it is intrinsically appealing to the general public.

A second problem with personality psychology is a generalized lack of concern for measurement validity. There are perhaps 2,500 test publishers in the United States, and only a very few pay attention to validity. In her recent book, *The Cult of Personality*, Annie Murphy Paul (2004) argued that personality tests have led us to "miseducate our children, mismanage our companies, and misunderstand ourselves" (p. 1). This indictment of personality testing is due almost entirely to the willingness of publishers to sell tests with no demonstrated validity. Not surprisingly, the reaction of the test publishing industry to the Paul (2004) book has been a big yawn. In part, this is a reflection of a long-standing lack of concern with the relevance of personality tests for predicting meaningful outcomes. For example, the pioneers of personality measurement—J.P. Guilford, Raymond Cattell, and Hans Eysenck—regarded correlations between test scores and real world criteria as "peripheral validity"; for them, real validity was the degree to which factor structures replicate across samples. Ironically, the empirical tradition from Minnesota, which focuses on criterion-related validity, is typically derided as "dust bowl empiricism." The "pioneers" were interested in replicating factor structures, whereas the empirical tradition was interested in predicting outcomes. The "pioneers" had an academic agenda that is of little use to consumers of assessment services, and the empirical tradition has an applied agenda that interests consumers but not academics.

The last problem with personality psychology concerns the quality of the research. Like the ability to play the piano, the ability to do research is normally distributed. A few people have a talent for research, but most people don't. The popularity of meta-analysis has exacerbated the problem because it allows people to conduct research in a variety of domains (including personality) even if they have little knowledge of the content in that particular area. As a result, many of the meta-analyses evaluating the validity of personality assessment (which are a source of much of the academic skepticism regarding personality) are significantly flawed. For example, researchers often include in the same analysis measures that are not commensurable. Thus, they combine measures of normal personality with measures of psychopathology and values and interests. In addition, they include well-validated measures (e.g., the California Psychological Inventory [CPI]) with poorly validated measures (e.g., the Myers-Briggs Type Indicator). They incorrectly often treat constructs with similar names as if they were interchangeable. For example, high scores on the Agreeableness scale of the NEO indicate people who try not to give offense, whereas high scores on the Likeability scale of the Hogan Personality Inventory (HPI) indicate people who are actively charming. These scales predict different things and don't belong in the same analysis, but they have been lumped together in certain meta-analytic studies.

Finally, many researchers ignore the problem of bidirectionality—measures of conscientiousness are likely to be positively correlated with some outcomes and negatively correlated with others, for sound theoretical reasons in both cases. Imagine that conscientiousness is negatively correlated with one kind of performance (rated creativity), but positively correlated with another kind of performance (rated compliance with rules). This suggests that conscientiousness is a robust predictor of performance. However, if you simply add the two sets of correlations together, they cancel each other out. This poorly informed practice of averaging correlations that are expected to differ in sign has, in some cases, contributed to the conclusion that personality is a weak predictor of performance (Tett, Jackson, Rothstein, & Reddon, 1999).

The best known meta-analyses regarding the validity of cognitive ability measures used one test, the General Aptitude Test Battery, allowing researchers to avoid the problems of classification and measurement equivalence (Hunter, 1980). In the same way, meta-analyses of personality research should only use one inventory rather than combining a bunch of them, all of which have different measurement goals.

We also believe that many of the critics of personality psychology begin with a pronounced bias. They are behaviorists, and most behaviorists will no more be persuaded by data supporting the validity of personality measurement than creationists will be persuaded by data supporting evolutionary theory. The most important claim of personality psychology is that there are structures inside people (hopes, dreams, fears, and aspirations) that determine their behavior. This claim is anathema to behaviorists, who assume that social behavior is caused or explained in terms of reward structures in the environment. B. F. Skinner, the best known advocate of behaviorism in the

20th century, was notoriously insensitive to human feelings (when his brother died unexpectedly, Skinner helped the county medical examiner with the autopsy and found it quite interesting). Skinner died denying the truth of evolutionary theory and the existence of instincts—that is, denying that internal structures influence social behavior. Although the modern cognitive behaviorists have discovered internal structures, they still don't really understand evolutionary theory. A good bit of the antipersonality sentiment in our profession is sheer ideology, promoted by critics who won't be persuaded by data.

EMPIRICAL SUPPORT FOR THE UTILITY OF PERSONALITY MEASURES

There have always been good data supporting the validity of personality measures. Consider some data from the 1960s. Gough (1965) reported a point-biserial correlation of .73 between a delinquency–nondelinquency criterion and scores on the Socialization scale of the CPI in a sample of 10,296 people. In a related study, Gough reported a cross-validated, point-biserial correlation of .63 between a CPI regression equation (Socialization had the largest beta weight) and the delinquency criterion in an American sample of 2,981 cases, and of .60 in a Japanese sample of 149 cases (Gough, DeVos, & Muzushima, 1968). In the best study of creativity ever published, Hall and MacKinnon (1969) reported a cross-validated multiple R of .61 between a three (personality) variable regression equation and a solid criterion of real-world creativity. Also in the 1960s, we put together a large sample of college students from two campuses in the Northeast and developed an index of marijuana use ranging from frequent use to principled non-use. A CPI-based discriminant function correctly classified 81% of all the users and 81% of all the non-users (see Hogan, Mankin, & Fox, 1970). These studies bear only indirectly on occupational performance, but they indicate the kind of correlations that one can expect from competent personality research.

More recently, Judge, Bono, Ilies, and Gerhardt (2002) conducted a careful meta-analytic study of the links between personality (defined in terms of the Five-Factor model) and leadership (defined in terms of emergence and effectiveness). They report the following estimated corrected correlations: Neuroticism -.24 (N = 8,025); Extraversion .31 (N = 11,705); Openness .24 (N = 7,221); Agreeableness .08 (N = 9,801); and Conscientiousness .28 (N = 7,510), with a multiple R, using the five dimensions, of .48.

In the best meta-analytic study of personality and job performance published to date, Hogan and Holland (2003) confined their investigation to one inventory (the HPI; Hogan & Hogan, 1995), rather than trying to combine scales across inventories, and they carefully aligned predictors with the relevant criteria. That is, they did not try to predict training performance using the HPI Adjustment scale or sales performance using the HPI Prudence scale. They reported the following estimated true validities: Emotional Stability .43 (N = 2,573); Extraversion/Ambition .34 (N = 3,698); Agreeableness .36 (N = 2,500); Conscientiousness .36 (N = 3,379); and Intellect/Openness .34 (N = 1,190).

ACADEMIC COMPLICITY IN FOSTERING EI BUSINESS FADS

So far we have argued that business is interested in EI because many business people understand that personality is important. For them, however, one personality measure is the same as the next, and many measures of EI come quickly to hand. It is worth noting again that *both* academics and business people are susceptible to fads, and sometimes the causes of their interest in fads are intertwined. Academic fads are stimulated by publication opportunities—the first paper to publish a new finding "wins" academic recognition and potential financial rewards in terms of grants or consulting opportunities. Ironically, the buzz created by the publication of a sexy new finding can create a business fad, because business trends are legitimized by being featured in such visible and popular "academic" outlets as the *Harvard Business Review (HBR)*.

In the case of EI, consider the HBR articles, *"What Makes a Leader"* (Goleman, 1998) and *"Building the Emotional Intelligence of Groups"* (Druskat & Wolff, 2001). HBR is also very savvy about its business market—it not only publishes the original articles, it also creates OnPoint executive "Cole Notes" versions for the busy executive who may not want to read a complete article. In HBR's words:

> HBR OnPoint articles save you time by enhancing an original *Harvard Business Review* article with an overview that draws out the main points .... This enables you to scan, absorb, and share the management insights with others.

And then HBR, using a tried-and-true marketing strategy to increase sales by simply repackaging the same product, recombines original articles into "new" groups of articles:

> HBR OnPoint collections save you time by synthesizing and distilling the essence of three *Harvard Business Review* articles that, together, help you meet a specific management challenge. One-page overviews draw out the main points.

For EI examples, consider *Best of HBR on Leadership: Emotionally Intelligent Leadership* (Harvard Business Review Online,

2001a), a collection of three previously published HBR articles by Goleman, and *Boosting Your Team's Emotional Intelligence—for Maximum Performance* (Harvard Business Review Online, 2001b), a collection of three HBR articles (which recycles one of Goleman's articles from the *Best of HBR on Leadership* just mentioned). Earlier, we noted that business people prefer quick, intuitive actions. The HBR strategy of packaging their regular articles with short, simplified (even simplistic) summaries fits this personality type perfectly.

Material published in HBR (and other less known B-school publications) provides the credibility that business consultants need to sell new services—consultants are *always* looking for the newest trend to differentiate themselves from their competition. Consequently, HBR is an important source for new management trends. Because the HBR summaries emphasize broad overviews rather than detailed statistical analyses, scientific merit takes a back seat to face validity when decisions are made about what to publish.

Business journalists have also contributed to the process of hyping EI. A few years ago, *Fast Company*, with its tagline "How Smart People Work," and *Business 2.0*, with its tagline "The Playbook for a New Generation of LeadersÔ," were *the* business trend/fad setters *par excellence* for the new wave of high-tech managers. In one *Fast Company* article, Schwartz (2000a) noted, "'Emotional intelligence' is starting to find its way into companies, offering employees a way to come to terms with their feelings—and to perform better. But as the field starts to grow, some worry that it could become just another fad."

Although this suggests a balanced view, the overall thrust of the article is that paying attention to EI competencies will have tangible business payoffs.

Similarly, Schwartz (2000b) wrote about how Gallup Organization's Buckingham and Coffman (1999) "have managed to crunch 25 years' worth of interviews with more than 1 million workers into a metric that clearly defines the bottom-line value of eliciting certain feelings from employees in the workplace" (p. 398). For time-pressured profit-oriented business executives, articles like these helped create the EI fad.

SUCCESSFUL EI COMPANIES SPEAK THEIR CUSTOMERS' LANGUAGE AND MEET THEIR NEEDS

Business leaders are preoccupied with financial models and competitive strategies. They are focused on getting good financial results every quarter, and, consequently, they rarely devote time to analyzing the merits of the latest management practices; even if they had the time, they are not temperamentally inclined to analyses of this sort. Moreover, they are no more interested in the psychometric properties of an assessment program, EI or otherwise, than they are in the computer programming code that drives their accounting processes, and all of this heightens their susceptibility to trends and fads. In particular, managers who are (rightly) convinced of the relevance of personality in the business world will naturally be attracted to personality-like measures that have at least the appearance of business relevance, and many EI measures fit the bill.

The proliferation of companies offering online assessment has also enhanced the availability of poor quality assessments. For online assessment providers, a good Web designer is more important than a good researcher. Many (perhaps even most) online test providers offer assessments that have never undergone academic peer review to ensure their psychometric integrity, and business consumers have no idea what they are buying. In the current Internet-enabled marketing universe, an important criterion for the success of a personality instrument is achieving first screen status (i.e., being the first set of items retrieved when searching for information on business applications of personality measures). From a business perspective, the reporting format, reselling price structure, and collateral materials describing how to use the assessment results are likely to be much more important than any technical manual in evaluating what test to purchase. The nonanalytic style favored by many business leaders contributes to the acceptance of poorly validated EI instruments by the business world.

Business leaders understand the importance of hiring decisions and how the personality issues of key players impact team performance from the executive team to the shop floor—these are very real problems. At senior corporate levels, placing the wrong executives in charge can lead to a collapse of the entire organization. There are many well-known examples in recent years of global public corporations being dragged into bankruptcy by greedy leaders with bad core values. Boards of directors are increasingly being held accountable for executive hiring mistakes, and shareholder class-action suits have raised the ante for board members. Nonetheless, boards of directors and senior executives have not become more capable of finding valid selection systems to evaluate candidates for key positions.

Rather, they must rely on their internal HR staff or executive search firms to do this for them. But most internal staff and executive search consultants lack the background or experience to discriminate between competently validated selection instruments and psychometric junk. As is the case with most other parts of the organization, technical expertise is not the key to management success in HR functions. As a result, decisions made by top HR managers and their consultants are rarely driven by technically sophisticated instruments or techniques.

To make things worse, business-savvy purveyors of unvalidated personality tests, a category that includes many EI-related test materials and EI consulting interventions, avoid trying to sell to I/O psychologists with professional qualifications, preferring to go directly to the end users (i.e., HR executives). For example, compare the assessment providers at a Society for Industrial and Organizational Psychology (SIOP) conference with the assessment providers at a meeting of the American Society for Training and Development (ASTD). The SIOP conference is geared toward academic research and science-based applications, whereas the ASTD meeting is geared toward solving business problems, and, for the most part, EI vendors avoid SIOP and flock to ASTD. By offering certification in their train-the-trainer programs, they qualify a cadre of nonpsychologists who attend meetings such as ASTD to market and deliver their assessment instruments. This creates a vastly larger pool of "qualified" users (and purchasers) and eliminates the constraints of dealing with a potentially skeptical academic market. This strategy can be attractive to the business community from the perspective of increased accessibility and lower price points.

Tests with professional and popular appeal must not only be properly researched, they must be effectively marketed to the business community—just as any business must do. But academics typically have neither the skills nor the orientation to successfully market their products and services to business. Businesses will seek out whatever works to meet their needs, hence the proliferation of low quality instruments by business minded nonacademic companies.

To summarize, although there are good published data supporting the validity of personality assessment, the academic community tends to ignore it and to argue that personality measures are only weak predictors of occupational performance. When business people ask academics for advice regarding using personality measures for selection purposes, they are typically told that the measures are unhelpful. But many business people understand that personality is an important determinant of occupational performance, and they go elsewhere for advice. The result is the impressive popularity of tests like the Myers-Briggs Type Indicator and many measures of EI, which are weak in terms of empirical validity but strong in terms of their apparent relevance to organizations.

Perhaps more importantly, there is a significant lesson here for academic psychologists, but it is one that they probably don't want to hear. The goal of their activity is the production of knowledge. But their product (knowledge) must compete in an intellectual marketplace, and that requires paying attention to the needs of the potential consumers of their products, and academic psychology's track record here is not very impressive. Many purveyors of EI tests and interventions have been successful in the business world because they listen to customers, provide a service business customers want, and speak the language of their customers.

EI marketers have approached the business world in a strategically sensible manner. First, their books, tests, and interventions make vague, broad claims that are intuitively appealing but rarely backed by data (e.g., see chaps. 1, 3, 6 , 8, 9, 10, & 11, this volume). However, from the perspective of business leaders, good psychometric data rank somewhere below good penmanship as a reason for adopting an intervention as appealing as an EI test. Second, EI marketers claim to solve problems business leaders care about, whereas personality psychologists focus on problems like convergent and discriminant validity. Finally, EI consultants do not come into an executive boardroom talking about reliability coefficients, fit indices, or other psychometric trivia. Rather, they claim to offer what executives need—that is, solutions to the people problems that make management so difficult.

Has EI then become yet another "fad" adopted by a business community seeking the latest idea to gain a competitive edge? Increasingly, the answer seems to be "yes." But the EI "fad" may be around for a long time and morph into a significant trend because of the changes in work and organizational structure brought about by the global knowledge economy. Organizations need to adopt progressively more effective ways to attract, develop, *and* retain knowledge workers—their human capital wealth creators; they need ways to improve working relationships between the employees themselves and between employees and management.

REFERENCES

Briggs, S. R., Cheek, J.M., & Buss, A.H. (1980). An analysis of the self-monitoring scale. *Journal of Personality and Social Psychology, 38,* 679–686.
Buckingham, M., & Coffman, C. (1999). *First, break all the rules:_What the world's greatest managers do differently.* New York: Simon & Schuster.
Chapanis, N. P., & Chapanis, A. (1964). Cognitive dissonance: Five years later. *Psychological Bulletin, 61,* 1—22.
Digman, J. M. (1990). Personality structure: Emergence of the five-factor model. *Annual Review of Psychology, 41,* 417—440.
Druskat, V. U., & Wolff, S. B. (2001, March). Building the emotional intelligence of groups. *Harvard Business Review, 79*(3), 81–90.
Festinger, L. (1957). *A theory of cognitive dissonance.* Palo Alto, CA: Stanford University Press.
Goleman, D. (1995). *Emotional intelligence.* New York: Bantam Books.
Goleman, D. (1998, November/December). What makes a leader? *Harvard Business Review, 76*(6), 92–102.
Gough, H. G. (1965). Conceptual analysis of psychological test scores and other diagnostic variables. *Journal of Abnormal Psychology, 70,* 294–302.

Gough, H. G., DeVos, G., & Muzushima, K. (1968). Japanese validation of the CPI social maturity index. *Psychological Reports, 22,* 143–146.

Hall, W. B., & MacKinnon, D. W. (1969). Personality inventories as predictors of creativity among architects. *Journal of Applied Psychology, 53,* 322–326.

Hammer, M., & Champy, J. (1993). *Reengineering the corporation: A manifesto for business revolution.* New York: HarperCollins.

Hare, R. D. (1985). Comparison of procedures for the assessment of psychopathology. *Journal of Consulting and Clinical Psychology, 53,* 7–16.

Harvard Business Review Online. (2001a, December). *Best of HBR on leadership: emotionally intelligent leadership.* Retrieved December 1, 2001, from http://harvardbusinessonline.hbsp.harvard.edu

Harvard Business Review Online. (2001b, March). *Boosting Your Team's Emotional Intelligence—for Maximum Performance.* Retrieved March 1, 2001, from http://harvardbusinessonline.hbsp.harvard.edu

Hogan, R. (2004). Personality psychology for organizational researchers. In B. Schneider & D. B. Smith (Eds.), *Personality and organizations* (pp. 3–24). Mahwah, NJ: Lawrence Erlbaum Associates.

Hogan, R., & Hogan, J. (1995). *Manual for the Hogan Personality Inventory.* Tulsa, OK: Hogan Assessment Systems.

Hogan, R., & Hogan, J. (1996). *The movtives, values, preferences inventory.* Tulsa, OK: Hogan Assessment Systems.

Hogan, R., Holland, B. W. (2003). Using theory to evaluate personality and job performance relations. *Journal of Applied Psychology, 88,* 100–112.

Hogan, R., Mankin, D., Conway, J., & Fox, S. (1970). Personality correlates of undergraduate marijuana use. *Journal of Consulting and Clinical Psychology, 35,* 58–63.

Holland, J. L. (1997). *Making vocational choices: A theory of vocational personalities and work environments* (3rd ed.). Odessa, FL: PAR.

Hunter, J. E. (1980). *Validity generalization for 12,000 jobs: An application of synthetic validity and validity generalization to the General Aptitude Test Battery (GATB).* Washington, DC: U. S. Department of Labor, Employment Service.

Judge, T. A., Bono, J. E., Ilies, R., & Gerhardt, M. W. (2002). Personality and leadership: A qualitative and quantitative review. *Journal of Applied Psychology, 87,* 765–780.

Kahneman, D. (2003). A perspective on judgment and choice: Mapping bounded rationality. *American Psychologist, 58,* 697–720.

Logan, R. K., & Stokes, L. W. (2004). *Collaborate to compete: Driving profitability in the knowledge economy.* Toronto, ON: Wiley.

Loehlin, J. C. (1992). *Genes and environment in personality development.* Newbury Park, CA: Sage.

Lucier, C., Schuyt, R., & Handa, J. (2004). CEO succession 2003: The perils of "good" governance. *Booz Allen: strategy + business, 35*(Summer), 70–93.

Paul, A. M. (2004). *The cult of personality.* New York: Basic Books.

Ross, L. (1977). The intuitive psychologist and his shortcomings. In L. Berkowitz (Ed.), *Advances in experimental social psychology* (Vol. 10, pp. 174–214). New York: Academic Press.

Schwartz, T. (2000a). How do you feel? *Fast Company, 35*(June), 296.

Schwartz, T. (2000b). Life/Work. *Fast Company, 40*(November), 398.

Seligman, M. E.P. (1975). *Helplessness: On depression, development, and death.* San Francisco: Freeman.

Snyder, M. (1987). *Public appearances/private realities: The psychology of self-monitoring.* New York: Freeman.

Stanovich, K. E., & West, R. F. (2000). Individual differences in reasoning: Implications for the rationality debate. *Behavioral and Brain Sciences, 23,* 645–665.

Tett, R. P., Jackson, D. N., Rothstein, M., & Reddon, J. R. (1999). Meta-analysis of bidirectional relations in personality-job performance research. *Human Performance, 12,* 1–29.

IV

Improving EI Research and Applications

The final section of this book looks at the possibility that the problems that have led to the emotional intelligence (EI) controversy might be resolved. In chapter 12, Murphy and Sideman describe the process by which fads like EI grow and collapse, and they suggest that the key to improving EI is to engage more mainstream research on the topic. They also suggest that it will be necessary to take this construct back from the cadre of committed EI enthusiasts ("true believers") who have so far dominated the scene.

In chapter 13, Daus makes an eloquent case for focusing on an ability-based model of EI. This chapter notes that the models developed by Salovey, Mayer, and their colleagues predated the current EI controversy and that they are likely to endure.

In chapter 14, Spector and Johnson present concrete ideas for improving the definition and measurement of EI. In part, their recommendations echo those in several other chapters—that is, that EI should return to its roots. In the early 1990s, EI emerged as a mainstream topic of study; most of the original work that led to the emergence of this construct appeared in peer-reviewed journals, and this work still forms the basis for the most attractive models of EI. Spector and Johnson go beyond the recommendation to concentrate on ability-based models to suggest how better measures of EI might be developed.

Chapter 15 summarizes four key conclusions that can be drawn from chapters 1 through 14, that (1) EI is poorly defined and even more poorly measured, (2) the relationships between EI and other similar constructs are still poorly understood, (3) the most influential claims about EI do not hold up to scrutiny, and (4) there are reasons for hope when considering the future of EI, but there is also a long way to go.

The bottom line of this section of the book is that many of the problems that have contributed to the controversy over EI can be resolved.

There is clear consensus that some models of EI are better than others; models that describe EI in terms of specific abilities and skills represent the only realistic prospects for progress in EI. Cleaning up the definition of EI would solve many of the problems noted in the first three sections of this book, by setting more concrete and definite boundaries between EI and other constructs, by providing a more consistent target for the development of measures, and by restoring some sanity to the claims about what EI can and cannot do for individuals and organizations. Better definitions would also contribute to better measures, which are critical if we hope to make real progress with EI.

The debate over EI seems to be moving beyond the early volleys EI proponents and EI skeptics lobbed at one another. As the authors of this volume document, there is a growing body of serious research on EI and a growing community of researchers asking important questions about the construct of EI. It is not clear yet how the answers to some of these questions will turn out, but there is a solid basis for a critical examination of EI research and practice as well as some reasons for optimism about the future of EI.

12

The Fadification of Emotional Intelligence

Kevin R. Murphy and Lori Sideman
Pennsylvania State University

Psychology, business, and education share a common curse: a susceptibility to fads. In all three domains, ideas, theories, and applications often follow the same general trajectory:

1. They emerge suddenly and capture popular attention.
2. They attract a dedicated core of "true believers," whose fervor and uncritical acceptance of the new idea or approach fuels both its growth and controversy over its value.
3. These true believers trumpet this new idea as a general solution to a wide range of problems.
4. These claims become the focus of bitter disputes.
5. The idea, approach, or solution collapses as suddenly as it arose, and it is replaced by a new fad or fashion.

Emotional Intelligence (EI) certainly exhibits many of the characteristics of this trajectory. First, interest in EI has shown this same pattern of explosive growth. Prior to 1995, there were only a handful of researchers seriously interested in EI, and there were few EI tests, training programs, or interventions. In mid-2005, a Google search using the keywords "emotional intelligence" produced 4,380,00 hits.

Second, EI has been described by enthusiasts as both highly important and broadly relevant (most notably, Goleman, 1995, 1998), and it has attracted both a dedicated core of true believers and an equally dedicated cohort of skeptics and critics. It is too soon to tell whether interest in EI will collapse as quickly as it grew (as is usually the case with fads), but if history is any guide, it is unlikely that current levels of enthusiasm for EI can be sustained over the long run.

Is EI a fad? If so, so what? Labeling something a fad does not mean that it is a bad idea (although many of the fads cataloged in this chapter represent profoundly bad ideas), nor does it mean that claims currently made for EI will turn out to be unsupportable. Fads come and go, but they nevertheless sometimes lead to products of enduring value. For example, some of

Picasso's most influential paintings (e.g., *Guernica*) were done in styles that seemed to spring from nowhere, to catch fire overnight, and then suddenly disappeared, virtually without a trace; a painting done in the same style today would be poorly received. We usually use terms like *fad* to describe things that are slightly foolish but inexplicably popular (e.g., hula hoops, pet rocks), but there is no reason to assume that ideas that are described as faddish are always wrong. Nevertheless, the possibility that current enthusiasm for EI represents a fad is a troubling one, for reasons that are laid out next.

The trouble with fads is not that they necessarily lead to the promotion of bad ideas, but rather that the process of sudden rise, intense debate, and sudden fall that characterizes so many fads tends to stifle or short-circuit the sort of constructive criticism that is critical to scientific progress. That is, even when a fad is launched on the basis of a good idea, the "fadification" process makes it unlikely that the idea will develop in a thoughtful, rigorous way. Proponents of fads are swept along by the ideas that define the fad, and they are unlikely to be appropriately critical. Opponents of fads are too focused on sinking the whole enterprise, and they often fail to give faddish ideas the serious and thorough examination more often given to proposals put forth in a more cautious, conservative fashion. As a result, fads inspire partisan bickering rather than dispassionate analysis. Fads provoke fistfights more readily than they provoke serious debate, and the proposition that EI may represent a fad has an important bearing on evaluating the scholarship on both sides of the EI debate.

DEFINITIONS AND LIFE CYCLE OF FADS

In a classic paper, Dunnette (1966) provided definitions of fads, fashions, and folderol in psychological research. *Fads*, as he describes them, are "practices and concepts characterized by capriciousness and intense, but short-lived interest," while *fashions* are described as "manners or modes of action taking on the character of habits and enforced by social or scientific norms defining what constitutes the 'thing to do'" (p. 343). Finally, Dunnette defines *folderol* as "practices characterized by excessive ornamentation, nonsensical and unnecessary actions, trifles and essentially useless and wasteful fiddle-faddle" (p. 343). It is not clear whether this distinction is always useful one, but it is clear that fads, fashions, and folderol influence research and practice in psychology. Dunnette's (1966) observation that psychological research is often infiltrated by theories, techniques, and practices that galvanize popular interest in the short term, but that lack strong scientific support or sustainability, remains a valid one.

It is tempting to attribute fads in the social and behavioral sciences to a combination of unscrupulous manipulation on the part of the a few key proponents and naiveté and gullibility on the part of the public that sustains the fad. Unfortunately, things are probably not that simple. Park (2000) notes that much of what we would think of as "junk science" (or to use his term, "voodoo science") consists of theories of what could be rather than evidence supporting was really is (p. 9). His review suggests that the process by which dubious ideas take a life of their own, overwhelming more valid but less captivating theories in the published literature, is similar to the placebo effect.

> The placebo works by fooling the brain into thinking the problem is being taken care of. Once the brain is persuaded that things are under control, it may turn the signal level down by releasing endorphins, opiate proteins found naturally in the brain. Rather than blocking the production of prostaglandins, the endorphins block their effect. As powerful as the placebo effect can be, it is extremely doubtful that placebos can cause hair to grown on bald heads or shrink tumors, as some have claimed, but there is no doubt that placebos can influence the perception of pain. Whether a person responds to a placebo depends almost entirely on how well the doctor plays his or her part. (p. 51)

Like placebos, fads often work, at least in the short run, because people believe they will work. However, belief in an emerging fad is not enough to ensure its growth. Rather, fads seem to take off only when two conditions are met: (1) The fad appears to solve problems that people care about, and (2) more traditional approaches do not seem to provide a solution for the same problem. That is, fads grow only in fertile soil, in conditions where the normal process of scientific progress and discovery does not seem to be making headway. One explanation for the frequency with which fads arise in business, education, and management is that scientific progress in these areas has been relatively slow.

As the placebo analogy suggests, fads are most likely to thrive if they make sweeping promises than if they make only limited ones. That is, a new idea that promises to help solve only narrow or technical problems is unlikely to attract a set of true believers, whereas fads that appear to address a wide range of important problems will have little trouble attracting adherents. One corollary is that fads have the strongest chance of initial success and ultimate failure if they promise more than they are can deliver. That is, the likelihood of rallying a cohort of true believers probably depends largely on the implicit or explicit promises made by the early proponents of a faddish idea, and the more substantial the promised outcomes of any particular fad, the easier it will be to attract true believers. However, the more sweeping the initial promise, the more difficult it will be to fulfill that promise. Therefore, in assessing the value of an apparent fad, Harvey and Pauwels (2003) suggest one must "peer into the future and speculate about whether the costs of the endeavor will be later justified by a valuable increase in our understanding of the human condition" (p. 125). Several authors (e.g., Lazarus, 2003; Lyubomirsky & Abbe, 2003) agree that "hot topics" must be put to rigorous tests and held to the highest standards of science (measurement and methodology) in order to guard against the suspension of disbelief that characterize public (and sometimes scientific) evaluations of the latest fad.

Several studies (e.g., Lanier, Carson, & Birkenmeier, 1999; Carson, Lanier, Carson, & Guidry, 2000; Ettorre, 1997) suggest that the life cycle of fads and fashions resembles a bell-shaped, normal curve. This curve begins with *invention*, wherein the awareness of the fad begins and the "buzz" about the phenomenon is born. Second is *acceptance*; the fad is implemented by some practitioners and the idea becomes more rampant. *Digestion* is the middle stage, where the phenomenon becomes broadly used but also begins to be subjected to criticism. *Disenchantment* occurs next, and this is where the idea is faced with frustration due to its inability to solve the problems it is proposed to explain. Finally, *decline* marks the end of the fad. The idea of a life cycle is a valuable one, particularly if fads can be detected and diagnosed early in the process. That is, if there is a reliable way to spot emerging fads before they become widely accepted, it might be possible to avoid much of the pointless controversy, wasted effort, and disappointment that marks most fads in management, education and psychology. One way to develop such a diagnostic scheme is to examine existing fads.

Psychology Fads

One of the fastest growing movements in psychology is the topic of "positive psychology." In a recent article in *Psychological Inquiry*, the late Richard Lazarus questions if the movement "has legs." In this controversial article, Lazarus (2003) declares his fear that the movement is in danger of being "just another one of the many fads that come and go in our field, which usually disappear in time, sometimes to return again in another form because the issues addressed are important but unresolved" (p. 93). While he makes clear that his business is not to speculate about why the field of psychology is like this, he affirms this is the case for several issues that researchers believe will be the next "God's gift" to research that ultimately disappear. He suggests a cycle of fad research in which many publications are written on a similar theme that ultimately dies off. With the positive psychology movement specifically, Lazarus suggests that people are merely caught up in the excitement of finding a new concept when, in fact, researchers have simply oversimplified theories and created exciting slogans for old concepts.

In response to his article, Diener (2003) answers Lazarus' question of the "fadness" of positive psychology by putting a different spin on the idea of fad. "My hope is that positive psychology is a movement that will eventually disappear because it becomes part of the very fabric of psychology" (p. 120). This sort of assimilation is not characteristic of fads, which usually decline as quickly as they arise; Diener's reply in essence makes the claim that positive psychology is not a fad at all but rather a sustainable trend in psychological research.

Interestingly, another commentary to Lazarus' article compares the positive psychology movement to that of EI research (Matthews & Zeidner, 2003). EI researchers sometimes use positive psychology terms (e.g., *well-being*, *flow*, *optimism*) in defining EI (Goleman, 1995). Matthews and Zeidner (2003) suggest that some of the same failings found in EI research also exist in positive psychology studies, such as "conceptual incoherence, neglect of measurement issues, and a tendency to make grandiose claims without supporting evidence" (p. 138).

The study of graphology represents a fad that has come and gone in multiple waves. The analysis of handwriting is sometimes used to assess honesty (Murphy, 1993) based on the belief that characteristics of a person's handwriting reveal some information about the person's personality. While still used in pre-employment screening, the validity of this method has been subjected to harsh criticism (e.g., Bar-Hillel & Ben-Shakhar, 1986). There is some evidence that graphologists can make valid predictions of job applicants' performance, but it seems that nongraphologists make equally valid predictions, given the same handwriting samples (Ben-Shakhar, 1989). In fact, nonexperts are often better than graphologists at making inferences about verifiable attributes of the writer, such as gender (Murphy, 1993). Furnham notes that because there is no useful theory explicating why graphology should work, it is no wonder we are not finding empirical evidence to support it; thus, graphology is thought to be "another pipe dream of those who want a quick and dirty decision...another in a long list of quack substitutes for hard work" (Carroll, 2002b, p. 2). Examination of publication rates for studies of graphology (specifically, studies that can be located using a title search for the term "graphology" in PsycINFO) suggest a multiple-wave cycle for this fad: 16 graphology articles published in the 1950s, 10 in the 1960s, and 1 in the 1970s; publication on this topic picked up again in the 1980s with 14 articles, 15 articles in 1990, and 4 (at the time of this writing) in the 2000s. These publication data suggest that the graphology fad that arose in the 1950s and died out in the 1970s reemerged in the 1980s and 1990s, and that it might not have died out completely yet (Murphy, 1993, notes that graphology is still very widely used in Israel and France, suggesting that in those countries, graphology has not yet reached the "disenchantment" stage).

Management Fads

The field of management is particularly susceptible to fads. Carson et al. (1999) suggest several reasons why management is so strongly fad-driven, including environmental pressures (e.g., competitive and unionized industries), forces for conformity (e.g., informational, normative, or social influences), and organizational characteristics (e.g., a history of implementing previous managerial innovations or when organizations are striving for differentiation). Carson et al. (1999) also suggest moderators that make fads more or less likely to be adopted as management practices. Fads may be more likely implemented if they are seen as "easy" or not seen as a harshly radical idea. Firms will be more likely to accept a fad if there is a plentiful supply of fads in existence.

Mazur (2002) suggests another reason why managers find fads so attractive. She suggests fads are comforting: "After all, how can you go wrong if everyone else is doing it?" (p. 16). However, she notes that many of the characteristics that make fads so popular also undermine them in the end. She reviews eight qualities that most business fads share, including their simplicity and ease in understanding/communicating, their prescriptive nature in solving management problems, their tendency to be rooted in a one-size-fits-all mentality, and their tendency to be in touch with the business problems of the current day. All of these qualities make it easier to sell a fad, but none of them contributes much to the long-term viability of fads. Carson et al. (2000) discuss the "fashion consciousness manager," who has a tendency to align himself to unproven yet intuitively appealing conjectures. These authors suggest the antifad movement has become quite trendy, in that "fad bashing" is now a fashion in and of itself (Carson et al.,

2000). Based on a review of various definitions of management fads and fashions, these authors suggest that a management fashions are (1) subject to social contagion because they are novel, (2) perceived as innovative and functional, (3) aimed at encouraging better organizational performance, (4) thought to be a remedy to a known problem, and (5) not supported by comprehensive research legitimizing their prolonged utility.

Total Quality Management (TQM) is often touted as a fad in the field of management. A PsycINFO search revealed 0 articles in the 1980s with Total Quality Management in the title, 89 in the 1990s, and 12 so far in the 2000s, resembling the bell-shaped curve of research suggested by Carson et al. (2000). Like other fads, TQM has been the subject of heated criticism. Matthews (1993) claims that TQM has now created a demand for cleanup and repair crews to help clean up the mess TQM created. Byrne (1997) reviews surveys that suggest that some of the most popular management remedies also draw the highest rates of dissatisfaction.

Another management system that has been discussed as faddish is Management by Objective (MBO). A combination of goal setting, participation in decision making, and objective feedback, MBO systems are thought to increase productivity when implemented in organizations. A meta-analysis (Rodgers & Hunter, 1991) supports this view, suggesting that 68 out of 70 studies reviewed show increases in productivity when MBO is introduced. Nevertheless, Carson et al. (2000) found MBO to fit the authors' operational definition of management fashion. A literature search on this topic using a title search on PsycINFO revealed 3 articles in the 1960s, 25 in the 1970s, 14 in the 1980s, 5 in the 1990s and 1 so far in the 2000s. This publication rate also seems to resemble the bell-shaped curve of research as suggested by Carson et al. (2000) and others (e.g. Ettorre, 1997), and it appears that interest in MBO is waning.

Quality circles represent another example of a fad. Abrahamson and Fairchild (1999) note that quality circles were invented in Japan and have been defined as "small groups of employees that meet regularly, without managerial supervision, to discuss ways of enhancing the efficiency of operations and the quality of outputs" (p. 710). Like other fads, this idea rose to prominence, attracted a great deal of attention, intense criticism, and a fairly precipitous decline, Examining data from 1967 (when the first article on quality circles appeared) to 1995, Abrahamson and Fairchild found that research on quality circles had a long latency phase prior to its popularity surge. Specifically, they found that after the first article in 1967, it wasn't until 14 years later when the number of articles on quality circles increased, and rose much more rapidly than fell, following a positively skewed pattern. Interestingly, it seems that popular press publications fell off much more quickly than did academic interest and publication on the topic. Furthermore, Abrahamson and Fairchild (1999) suggested that the decline of the quality circle fad served as a trigger for a series of subsequent fads in management.

Education Fads

Education policy represents a third area hard hit by fads. Finn and Petrilli (1998) use the word *promiscuous* to describe the trend in federal education policy. Since the 1990s, numerous educational fads have been transformed into government programs, such as character education, requiring school uniforms, paying for teachers to be appraised by a national standards board, ensuring "equity" in textbooks, replacing textbooks with laptops, and connecting all classrooms to the Internet. Finn and Petrilli (1998) note that "the arena of federal education policy resembles a vast flea market, where practically any program idea can be displayed and offered for purchase without regard to its soundness or effectiveness" (p. 56).

Why are programs that have failed to demonstrate their effectiveness (or that have shown their uselessness) still hanging around? Finn and Petrilli (1998) suggests that this is because education presents a set of problems that voters want solved: "The simplest way to give at least the appearance of action is to propose another program" (p. 56). The best way to get votes is to appeal to voters and offer instant solutions, which ultimately will not solve any real problems. The idea of the "quick fix" that will appease voters seems to be a theme running through educational policy fads. Chaddock (1998) believes this plague is partly due to the fact that key decision makers typically hold jobs for 3 years and feel pressure to show fast results. Further, she suggests that a large number of unjuried professional journals let inadequate research pass uncritically. Additionally, because educational research is poorly funded, governmental figures tend to support what is new, as opposed to what has proven effective.

Chaddock (1998) details some of the educational fads (the "reform du jour") over the years. While 1970s promoted open classrooms, the 1980s promoted the idea of whole-language instruction as opposed to learning word by word. Chaddock notes that "the new books were engaging, but many kids weren't learning to read ... [and] teachers were ordered to dig out the flash cards" (p. 1). The 1990s brought the idea of teaching to individual learning styles, despite a lack of research on the measurement of learning styles or whether it is more appropriate to teach to a style versus help students overcome it. At the end of her article, Chaddock notes some tips of "how to fad-proof your school."

One of the most useful is to remember that the most entertaining consultant does not always have the best ideas. Further, Chaddock suggests the need to take a hard look at the research base behind a proposal: What's the evidence that students will learn more under the new program than under the program it is replacing? What is the experimental design of the study, and how strong is the evidence? How similar are students in this study to those in your classroom?

One well-known fad in this area is the idea of facilitated communication (FC). First proposed by Crossley in Australia, it was brought to the United States by Bilken in the 1990s and has been used as an intervention targeted at children with autism and other communication disorders (Mostert, 2001). Bilken believed that people with autism simply had problems expressing themselves, as opposed to a meaningful cognitive deficit, which prohibited appropriate use of language. He saw FC as a tool that would bypass the expression problem and allow natural language to emerge. This technique involves a patient communicating through her facilitator, who expresses what she understands the patient is trying to say (it is more likely that the communication reflects the facilitator rather than the patient; Carroll, 2002a). There have been several reviews of using FC as an intervention, usually finding a complete lack of support for the method (e.g., Cummins & Prior, 1992; Jacobson, Mulick, & Schwartz, 1995; Mostert, 2001). Because of its relatively short-lived life span, a title search on facilitated communication on PsycINFO revealed 38 hits in the 1990s and only 3 so far in the 2000s.

Another fad in the education research is discovery learning. Discovery learning, known as a constructivist method, has been defined as a method of instruction in which students are free to work in a learning environment with little or no guidance and involves them being cognitively active in the learning process. In an *American Psychologist* article in 2004, Mayer reviews the research on discovery learning and proposes that there is ample research questioning the benefits of using a pure discovery learning method with students. He suggests that when students have too much freedom, "they may fail to come into contact with the to-be-learned material .... If a learner fails to come into contact with the to-be-learned material, no amount of activity or discussion will be able to help the learner make sense of it" (p. 17). In a title search in PsycINFO, we found 7 articles in the 1970s, 3 in the 1980s, 14 in the 90s, and 5 so far in the 2000s.

DIAGNOSING FADS

There are a variety of signs and diagnostic tests that might be used to determine whether a particular idea, intervention, or theory is a fad.

Before examining the methods that might be used in diagnosing and recognizing fads, it is useful to consider the question of what is accomplished by making such a diagnosis. It is also useful to consider the costs and benefits of labeling something a fad; surely there were physicians in the 1940s who labeled antibiotics as a passing fad, much to their chagrin (and the chagrin of their patients). Before we go too far down the path of fad diagnosis, we should have a clear idea of what we might gain by the early identification of fads and what we might lose by dismissing good, sustainable ideas as fads.

We would argue that there is a great deal to be gained by identifying fads early in their life cycle. If nothing else, fads consume nonrenewable resources such as funding, public support, and the time and energy of researchers. Almost by definition, fads are wasteful, and if it were possible to reliably determine what is or is not a fad before the entire life cycle of growth, controversy, and decline has played out, it would be possible to minimize the waste. More generally, fads are a bit like secondhand smoke: They seem to harm everyone in the vicinity. The proponents of fads end up running down blind alleys. The individuals who receive fad-driven treatments, placement, or interventions are unlikely to be helped and could suffer real harm. Even the opponents of fads are harmed, because they receive reinforcement for criticism that is too often superficial and insipid. Fad bashing, although it might receive approval from like-minded critics, rarely inspire the sort of detailed, careful, and thoughtful criticism that is given to a theory, intervention, or idea that is taken seriously by its critics. Early and accurate diagnosis of a looming fad might give people a chance to jump off the bandwagon before too much harm is done.

There is some possibility that genuinely good and useful ideas could be prematurely dismissed as fads, leading researchers to abandon promising lines of work. This suggests that any diagnosis of fads will have to be done in a way that is sensitive to false-negative errors (i.e., declaring an idea that is actually worthwhile and sustainable to be a fad). In our view, the risk of false-negative errors is probably small, because proponents of a truly worthwhile idea have multiple outlets for demonstrating that the idea they champion is not a fad at all. For example, in the early history of the use of meta-analysis in psychological research, there were numerous authors who dismissed this method as a fad and its conclusions as silly (e.g., Eysenck, 1978). The repeated success of meta-analytic studies eventually convinced most critics. When a real fad is dismissed as a fad, its proponents often have little ammunition for countering this criticism (they are more likely to dismiss the critics). When good ideas are dismissed as fads, it is often possible to demonstrate empirically or analytically that the idea being attacked is, in fact, a viable one.

The fads reviewed in the preceding section differ in a number of ways. Some are based on ideas that seem reasonable but that don't pan out (e.g., MBO). Others are based on ideas that seem implausible but that nevertheless attract a core of true believers (e.g., FC). As our quick glimpse into some notable fads in psychology, management, and education suggests, it is difficult to determine whether a particular idea, theory, or intervention will become a fad on the basis of an examination of its content alone. However, although fads vary in their content, they share some structural characteristics that may be useful in diagnosing them. We have already noted three distinctive characteristics of fads: the fast growth trajectory, the tendency to promise a great deal more than they can deliver, and the intensity of reactions. That is, fads seem to spring up overnight (and they often collapse just as quickly), and it is likely that this fast growth is related to the apparent promise that the fad will provide quick solutions to pressing problems. Fads also tend to provoke intense reactions, being greeted as a panacea by proponents and derided as hogwash by critics.

These three characteristics are all potentially useful in spotting fads as they develop, and it pays to be wary of theories and practices that emerge quickly, promise a great deal, and become the quick target of intense and bitter controversy. There are a number of additional diagnostic tools that are likely to prove useful for evaluating potential fads. First, it is useful to closely examine the developmental trend of research in an area that looks like an emerging fad. In normal scientific research, theories, ideas, and interventions tend to develop slowly but consistently over time. To be sure, there are peaks and valleys in the developmental tracks of many scientific theories, and sudden changes in the trajectory along which theories develop can play a critical role in the progress of scientific knowledge (Kuhn, 1962). Fads, on the other hand, often emerge almost fully formed and don't seem to make much progress over time. This is particularly true if the fad originates from the ideas of a charismatic or eloquent founder. In this case, fads tend to quickly fossilize around the founder's vision. Thus, one good marker for a fad is the failure to advance and improve over time.

Fads are also distinguished by an imperviousness to disconfirming evidence. As noted earlier, there have been numerous studies casting serious scientific doubt on fads such as FC and the use of handwriting analysis to make inferences about personality, truthfulness, and so forth. These studies have had remarkably little influence on the true believers in either of these two. More important, proponents of FC and handwriting analysis have substantially not changed their methods, their claims, or their inferences as a result of evidence questioning their utility and validity. In normal scientific research, the emergence of substantial bodies of disconfirming evidence tends to lead to abandonment of, or changes to, a theory. Fads remain stagnant even in the face of the most withering empirical criticisms.

Fads are rarely disseminated through scientific journals. Furnham (2003) noted that one of the key markers of management fads is dissemination by way of one or more best-selling, popular-press books. For example, popular-press publications have been extremely important in the growth of some variants of EI (in chap. 2 of this volume, we noted that there are at least two distinct versions of EI, only one of which has relied extensively on the popular press for its dissemination). One can argue that the status of EI changed virtually overnight in 1995 as a result of the publication of Goleman's *Emotional Intelligence*, together with the October issue of *Time* magazine, whose cover story was devoted to the concept of emotional intelligence. This reliance on the popular press as a means of advancing an idea is not by itself evidence of faddishness.

Finally, fads are distinguished by a generally weak ratio of supporting evidence to claims of success. That is, fads often start with a strong claim that they will solve an important problem. These claims are rarely accompanied by evidence that will stand public scrutiny. The very fact that substantial claims are accepted in the absence of credible evidence suggests that a fad has succeeded in attracting its corps of true believers. The cover of Goleman's 1995 book staked out a claim that helps to account for EI's surge of popularity: that EI might matter more than IQ. His subsequent works (e.g., Goleman, 1998) made equally bold claims, suggesting that EI might be considerably more important that IQ is some domains. These claims have not, to date, held up well to empirical tests (Matthews, Zeidner, & Roberts, 2003; Van Rooy & Viswesvaran, in press).

Table 12.1 summarizes a number of signs and symptoms that might be used to diagnose fads well before they reach their swift decline stage. Unlike a medical or psychiatric handbook (e.g., *DSM-IV*),

TABLE 12.1   **Signs That an Emerging Idea Is Likely to Be a Fad**

Sudden emergence and fast growth

True believers

Reliance on public press

Intense and bitter debates over the legitimacy of the idea

Substantial promises based on weak evidence

The failure to develop over time

Imperviousness to disconfirmatory evidence

we do not claim that the presence of a fixed number or combination of symptoms is a certain sign that the concept in question will pan out to be a fad. However, we do believe that ideas, theories, and interventions that share many of the characteristics laid out in Table 12.1 pose a substantial risk of falling apart almost as quickly as they emerge.

Suppose that you decide that the new "hot topic" is likely to be a fad (e.g., because it shows several of the characteristics illustrated in Table 12.1). What should you do? One suggestion encountered in the literature is that you should insist on the highest scientific and evidentiary standards before investing in a potential fad (Lazarus, 2003; Lyubomirsky & Abbe, 2003). In our view, this suggestion is not completely realistic. As Table 12.1 suggests, an idea or intervention that is supported by data that will stand up to rigorous analysis has little chance of being diagnosed as a fad. A more realistic version of this suggestion is that the tentative diagnosis of "fad" should lead you to be skeptical, to pay careful attention to the relevance and reliability of whatever evidence is offered to support the potential fad, and to be watchful for the course of research on the potential fad over time. The less credible the evidentiary base and the more static the development of ideas that look faddish, the more thought you should give to jumping off the bandwagon.

IS EI A FAD?

In chapter 2 of this volume, we argued that there are two distinct conceptions of EI: one that is largely science-driven, drawing on the work of Salovey, Mayer, and their colleagues, and another that is largely practice-driven, drawn largely from the work of Goleman, and to a lesser extent, Bar-On. In our judgment, the practice-driven version of EI looks like a fad, whereas the science-driven version seems less fad-like. Goleman's conception of EI has been characterized by rapid growth, a high proportion of the most important publications in this area have appeared in popular press, it is already the focus of fairly heated controversy, and the debate over this version of EI seems to be characterized by unresolveable gaps between the true believers and the devoted skeptics. In terms of the life-cycle models described earlier, this version of EI appears to be in the *Digestion* phase, in which the growth curve for EI is likely to level off and in which the criticisms of EI are likely to grow. There is no clear evidence of widespread public disenchantment with this version of EI yet, but the bell-curve model does suggest that the rise of this practice-driven version of EI has probably run its course and that a steep decline can be expected sometime in the fairly near future. This life-cycle model would suggest that now is a very good time to start jumping off the EI bandwagon.

There are two significant cautions that need to be offered along with the "jump off the bandwagon" advice. First, the bell-curve model is descriptive, not prescriptive. That is, this model describes the typical life cycle of fads, but it does not provide clear guidelines for predicting the duration of stages or even a certain prediction that interest in the version of EI offered by Goleman and his colleagues will decline. As a result, any advice based on such a model must be tentative and imprecise. We do think it is a good idea to jump off the EI bandwagon soon, but there is no good way to determine whether "soon" refers to weeks, months, or years. Even if we could be confident that EI will someday experience the same sort of sudden collapse that is characteristic of other fads, it is hard to tell when that will happen, and someone who jumps off a profitable bandwagon several years too early might not find our advice very useful.

More important, there are two quite different versions of EI, and in our view, the Salovey-Mayer model is unlikely to suffer the same catastrophic collapse (in part because it has not experienced the same sort of sudden emergence) that the life-cycle model predicts for the Goleman model of EI. The Salovey-Mayer model has emphasized the links between EI and more traditional models of ability and personality (Mayer, Caruso, & Salovey, 1999; Mayer & Salovey, 1993, 1997; Mayer, Salovey, & Caruso, 2000; Mayer, Salovey, Caruso, & Sitarenios, 2001) and has maintained linkages with the broader scientific community that are likely to make it a less flashy but more durable concept than the Goleman model of emotional intelligence. The science-driven version of EI that is exemplified by the Salovey-Mayer model does not seem to show many of the characteristics of fads illustrated in Table 12.1, and the answer to the question "Is EI a fad?" probably depends on which EI you are talking about.

The mixed status of EI (half fad, half not) presents both risks and opportunities to researchers and practitioners. The risks are obvious: If the EI fad comes to a catastrophic, crashing halt, it is likely that much of the well-grounded research in the Salovey-Mayer tradition will also go by the wayside. No matter how good or how careful the work, research that is seen as part of a failed fad is unlikely to get much attention or respect in the scientific community. The opportunities are less obvious, but every bit as real. EI is in the public eye. A number of agencies and institutions have expressed real interest in EI and related constructs. There is some very good research out there, and if EI enthusiasts can succeed in separating the valid work from the hype, there is still hope for the construct.

In the long run, EI's most dangerous enemy is probably the "true believer." Fads, like football teams, flourish as a result of the loyalty of the fans, and even when the team is a hopeless loser, there are always fans willing to support the team. The same is true of EI. There are a number of individuals, firms, and organizations truly devoted to EI, and the uncritical devotion that characterizes the true believers in this field makes progress, critical analysis, and restraint difficult. The best opportunity for EI to develop and flourish, therefore, will probably require more constructive involvement on the part of EI skeptics. It is easy, but ultimately unproductive, for EI skeptics to take potshots at the excesses of the true believers. It will be harder but, in the long run, much more productive for scientists who are skeptical about EI to become involved in improving EI measures, theories, applications, and so forth. The downward slide typical of fads is not inevitable, and there are still opportunities to rescue EI from the faddification process, but it will require transforming EI skeptics into EI researchers.

SAVING EI FROM FADIFICATION

If EI's worst enemies are the true believers, the group that has the greatest potential to save EI from the usual boom–bust cycle of other fads in psychology, business, and education is probably the subset of EI skeptics who have not dismissed EI wholesale but who have raised reasonable questions about the construct, its measurement, and its meaning; many of these skeptics have contributed to this volume. There are at least three critical questions about EI that have not been fully answered to date; a program of research that answered all three would pull EI from the status of a fad to the less exciting but more sustainable status of an individual difference construct that is likely to be useful for understanding performance in some specified range of settings. The questions are (1) What is EI and how does it relate to other well-researched constructs? (chaps. 1, 2, 4, 7, 8, 9, & 10, this volume); (2) What are the things that a person high on emotional intelligence does better than a person low on emotional intelligence? (chaps. 1, 3, 5, & 10, this volume); (3) How can we measure a person's level of EI? (chaps. 2, 3, 13, & 14, this volume). The first two questions relate to the issue of construct explication; the more we know about the meaning and implications of EI and about its relationship with other individual differences, the less likely it is that EI will be dismissed as a meaningless fad. The third question, how to best measure EI, may be the most challenging one to address. There are several EI measures in use, but none achieves the level of sophistication, reliability, and validity that is common for measures of most other well-documented individual difference constructs. As long as EI is measured crudely, applications of this construct and evidence that this construct is, in fact, useful will be similarly crude.

To be blunt, progress on construct explication and measurement is not likely to be made by the true believers; they already think EI is wonderful in its current state. Progress will depend on bringing a larger cadre of researchers into the EI tent who are not committed to current conceptions of EI (or at least sufficiently flexible to consider the available evidence and modify their models as new evidence emerges) and who are well versed in areas such as test construction, individual difference theory, and validation. We end this chapter with a plea to EI skeptics: Help save EI from the true believers!

REFERENCES

Abrahamson, E., & Fairchild, G. (1999). Management fashion: Lifecycles, triggers, and collective learning processes. *Administrative Science Quarterly, 44,* 708–740.

Bar-Hillel, M., & Ben-Shakhar, G. (1986). The a priori case against graphology: Methodological and conceptual issues. In B. Nevo (Ed.), *Scientific aspects of graphology* (pp. 263–279). Springfield, IL: Charles C Thomas.

Ben-Shakhar, G. (1989). Non-conventional methods in personnel selection. In P. Herriot (Ed), *Handbook of assessment in organizations: Methods and practice for recruitment and appraisal* (469–485). Chichester, UK: Wiley.

Byrne, J. A. (1997, June 23). Management theory or fad of the month? *Business Week, 47.*

Carroll, R. T. (2002a). *Facilitation communication.* Retrieved June 3, 2004, from http://skeptic.com/facilcom.html

Carroll, R. T. (2002b). *Graphology.* Retrieved June 3, 2004, from http://skeptic.com/graphol.html

Carson, P. P., Lanier, P. A., Carson, K. D., & Birkenmeier, B. J. (1999). An historical perspective on fad adoption and abandonment. *Journal of Management History, 5,* 320–333.

Carson, P. P., Lanier, P. A., Carson, K. D., & Guidry, B. N. (2000). Clearing a path through the management fashion jungle: Some preliminary trailblazing. *Academy of Management Journal, 43,* 1143–1158.

Chaddock, G. R. (1998, August 25). Perils of the pendulum resisting education's fads. *Christian Science Monitor,* p. 1.

Cummins, R. A., & Prior, M. P. (1992). Autism and assisted communication: A response to Biklen. *Harvard Educational Review, 62,* 228–241.

Diener, E. (2003). What is positive about positive psychology: The curmudgeon and pollyanna. *Psychological Inquiry, 14,* 115–120.

Dunnette, M. D. (1966). Fads, fashions, and folderol in psychology. *American Psychologist, 21,* 343–352.

Ettorre, B. (1997). What's the next business buzzword? *Management Review, 86,* 33.

Eysenck, H.J. (1978). An exercise in mega-silliness, *American Psychologist, 33,* 517.

Finn, C. E., & Petrilli, M. J. (1998, Fall). Washington versus school reform. *Public Interest, 133,* 55.

Furnham, A. (2003). *Mad, sad and bad management.* Cirnester, UK: Kemble Management Books.

Goleman, D. (1995). *Emotional intelligence.* New York: Bantam Books.
Goleman, D. (1998). *Working with emotional intelligence.* New York: Bantam Books.
Harvey, J. H., & Pauwels, B. G. (2003). The ironies of positive psychology. *Psychological Inquiry, 14,* 125–128.
Jacobson, J. W., Mulick, J. A., & Schwartz, A. A. (1995). A history of facilitated communication: Science, pseudoscience, and antiscience. *American Psychologist, 50,* 750–765.
Kuhn, T. (1962). *The structure of scientific revolutions.* Chicago: University of Chicago Press.
Lazarus, R. S. (2003). Does the positive psychology movement have legs? *Psychological Inquiry, 14,* 93–109.
Lyubomirsky, S., & Abbe, A. (2003). Positive psychology's legs. *Psychological Inquiry, 14,* 132–136.
Matthews, J. (1993, June 6). Totaled quality management: Consultants flourish helping firms repair the results of a business fad. *The Washington Post,* p. 1.
Matthews, G., & Zeidner, M. (2003). Negative appraisals of positive psychology: A mixed-valence endorsement of Lazarus. *Psychological Inquiry, 14,* 137–143.
Matthews, G., Zeidner, M., & Roberts, R. D. (2003). *Emotional intelligence: Science and myth.* Boston: MIT Press.
Mayer, J. D., Caruso, D. R., & Salovey, P. (1999). Emotional intelligence meets traditional standards for an intelligence. *Intelligence, 27,* 267–298.
Mayer, J. D., & Salovey, P. (1993). The intelligence of emotional intelligence. *Intelligence, 17,* 433–442.
Mayer, J. D., & Salovey, P. (1997). What is emotional intelligence? In P. Salovey & D. Sluyter (Eds.), *Emotional development and emotional intelligence: Implications for educators* (pp. 3–34). New York: Basic Books.
Mayer, J. D., Salovey, P., & Caruso, D. R. (2000). Emotional intelligence as zeitgeist, as personality and as a mental ability. In R. Bar On & J. Parker (Eds.), *The handbook of emotional intelligence: Theory, development, assessment and application at home, school and in the workplace* (pp. 92–117). San Francisco: Jossey-Bass.
Mayer, J. D., Salovey, P., Caruso, D. R., & Sitarenios, G. (2001). Emotional intelligence as standard intelligence. *Emotion, 1,* 232–242.
Mayer, R. E. (2004). Should there be a three-strikes rule against pure discovery learning? The case for guided methods of instruction. *American Psychologist, 59,* 14–19.
Mazur, L. (2002, October 17). Fad bandwagon is no cure-all for ailing business. *Marketing,* 16.
Mostert, M. P. (2001). Facilitated communication since 1995: A review of published studies. *Journal of Autism and Developmental Disorders, 31,* 287–313.
Murphy, K. R. (1993). *Honesty in the workplace.* Monterey, CA: Brooks/Cole.
Park, R. L. (2000). *Voodoo science: The road from foolishness to fraud.* New York: Oxford University Press.
Rodgers, R., & Hunter, J. E. (1991). Impact of management by objectives on organizational productivity. *Journal of Applied Psychology, 76,* 322–336.
Van Rooy, D. L., & Viswesvaran, C. (in press). Emotional intelligence: A meta-analytic investigation of predictive validity and nomological net. *Journal of Vocational Behavior.*

13

The Case for an Ability-Based Model of Emotional Intelligence

Catherine S. Daus
Southern Illinois University, Edwardsville

One analogy that is often used in describing the explosive growth of interest in emotional intelligence (EI) is to liken it to a bandwagon. The *bandwagon effect* is the observation that people often do (or believe) things because many other people do (or believe) the same. Without examining the merits of the particular thing, people tend to "follow the crowd" (Lavine, 1996; http://www.fact-index.com/b/ba/bandwagon _effect.html).

> In 19th and early 20th century America, a bandwagon was exactly what it sounds like, a wagon, usually horse-drawn, which carried a musical band. Bandwagons were used in circuses, to lead parades, and at political rallies. Hence to join or *jump on the bandwagon* was to follow the crowd, and in a political context with the connotation that one was there for the entertainment and excitement of the event, rather than from deep or firm conviction. (Lavine, 1996; http://www.wordorigins. org/wordorb.htm)

Unfortunately, the term *bandwagon* seems to apply to much of the field of EI. There exist unreasonable claims and seemingly unthinking acceptance, among other issues, with what the concept has morphed into. In essence, there are two approaches labeled EI: a mixed-model approach and an ability approach. These approaches to EI have little in common, other than the use of the term *emotional intelligence*.

It is equally true, however, that those who criticize the area without investigating it may be subject to another kind of issue, which here I refer to as the "broken oxcart" phenomenon. This involves sitting in a stationary, broken-down vehicle—unable or unwilling to move with the times and failing to realize that one's cart is broken. To those on the bandwagon, the people in the broken oxcart seem behind the times, stagnant, and unable to move. To those viewing the bandwagon from the oxcart, however, the cheerleaders must seem to have lost their senses. For those who have the time to take the walk to the local school, however, there is knowledge to be gained, and that is, of course, the point of this chapter, and more generally, this book.

The specific focus of this chapter is to hold up for examination what I regard as the most promising line of scientific research in the field of EI: the ability approach to emotional intelligence. To accomplish this, I first address aspects of EI that have, indeed, led people to "follow the wrong crowd," and I then discuss reasons why I believe that to follow advocates of the ability approach to emotional intelligence is to "follow the right crowd."

WHERE AND WHY HAVE PEOPLE BEEN LED ASTRAY REGARDING EMOTIONAL INTELLIGENCE?

Overstated Claims

Perhaps the (in)famous *Time* magazine article from 1995 (Gibbs, 1995) which quipped on its front cover: "What's your EQ?" (byline reads: "It's not your IQ. It's not even a number. But emotional intelligence may be the best predictor of success in life, redefining what it means to be smart") did more harm than good—at least for the acceptance of the legitimacy of the construct in the *scientific and academic community*. This article referred to a book called *Emotional Intelligence*, by Daniel Goleman (who "borrowed" the term for his book, originally to be about emotional literacy in education; Ashkanasy & Daus, 2005). According to Goleman (1995), evidence suggests that it is "as powerful, and at times more powerful, than IQ" (p. 34), and is advantageous in most aspects of life. "EQ" then, spread like wildfire in the popular press and in businesses, and several other books and consultancies quickly arose, making further, unsubstantiated claims and offering businesses and individuals EI training as the panacea to many (all) organizational and personal problems.

While these events ultimately led to a wave of management consulting, they somewhat simultaneously served to place EI in the minds of many academics in the realm of those unscientific, popular, quick fix, organizational "flavor-of-the-month" programs that might not meet the standards of scientific discourse. A great deal of discussion and effort has been devoted to debunking such claims as were made, particularly by the originators of the EI construct and architects of the ability approach (see, e.g., Mayer & Cobb, 2000; Mayer, Salovey, & Caruso, 2000). Nevertheless, it may be the case that academics less intimately familiar with this particular scientific discourse have unwittingly denied the legitimacy of the ability-based EI construct based on the incredible claims of some proponents of alternative models of EI.

Lack of Integrity in Scientific Inquiry

In psychology, one of the core ideals and mantras is critical thinking. Virtually any psychology program has "teaching critical thinking" as an integral part of its mission statement (core values, goals, etc.). Students and professionals are trained on the power and critical nature of the logic behind the scientific method: gathering data to test hypotheses and not simply relying on intuition or claims. When we want to know something, what do we do? Gather data. If a student or friend shows an interest in something we know a reasonable amount about, we shower them with (probably unwanted) books and/or articles.

It is uncharacteristic that so many in the academic community have seemingly taken such a strong stance against EI, based on inappropriate or limited knowledge, data, and evidence. Curiously, one quite freqently sees researchers using one framework to define emotional intelligence (e.g., the Salovey & Mayer, 1990; or Mayer & Salovey, 1997 model), but then another to measure it (with, for e.g., Goleman's Emotional Competency Index [ECI]; Sala 2002; or Schutte's self-report measure of EI, the Assessing Emotions Scale; Schutte et al., 1998). And these are *often* at odds with each other.

Although most scholars and writings do agree, however, on the definition of emotional intelligence—the ability to perceive, understand, regulate, and use emotions well in the self and others (Mayer & Salovey, 1997; Salovey & Mayer, 1990)—the differing models vary greatly in how well they capture this definition and how far they stray from it. It is therefore odd when we hear and read people making claims about *emotional intelligence* that are based on reviews, books, and such, that have inappropriately made claims and inappropriately reviewed the "evidence" for the mixed and self-report models, and then lumped them together with the ability model (e.g., Conte, 2005; Davies, Stankov, & Roberts, 1998; Matthews, Zeidner, & Roberts, 2002; Roberts, Zeidner, & Matthews, 2001; Van Rooy & Viswesvaran, 2004). To be sure, it is troubling, as I have alluded to, that such disparate models are called the same thing, but that de facto does not invalidate anything calling itself "emotional intelligence." Next, I attempt to give an overview of the most common measures of EI and compare them to the ability approach model.

FOUR APPROACHES TO EMOTIONAL INTELLIGENCE

The most commonly used measures of emotional intelligence are the Bar-On Emotional Quotient Inventory (EQ-I; Bar-On, 1997); Goleman's ECI, Schutte's Assessing Emotions Scale (Schutte et al., 1998), and Mayer, Salovey, and Caruso's measure(s)—the Multifactor Emotional Intelligence Scale (MEIS; Mayer, Caruso, & Salovey, 1999) and the Mayer-Salovey-Caruso Emotional Intelligence Test (MSCEIT; Mayer, Salovey, & Caruso, 2002). The first two measures, Goleman's and Bar-On's, are broad-based, multidimensional, self-report questionnaires. They both, basically, were developed by researchers who came across the Mayer and Salovey definition of EI and incorporated the term into their measures and/or models (Ashkanasy & Daus, 2005). Notice that Goleman refrains from even calling it *emotional intelligence*. Their measures assess a multitude of things (each having more than 15 scales[1]) from self-rated leadership to empathy to teamwork to decision making, thus prompting Mayer and colleagues (Mayer, Salovey, & Caruso, 2000) to call these models "mixed." People may question such broad-based scales and wonder, for example, *how* is decision making a *part of* emotional intelligence specifically. The question is not "Is effective decision making likely *related* to high emotional intelligence?" but rather "Is decision making *a part of* emotional intelligence?" Use of such broad-based scales would imply the latter, but my perspective fits more with the former. Thus, a question that arises is does it even make sense to call these scales emotional intelligence, when they are measuring a multitude of extraneous factors? It is my opinion, as well as that of many of the critics who contributed chapters to this edited book, that one is hard pressed to reconcile these measures with the focused definitions of EI originally proposed in the literature. As Locke quipped in a debate (DeNisi, 2003) on the topic, "According to Goleman, emotional intelligence is anything that isn't cognitive ability and is related to successful leadership!"

Another common measure is Schutte's self-judgment measure of EI, the Assessing Emotions Scale (Schutte et al., 1998), and as mentioned, Goleman's and Bar-On's measures are self-judgment. Self-judgment scales are crucial to mental measures of all types; yet they have certain applications that make more or less sense. Self-judgment is important for understanding how an individual feels about himself. It may be less suitable, however, as a measure of ability.

Here, we can draw a parallel to the criticisms lodged at self-report organizational citizenship behaviors (OCBs; Organ & Ryan, 1995). Am I a helpful person? (OCB item). Do I often stay late to help my co-workers? (another OCB item). Do I often help others feel better when they are down? (an item from Schutte's self-judgment measure). People naturally want to answer these in the affirmative. Critics often rightly conclude that a lot more than the reality of a person's behavior goes into answering these questions. This is perhaps due to the fact that self-report scales correlated positively with positive affect (Mayer & Cobb, 2000).

The MSCEIT, in contrast, is an ability-based measure of the construct. It is based on the four-branch (Mayer & Salovey, 1993, 1997) hierarchical model of EI, with perceiving or identifying emotions at the base followed by using emotions, understanding emotions, and, finally, managing emotions. Mayer, Salovey, and Caruso have constructed a series of scales to measure EI (Mayer et al., 1999; Mayer, DiPaolo, & Salovey, 1990; Mayer & Geher, 1996; Mayer et al., 2002), of which, the MSCEIT is the most recent (2002). The MSCEIT comprises eight tasks: two each to test the four abilities/branches. Each task has a solid empirical and psychometric history based in classic psychological literature (e.g., Ekman & Friesen, 1975; Isen, 2001; Ortony, Clore, & Collins, 1988; Thayer, 1966). Sample tasks on the MSCEIT include identifying emotions in faces and pictures (to test Branch 1); identifying emotions that would best facilitate a type of thinking or decision making (such as planning a birthday party); and presenting participants with a hypothetical scenario involving an emotionally laden event with a friend and asking how they would behave to achieve a desired outcome (e.g., make their friend feel better). In a later section, I address the psychometric properties of the MSCEIT which give quite solid evidence and support for its reliability and validity.

WHY THE ABILITY APPROACH IS THE APPROPRIATE HORSE TO DRIVE THE EMOTIONAL INTELLIGENCE CART

In this second section, I outline why I feel it justifiable that people and organizations consider EI (an ability-based model) as a viable and valuable construct. I delineate three primary reasons for my justification:

1. Emotion is as basic as cognition.
2. Emotional intelligence is supported by solid, empirical research.
3. Emotional intelligence has intuitive value (face validity).

The Fundamental Nature of Emotion and Cognition

For centuries, there has seemingly existed an antagonism between emotion and cognition (see, e.g., classic debates regarding the relative importance of each, DeSousa, 1987; Leeper, 1948, p. 17; Young, 1943, pp. 457–458; or the relative primacy of each, Arnold, 1960; Arieti, 1970; Lazarus, 1982; 1984; Lazarus, Averill, & Option; 1970; Tomkins, 1970; Zajonc, 1980; 1984; Zajonc & Marcus, 1982; 1985). For example, in what is now considered to be a classic work on the topic, *The Rationality of Emotion*, DeSousa (1987) has this to say about the issue:

> Despite a common prejudice, reason and emotion are not natural antagonists. On the contrary: I shall argue that when the calculi of reason have become sufficiently sophisticated, they would be powerless in their own terms, except for the contribution of emotion. (p. 21)

DeSousa discussed how as far back as Plato, who broke down the soul into the three parts of reason, desire, and emotion, and Descartes, who recognized the interdependence of thinking, feeling, and behavior, humans have consistently considered emotions *and* cognition as being central to the human experience (and distinct from each other, worthy of study independently and interdependently). This remains one of the fundamental issues in psychology (Forgas, 1992; Hilgard, 1980).

Yet for years, during the cognitive revolution in psychology, affect was considered (in the cognitive paradigm) as noise, or "error variance," an annoyance to be controlled, at best: "Affect was at best seen as a potentially 'disruptive' influence on normal (that is, affectless) cognition" (Forgas, 1992, p. 229). This time period in psychology's history did much to advance psychological thought but also did a disservice in maintaining the legitimacy of emotion as important a human aspect, in its own right, as cognition. Now, however, the tides have again shifted, and it is somewhat universally recognized that affect and cognition should be recognized and considered as parts of a universal, integrated system (e.g., see Bower, 1981; Bower & Cohen, 1982; Forgas, 1992; Isen, 1984; Laird & Bresler, 1990; Mayer, 1986; Salovey & Rodin, 1985). Most current theories of attitudes (e.g., see Miller & Tesser, 1992), for example, conceive of attitudes as being global evaluations having both a cognitive and an affective component (many consider behavior to be a third component, i.e., the classic *Tripartite Model of Attitudes*, Breckler, 1984; and others consider behavior to be an attitudinal outcome or correlate).

I feel that evidence supports my contention that EI as a construct and the ability model of operationalization reflect both classic and recent thought regarding the primacy of both cognition and emotion. The ability model of EI captures the integrity of the distinctiveness of emotion from cognition and has demonstrated that both are critical, independent predictors of life and work outcomes. Thus, this approach integrates nicely the most advanced theorizing about the interplay, interdependence, and independence of cognition and emotion.

But How, Exactly, Do Emotion and Intellect Interact?

Antagonists of the EI perspective have argued that because emotions are information, just like everything else, we therefore don't need to postulate a distinct ability to process this information. We don't have separate abilities for every possible domain, so why should we for emotions? In the previous section, I argued for the primacy of emotion along with cognition, which is an initial response to the reason for elevating emotions in importance (compared to anything else that may contain important information to process). If we give primacy to both emotion and cognition as parts of the mind, thinking about their interaction leads to four possibilities: (1) Emotions serve intellect, (2) intellect serves emotions, (3) they both serve and/or are served by other parts, or (4) neither serves the other. The first three possibilities are all supported. First, we know emotions serve (and possibly inhibit) intellect. For example, research has established that emotions require attention and can, and do, interrupt cognitive processing (Forgas, 1992; Morris, 1989; Simon, 1982; Thayer, 1989). In a recent discussion, John Cacioppo and Gary Bernston (1999) described the intertwining of affect and emotion thus: "The affect system works hand in glove with the cognitive system to appraise the significance of stimuli and to execute appropriate actions. It directs attention, guides decision making, stimulates learning, and triggers behavior" (p. 133).

Yet, there has long been a tradition of regarding emotions as irrationally interfering with cognition, rather than as possibly positively contributing to it (Forgas, 1992; Mayer & Salovey, 1997). Some research does support this. Within the domain of emotional regulation, researchers have found that emotion "work," such as suppressing emotions and/or exaggerating emotions, may impair cognitive performance (Baumeister, Bratslavsky, Muraven, & Tice 1998). Emotion can positively contribute to cognition, as well. Emotion can signal and direct one to cognitively attend to what is most important; that is, to "prioritize cognition" (de Sousa, 1987; Mayer & Salovey, 1997) and thus positively contribute to thought. Related, de Sousa (1987) argued that emotion is necessary for "task-oriented cognition," enabling one to decide what information is important and relevant for problem solution. Some researchers have suggested that the performance implications of negative emotions are more pronounced than for positive ones, because a negative emotion signals that something is wrong (Isen & Baron, 1991; Morris, 1989).

Related, within the mood research domain, we have similar evidence that emotion serves cognition. Positive moods may impair some cognitive (and other types) activity if the person actively seeks to maintain her positive mood and avoids activities that may threaten that mood (Clark & Isen, 1982). Positive mood, in some research, has been found to lead to poorer problem solving and reduced cognitive processing. In fact, there is a (generally) consistent effect across bodies of research that suggests that a positive mood tends to lead to the use of more heuristics in decision making and problem solving. Possibly an alternative way to frame it is that people in a positive mood will expend less cognitive effort. In other research, positive mood was found to facilitate creativity and divergent thinking. In general, the research is fairly consistent that positive mood tends to facilitate creativity and inhibits more considered, structured problem solving.

Compared to the increased use of heuristics of people in a positive mood, people in a negative mood are more likely to engage in systematic and deeper cognitive processing (Schwarz & Bohner, 1996). Negative emotions and mood states signal to the organism that something is wrong (Frijda, 1988; Schwarz & Bohner, 1996) and thus promote effortful cognitive processing strategies:

> Increased accessibility of procedural knowledge, however, would also increase the likelihood that the respective procedures are applied to other tasks that people work on while in a bad mood, resulting in a generalized use of analytic reasoning procedures during bad moods. (Schwarz & Bohner, 1996, p.121)

Yet, there is some evidence that a depressed mood can impair cognitive recall (unless the required recall is for depressed or negative information). However, the literature is quite consistent in suggesting that negative moods should facilitate a more analytic cognitive strategy.

Thus, emotions can and do service intellect. But what about the other direction: Does/can cognition serve emotion? I argue that emotional intelligence is at the very heart of this alternative direction. Emotional intelligence is the effective use of emotions as information—it is cognition serving emotion.

EMOTIONAL INTELLIGENCE IS EMPIRICALLY RELIABLE, VALID, AND HAS FUNDAMENTAL, PREDICTIVE VALUE

I have already argued that the ability model is the best operationalization of EI, and thus in this section, I restrict my review to evidence that is based in this paradigm and tradition.

Psychometric Evidence

The MSCEIT has solid psychometric properties. Current evidence for the MSCEIT shows strong internal consistency reliability: The MSCEIT's overall internal consistency reliability is $r = .91$ (using expert scoring) and .93 (using consensus scoring[2]), with branch score reliabilities (representing the four branches listed earlier) ranging from .76 to .91 (Mayer, et al., 2002; Mayer, Salovey, & Caruso, 2004a; Palmer, Gignac, Manocha, & Stough, 2004). Regarding the factorial validity, confirmatory factor analyses support evidence of an overall emotional intelligence factor (Palmer et al., 2004; Mayer et al. 2003). Further, four-factor solutions representing each of the four abilities/branches supply an excellent fit to the data (Day & Carroll, 2004; Mayer et al., 2003; Mayer et al., 2004a; Palmer et al., 2004; Roberts et al., 2001).[3]

By far, the most numerous and consistent criticisms against the EI construct have been levied at its discriminant validity (or lack thereof). The claim is that EI is nothing more than a particular constellation of personality factors. For example, an early, well-known and oft-cited comment regarding emotional intelligence was that "little remains of emotional intelligence that is unique and psychometrically sound" (Davies, Stankov, & Roberts, 1998, p. 1013). The strongest criticism by Landy (2005), Locke (2005), and others (Conte, 2005; Davies, Stankov, Roberts, 1998; Matthews, Zeidner, & Roberts, 2002; Roberts, Zeidner, & Matthews, 2001; Van Rooy & Viswesvaran, 2004) argued that EI is nothing more than a constellation of the Big Five factors and is thus not distinct from personality. Yet this issue is misleading regarding the ability model of EI, as most reports examining the evidence have collapsed across all measures—ability, self-judgment, mixed models—and found the results to be damning for concluding that EI is distinct from personality (Daus & Ashkanasy, 2005).

When a more focal definition and test are considered, there is considerable discriminant validity. Regarding the MSCEIT's discriminant validity, examining the evidence for the MSCEIT separately provides solid, replicable evidence that the MSCEIT diverges from both personality characteristics and cognitive ability.

The evidence for the discriminant validity of emotional intelligence (ability-based measure) and personality is quite compelling: Average correlations across five studies (with sample sizes > 150) for each of the five factors and total EI ranged from a low of .06 (Extroversion) to .21 (Agreeableness). The highest single correlation found between any branch and a Big Five factor was between Management of Emotion and Agreeableness at .39 (see Mayer et al., 2004a, for a comprehensive review of this data). Of note and for clarity, two widely used measures of EI (both self-judgment) suffer from substantial overlap with the Big Five: Bar-On's EQ-I (Bar-On, 1997) had a multiple R of .75 with the Big Five, and Schutte's (Schutte et al., 1998) scale's multiple R was .52 and correlated strongly with many other personality constructs (e.g., anxiety, alexithymia, optimism, impulse control) and social/emotional functioning (Brackett & Mayer, 2003).

Similar criticisms (Davies, Stankov, Roberts, 1998; Matthews, Zeidner, & Roberts, 2002; Roberts, Zeidner, & Matthews, 2001; Van Rooy & Viswesvaran, 2004) have been lodged at EI and its overlap with cognitive ability. Regarding cognitive ability, the highest level of relationship between an EI branch and cognitive ability is with the understanding emotions branch (involving labeling emotions and understanding how emotions are corelated): correlations range between .25 and .40 (sharing at most 16% of the variance); the range of correlations for overall emotional intelligence and cognitive ability is .14 to .36 (see Mayer et al., 2004a, for a comprehensive review). Thus, the data and evidence strongly support the claim that the ability model of EI shows discriminant validity from both cognitive ability and the Big Five model of personality.

Predictive Evidence

In this section, I briefly summarize the research substantiating that EI has garnered a solid amount of empirical support showing that it is related to important life and work outcomes.

Social and "Life" Outcomes

Emotional intelligence, as conceptualized by the ability model, predicts aspects of social relationships. For example, Lopes and colleagues have recently demonstrated (Lopes, Brackett, Nezlek, Schutz, Sellin, & Salovey, 2004; Lopes, Salovey, Côté, & Beers, 2004) that the ability to manage emotions and regulate emotions contributes positively to the quality of social interactions with friends, above and beyond personality (the Big Five) and intelligence (in Lopes, Salovey, Côté, & Beers, 2004). Participants who could manage emotions well were also more liked and valued by members of the opposite sex. Indeed, there is evidence that suggests that the emotionally intelligent are simply more social and/or socially adept and more securely attached; Fullam (2004) found that those who were more emotionally intelligent rated their social support networks higher; and Brackett (2001) found that those who were more emotionally intelligent were more likely to have evidence or objects of attachment around (e.g., photos of family, letters). Further, Brackett also found that the more emotionally intelligent were more likely to choose the social work job of caretaker.

Additionally, EI tends to protect people from deviant and/or violent behavior. Aspects of EI are significantly inversely related to aspects of mental health, specifically anxiety and depression. Emotion recognition is associated with less drug-related and violent behavior (Mayer, Caruso, & Salovey, 1999). More recently, Brackett, Mayer, and Warner (2004) have confirmed these findings and found that overall EI in men was significantly related to less illicit drug use and less fighting and vandalizing. Trinidad and Johnson (2002) also found that EI was inversely related to alcohol and tobacco use in adolescents, as well as with overall smoking risk factors for adolescents (Trinidad, Unger, Chou, & Johnson, 2004). In childhood, a form of violent behavior, bullying, also shows significant relationships with EI: The less emotionally intelligent kids bullied more (Rubin, 1999). Progressing along the continuum of violent behavior, Brackett, Mayer, and Warner (2004) demonstrated an inverse association between social deviance (operationalized by number of physical fights, number of vandalization events, etc.) and EI, and Swift (2002), studying individuals in an actual court-mandated violence prevention program, found an inverse relationship between perceiving emotions and aggression but a positive relationship between managing emotions and aggression.

Work Outcomes—Leadership[4]

Academics agree that leadership effectiveness has an intuitively compelling relationship with EI (Ashkanasy & Tse, 2000; Caruso, Mayer, & Salovey, 2002; George, 2000). Specifically, transformational leadership and distinct aspects of EI (emotion management) have natural linkages that research has illustrated. Daus and Harris (2003) studied leader emergence, transformational leadership, and EI over a semester using a student sample of a small groups class with a complex final group project (organizing a fundraiser and donating the proceeds to charity) required. We found that EI predicted leader emergence and is related to transformational leadership. Specifically, leadership emergence rated by group members was significantly related to the managing others' emotions branch of EI, and overall transformational leadership (as well as all five dimensions of transformational leadership) was significantly associated with the understanding emotions branch of EI (Daus & Harris, 2003). Others (Coetzee & Schaap, 2004) have reported similar findings from a survey study of 100 South African managers regarding transformational leadership, transactional leadership, and EI, showing that transformational leadership is related to overall EI as well as two branches (identifying and managing emotion); further, transactional leadership was related to the managing emotion branch, and nontransactional, or "laissez-faire" leadership, was inversely related to the using emotion branch. Also, Lopes et al. (2004) found that EI was related to both peer-rated leadership potential (marginally) and supervisor-rated leadership potential (strongly) in a sample of 44 analysts and clerical employees; these relationships remained even after controlling for the Big Five, education, and cognitive ability (verbal ability), among other variables (e.g., age, gender, trait affect, and coping approach).

Also, there is evidence that the level of EI apparently critical for leadership success is a function of how central EI may be to the career. Collins (2001) studied 59 senior executives from a large international production and service organization and found that emotional intelligence was less predictive the higher up the corporate hierarchy for career tracks where EI skills were not critical or necessary. And subordinates whose supervisors have higher EI are more committed to the organization (Giles, 2001). Part of transformational leadership is developing, communicating, and garnering commitment to a vision (Avolio & Bass, 1999; Kouzes & Posner, 1990), and indeed, those with higher EI write higher quality vision statements than others (significant effects remained even after controlling for the Big Five; Côté, Lopes, & Salovey, 2004). Finally, the understanding emotions branch of EI appears to predict accuracy in self-ratings of leaders—those with lower levels of this ability overrated their own leadership (as assessed by direct reports), whereas those with higher levels underrated their own leadership (Collins, 2001).

Work Outcomes—Job Performance

In general, we see that EI is related to overall performance and work outcomes. Studying analysts and clerical employees in a finance company, Lopes, Côté, Grewal, Kadis, Gall, and Salovey (in press) found that those higher in EI received greater merit increases, held higher company rank, and were rated higher by peers and supervisors on interpersonal skills, stress tolerance, and leadership potential. It appears that the higher level abilities of understanding and managing emotion were most strongly related to the more objective criteria (salary and company rank), and the lower level abilities of perceiving and using emotion were most strongly predictive of the more subjective, peer- and supervisor-rated variables.

It is particularly with jobs that seem to require high levels of EI where the research substantiates the linkage between EI and job performance. Daus (2002) and colleagues (Cage, Daus, & Saul, 2005; Daus, Rubin, & Cage, 2004; Daus, Rubin, Smith, & Cage, 2005) have conducted a series of studies to show that for jobs that require a high level of EI, there is indeed a positive relationship between EI and job performance. Police officers are employed in a career that has one of the highest emotional labor demands (Glomb, Kammeyer-Mueller, & Rotundo, 2004), which Hochchild (1983) has defined as managing emotions in the service of one's job. Given that there is a high demand for officers to manage their own and others' emotions, high levels of EI should predict aspects of officer performance. In an ongoing series of research projects regarding police officers, both qualitative data (intensive semistructured interviews with patrol officers and their supervisors, investigators, dispatchers, and police chiefs; Daus, Rubin, & Cage, 2004) and quantitative data (Daus, Rubin, Smith, & Cage, 2005) support that aspects of EI are critical for effective job performance and the prevention of negative stress outcomes from the job. Furthermore, aspects of EI predicted job satisfaction and inversely predicted turnover intentions (Daus et al., 2005).

Another type of job with strong EI implications is that of customer service and/or retail sales. The sheer amount of interaction with customers and the fact that job performance is largely determined by customer interaction speak to the necessity of having emotional skills and abilities, both in self and in dealing with others. Daus (2002), in a laboratory simulation of a customer service event, demonstrated the link between EI of the customer service representative (the participants in the experiment) and job performance in relation to the handling of an angry customer (played by confederates in the experiment). Whereas the dimension of reading emotions was inversely related to rated job performance, managing emotions in self was positively related to job performance as rated by independent observers/raters. As well, dimensions of EI (reading emotions in faces, managing emotion in self) were related both to work attitudes (job satisfaction) and emotional labor (discussed next). Recently, Cage, Daus, and Saul (2005) extended these results with a field sample of sales/customer service reps in a department store, with both subjective ("secret shopper" ratings) criterion data and more "objective" criterion data (sales). Results essentially expand and mirror Daus (2002): The utilizing emotions branch of EI was significantly associated with rated customer service performance, the managing emotions branch was significantly associated with actual sales performance, and understanding emotions was significantly associated with job satisfaction (Cage, Daus, & Saul, 2005). Clearly, evidence from all these recent studies indicates that EI skills are important in predicting job performance for some types of jobs.

Group Performance.   Emotional intelligence is also important in work groups or teams. Rice (1999) studied 26 teams of claims adjusters working in the financial services center of a large insurance company. She found that teams with higher average EI received higher performance ratings for managers, particularly for customer service. However, her results were mixed and did not uniformly support an EI–team performance relationship. Lopes, Cote, Salovey, and Beers (2003) examined the EI of 91 students working on a 10-week project in small teams. Individuals who were better able to manage emotions were more satisfied with other group members and with the communication and also reported receiving more social support.

Emotional Labor

As mentioned earlier, emotional labor is defined as managing emotion in the service of one's job (Hochschild, 1983) and, as such, it has obvious apparent relationships with EI (Ashkanasy & Daus, 2002). Research on emotional labor has developed quickly recently with empirical demonstrations of the frequent negative effects of emotional labor on employees (e.g., regarding high stress, burnout, lower job satisfaction, etc.; Grandey, 2000; Kruml & Geddes, 2000). Thus, an individual skill such as EI, which might moderate or ameliorate the negative consequences of emotional labor, would be critical to explore. Emotional labor is highest in jobs with a high amount of contact with clients and customers (such as in customer service occupations and the helping professions). Indeed, both laboratory and field research has begun to demonstrate the important relationships between EI and emotional labor. In studies (mentioned earlier) with simulated customer service representatives (Daus, 2002) and actual customer service reps/sales personnel (Cage, Daus, & Saul, 2005), relationships between EI and emotional labor were confirmed. Daus (2002) found that people who could better read emotions in faces felt less of an emotional load from the job, and people who could better manage emotions in themselves felt more of an emotional load. Also, Cage and colleagues (2005) found that the understanding emotions dimension of EI was positively associated with the faking positive aspect of emotional labor. Further, expressing negative emotions was inversely associated with actual sales performance. The study with the police officers (Daus, Rubin, Smith, & Cage, 2005) additionally demonstrated a definitive link between aspects of emotional labor and EI. Overall, EI was significantly associated with both deep acting (actually feeling the emotion) of emotional labor and suppressing negative emotions. Further, all four branches of EI were significantly associated with deep acting; one (understanding emotions) was associated with surface acting; three (all but understanding emotions) were significantly associated with suppressing negative emotions; and one (using emotions) was associated with faking positive emotions.

In another study, Brotheridge (2003) found that additional incremental variance in surface acting (expressing the appropriate emotions without actually feeling them) was explained (beyond emotional labor antecedents and the personality variable of emotional expressivity) by the managing emotions in self and others branch of the MSCEIT. Also, like with leadership, EI seems to predict better in those jobs requiring more of it (and requiring more emotional labor): Janovics and Christiansen (2002) found that in those jobs with the most direct contact with customers, higher EI scores predicted better supervisor ratings, even after controlling for the effects of cognitive intelligence. Finally, and related in this vein, Rice (1999) found that customer satisfaction was higher with claims adjustments made by teams whose average EI was higher.

In summary, it appears that EI clearly has much to offer the domain of emotional labor and jobs that require high amounts of it such as customer and social service types of occupations, and those that require a high amount of interaction with the public. It is critical that researchers specify which roles require high degrees of EI and also to determine what sort of outcomes EI should relate to. EI, in the ability model, is not supposed to predict twice as much variance as IQ, nor is it believed to be an advantage in all roles.

Emotional Intelligence Has Face Validity and it Makes Intuitive Sense

While face validity, or the appearance of a measure being legitimate and/or measuring the underlying construct it purports to measure, is not legally or empirically defensible evidence for the validity of a measure/construct, it can do a service or disservice to the construct by raising questions (if it has suspect face validity) or suppressing issues (if it has solid face validity). Because I have already reviewed the empirical evidence and demonstrated that the ability model of EI has solid psychometric evidence and worthwhile predictive power regarding both overall social and life functions/relationships and workplace outcomes, I feel comfortable ending on this more intuitive note.

Regarding EI, it seems that the ability perspective has unquestionable face validity and makes intuitive sense as a construct worthy of study in predicting important workplace outcomes. I ask the reader, for example, does it not make sense (and has been borne out in personal interactions) that some people have no real sense of their and others' emotional worlds? And further, that this is independent from their cognitive intelligence? (i.e., there are quite intelligent people who may be emotionally bereft, and there are not-so-intelligent people who are also emotionally bereft). And might this be a quite important, and distinct, aspect of their life, predicting success in various life and work domains? All of these questions, of course, have been definitively empirically answered in the affirmative, as I have reviewed. Regarding the ability measure of EI, no one questions us regarding the face validity (in empirical or applied uses) of the ability measure of EI (not so for some of the other measures of emotional intelligence). It makes intuitive sense to people that those who have higher EI should be better at, for example, reading people's emotions in faces, responding with appropriate actions to emotional events, and understanding how emotions transition and blend with each other!

History is rife with examples of persons and occupations where emotions and emotion work were critical and naturally fused with success. Artist is one such occupation where there appears to be a natural core element of EI underlying much successful work. By way of illustration, I briefly discuss Rembrandt van Rijn, truly and incontrovertibly one of the world's greatest artists of all time.

I was thrilled to be able to attend a special exhibit of Rembrandt in Chicago (in April, following the Society of Industrial Organizational Psychology Conference, 2004). What was even more thrilling was to find that Rembrandt, early in his career, devoted much time to trying to depict himself expressing a wide range of sentiments (e.g., there was a series of more than 15 small self-portrait etchings, made between 1627 and 1630, where "Rembrandt appears to try out a wide range of sentiments, as if putting on so many masks"; Westermann, 2000, p. 42). Rembrandt felt that if an artist were to be successful, he had to make certain that he could both capture the "strong expression [that] can happen to elegant faces" (Westermann, 2000, p. 42), as well as convey that emotion so that beholders could accurately interpret it. Rembrandt believed "that an artist would benefit from depicting his passions as he sees them in a mirror, where he is simultaneously the performer and the beholder" (Wheelock, 2000, p. 17). Rembrandt, almost 400 years ago, thought that emotional skills were critical to the success of any person in his occupation. Today, we agree that there are indeed, some occupations where EI might make the difference between success and failure. Although it is too soon to for a wide body of evidence to be available to delineate such occupations, I concur with Landy (2005) that there certainly are some that make more sense than others to examine. Ones that readily are apparent are police officer, customer service worker, social service worker (any of the human service professions, really), and certain managerial and leadership roles. It is likely that high EI in people performing such roles will only be apparent over the long haul and will impact outcomes such as employee/customer satisfaction, quality of social support, and engaging in constructive behaviors.

ENDING COMMENTARY

I end with a hypothesis about what I feel is both a contributor to, and an outcome of, the EI bandwagon phenomenon. Organizations (and people) tend to want things faster and faster and want "quick fixes" to problems (Buy a pill to lose weight without exercise and diet! Read this book to find the seven ways to become a more successful manager!). As such, they often lack discrimination in choices for programs—individually and organizationally—refusing to weigh carefully the evidence both for and against. I name this phenomenon and describe it here: *"The Organizational Veruca Salt Phenomenon"*: *"I want it all, and I want it now!"*

To refresh readers' memories, Veruca Salt was the character in *Willy Wonka and the Chocolate Factory* who was the spoiled, rich brat whose father indulged her every whim. Her infamous, somewhat evil declaration of "I want it now" (which got her sent down the "bad egg" chute) reminds children (!) of what can happen when we get too greedy. Perhaps adults in organizations making decisions about budgets and programs need also to be reminded of this. The history of organizational behavior is riddled with examples of sexy ideas with little empirical support being quickly adopted and used in organizations. Several examples serve to illustrate.

Every good introductory industrial/organizational psychology and human resource management textbook has a section on criterion-related validity. Most of them describe the difference between concurrent (measuring predictor and criterion at the same time, usually with current employees) and predictive (measuring predictor initally, typically with job applicants or new hires, holding the data, and measuring the criterion at some later point in time) criterion-related validity. Some of these same textbooks further may (should) explain that although the predictive strategy is a more psychometrically sound strategy (doesn't have the range restriction due to employees having been deemed "successful" as applicants and hired based on some criterion, that the criterion-related strategy suffers from), it is often quite difficult to convince organizations of the value of not using the new predictor which you are arguing is going to be much better, until you have actually demonstrated in their organization, that this is so. They want the purported benefits now!

Management by Objectives (MBOs)—which is an approach that suggests using a participative management style and argues for managers sitting down with employees and collectively deciding on short- and long-term goals (objectives), aligning individual goals with corporate goals, identifying strategies to achieve them, and acknowledging possible associated outcomes (consequences)—was touted as a surefire way to an organization's making incredible gains in productivity. Many organizations adopted MBOs, particularly in the 1960s and 1970s, while research lagged far behind. Unfortunately, the research (and anecdotal evidence) failed to establish the utility of MBOs decades after many companies had spent considerable efforts on them (see Dinesh & Palmer, 1998; Van Tassel, 1995, for overviews of MBOs and their failure): "Ironically, the same organizations that adopted MBO as a performance management system later claimed that MBO proved to be more of a hindrance rather than a help" (Van Tassel, 1995, p. 367). What research elucidated was that if employees are given a goal by a respected authority figure (most supervisors), participation does nothing to increase goal acceptance. In other words, if my boss tells or asks me to do something, as long as I view his request (goal) as legitimate, I will be committed to it. Also, partial implementation and failure to shift thinking to a human relations perspective were cited as critical reasons for MBO's failure (Dinesh & Palmer, 1998).

Another example is that of consensual decision making (CDM)—not moving forward on something until all the major stakeholders have given their approval. On the surface, CDM makes sense in that we should want the people who have a major interest in, and responsibility for, the decision and outcomes to be on board with it. It also, on the surface, appears to be a very fair, highly democratic approach. However, what this translated to is many companies spinning their wheels and wasting valuable time trying to reach consensus. We *now* understand that there are times and conditions that make consensus unlikely or impossible—"bounded" consensus. Such things include personal/hidden agendas, personality clashes, and different budgetary ideologies, to name a few. In addition, many difficulties, problems, and issues with consensus have been recognized (adapted from http://www.oktobra.net/kreativ/text3.html):

1. Consensus is often lengthy. "the requirement of consensus often leads to prolonged, marathon sessions, or meetings where nothing is decided" (http://www.oktobra.net/kreativ/text3.html).
2. Consensus can silence the dissenting minority (through subtle or direct psychological coercion guilt, etc.)
3. Consensus limits the vital and creative function of disagreement in group discussion.
4. Often, groups will adopt a "minimalist" strategy: Choose the solution that has the fewest number of people disagreeing, rather than choose the optimal choice.
5. It is impractical, especially in large groups.
6. It unfairly advantages the self-confident and articulate.
7. Consensus is actually contradictory to democracy, that is, it is antidemocratic. "A small minority does not have the right to

prevent the majority of members from doing what they want to do" (http://www.oktobra.net/kreativ/text3.html).

In short, consensus tends to "subvert individuality in the name of community and dissent in the name of solidarity" (http://www.oktobra.net/kreativ/text3.html).

Emotional intelligence has suffered the same fate, largely because of the unsubstantiated claims discussed earlier. In other words, people and organizations have been led astray regarding EI, and have jumped onto the wrong emotional intelligence bandwagon, the one that uses broad-based mixed models. Largely, these models have not been solidly empirically substantiated, and further, as I have already discussed, they have suspect construct validity (I claim many of them are not even the same construct as the ability model of EI). Thus, the psychometrically and construct-valid approach of the ability model, has somewhat been overshadowed by these other models. I hope that my chapter has convinced a few and enlightened many.

ACKNOWLEDGMENTS

The author would like to thank John Mayer, David Caruso, Peter Salovey, and Kevin Murphy for their helpful comments on this manuscript.

ENDNOTES

[1] Basic, psychometric principles of factor analyses call into doubt the reliability and construct validity of a 15-scale measure (see, e.g., Kim & Mueller, 1978; Tabachnick & Fidell, 2001).

[2] Use of expert scores consists of comparing answers to a panel of experts, while consensus scoring compares answers to a normed group's scores.

[3] One set of findings (Palmer et al., 2004) with an Australian sample suggest that there is no discernible difference between the three and four-factor models, with Branches 2 and 4 being indistinguishable.

[4] Much of this material in the next section is adapted from Daus and Ashkanasy (2005).

REFERENCES

http://www.wordorigins.org/wordorb.htm; accessed July 9, 2004

http://www.fact-index.com/b/ba/bandwagon_effect.html; accessed July 9, 2004

http://www.oktobra.net/kreativ/text3.html; accessed October 14, 2004.

Arieti, S. (1970). Cognition and feeling. In M. B. Arnold (Ed.), *Feeling and Emotion: The Loyola Symposium*. Orlando, FL Academic Press.

Arnold, M. B. (1960). *Emotion and personality*. New York: Columbia University Press.

Ashkanasy, N. M., & Daus, C. S. (2005). Rumors of the death of emotional intelligence in organizational behavior are vastly exaggerated. *Journal of Organizational Behavior, 26,* 441–452.

Ashkanasy, N. M., & Tse, B. (2000). Transformational leadership as management of emotion: A conceptual review. In N. M. Ashkanasy & C. E. J. Härtel (Eds.), *Emotions in the workplace: Research, thoery, and practice* (pp. 221–235). Westport, CT: Usenwood Publishing Group.

Avolio, B. J., & Bass, B. M. (1999). Re-examining the components of transformational and transactional leadership using multifactor leadership questionnaire. *Journal of Occupational & Organizational Psychology, 72*, 441–467.

Bar-On, R. (1997). *Bar-On Emotional Quotient Inventory (EQ-I): Technical Manual.* Toronto, ON: Multi-Health Systems.

Baumeister, R. F., Bratslavsky, E., Muraven, M., & Tice, D. M. (1998). Ego depletion: Is the active self a limited resource? *Journal of Personality and Social Psychology, 74*, 1252–1265.

Bower, G. H. (1981). Mood and memory. *American Psychologist, 36*, 129–148.

Bower, G. H., & Cohen, P. R. (1982). Emotional influences in memory and thinking: Data and theory. In M. S. Clar & S. T. Fiske (Eds.), *Affect and cognition.* Hillsdale, NJ: Lawrence Erlbaum Associates.

Brackett, M. A. (2001). *Personality and its expression in the life space.* Unpublished master's thesis, University of New Hampshire, Durham.

Brackett, M. A., & Mayer, J. D. (2003). Convergent, discriminant, and incremental validity of competing measures of emotional intelligence. *Personality and Social Psychology Bulletin, 29*, 1147–1158.

Bracket, M., Mayer, J. D., & Warner, R. M. (2004). Emotional intelligence and the prediction of behavior. Personality and Individual Differences, 36, 1387–1402.

Breckler, S. J. (1984). Empirical validation of affect, behavior, and cognition as distinct components of attitude. *Journal of Personality and Social Psychology, 47*, 1191–1205.

Brotheridge, C. M. (2003). Predicting emotional labor given situational demands and personality. Paper presented at the 18th Annual Meeting of the Society for Industrial/Organizational Psychology, Chicago, IL.

Cacioppo, J. T., & Bernston, G. G. (1999). The affect system: Architecture and operating characteristics. *Current Directions in Psychological Science, 8*, 133–137.

Cage, T., Daus, C. S., & Saul, K. (2005, August). *An examination of emotional skill, job satisfaction, and retail performance.* Paper presented at the 19th Annual Society for Industrial/Organizational Psychology. Washington, DC.

Caruso, D. R., Mayer, J. D., & Salovey, P. (2002). Emotional intelligence and emotional leadership. In R. E. Riggio, S. E. Murphy, & F. J. Pirozzolo (Eds.), *Multiple intelligences and leadership* (pp. 55–74). Mahwah, NJ: Lawrence Erlbaum Associates.

Clark, M. S., & Isen, A. M. (1982). Toward understanding the relationship between feeling states and social behavior. In A. H. Hastorf & A. M. Isen (Eds.), *Cognitive social psychology.* New York: Elsevier North-Holland.

Coetaee, C., & Schaap, P. (2004). *The relationship between leadership styles and emotional intelligence.* Paper presented at the 6th Annual Conference for the Society of Industrial and Organizational Psychology, Sandton, South Africa.

Collins, V. L. (2001). Emotional intelligence and leadership success. Unpublished doctoral dissertation. University of Nebraska, Lincoln.

Conte, J. M. (2005). A review and critique of emotional intelligence measures. *Journal of Organizational Behavior, 26*(4), 433–441.

Dause, C. S. (2002, April). *Dissatisfaction as a function of emotional labor.* Paper presented at the 17th Annual Meeting of the Society for Industrial and Organizational Psychologists, Toronto, Canada.

Daus, C. S., & Ashkanasy, N. M. (2005). The case for the ability based model of emotional intelligence in organizational behavior. *Journal of Organizational Behavior, 26,* 453–466.

Daus, C. S., & Harris, A. (2003). *Emotional intelligence and transformational leadership in groups.* Paper presented at symposium at the 18th Annual Meeting of the Society for Industrial and Organizational Psychologists, April, Orlando, FL.

Daus, C. S., Rubin, R., & Cage, T. (2004). *A qualitative study of the emotional aspects of police work.* Unpublished manuscript.

Daus, C. S., Rubin, R. S., Smith, R. K, & Cage, T. (2005). *Police performance: Do emotional skills matter?* Paper presented at the 19th Annual Meeting of the Society for Industrial and Organizational Psychologists, April, Los Angeles.

Davies, M., Stankow, L., & Roberts, R. D. (1998). Emotional intelligence: In search of an elusive construct. *Journal of Personality and Social Psychology, 75,* 989–1015.

Day, A. L., & Carroll, S. A. (2004). Using an ability-based measure of emotional intelligence to predict individual performance, group performance, and group citizenship behaviors. *Personality & Individual Differences, 36,* 1443–1458.

Denisi, A. S. (Chair; 2003). *Emotional intelligence.* Special even presented at the 18th Annual Meeting of the Society for Industrial and Organizational Psychology, Chicago, IL.

DeSousa, R. (1987). *The rationality of emotion.* Cambridge, MA: MIT Press.

Dinesh, D., & Palmer, E. (1998). Management by objectives and balanced score card. Will Rome fall again? *Management Decision, 5,* 363–370.

Ekman, P., & Friesen, W. V. (1975). *Unmasking the face: A guide to recognizing the emotions from facial cues.* Englewood Cliffs, NJ: Prentice Hall.

Forgas, J. P. (1992). Affect in social judgments and decisions: A multiprocess model. In M. Zanna (Ed.), *Advances in Experimental and Social Psychology* (Vol. 25, pp. 227–275). San Diego, CA: Academic Press.

Frijda, N. H. (1998). The laws of emotion. *American Psychologist, 43,* 349–358.

Fullam, A. (2002). Adult attachment, emotional intelligence, health, and immunological responsiveness to stress. *Dissertation Abstracts International, 63(2-B),* 1079.

George, J. M. (2000). Emotions and leadership: The role of emotional intelligence. *Human Relations, 53,* 1027–1055.

Gibbs, N. (1995, October 2). The EQ factor, *Time Magazine, 146,* 60–68.

Giles, S. J. S. (2001). *The role of supervisory emotional intelligence in direct report organizational commitment.* Unpublished master's thesis. University of New South Wales, Sydney, Australia.

Glomb, T. M., Kammeyer-Mueller, J. D., & Rotundo, M. (2004). Emotional labor demands and compensating wage differentials. *Journal of Applied Psychology, 89,* 700–714.

Goleman, D. (1995). *Emotional intelligence.* New York: Bantam Books.

Grandey, A. (2000). Emotion regulation in the workplace: A new way to conceptualize emotional labor. *Journal of Occupational Health Psychology, 5,* 95–110.

Hilgard, E. R. (1980). The trilogy of mind: Cognition, affection, and conation. *Journal of the History of the Behavioral Sciences, 16,* 107–117.

Hochschild, A. R. (1983). *The managed heart: Commercialization of human feeling.* Berkeley: University of California Press.

Isen, A. M. (1984). Towards understanding the role of affect in cognition. In R. S. Wyer & T. K. Srull (Eds.), *Handbook of Social Cognition, Vol. 3*, Hillsdale, NJ: Lawrence Erlbaum Associates.

Isen, A. M. (2001). An influence of positive affect on decision making in complex situations: Theoretical issues with practical implications. *Journal of Consumer Psychology, 11*, 75–86.

Isen, A. M., & Baron, R. A. (1991). Positive affect as a factor in organizational behavior. *Research in Organizational Behavior, 13*, 1–54.

Janovics, J., & Christiansen, N. D. (2002). *Emotional intelligence in the workplace*. Paper presented at the 16th Annual Conference of the Society of Industrial and Organizational Psychology, San Diego, CA.

Kim, J., & Mueller, C. W. (1978). *Introduction to factor analysis: What it is and how to do it*. Newbury Park, CA: Sage.

Kouzes, J., & Posner, B. (1990). Leadership practices: An alternative to the psychological perspective. In K. E. Clark & M. B. Clark (Eds.), *Measures of leadership* (pp. 205–215), West Orange NJ: Leadership Library of America.

Kruml, S. M., & Geddes, D. (2000). Catching fire without burning out: Is there an ideal way to perform emotional labor? In N. M. Ashkanasy, C. E. J. Härtel, & W. J. Zerbe (Eds.), *Emotions in the workplace: Theory, research, and practice* (pp. 177–188). Westport, CT: Quorum.

Laird, J. D., & Bresler, C. (1990). William James and the mechanisms of emotional experience. *Personality and Social Psychology Bulletin, 16*, 636–651.

Landy, F. L. (2005). Some historical and scientific issues related to research on emotional intelligence. *Journal of Organizational Behavior, 26*, 411–424.

Lavine, C. L. (1996). What are they really saying? *Cobblestone, 17*(7), 34–38.

Lazarus, R. S. (1982). Thoughts on the relations between emotion and cognition. *American Psychologist, 37*, 1019–1024.

Lazarus, R. S. (1984). On the primacy of cognition. *American Psychologist, 9*, 124–129.

Lazarus, R. S., Averill, J. R., & Opton, E. M., Jr. (1970). Toward a cognitive theory of emotion. In M. B. Arnold (Ed.), *Feeling and emotion: The Loyola Symposium*. Orlando, FL: Academic Press.

Leeper, R. W. (1948). A motivational theory of emotions to replace "Emotions as a disorganized response." *Psychological Review, 55*, 5–21.

Locke, E. A. (2005). Why emotional intelligence is an invalid concept. *Journal of Organizational Behavior, 26*, 425–431

Lopes, P. N., Côté, S., Grewal, D., Kadis, J., Gall, M., & Salovey, P. (in press). Evidence that emotional intelligence is related to job performance, interpersonal facilitation, affect, and attitudes at work, and leadership potential. *Psicothema*.

Lopes, P. N., Brackett, M. A., Nexlek, J. B., Schutz, A., Sellin, I., & Salovey, P. (2004). Emotional intelligence and social interaction. *Personality and Social Psychology Bulletin, 30*, 1018–1034.

Lopes, P. N., Salovey, P., Côté, S., & Beers, M. (2004). Emotion regulation ability and the quality of social interaction. *Emotion, 5*, 113–118.

Matthews, G., Zeidner, M., & Roberts, R. D. (2002). *Emotional intelligence: Science and myth*. Cambridge, MA: MIT Press.

Mayer, J. D. (1986). How mood influences cognition. In N. E. Sharkey (Ed.), *Advances in Cognitive Science* (Vol. 1, pp. 290–314). Chichester, UK: Ellis Horwood.

Mayer, J. D., Caruso, D. R., & Salovey, P. (1999). Emotional intelligence meets traditional standards for an intelligence. *Intelligence, 27*, 267–298.

Mayer, J. D. & Cobb, C. D. (2000). Educational policy on emotional intelligence: Does it make sense? *Educational Psychology Review, 12,* 163–183.

Mayer, J. D., DiPaolo, M. T., & Salovey, P. (1990). Perceiving affective content in ambiguous visual stimuli: A component of emotional intelligence. *Journal of Personality Assessment, 54,* 772–781.

Mayer, J. D., & Geher, G. (1996). Emotional intelligence and the identification of emotion. *Intelligence, 17,* 89–113.

Mayer, J. D., & Salovey, P. (1993). The intelligence of emotional intelligence. *Intelligence, 17,* 433–442.

Mayer, J. D., & Salovey, P. (1997). What is emotional intelligence? In P. Salovey & D. Sluyter (Eds.), *Emotional development and emotional intelligence: Educational applications* (pp. 3–31). New York: Basic Books.

Mayer, J. D., Salovey, P., & Caruso, D. R. (2000). Models of emotional intelligence. In R. J. Sternberg (Ed.), *Handbook of intelligence* (pp. 396–420). Cambridge, England: Cambridge University Press.

Mayer, J. D., Salovey, P., & Caruso, D. (2002). *Mayer-Salovey-Caruso Emotional Intelligence Test (MSCEIT) User's Manual.* Toronto, ON: Multi-Health Systems.

Mayer, J. D., Salovey, P., & Caruso, D. R. (2004a). Emotional intelligence: Theory, findings, and implications. *Psychological Inquiry, 60,* 197–215.

Miller, M. G., & Tesser, A. (1992). The role of beliefs and feelings in guiding behavior: The mismatch model. In L. L. Martin & A. Tesser (Eds.), *The Construction of Social Judgments* (pp. 277–300). Hillsdale, NJ: Lawrence Erlbaum Associates.

Morris, W. N. (1989). *Mood: The frame of mind.* New York: Springer-Verlag.

Organ, D. W., & Ryan, K. (1995). A meta-analytic review of attitudinal and dispositional predictors of organizational citizenship behavior. *Personnel Psychology, 48,* 775–802.

Ortony, A., Clore, G. L., & Collins, A. M. (1988). *The cognitive structure of emotions.* Cambridge, England: Cambridge University Press.

Palmer, B. R., Gignac, G., Manocha, R., & Stough, C. (2004). *A psychometric evaluation of the Mayer-Salovey-Caruso Emotional Intelligence Test Version 2.0.* Unpublished manuscript.

Rice, C. L. (1999). *A quantitative study of emotional intelligence and its impact on team performance.* Unpublished master's thesis, Pepperdine University, Malibu, CA.

Roberts, R. D., Zeidner, M., & Matthews, G. (2001). Does emotional intelligence meet traditional standards for an intelligence? Some new data and conclusions. *Emotion, 1,* 196–231.

Rubin, M. M. (1999). *Emotional intelligence and its role in mitigating aggression: A correlational study of the relationship between emotional intelligence and aggression in urban adolescents.* Unpublished doctoral dissertation. Immaculata College, Immaculata, Pennsylvania.

Sala, F. (2002). *Emotional competence inventory: Technical manual.* McClelland Center for Research: Hay Group. Philadelphia, PA.

Salovey, P., & Rodin, J. (1985). Cognitions about the self: Connecting feeling states and social behavior. In P. Shaver (Ed.), *Self, Situations, and Social Behavior* (Vol. 6, pp. 143–166). Beverly Hills, CA: Sage.

Salovey, P., & Mayer, J. D. (1990). Emotional intelligence. *Imagination, Cognition, and Personality, 9,* 185–211.

Schwarz, N., & Bohner, G. (1996). Feelings and their motivational implications: Moods and the action sequence. In P. Gollwitzer & J. Bargh (Eds.),

The psychology of action: Linking cognition and motivation to behavior (pp. 119–145). New York: Guilford.

Schutte, N. S., Malouff, J. M., Hall, L. E., Haggerty, D. J., Cooper, J. T., Golden, C. J., & Dornheim, L. (1998). Development and validation of a measure of emotional intelligence. *Personality and Individual Differences, 25,* 167–177.

Simon, H. A. (1989). Comments. In M. S. Clark & S. T. Fiske (Eds.), *Affect and cognition* (pp. 333–342). Hillsdale, NJ: Lawrence Erlbaum Associates.

Swift, D. G. (2002). *The relationship of emotional intelligence, hostility, and anger to heterosexual male intimate partner violence. Dissertation Abstracts International, Section B: The Sciences and Engineering, 62*(10-B). New York University, New York.

Tabachnick, B. G., & Fidell, L. S. (2001). *Using Multivariate Statistics.* Boston, MA: Allyn & Bacon.

Thayer, R. E. (1966). *The origin of everyday moods.* New York: Oxford University Press.

Thayer, R. E. (1989). *The biopsychology of mood and arousal.* New York: Oxford University Press.

Tomkins, S. (1970). Affect as the primary motivational system. In M. B. Arnold (Ed.), *Feeling and Emotion: The Loyola Symposium* (pp. 101–110). Orlando, FL: Academic Press.

Trinidad, D. R., & Johnson, C. A. (2002). The association between emotional intelligence and early adolescent tobacco and alcohol use. *Personality and Individual Differences, 32,* 95–105.

Trinidad, D. R., Unger, J. B., Chou, C. P., & Johnson, C. A. (2004). The protective association between emotional intelligence with psychosocial smoking risk factors for adolescents. *Personality and Individual Differences, 36,* 945–954.

Van Rooy, D. L., & Viswesvaran, C. (2004). Emotional intelligence: A meta-analytic investigation of predictive validity and nomological net. *Journal of Vocational Behavior, 65,* 71–95.

Van Tassel, J. D. (1995). Death to MBO, *Training & Development, 49,* 2–5.

Westermann, M. (2000). Making a mark in Rembrandt's Leiden. In Chong (Ed.), *Rembrandt creates Rembrandt: Art and ambition in Leiden,* 13–23. Zwolle, Netherlands: Waanders Printers.

Wheelock, A. K. (2000). Rembrandt inventing himself. In Chong's (Ed.) *Rembrandt creates Rembrandt: Art and ambition in Leiden,* 25–49. Zwolle, Netherlands: Waanders Printers.

Young, P. T. (1943). *Emotion in man and animal: Its nature and relation to attitude and motive.* New York: Wiley.

Zajonc, R. B. (1980). Feeling and thinking: Preferences need no inferences. *American Psychologist, 35,* 151–175.

Zajonc, R. B. (1984). On the primacy of affect. *American Psychologist, 39,* 117–123.

Zajonc, R. B., & Markus, H. (1982). Affective and cognitive factors in preferences. *Journal of Consumer Research, 9,* 123–131.

Zajonc, R. B., & Markus, H. (1985). Affect and cognition: The hard interface. In C. E. Izard, J. Kagan, & R. B. Zajonc (Eds.), *Emotions, Cognition, and Behavior.* New York: Cambridge University Press.

Improving the Definition, Measurement, and Application of Emotional Intelligence

Paul E. Spector
Hazel-Anne M. Johnson
University of South Florida

There is perhaps no construct in the social sciences that has produced more controversy in recent years than emotional intelligence (EI). Much of the controversy arises from the extent to which exaggerated, and even ridiculous, claims have been made about its superiority over more established constructs in predicting (and causing) organizational outcomes such as job performance and leadership success. Such claims have been made, at times, in the absence of fully disclosed and peer-reviewed scientific evidence (Landy, 2005). Nevertheless, the idea that EI can predict important outcomes has captured the imagination of practitioners who market EI-based products and their clients who purchase them. The combination of provocative claims with widespread marketing and application of EI tests and interventions despite the weak body of evidence supporting these applications has elicited alarm in the scientific community.

Perhaps not unexpectedly, extreme claims for the importance of EI to success in a broad range of human endeavors have led to strong criticism of the entire EI idea (e.g., Landy, 2005; Locke, 2005). Landy

(2005), for example, challenged EI researchers to meet a very high standard of validity evidence, far in excess of what is typically required for claiming the viability of a new construct. This counterweight to the more journalistic and popular psychology literature trumpeting EI has had the effect of marginalizing the more serious scientific work on EI that has emerged in the organizational literature, mainly since about 2000, and in the more general psychology literature beginning in the early 1990s. Thus, EI researchers are not only faced with the normally difficult task of conceptually and operationally developing a new construct, but are also saddled with convincing an alarmed and somewhat hostile audience that the endeavor has merit in the first place.

Our purpose in this chapter is to explore EI as a potentially useful scientific construct that can help explain human behavior in a wide range of settings and perhaps lead to valid application in the workplace. Our focus is on what might be done in the future rather than on a critique or defense of what has been done in the past, as other chapters in this volume have addressed these issues. We adopt the point of view that the notion of EI has potential, but that the jury is out and has just started deliberating. There is a great deal of both conceptual and empirical work that needs to be done before we can either claim EI is an important advance or conclude that it is nothing more than a repackaging of older established constructs. Some of that work has been published, but more is still needed to convince the field that EI has sufficient value to justify continued serious research on this new construct.

As the critics well describe (e.g., Conte, 2005; Landy, 2005; Locke, 2005; Zeidner, Matthews, & Roberts, 2004), there are two major areas of concern with EI. First, there are basic definitional issues in that there is no consensus on the definition of EI, so the field has yet to decide on exactly what it is. Generally, we can say that EI is an ability (or constellation of abilities) involving emotions in self and others (Mayer & Salovey, 1997; Wong & Law, 2002). However, the specific nature and number of those abilities is a matter of debate. Definitions of EI can be extremely broad, listing a variety of different abilities and human attributes. Thus, some definitions characterize EI not as a single construct but as a composite of distinct constructs or subconstructs that may or may not be related (Bar-On, 1997; Boyatzis, Goleman, & Rhee, 2000). Two individuals might have the same overall level of EI, for example, because one is skilled in regulating emotions in others but not self, and the other is skilled in regulating emotions in self but not others. Thus far, the somewhat complementary and more proscribed definitions of EI proposed by Mayer and Salovey (1997) and Wong and Law (2002) have received the most empirical support, but they have

not received universal acceptance. The definitions of EI often encountered in the popular press or in marketing brochures are generally
broader and fuzzier than the Mayer and Salovey (1997) and Wong and
Law (2002) definitions.

The second issue concerns EI assessment. Different researchers
have devised their own EI measures that take different approaches
and do not necessarily demonstrate strong convergent validity with
one another. Some measures assess EI as an ability by using items
that mirror cognitive ability or IQ tests (e.g., Mayer, Salovey, Caruso, &
Sitarenios, 2003). In these tests, each item is a problem that has a correct solution to be indicated in multiple-choice format. Other measures have taken more of a personality assessment approach with
items asking for self-descriptions, usually in the form of rating the extent to which each item describes the examinee (Wong & Law, 2002).
Complicating matters further is that the best established measures
are commercial and proprietary tests, and researchers have been
given limited data concerning psychometric properties for some of
them.

The final issue, that has received far less attention, is whether or
not EI measures are useful in applied settings. As a selection device,
the concern is whether EI measures have predictive validity, and if
they do, is there incremental validity over established measures? It is
certainly possible that the answer is yes to both questions, even
though the EI measures have little or no construct validity. In other
words, a given measure might merely assess some characteristic associated with job performance that has little to do with emotion, such
as cognitive ability or some other cognitive skill. Likewise, a training
program designed to enhance EI might improve performance, but for
reasons that have little to do with EI. For example, EI training might
enhance problem-solving strategies that have little to do with emotions. In order to fully understand the potential value of EI measures,
it is important to learn what these tests measure, what criteria they
predict, and what unique contributions these tests make to predicting
criteria.

DEFINITIONAL ISSUES

The first step in developing a construct is to articulate a clear conceptual definition that helps place that construct in a theoretical
nomological network of relationships with other constructs. At the
heart of all EI definitions is that it concerns emotion-related mental
abilities. The use of the term *intelligence* implies that cognitive and
problem-solving abilities are involved. However, some of the existing
definitions of EI can be quite broad, including elements that either are

not entirely problem solving by nature or have only a loose connection to emotions. Furthermore, it is unclear if EI can reasonably be considered a single construct or if it is a label for a variety of conceptually independent constructs. Certainly IQ, on which EI is loosely based, comprises different subabilities, such as mathematical and verbal reasoning, but at the core of each is the idea that IQ concerns a certain class of reasoning abilities. It is not as clear that the various EI components are similarly connected. So should EI be considered a single construct like IQ, with perhaps several separable components, or should it be considered a class of distinct constructs that may even be unrelated, such as Type A Behavior (Edwards, Bagliono, & Cooper, 1990) that comprises unrelated elements such as achievement striving and time urgency (Spector & O'Connell, 1994)? The answer to these questions requires both conceptual and empirical work.

Of the multiple definitions for EI, there are three that have been widely used: Goleman (1995) defined EI as "abilities that include self-control, zeal and persistence, and the ability to motivate oneself" (p. xii). Bar-On (1997) defined EI as "an array of noncognitive capabilities, competencies, and skills that influence one's ability to succeed in coping with environmental demands and pressures" (p. 14). Mayer and Salovey (1997) defined EI as "the ability to accurately perceive and express emotion; the ability to access and/or generate feelings when they facilitate thought; the ability to understand emotion and emotional knowledge; and the ability to regulate emotion in the self and others" (p. 10). The key distinction among these definitions is that the first two conceptualize EI as an ability that encompasses characteristics such as self-control and persistence that seem to overlap with personality (Bar-On, 1997; Goleman, 1995), whereas the third definition primarily emphasizes a number of discrete emotional abilities (Mayer & Salovey, 1997). The inclusion of personality characteristics in the Goleman (1995) and Bar-On (1997) definitions leads to their characterization as mixed models (Mayer, Salovey, & Caruso, 2000a), whereas Mayer and Salovey's (1997) tighter focus on the relationship between emotion and thought is more closely aligned with the notion of EI as a strict form of intelligence.

Mayer, Caruso, and Salovey (1999) provide theoretical justification for the existence of EI as a form of intelligence, and they have shown how it is correlated to, yet distinct from, other types of intelligence such as verbal IQ. They outline three criteria required for scientific consideration of a construct as an intelligence. First, one should be able to operationalize the intelligence as a set of abilities, which is clearly done in their four-branch model (Mayer & Salovey, 1997). By this criterion, the Goleman (1995) and Bar-On (1997) definitions of EI are not, strictly speaking, just types of intelligence, but rather are a mix of abilities, interests, and personality characteristics. Second, the abilities that intelligence comprises should be intercorrelated and related to preexisting intelligences while still exhibiting unique variance. Mayer et al. (1999) present a positive correlation in the mid-30s for EI and verbal intelligence, which is moderate but low enough to suggest that EI will likely contribute unique variance in the prediction of various criteria. The third criterion is developmental, such that intelligence should develop with age and experience. A comparison of adult and adolescent samples revealed higher levels of EI in adults, thereby suggesting that it may improve with age and experience (Mayer et al., 1999).

All the EI definitions provide a list of distinct abilities/characteristics that make up the overall construct. Factor-analytic research conducted by Mayer et al. (2003) on their EI measure demonstrated that their four-branch model provides the best fit to the data, which lends support to their notion that EI is composed of distinct factors. What is less clear is the extent to which their four branches, as well as other proposed characteristics, form a reasonable meta-construct of EI as opposed to a constellation of distinct, albeit related, abilities. Furthermore, are there some lower level abilities that might comprise the various theoretical components? For example, Mayer et al.'s (2003) four EI branches involve more than just problem solving, which might be implied by the idea of an intelligence. Elements of EI also include perceptual accuracy, emotional expression, emotional control, and motor and verbal behavior. Knowledge about emotion is included with the ability to reason about emotion. One might presume that a high level of knowledge presupposes a high level of ability to acquire that knowledge, but is knowledge the same as intelligence?

One of the important distinctions in the EI literature concerns the ability to recognize versus regulate emotions, both of which are elements of Mayer and Salovey's (1997) model. Are these abilities related or are they entirely distinct? In other words, must one be able to recognize emotions in order to regulate them? A person might regulate emotions in others through a highly effective learned repertoire of body language, facial expression, and verbalization. This emotion regulation might be performed in a rather rote fashion and not in response to the recognition of emotional states in others, much like a skilled movie actor might perform in front of a camera. Furthermore, it might be performed for an entire audience of individuals at one time (e.g., a political candidate making an emotionally stirring stump speech), without emotional cues from the individuals whose emotions are being regulated. Therefore, it is plausible that one might successfully regulate without recognition.

One place where we might see regulation as a performance is with emotional labor, which is the regulation of feelings and emotions in order to express the appropriate emotions in accordance with organizational display rules (Grandey, 2000). The performance of emotional labor can take two forms, surface acting or deep acting, where surface acting is the modification of the behavioral display to match the organization's requirements, and deep acting is the conscious effort to modify feelings to match the required emotional display (Hochschild, 1983). Thus, surface acting is just emotional expression, whereas deep acting also involves emotion regulation. It is easy to envision a scenario in which an employee regulates his emotions in accordance with organizational display rules without awareness or recognition of emotions in a target person. Where emotion recognition may play an important role is that performances of emotional displays such as smiling may not be as effective as performances that are flexible and respond to the emotional states of the target. At times, it may not be effective for the employee to smile at the target, as the smile might be perceived as inappropriate or phony if it is in response to a certain emotional display by the target. It may be that regulation of emotion can operate without recognition, but perhaps the pairing of the two processes leads to the most effective regulation. More importantly for the theory of EI is the issue as to whether there is an underlying set of abilities that lead to both recognition and regulation. The connection between recognition and regulation needs investigating as it goes to the heart of whether EI can be reduced to a single underlying construct or must remain a series of conceptually related but distinct constructs. Of course, emotional labor is concerned with performance and not ability. It is certainly possible that those individuals who have high ability to regulate also have high ability to recognize, even though in a given situation they may be using only one of the abilities.

Another distinction cutting across recognition and regulation is self versus others. It is not entirely clear that there is a general ability that encompasses both recognition and regulation of one's own and others' emotions. Indeed it is possible that these are entirely different abilities or that perhaps they are even negatively related. Some EI researchers have used the level of emotional traits such as negative affectivity (Fox & Spector, 2000) as a proxy for the ability to self-regulate, assuming that high negative affectivity represents an inability to regulate negative emotion. However, it is not clear that high levels of affective traits represent a breakdown in regulation as much as internal physiological functioning and thresholds for emotionality. Individuals high in positive or negative affective traits might just have lower physiological thresholds for arousal in response to stimuli. In fact, the individual high in these traits might, through necessity, develop enhanced regulatory abilities in order to cope with a constant flood of emotional arousal that, in the absence of regulation, would leave the person in a chronic state of extreme emotionality. Their regulation abilities might be superior to individuals who have high thresholds for emotional arousal and do not often experience those emotions. Furthermore, it is conceivable that those who are high in negative affectivity are more sensitive to emotional states in themselves and others and therefore might develop enhanced ability to recognize emotions in others. Of course, all this is speculation that needs empirical research to confirm or refute.

Even a cursory review of various existing EI definitions will find several additional abilities and characteristics that are thought to be parts of EI, leading to questions about how many distinct constructs underlie EI and whether there is a core that can be reduced to a single construct. What is needed is systematic research to investigate the connections among the various abilities and characteristics to answer the question about which (if any) are manifestations of the same underlying constructs, which are manifestations of related but distinct constructs, and which are manifestations of independent constructs. Likely some will fall into each category. This work can be done by assessing the individual abilities and characteristics with sound measures and then proceeding with a series of construct validity tests. First, we would investigate the strength of relationships among measures. We would expect that measures of the same underlying construct should be strongly related. Correlations approaching internal consistency estimates would clearly suggest the same construct is being assessed, but it is possible for more moderate levels of convergence if the underlying construct is reasonably heterogeneous, consisting of different components. Of course, in that case one might wonder if the subcomponents are really manifestations of a single core construct or if they are really just related but distinct constructs.

Second, the nomological networks of each component should be investigated. If the various components tend to have different correlates, this would argue against a single underlying construct. However, if components tend to relate to the same variables, theoretically expected to be related to EI, the evidence would support a single construct. Finally, one might study whether changes in different components as the result of experiences co-occur. For example, does EI training produce improvement in all component abilities and characteristics or only in some of them? Are some components more stable over time than others? Are some more affected by life events, such as emotional trauma? Co-occurrence of change will argue for a single construct, whereas lack of co-occurrence argues for separate constructs.

To date there have been too few research studies that have attempted to establish the construct and criterion-related validity of the various versions of the EI construct, with findings across different studies sometimes being inconsistent. Perhaps the strongest support has been found for the Mayer and Salovey (1997) model (see Daus & Ashkanasy, 2005, for an overview of empirical support). Evidence for the other measures/models as well as convergence among them is more mixed. For example, Brackett and Mayer (2003) demonstrated that there was low convergence between ability EI, as measured by the Mayer-Salovey-Caruso Emotional Intelligence Test (MSCEIT v. 2.0; Mayer, Salovey, & Caruso, 2002), and mixed-model EI, as measured by the Emotional Quotient Inventory (EQ-I; Bar-On, 1997) and the self-report EI test (SREIT; Schutte et al., 1998). Limited convergence of these measures is to be expected as their definitions of EI vary widely. Brackett, Mayer, and Warner (2004) provide criterion-related and incremental validity evidence for the MSCEIT v. 2.0 through its ability to predict negative behaviors in a group of college-age males even after controlling for personality (the Big Five) and academic achievement. In addition, they demonstrate discriminant validity for the EI construct as the MSCEIT scores displayed small correlations with Agreeableness and Intellect and moderate correlations with verbal SAT scores. These results are encouraging, as the conceptualization of ability EI requires that it does not overlap significantly with personality but moderately correlates with IQ, which in this instance is approximated by the verbal SAT scores.

On the other hand, in a study utilizing an earlier version of the MSCEIT (Mayer, Salovey, & Caruso, 2000b), Day and Carroll (2004) found mixed support for the factor structure of the EI scale and little support for its criterion-related validity. An exploratory factor analysis of the eight subscales produced two, rather than the expected four, underlying factors, with subscales from Emotional Understanding and Emotional Management loading on one factor, subscales from Emotional Integration loading on the second factor, and one subscale from Emotional Perception loading on each factor. A confirmatory factor analysis found similar fit for both the two-factor and four-factor structure proposed by Mayer et al. (2000b). This set of findings call for further research to determine whether the MSCEIT v. 2.0 will exhibit a more stable factor solution.

Law, Wong, and Song (2004) present recent construct validity evidence of EI as assessed by the Wong and Law Emotional Intelligence Scale (WLEIS; Wong & Law, 2002). They employ a four-dimensional definition of EI, which is based on Mayer and Salovey's (1997) ability model of EI. Law et al. (2004) reported that EI, as measured by the WLEIS, may be distinct from the Big Five dimensions, however, there were some moderate correlations with Neuroticism and Conscientiousness (rs = .44 to .59) that are greater than those between the

MSCEIT v. 2.0 and the Big Five dimensions (Brackett & Mayer, 2003). These findings suggest that EI, as assessed by the WLEIS, may be more closely related to personality, than as assessed by the MSCEIT v. 2.0. Law et al. (2004) also provided construct validity evidence by demonstrating convergent and discriminant validity of EI through use of the MTMM technique to examine measures of EI and other related constructs from multiple assessors.

All this suggests the need for a program of research that will continue to inform the conceptual definition and scope of EI. Some researchers feel that the Mayer and Salovey (1997) model is sufficiently developed and supported to be adopted as the basis for research at the current time (e.g., Ashkanasy & Daus, 2005), but this position does not enjoy consensus of the field. If research provides consistent answers, we will likely see consolidation of the variety of definitions currently in existence, reducing EI to a fairly parsimonious construct or set of constructs that is widely accepted. The results of such research will also help settle the question about whether EI is a useful construct or nothing more than a repackaging of existing constructs that offers little value to the literature. Of course, these conceptual issues are closely tied to issues of how best to assess EI.

MEASUREMENT ISSUES

One of the major controversies in EI concerns assessment (Conte, 2005). Different theorists/researchers have developed their own measures, many proprietary, that seem to assess, in many cases, quite different constructs (Bar-On, 1997; Boyatzis et al., 2000). Furthermore, it is not always clear that the measures are assessing anything distinct from other established constructs (Landy, 2005), such as empathy or cognitive ability. There have been two major types of measures: summated rating scales similar to personality tests (Wong & Law, 2002) and direct ability measures similar to cognitive ability tests (Mayer et al., 2003). The former ask respondents to rate their standing on items that reflect EI, presuming that individuals are willing and able to accurately report on their own characteristics or experiences that reflect those abilities. The latter ask respondents to choose the correct answers, presuming that EI can be reflected in the ability to choose the correct answer to questions concerning emotions. Both types of measures have been highly criticized by a number of authors, including some in this volume (e.g., Conte, 2005; Landy, 2005).

Of course, the development of sound measures begins with a clear articulation of the construct in question. Given the breadth of the EI concept, with a variety of subcomponents, a sound EI measure will most likely be multidimensional. The nature of those dimensions will help determine the types of measures that should be employed. Mayer and Salovey's (1997) conception of EI includes perception, understanding, and regulation of emotions. Although all these abilities involve cognitive problem-solving processes, there are also elements of motor abilities involved, such as the ability to use facial expressions and body postures to communicate emotions or emotion-eliciting information. Can all of these abilities plus those proposed by other theorists be reasonably tapped with paper-and-pencil measures? If so, can self-reports tap the constructs of interest, or do we need ability-type items? Alternatively, would other kinds of assessments be required? These are not easy questions to answer in cases where there are no distinct and precise definitions of subcomponents. Furthermore, extensive construct validity data will be needed to convince the scientific community that measures can be meaningfully interpreted to represent EI as opposed to other constructs. This does not mean just showing that an EI measure is distinct from a measure of cognitive ability or personality (in most studies, the Big Five dimensions), as a measure of EI might assess something else that is unrelated to emotion. Better evidence will be provided by theory-driven studies that show how EI can confirm hypotheses about relationships with other variables. Furthermore, studies need to go beyond showing relationships entirely with paper-and-pencil criteria. Such studies are valuable but are insufficient in establishing construct validity.

Paper-and-Pencil Measures

It certainly seems reasonable for researchers to continue to pursue paper-and-pencil measures of both types. Some aspects of EI might be measurable with self-reports, whereas others could be better measured with ability-type tests. Self-reports might be approached in at least two ways. First, one might ask people directly to self-rate their abilities on a variety of subdimensions, such as the ability to read other people's emotions or the ability to manipulate other people's moods. Although it is tempting to guess that those low in EI will be unaware that they can not recognize or regulate, it is certainly possible that people are quite aware of their emotion-related skills. Likewise, people might be quite aware of their abilities to self-recognize and self-regulate. It is even possible that a high score might indicate low EI; people who give their own ability to recognize and manipulate emotion unrealistically high ratings might be exhibiting low levels of EI. Finally, this direct method might reflect emotional self-efficacy (beliefs about ability) rather than EI itself, but this is an empirical question.

Second, one might ask questions that tap EI less directly, by asking about experiences that are the result of high or low EI. For example, individuals might be asked about relationships with other people, their level of comfort in various social situations, or their success in dealing with others. Such issues might be more accessible to individuals than direct ratings of their own abilities, and it is certainly possible that the proper set of questions will do a reasonable job of indicating at least some aspects of EI.

On the other hand, some components of EI might be best assessed with ability-type measures in which individuals are asked to choose the "correct" answer on items concerning emotions. Of course, such tests tap knowledge about emotions rather than the actual skill in recognizing/regulating emotions. To the extent that knowledge is a component of EI, this approach has promise. However, it is possible that the assessment of knowledge in the abstract does not reflect the live performance of EI in the rich social situation of real life. Just as a physicist is not a skilled gymnast merely from knowledge of the physics of the activity, an individual might not be skilled at emotion expression, recognition, or regulation just by knowing underlying principles. One might understand that smiling at someone can be an effective means of producing a positive emotional reaction, but recognizing in a live encounter the moment to smile and doing so in a way that does not seem false or insincere may well be a different ability. Likewise, knowing that negative emotion can be managed through cognitive restructuring is not the same as being able to effectively apply such a technique. The extent to which knowledge reflects performance is a topic in need of careful study. It might be that EI is only part of the story and that additional abilities will have to be included in our studies and theories. It also might be that our models of EI are too broad and include components that are really something different.

Even within the well-developed four-dimension model proposed by Mayer and Salovey (1997), there might be room to consider alternative types of measures to paper-and-pencil. For example, we might assess the Perceiving Emotions dimension by presenting participants with pictures or movies of people displaying various emotions, and requiring they correctly identify the emotions. Target scoring could be employed for this dimension where the individuals (targets) whose faces are used record what emotions they were feeling at the time, and ability to perceive emotion would be judged by correspondence of emotion identified with displayed emotion. The next two dimensions in the four-branch model, Facilitation of Thought and Understanding Emotions, are more concerned with knowledge about emotions; therefore, ability measures such as the MSCEIT v. 2.0 may be most appropriate to assessing these dimensions. Expert consensus can be utilized to score the ability measures, because groups of emotions experts have been shown to display acceptable inter-rater agreement (Mayer et al., 2003).

The experts, by nature of their training, are better able to identify the correct answer by attending to the consensual information of the group. However, to avoid an earlier criticism of Roberts, Zeidner, and Matthews (2001), efforts must be made to select a demographically diverse group of experts, so that their scores are not biased on the basis of gender, ethnicity, or intelligence. The fourth dimension of Managing Emotions might be assessed by observation of the individual in the process of managing emotions, so methods such as those described in the following section would be most appropriate.

Interpersonal Simulation Tests

An entirely different assessment approach that might prove to have advantages over paper-and-pencil is the interpersonal simulation that might be patterned on exercises included in assessment centers (Cascio, 1998; Lievens & Klimoski, 2001). These centers, used frequently by organizations to select managers, involve a variety of paper-and-pencil measures with simulation exercises to assess a variety of abilities and personal characteristics. Many of the exercises are designed to determine how effectively an individual can handle an interpersonal situation, such as leading a group or disciplining an employee. This approach might be applied to some of the components of EI, particularly the regulation of emotions in self and others.

There has been an assumption by some researchers and theorists that EI is akin to IQ and that ability-type tests make the most sense. However, there are differences between the two in that IQ is concerned primarily with mental tasks, that is, solving logical, mathematical, and verbal problems. The items on an IQ test are samples of such problems. EI involves the performance of tasks that involve more than mental problem solving, although there are certainly cognitive elements in all of them, as is true of all (or almost all) human activities beyond reflexes. For example, recognizing emotional states in others involves perception in the ability to detect subtle nuances of facial expression and body language. Regulation of emotions in the self can involve a variety of strategies, including motor performances such as using physical activity to reduce emotional arousal by "working it off." Regulation of emotions in others requires the performance of an extensive repertoire of body language, facial expression, verbalization, and emotional expression. Such performances might involve more than mere cognitive ability but include motor activities as well; consequently, paper-and-pencil tests might not be sufficient.

Simulations can be done with a variety of exercises that are designed to assess different subcomponents of EI. For example, some exercises might determine if an individual is able to self-regulate by concealing negative emotions or expressing positive ones, appropriate to the situation at hand. The assessment of success at controlling negative emotion might even be informed by use of physiological measures. Other exercises might assess how well the individual can regulate positive or negative emotions in others. Individuals might be aware that emotion regulation is the point of the exercise, or they might not be, in order to determine if they figure out on their own that this is required. Exercises might be designed to see if individuals spontaneously make efforts to regulate emotions in the context of the simulated situation where a confederate's emotions should be regulated to best perform the expressed purpose of the exercise. Alternatively, assessees might be explicitly instructed to regulate the emotional response in a confederate (or another assessee), either by attempting to elicit a positive response or reduce a negative one. For example, a role-play exercise might ask the assessee to comfort a coworker or subordinate who is upset.

These exercises can be scored by trained observers who rate the person's performance directly. Just as with assessment centers, multiple raters could be asked to indicate how well individuals do on a variety of dimensions. They can be focused on broad dimensions, such as rating the person on regulating the emotions of others. An alternative would be to focus on more microscopic behaviors that are relevant to regulation, such as smiling, making eye contact, or making particular types of statements that might affect emotions (e.g., reassuring the person that everything will be fine). The more global approach is simpler and takes less time, but may be less accurate unless raters can be trained to accurately recognize performance. The latter requires more effort, and considerable work will be required to determine the relevant behaviors that need to be rated. Although it would seem this approach would result in more accurate assessment, that assumption would have to be empirically verified.

An alternative approach might be to interview the individual after the exercise to find out what she observed and what she was trying to accomplish. For example, an individual high in EI might report that he noticed another person appeared unhappy with the situation, noting the cues on which he relied to reach that conclusion. He might explain how humor was used to lift the person's mood. Trained observers could rate the effectiveness of recognition (whether the person grasped the emotional situation) and regulation (whether the assessee was carrying out what he claimed was being attempted).

Of course, a great deal of work would be required to develop the exercises and scoring. As with the ability-type measures, the criterion for what behavior constitutes high versus low EI is a potential weakness. However, if EI is an ability to actually affect emotions in self and others, it might be necessary to assess actual performance on regulation tasks, treating each exercise as a test item, rather than assessing knowledge about that performance.

Alternatively, the EI assessment center could be used as a criterion for validation studies of paper-and-pencil measures of EI. Would such measures predict who will perform best in role plays and other interpersonal simulations? Would those subscales most closely linked to the nature of the exercise relate most strongly? For example, would an emotion regulation subscale relate most strongly to an emotion regulation exercise? Would such paper-and-pencil measures correlate similarly to different types of exercises; that is, is the same ability reflected in regulation of both positive and negative emotions in others? Research on such issues would help determine the viability of the EI construct.

APPLICATION ISSUES

As well argued by Zeidner et al. (2004), EI measures are being used for selection and other purposes in the absence of sufficient scientific evidence supporting their validity. They point out, for example, that results linking various measures to performance have been inconsistent. Furthermore, it is not clear when EI measures relate to criteria that the shared variance represents something other than IQ or existing personality variables. Consequently, there might be predictive validity in the absence of construct validity.

Validation studies are necessary to demonstrate how existing or future measures can be valid predictors of performance or other criteria consistently across studies. Equally important will be a demonstration of incremental validity over and above existing constructs in order to demonstrate that EI is something unique. This does not mean that there cannot be overlap, as it is certainly possible that EI relates to IQ and personality at the construct level. Of course, it is possible that EI is a distinct ability that underlies other established variables, such as personality. For example, suppose the development of empathy depends on having the innate ability to recognize emotions in others. One cannot develop empathy without being able to recognize emotions, so only those with reasonably high EI will be fully empathic. If this is the case, empathy might relate strongly to EI and have many of the same correlates. It might well be that empathy mediates the relation between EI and some criteria because EI is a cause of empathy, and empathy is a cause of a criterion. In such a case EI might not show incremental validity at all, although it might be an important ability underlying the performance of the criterion. Whether one would be better off using a measure of empathy or EI is a matter of taste unless one proves to be a better predictor than the other. Incremental validity can support the viability of an EI construct, but failure to find it is far less conclusive and does not automatically invalidate it.

Research to date has provided somewhat mixed support for the predictive and incremental validity of EI, depending in large part on the particular scales that are used and the criterion in question. For instance, Daus and Ashkanasy (2005) summarized studies showing relationships between the Mayer et al. (2002) MSCEIT and a variety of criteria, including job performance and leadership emergence. Johnson (2004) explored how EI might facilitate the performance of emotional labor, with the more emotionally intelligent showing lower levels of strain. As hypothesized, Johnson's study showed that EI, as assessed by the WLEIS (Wong & Law, 2002), served as a moderator in the relationship between emotional labor and strain. At high levels of emotional labor, high-EI individuals experienced higher job satisfaction and affective well-being, as well as lower emotional exhaustion (Johnson, 2004). Therefore, we might expect that EI would moderate the relationship between emotional labor and other individual outcomes, as well as organizational outcomes, such as service performance. In addition, EI was positively related to employee affective well-being and negatively related to emotional exhaustion across a wide range of service organizations, so it appears to have direct effects on the well-being of service employees.

Not all research, however, has been as supportive. Day and Carroll (2004), for example, found that the MSCEIT v. 1.1 was not predictive of job performance or citizenship behavior in a laboratory setting. Brackett et al. (2004) demonstrated criterion-related validity of the MSCEIT v. 2.0 only for males in predicting negative behaviors such as drug or alcohol abuse. In a general sense, women score consistently higher than men in the realm of EI, which is possibly attributable to social roles; that is, women are socialized to be alert to and perceptive of emotions (Eagly, 1987). On the other hand, if the observed gender difference in EI is a function of measurement bias rather than actual gender differences in EI, this may be problematic for its implementation as a selection measure, as it may provide an unfair advantage for women.

It also does not seem likely that EI (assuming it is an important ability for success) will be equally important for all performance criteria or for all jobs (Daus & Ashkanasy, 2005). In fact, differential patterns of validity might provide useful construct validity evidence. For example, the recognition and regulation of emotions in others will probably be more important for sales performance than computer programming. Part of the validation evidence that EI is a viable construct would be to show that it predicts performance on tasks involving interpersonal interaction, particularly tasks involving interpersonal influence (see Daus & Ashkanasy, 2005, for evidence of this). EI should predict performance in sales, the interpersonal side of management, and counseling. One might argue that self-regulation of emotion might be important for all tasks, as negative emotion would interfere with task performance. Here too, the type of task should be a factor, as negative emotion would be expected to interfere with new learning and complex tasks rather than well-learned simple tasks (Yerkes & Dodson, 1908). Miller (2004) developed a job analysis method to determine the emotional requirements for a job that might be a useful tool for investigating where EI might be especially relevant in predicting job performance.

A program of research showing relations of EI measures with established measures of other variables would help establish the nomological network of EI relationships. Contextual variables, such as emotional demands of the job, should be considered as moderators. It would be most useful for theory to guide this research as opposed to blind empirical approaches of correlating EI measures with criteria across a variety of jobs chosen by convenience. Such an approach is likely to lead to inconsistency in results if characteristics of jobs and tasks moderate the EI–performance relationship. It also might lead to an erroneous impression that EI is not viable because results seem inconsistent across studies.

TYING THINGS TOGETHER

EI research is really in a very early stage, and at the current time we have little consensus about the definition or assessment. Although the state of affairs creates confusion, as different researchers are using the EI term to mean different things, one should keep in mind that the study of EI is evolving quickly, and likely there will eventually be a shakeout in terms of which components and definitions become established in the research community and which will be set aside. At the current time, it is important for researchers to continue to work on refining constructs and measures and amassing empirical support for the construct validity of various measures. These activities of defining constructs and empirical validation go hand in hand.

A comprehensive list of subdimensions suggested as part of EI would be quite long, with many being linked closely to other constructs. Some of those constructs, such as empathy, seem related to emotions, but others seem farther removed. Perhaps the first shakeout that needs to occur is to target dimensions that are strongly and directly related to emotions. It is certain that emotion recognition and regulation are central, but there may be other related components that are also important. Those that are distally or indirectly related to emotions will likely be eliminated from future definitions.

The Mayer and Salovey (1997) model seems the most carefully limited to emotion-related abilities, and it is the best developed, having enjoyed a long period of research and refinement. Daus and Ashkanasy's (2005) recent summary includes quite a few studies providing encouraging results based on this model and using Mayer et al's (2002) MSCEIT v. 2.0. This may well emerge as the consensus model, at least for the near future, in guiding research on EI. The recent availability of Wong and Law's (2002) self-report scale of the model's four dimensions may encourage even more research.

The second shakeout should focus on whether or not various components of EI are nothing more than the repackaging of existing established constructs. Some components of self-report measures used to assess EI relate to established personality measures, so one wonders if such dimensions of EI represent an advance. Is EI just empathy, negative affectivity, or some other personality variable? This is not to say that if there is overlap, EI automatically loses. It is certainly possible that EI would represent a more useful framework with which to understand certain phenomena than a more established construct. However, such advantages need to be demonstrated and not merely claimed. It would be premature at this point to draw a conclusion about the viability of these sorts of EI measures.

A distinction needs to be kept clear between the construct of EI and the current operationalizations. We are not so certain that existing measures have always done EI full justice, and failures to find support for EI predictions may say more about the quality of measures than about the EI concept and theories. Perhaps some measures contain biases shared with other personality variables, such as social desirability, that inflates their intercorrelation. There is still a great deal of work to be done, and perhaps completely adequate measures of EI have yet to be developed.

On a final note, we are not convinced that the ultimate value in this line of research will hinge on whether EI is a single construct like IQ, as opposed to a collection of independent emotion-related abilities, or if it is even reasonably a form of intelligence at all. To some extent, the debate over whether it is appropriate to call EI an intelligence (e.g., Locke, 2005) is a rhetorical issue that distracts from the more important questions. Is there an ability or constellation of abilities, largely cognitive in nature, which allow for expression, perception, regulation and understanding of emotion in self and others? Do these abilities help us predict and understand people's behavior?

In a way, it is unfortunate that EI has caught on prematurely in the consulting world and popular press in the absence of sufficient scientific support for its application. In these venues, expert opinion and subjective appeal often substitute for empirical evidence. This has produced a backlash from the scientific community that is rightly skeptical of both the exaggerated claims for the usefulness of EI as a selection tool in organizations and the efficacy of EI training. On the other hand, the publicity given the concept has stimulated researchers to conduct research to see if EI might be something of value. In other words, is there any truth at all to claims that EI is important for job performance and other aspects of organizational life? The often mixed results published so far are tantalizing and suggest that EI might be an important construct to study. However, it is too soon to tell if the scientific community will largely remain unimpressed, assuming that EI results are attributable to other explanations, or if EI will become a scientifically respected and useful construct.

REFERENCES

Ashkanasy, N. M., & Daus, C. S. (2005). Rumors of the death of emotional intelligence in organizational behavior are vastly exaggerated. *Journal of Organizational Behavior, 26*, 441–452.

Bar-On, R. (1997). *Bar-On Emotional Quotient Inventory: A measure of emotional intelligence.* Toronto, ON: Multi-Health Systems.

Boyatzis, R. E., Goleman, D., & Rhee, K. (2000). Clustering competence in emotional intelligence. In R. Bar-On & J. Parker (Eds.), *The handbook of emotional intelligence* (pp. 343–362). San Francisco: Jossey-Bass.

Brackett, M. A., & Mayer, J. D. (2003). Convergent, discriminant, and incremental validity of competing measures of emotional intelligence. *Personality and Social Psychology Bulletin, 29*, 1147–1158.

Brackett, M. A., Mayer, J. D., & Warner, R. M. (2004). Emotional intelligence and its relation to everyday behavior. *Personality and Individual Differences, 36*, 1387–1402.

Cascio, W. F. (1998). *Applied psychology in human resource management* (5th ed.). Upper Saddle River, NJ: Prentice Hall.

Conte, J. M. (2005). A review and critique of emotional intelligence measures. *Journal of Organizational Behavior, 26*, 433–440.

Daus, C. S., & Ashkanasy, N. M. (2005). The case for the ability based model of emotional intelligence in organizational behavior. *Journal of Organizational Behavior, 26*, 453–466.

Day, A. L., & Carroll, S. A. (2004). Using an ability-based measure of emotional intelligence to predict individual performance, group performance, and group citizenship behaviors. *Personality & Individual Differences, 36*, 1443–1458.

Eagly, A. H. (1987). *Sex differences in social behavior: A social-role interpretation.* Hillsdale, NJ: Lawrence Erlbaum Associates.

Edwards, J. R., Bagliono, A. J., Jr., & Cooper, C. L. (1990). Examining the relationships among self-report measures of the Type A behavior pattern. The effects of dimensionality, measurement error, and differences in underlying constructs. *Journal of Applied Psychology, 75*, 440–454.

Fox, S., & Spector, P. E. (2000). Relations of emotional intelligence, practical intelligence, general intelligence, and trait affectivity with interview outcomes: It's not all just 'G'. *Journal of Organizational Behavior, 21,* 203–220.

Goleman, D. (1995). *Emotional intelligence.* New York: Bantam Books.

Grandey, A. A. (2000). Emotion regulation in the workplace: A new way to conceptualize emotional labor. *Journal of Occupational Health Psychology, 5,* 95–110.

Hochschild, A. R. (1983). *The managed heart: Commercialization of human feeling.* Berkeley: University of California Press.

Johnson, H. M. (2004). *The story behind service with a smile: The effects of emotional labor on job satisfaction, emotional exhaustion, and affective well-being.* Unpublished master's thesis, University of South Florida, Tampa, FL.

Landy, F. J. (2005). Some historical and scientific issues related to research on emotional intelligence. *Journal of Organizational Behavior, 26,* 411–424.

Law, K. S., Wong, C. S., & Song, L. J. (2004). The construct and criterion validity of emotional intelligence and its potential utility for management studies. *Journal of Applied Psychology, 89,* 483–496.

Lievens, F., & Klimoski, R. J. (2001). Understanding the assessment centre process: Where are we now? In C. L. Cooper & I. T. Robertson (Eds.), *International Review of Industrial and Organizational Psychology* (Vol. 16, pp. 245–286). Chichester, UK: Wiley.

Locke, E. A. (2005). Why emotional intelligence is an invalid concept. *Journal of Organizational Behavior, 26,* 425–431

Mayer, J. D., Caruso, D. R., & Salovey, P. (1999). Emotional intelligence meets traditional standards for an intelligence. *Intelligence, 27,* 267–298.

Mayer, J. D., & Salovey, P. (1997). What is emotional intelligence? In P. Salovey & D. Sluyter (Eds.), *Emotional development and emotional intelligence: Educational Implications* (pp. 3–31). New York: Basic Books.

Mayer, J. D., Salovey, P., & Caruso, D. R. (2000a). Emotional intelligence as zeitgeist, as personality, and as a mental ability. In R. Bar-On & J. Parker (Eds.), *The handbook of emotional intelligence* (pp 92–117). San Francisco: Jossey-Bass.

Mayer, J. D., Salovey, P., & Caruso, D. R. (2000b). *Test manual for the Mayer-Salovey-Caruso Emotional Intelligence Test: Research version 1.1* (3rd ed.). Toronto, ON: Multi-Health Systems.

Mayer, J. D., Salovey, P., & Caruso, D. R. (2002). *Mayer-Salovey-Caruso Emotional Intelligence Test (MSCEIT), Version 2.0.* Toronto, ON: Multi-Health Systems.

Mayer, J. D., Salovey, P., Caruso, D. R., & Sitarenios, G. (2003). Measuring emotional intelligence with the MSCEIT v. 2.0. *Emotion, 3,* 97–105.

Miller, J. A. (2004). *Assessing emotional characteristics of jobs.* Unpublished doctoral dissertation, University of South Florida, Tampa.

Roberts, R. D., Zeidner, M., & Matthews, G. (2001). Does emotional intelligence meet traditional standards for an intelligence? Some new data and conclusions. *Emotion, 1,* 196–231.

Schutte, N. S., Malouff, J. M., Hall, L. E., Haggerty, D. J., Cooper, J. T., Golden, C. J., et al. (1998). Development and validation of a measure of emotional intelligence. *Personality and Individual Differences, 25,* 167–177.

Spector, P. E., & O'Connell, B. J. (1994). The contribution of individual dispositions to the subsequent perceptions of job stressors and job strains. *Journal of Occupational and Organizational Psychology, 67*, 1–11.

Wong, C. S., & Law, K. S. (2002). The effects of leader and follower emotional intelligence on performance and attitude: An exploratory study. *The Leadership Quarterly, 13*, 243–274.

Yerkes, R. M., & Dodson, J. D. (1908). The relation of strength of stimulus to rapidity of habit-formation. *Journal of Comparative Neurology and Psychology, 18*, 459–482.

Zeidner, M., Matthews, G., & Roberts, R. D. (2004). Emotional intelligence in the workplace: A critical review. *Applied Psychology: An International Review, 53*, 371–399.

15

Four Conclusions About Emotional Intelligence

Kevin R. Murphy
Pennsylvania State University

The debate over emotional intelligence (EI) has been loud and sometimes bitter, and it can be difficult to reconcile competing viewpoints that dominate this debate. On the one end of the continuum, EI enthusiasts promote this concept as a broad solution to many of the problems that beset organizations, schools, and the like. On the other end of this same continuum, there are many authors who dismiss the concept of EI altogether. Arguments between these two camps tend to generate more heat than light.

The contributors to this volume have, for the most part, been drawn from the middle ground. For the most part, the authors of chapters 1–14 seem skeptical of the more extravagant claims about EI, but many seem willing to give the concept of EI some credence. It is fair to say that the majority of the chapters lean more strongly in the direction of skepticism than enthusiasm, but chapters 1–14 of this volume do, in my view, give a sufficiently thorough and wide-ranging assessment to allow readers to evaluate the strengths and weaknesses of EI research and practice.

Chapters 1–14 lead me to a number of important conclusions, several of which are reflected in the overall structure of this book. In particular, I believe the material reviewed by the authors of these chapters leads directly to four broad conclusions about the current status of emotional intelligence:

1. Emotional intelligence is often poorly defined and poorly measured.
2. The relationship between emotional intelligence and other concepts, including general intelligence, social skills, and personality, is not adequately understood.
3. The most widely publicized claims about the relationship between emotional intelligence and success in school, in the workplace, and in life are not supported and, in some important cases, are almost certainly untrue.
4. There are some reasons for optimism about the future of emotional intelligence, but there is still a long way to go before this concept will come close to living up to the hype.

In this chapter, I hope to summarize the main messages of this book by laying out these conclusions in some detail. Rather than citing new literature to support these conclusions, I tie each of the four conclusions back to the specific chapters in this volume that offer the most direct support for particular points. All of these chapters make extensive reference to the relevant research literature, and readers who want to consider the primary research that forms the basis for each of these conclusions will find better, more expert review of the literature in each of these chapters than I could provide here. My intention is to draw out the main threads running through chapters 1–14 rather than introducing new arguments or observations into the debate over EI, so in this chapter I will restrict myself to referring to points raised by the authors of the preceding chapters.

EMOTIONAL INTELLIGENCE IS POORLY DEFINED AND POORLY MEASURED

Emotional intelligence has been defined in very different ways by different authors. Mayer, Salovey, and their colleagues define EI in terms of a set of abilities focuses around identifying emotions, using emotions, understanding emotions, and managing emotions. Bar-On and Goleman define EI in terms of a mix of abilities and personality characteristics. Goleman's definition is probably the broadest, including abilities and competencies such as self-control and emotional awareness, broad personality characteristics (e.g., conscientiousness), and even temperament factors (e.g., optimism).

It seems clear that mixed models of emotional intelligence are profoundly flawed (chaps. 1–3 discuss the weaknesses of these models in detail). Most generally, there are two problems with these definitions of EI. First, there is not a strong empirical basis for these models. The evidence linking the various abilities, competencies, personality characteristics, and other attributes that are included in these mixed models of EI is generally weak and unconvincing. Second, and more important, it is hard to make real sense of what it would mean to have high versus low EI when EI is defined as a broad mix of abilities, personality characteristics, and other attributes. For example, Goleman defines EI in terms of over 20 diverse competencies. It is unlikely that someone with a high level of EI will be strong in all of these areas or that someone with low EI will be weak in everything. Unlike the cognitive ability domain, there is no strong evidence of a general factor underlying all of the elements that are included in mixed-model definitions of EI. As a result, a statement like "Joe has a high level of emotional intelligence" might mean many different things. If the definition of EI is sufficiently broad and diverse, a statement like "Joe has a high level of emotional intelligence" will not mean anything at all.

Assessments of ability-based models of EI are generally more favorable (e.g., see chaps. 13 and 14), but these models are nevertheless open to criticism. In chapter 3, Conte and Dean note that ability-based models look strong in part because of a contrast effect. In comparison to the clear and obvious weaknesses of the mixed models, ability-based models don't look so bad, but this does not mean that ability-based models are good or useful. It merely means that models that focus on the abilities that describe and define emotional intelligence are less problematic than mixed-model definitions of EI.

There are three broad criticisms of ability-based models of EI. First, there is not a clear rationale for including some emotion-related tasks and not others (e.g., showing empathy) in one's definition of EI. The boundaries of EI have always been difficult to define, and none of the ability-based models has presented a good explanation for why some tasks that seem to involve emotion might be a part of EI and some others are not. Second, these models have not yet led directly to measures that are generally accepted as adequate by a wide range of scholars. Chapters 1 and 14 describe in some detail the deficiencies of existing EI measures; I expand on some of these later in this chapter. Finally, there is a long history of interest in EI and similar constructs, but as Landy notes (chap. 4) efforts to date to develop practical and valid measures of the abilities that are thought to underlie EI have been far from successful. It is possible that the current generation of EI scholars will succeed where so many others have failed, but the long and sorry track record of attempts to define and measures social abilities and skills suggests that this will not be a simple task.

Given the difficulties in defining EI, it is perhaps no surprise that there are also concerns with the adequacy of EI measures (e.g., see chaps. 1, 3, & 14). I believe it will be virtually impossible to develop adequate measures of the types of EI described by the mixed models of Goleman and Bar-On. Given the difficulty in even defining exactly what EI means in models that treat this construct as a broad amalgam of abilities, competencies, and personality characteristics, it is hard to see how one would go about developing valid measures or how one would tell whether particular measures provided an adequate index of EI. Ability-based definitions of EI are likely to be more amenable to the development of valid measures, but there are some problems particular to ability-based EI measures that have not been adequately solved to date.

As Matthews, Emo, Roberts, and Zeidner point out in chapter 1, ability-based EI measures differ from measures of many other abilities in that they ask respondents to answer questions and complete tasks in which there is no answer or response that is, by definition, correct. Rather, ability-based EI scales rely heavily on expert scoring or consensus scoring. That is, measures of people's ability to perceive, understand and manage emotions typically involve a comparison between the responses of an individual and the opinions of experts or the responses of other similar examinees, and a person who perceives emotions in a different way from experts or from other similarly situated examinees is presumed to be wrong. The use of expert and consensus-based scoring is not completely unique to ability-based EI measures; there are measures of artistic judgment that employ a similar strategy. The problem, of course, is that people might have different opinions about both art and emotions for a variety of reasons, and it is unclear whether a person who thinks about the emotional domain differently from experts or from the average of several peers is low on that ability, or whether that person simply has a a new (and perhaps better) way of thinking. In the absence of objective criteria for scoring ability-based EI measures, there will always be the possibility that unusual responses to questions about emotion will turn out to be better than the choice of the majority of so-called experts, making the scoring of these measures somewhat questionable.

THE RELATIONSHIP BETWEEN EI AND OTHER RELEVANT CONSTRUCTS IS UNCLEAR

Suppose one accepts ability-based models as the best existing approach to defining of the construct of EI. Suppose further that some of the questions raised in the preceding section (e.g., why include some emotions but not others, why focus on some tasks, such as perceiving and managing emotions, and not others) could be settled. There would still be some fundamentally important questions about EI that would need to be answered, including:

- Is EI really a type of intelligence?
- What does a measure of EI do for you that measures of other related constructs do not?
- How is EI similar to and different from related concepts such as social skills, empathy, or self-monitoring ?

As the authors of chapters 7 and 10 note, part of the appeal of EI is that it goes beyond the seemingly narrow domain of academic intelligence. Traditional intelligence tests produce outcomes that are deeply worrisome to many potential users (e.g., the use of cognitive ability tests in employment settings typically leads to reductions in employment opportunities for members of several racial and ethnic groups), and the idea of measuring new types of "intelligence" is appealing to many test users. It is fair to ask, then, whether EI is actually a new and distinct type of intelligence.

It does seem reasonable to conclude that EI shares some characteristics with other aspects of intelligence (see Daus, chap. 13, for a discussion of this evidence). Like virtually all other aspects of intelligence, EI involves active information processing. Like many other specific abilities (e.g., spatial visualization, calculation speed), EI deals with a specific domain and a specific type of information (i.e., emotions). However, EI seems different from the cognitive abilities that are traditionally studied in at least two ways.

First, all abilities are ultimately defined in terms of the examinee's capacity to do some particular thing well (e.g., solve mathematical problems, answer factual knowledge questions, extract meaning from passages one has read). The abilities that make up EI also refer to doing specific things with emotions (e.g., understanding, managing, perceiving), but it is often quite hard to tell whether an individual is really doing them well or poorly. In a previous section, I noted that concerns have been raised about the need to rely on expert or consensus scoring in constructing ability-based measures of EI. Unlike many other abilities, there may not be any objective benchmark to determine whether a specific individual performs EI-type tasks well.

Second, there is little good evidence of where EI-related abilities reside in a general taxonomy of cognitive abilities. As VanRooy, Dilchert, Viswesvaran, and Ones note in chapter 10, one of the defining features of cognitive abilities is that measures of virtually all abilities show positive manifold (i.e., they are positively intercorrelated). This makes it possible to construct well-organized, hierarchically structured taxonomies for understanding the relationships among cognitive abilities and the relationships between each specific ability and "g" (general cognitive ability). There has been little apparent attention to, or even interest in, the relationships between the abilities that are thought to define EI and other specific abilities. Several studies have documented correlations between measures of EI and measures of general cognitive ability, but it is hard to evaluate the proposition that EI is a type of ability until we know how measures of the specific components that are thought to define EI relate to other well-understood abilities.

One of the recurring criticisms of EI is that the construct of EI is simply a new name for constructs that have long been studied by psychologists, such as social skill, empathy, and self-monitoring. It seems likely that EI is related to all of these constructs, and it also seems plausible that it is distinct from each one in meaningful and important ways. However, there has still been too little research or theory laying out the relationship between EI and other relevant constructs to allow researchers to fully evaluate the value of the EI construct.

There are several ways of examining the hypothesis that considering EI as a construct tells you something about a person that is not adequately captured by more traditional constructs (e.g., broad personality dimensions). One way to demonstrate the value of EI is to show that measures of this construct allow you to predict or explain outcomes not adequately predicted on the basis of other constructs. The authors of several chapters (e.g., chaps. 7, 10, & 14) note that when predicting outcomes that *should* be related to EI, such as success in schools or in the workplace, measures of EI do not seem to add much that cannot be adequately accounted for by measures of normal personality and general intelligence. There are many potential explanations for this finding (e.g., it is possible that stronger relationships would be found if better EI measures were used), but the hypothesis that EI is both new *and* useful is one that has not received a great deal of support. Evidence that EI is different from other similar constructs widely studied by psychologists is surprisingly difficult to come by; there are relatively few studies that include adequate measures of EI and of related constructs such as social skills, self-monitoring, and so forth. Evidence that helps in predicting outcomes that cannot be predicted on the basis of normal personality and general intelligence seems even more rare.

THE MOST INFLUENTIAL CLAIMS DON'T HOLD UP

As the authors of chapters 1, 2, 6, 8, 9, 10, and 12 note, extravagant claims have been made about EI, including:

- EI is as important as, or more important than, IQ in determining success in school and the workplace.
- EI I not strongly related to race, class, education, or socioeconomic status.
- EI can be described as a set of competencies that can be developed with relative ease.
- Because there are so many ways to be emotionally intelligent, many people, and perhaps most people, have or could have high levels of EI.

Claims of this sort have been extremely important in explaining the popularity of EI; the controversy over these claims has been extremely important in explaining the harsh and skeptical stance taken by many academic critiques of EI.

Murphy and Sideman note (chap. 2) that the strongest claims have been made for the weakest variants of EI. That is, broad mixed-model definitions of EI, in which EI is viewed as a combination of a fairly diverse set of traits, competencies, and abilities, are the most likely to be associated with sweeping claims about the importance of EI, the fairness of EI tests, and the success of EI training programs. Research on ability-based versions of EI typically leads to more modest claims. Murphy and Sideman attribute this pattern of strong claims coupled with weak evidence versus arguably stronger evidence and demonstrably weaker claims to a clash of cultures. These claims are not targeted toward an academic or scientific audience (where debates about the weight of evidence would make a real difference) but rather to an audience that is neither inclined nor equipped to evaluate the underlying evidence (see chaps. 6 & 11).

It is clear from the evidence reviewed in chapters 1–14 that none of the sweeping claims described at the beginning of this section is likely to be true. There is meager supporting evidence for *any* of these claims, and at least in the case of claims about the relative importance of IQ versus EI, there is a wealth of evidence that directly discredits the idea that EI is as important as IQ. Broad claims about the relevance and importance of EI not only fail the test of empirical support (the evidence simply does not support such claims), they also fail the plausibility test. As is noted in chapters 8 and 9, it is almost certain that EI is more important in some settings than in others, suggesting, at a minimum, the need to substantially qualify claims made about EI. Thus, for example, there might be some jobs in which EI turns out to be fairly important (e.g., jobs in which there is a frequent need to communicate with a diverse audience or in which interpersonal stressors are especially common) and others in which it makes little difference (e.g., many technical jobs, in which much of the work is done individually and in which interactions with coworkers are heavily structured as a result of the demands of the tasks performed). The ability to work well with emotional information, to manage emotions, and so forth is simply unlikely to make much difference in a wide range of situations where emotions are peripheral to the task at hand.

Imagine an alternate scenario in which more modest claims were made about EI. I believe the evidence reviewed in chapters 1–14 supports the following conclusions:

- People differ in their skill in perceiving, understanding, and managing emotions.
- These skills develop over long periods of time and are probably difficult to improve with short interventions.
- These skills are relevant in some jobs and some social settings and not in others.
- The abilities that make up EI are (like virtually all abilities that involve active information processing) distinct from, but related to, general intelligence.
- It is possible to develop reliable measures of these abilities, but their validity is still an open question.

If EI proponents had limited themselves to claims like these, it is likely that the construct of EI would never have appeared on the cover of *Time* magazine. It is also likely that EI tests and training programs would be a relatively modest part of a consultant's arsenal and that there would be little controversy over EI. More to the point, it is unlikely you would be reading this book right now. If EI proponents had limited themselves to claims this modest, there would be relatively controversy over this construct and little need for extended commentaries or critiques.

The extravagant claims made by some proponents about the importance of EI are at the heart of the EI debate, but in many ways, the claims themselves are not being debated at all. For example, there is no serious debate about the claim that EI is more important than IQ; there is abundant evidence that this claim is wrong and that there is virtually no real evidence to support this assertion. EI proponents who make claims of this sort essentially ignore the literature (mainly academic) that questions the evidentiary basis for these claims and instead go straight to the popular press and to trade journals, in which a combination of strong claims and weak evidence is hardly unusual. As chapters 6 and 11 note, this might be the only effective strategy for reaching an audience of organizational decision makers, few of whom have the time, the background, or the inclination to wade through the academic journals. Academics often deride these claims, but usually only from the safety of their backyards (i.e., academic journals and conferences). As long as most academics and most market-oriented consultants continue to approach EI from completely different perspectives (see chap. 2), it is likely that the two camps will continue talking past one another rather than debating the topic of EI in a meaningful way. Luckily, there are good reasons to believe that discussions of EI will soon mature beyond the name-calling phase that has characterized so much of the EI controversy to date.

THERE IS ROOM FOR HOPE, BUT A LONG WAY TO GO

Chapters 12 and 14 outline a number of reasons for optimism when thinking about the future of EI research and practice. First, it is quite possible that the EI fad has already peaked. EI has clearly shown the pattern explosive growth and backlash that is characteristic of most fads (chap. 12), but the research reviewed in chapters 1–14 suggests that the EI debate has progressed to the point where a substantial number of researchers are taking this construct seriously. I should note that "taking this construct seriously" is different from believing EI is a useful construct. Many of the scholars who have taken a serious look at issues such as the measurement of EI (e.g., chaps. 3 & 14), the relationships between EI and other relevant constructs (e.g., chaps. 4 & 10), and the way EI is represented to the potential community of users (e.g., chaps. 2, 6, & 9) are not particularly impressed by what they see. However, it does seem clear that enough people are taking a serious look at the strengths and weaknesses of EI theories, measures, and interventions to form the basis for a thorough, well-researched critique.

Second, the EI controversy has helped transform EI from a somewhat isolated area of research, carried out by a small group of talented researchers (Salovey, Mayer, and their colleagues have been involved in EI research for over 15 years), into a hot topic for research. It is true that much of the growth in the EI research community has come by adding skeptics and debunkers, but many of the authors of this volume (e.g., Ashkanasy and his colleagues, Daus and her colleagues) have taken a more optimistic tack, suggesting ways EI research and practice might be improved and extended. The best hope for the future of EI is to recruit a large (and generally skeptical) group of researchers. If it turns out that the major problems with current EI models can be solved to the satisfaction of a suitably skeptical audience *and* that the data show real advantages of this construct over other related constructs, EI will move solidly into the mainstream of research on individual differences. The sort of work needed to get EI to this point requires a substantial large body of serious and careful work. A useful groundwork has been laid by Salovey, Mayer, and their colleagues; it is now time to see whether this line of inquiry will actually take us anywhere worth going.

The most pressing issue for proponents of ability-based models is the need to improve the measurement of EI. Measures of EI-related abilities are still far from perfect (see chaps. 3 & 14), and better measures will contribute substantially to EI research and practice. There is a need to develop both the theoretical and the empirical bases of support for EI and to build a comprehensive understanding of the relationship between EI and other abilities, as well as the relationships between EI and personality characteristics, preferences, and attitudes. The development of better EI measures is the first step in building this network of supportive evidence.

It is unlikely that ability-based versions of EI will ever capture the attention or match the claims made for the mixed-model versions of this construct. Rather, EI researchers should aim for a less ambitious goal, that is, demonstrating that the construct of EI has some value as a basis for predicting, explaining, and influencing behavior across some reasonable range of relevant situations and that this concept allows one to explain things not adequately explained by other similar constructs. The jury is still out on the question of whether EI has sufficient value as a construct to justify its use, but it does seem reasonable to believe that we will know the answer to this question before long.

Author Index

A

Abbe, A., 286, 295, *299*
Abrahamson, E., 289, 290, *298*
Ackerman, P. L., 17, *30*, 170, *182*, 240, *256*
Aderman, D., 110, *117*
Adler, M., 190, *206*
Aicher, C., 21, *30*
Alexander, W., 133, *137*
Allen, J., 131, 133, *136*
Allen, N. J., 193, *206*
Alonso, A., 72, *77*, 246, *261*
American Educational Research, 6, *30*, 71, *74*
American Psychological Association, 6, *30*, 53, *55*, 71, *74*
Ammeter, A. P., 202, *210*
Amo, L., 15, *33*
Anastasi, A., 103, *117*
Anderson, J. R., 7, *31*
Anderson, N., 238, *260*
Anderson, S., 19, *31*
Antonakis, J., 203, *206*
Arieti, S., 306, *319*
Arnold, M. B., 306, *319*
Aronson, J. A., 128, *139*

Arthur, W., Jr., 229, *232*
Arvey, R. D., 224, *232*
Ash, S. R., 225, *232*
Ashforth, B. E., 223, *232*
Ashkanasy, N. M., 23, *31*, 27, *32*, 38, *56*, 44, *55*, 68, *74*, 190, 191, 193, 194, 196, 197, 202, 203, 204, *206*, *207*, *208*, *210*, 302, 304, 309, 311, 314, *319*, 332, 333, 339, 340, 341, *342*
Ashton-James, C., 190, 194, 196, 197, *206*
Atwater, L., 203, *206*
Austin, E. J., 14, *31*, 34, 66, *74*, 76, 151, *157*
Averill, J. R., 306, *322*
Avolio, B. J., 201, 203, *206*, 312
Ayers, L. R., 133, *136*

B

Bagby, R. M., 12, *35*
Bagliono, A. J., Jr., 328, *342*
Bailey, J. R., 195, 197, *210*
Bajgar, J., 20, 21, *31*

Baldridge, D. C., 200, *207*
Baldwin, T. T., 228, *232*
Barchard, K. A., 14, *31*, 69, *74*, 242, *256*
Bar-Hillel, M., 287, *298*
Barnhart, D. L., 241, *259*
Bar-On, R., 5, 6, 9, 10, 12, 13, 14, 20, 21, *31*, 39, *56*, 61, 63, 64, *74*, 85, 112, *117*, 142, 153, *157*, 217, 227, *232*, 240, 246, 247, 255, *256*, 304, 310, *320*, 326, 328, 332, 333, *342*
Baron, R. A., 199, *208*, 308, *322*
Barrett, G. V., 214, 225, *232*
Barrick, M. R., 198, *206*, *209*
Barsade, S. G., 193, 197, *206*, *209*
Bartrum, D., 200, *207*
Bass, B. M., 201, 203, *206*, 312
Baumeister, R. F., 19, *31*, 307, *320*
Becker, T., 23, *31*
Bedell, B. T., 20, 21, *34*
Beers, M., 202, 204, *209*, 310, 314, *322*
Beier, M. E., 170, *182*
Bell, S. T., 229, *232*
Benbow, C. P., 181, *184*
Benjamin, L. T., 87, 90, *117*
Bennett, B., 163, *182*
Bennett, W., Jr, 229, *232*
Ben-Shakhar, G., 287, *298*
Benson, J. B., 165, *182*
Berkowitz, L., 110, *117*
Berkowitz, M. W., 126, 131, *136*, *137*
Berman, S., 135, *139*
Bernardin, H. J., 226, *232*
Bernston, G. G., 307, *320*
Bertua, C., 238, *260*
Bevier, C. A., 238, *260*
Bier, M. C., 126, 131, *136*, *137*
Billig, S. H., 135, *137*
Binet, A., 162, *182*
Bingham, W. V. D., 94, 98, *117*
Binning, J. F., 214, 225, *232*
Birkenmeier, B. J., *186*, 288, *298*
Blanchard, K. H., 204, *208*
Blau, R. D., 98, *121*
Bloodworth, M. R., 129, 130, *139*
Bluestein, J., 131, *137*
Blum, M. L., 104, *117*
Blum, R. W., 131, *137*, *138*

Bobik, C., 154, *159*
Bobko, P. L., 238, *260*
Boden, J. M., 19, *31*
Bohner, G., 308, *323*
Bommer, W. H., 202, *210*
Bonanno, G. A., 19, *31*
Bond, F. W., 24, *32*
Bono, J. E., 203, *208*, 273, *279*
Booth, R. J., 18, *34*
Bordin, E. S., 194, *206*
Borman, W. C., 244, *256*
Boudreau, J. W., 200, *208*
Bower, G. H., 193, *208*, 306, *320*
Boyatzis, R. E., 13, 39, 42, *56*, 60, 63, *74*, 112, *117*, 201, 204, *208*, 227, *232*, 244, *258*, 326, 333, *342*
Brackett, M. A., 14, 16, 17, 26, *31*, 69, *74*, 199, *209*, 240, 242, 243, *257*, 310, 312, *320*, *322*, 332, 333, 339, *342*
Bradbury, T., 42, *56*
Braden, J. P., 167, *182*
Brand, C., 237, 238, *257*
Brass, D. J., 198, *209*
Bratslavsky, E., 307, *320*
Braverman, E. P., 178, *184*
Breckler, S. J., 306, *320*
Bregman, E. O., 88, 92, 95, *123*
Bresler, C., 306, *322*
Bretz, R. D., 200, *206*, *208*, *209*
Brienza, D., 245, *257*
Briggs, S. R., 267, *278*
Brody, N., 15, 16, 17, 26, *31*, 172, 173, 175, 177, 179, 180, *182*, 255, *257*
Broom, M. E., 94, 96, *118*
Brotheridge, C. M., 219, *232*, 315, *320*
Broussine, M., 223, *234*
Brown, A. S., 15, *32*
Brown, J., 198, 201, *206*
Bruner, J. S., 102, *118*
Buckingham, M., 269, 275, *278*
Buckley, M. R., 202, *210*
Burke, R. S., 94, 99, *119*
Burks, F. W., 96, *118*
Burley, P. M., 109, *118*
Buros, O. K., 92, *118*
Burtt, H. E., 94, 95, *118*
Buss, A. H., 267, *278*

Byham, W., 228, *233*
Byrne, J. A., 289, *298*

C

Cable, D. M., 200, *208*
Cacioppo, J. T., 307, *320*
Cage, T., 312, 313, 314, 315, *321*
Callender, J. C., 237, *257*
Cambron-McCabe, N., 135, *139*
Campbell, D. T., 215, *232*
Campbell, F. A., 166, *182*
Campbell, J. P., 237, *257*
Campion, M. A., 178, *184*
Cannon-Bowers, J., 237, *259*
Cantor, N., 5, *33*
Caputi, P., 19, 20, 21, 22, *31*
Carretta, T. R., 68, *76*, 179, *184*, 238,
    240, 256, *260*, *261*
Carroll, J. B., 17, *31*, 88, *118*, 162,
    163, 176, *183*, 236, *257*
Carroll, R. T., 288, 291, *298*
Carroll, S. A., 73, 74, 195, *207*, 244,
    246, 255, *257*, 309, *321*,
    332, 339, *342*
Carson, K. D., 286, 288, 289, *298*
Carson, P. P., 286, 288, 289, *298*
Carter, G. W., 226, *233*
Cartwright, S., 73, 76, *77*
Cartwright, S., 245, *261*
Cartwright, S., 24, 25, *35*, 64
Caruso, D. R., 4, 6, 11, 12, 13, 14, 15,
    16, 26, *33*, 34, 39, 43, *57*,
    62, 66, 69, 71, 72, *74*, 75,
    76, 112, *121*, 142, 144, 152,
    153, *158*, 175, *184*, 191,
    196, *209*, 216, 217, 227,
    233, 240, 246, 247, 255,
    259, 296, *299*, 303, 304,
    305, 309, 310, 311, *320*,
    322, *323* 327, 328, 329, 332,
    333, 335, 339, 341, *343*
Cascio, W. F., 51, 52, *56*, 215, *232*,
    336, *342*
Caspi, A., 249, *257*
Catano, V. M., 14, *34*, 64, *76*, 242, *259*
Cattell, R. B., 163, *183*
Cavallo, K., 245, *257*
Chaddock, G. R., 290, *298*
Chambless, D. L., 50, *56*
Champy, J., 269, *279*

Chan, A. Y. C., 19, 20, 21, 22, *31*
Chan, D. W., 21, *31*, 151, *157*
Chang, J., 131, 133, *136*
Chapanis, A., 267, *278*
Chapanis, N. P., 267, *278*
Chapin, F. S., 96, 100, 109, *118*
Charbonneau, D., 24, *31*
Cheek, J. M., 267, *278*
Cherniss, C., 190, 199, *206*, *207*,
    213, *232*
Cherny, S. S., 165, *182*
Chou, C. P., 311, *323*
Christiansen, N. D., 254, *258*, 315,
    322
Ciarrochi, J. V., 19, 20, 21, 22, *31*
Clark, J. H., 105, *118*
Clark, L. F., 109, *118*
Clark, M. S., 308, *320*
Clarke, H. M., 96, *118*
Cleary, T. A., 239, *257*
Cleeton, G. U., 104, *118*
Clinkenbeard, P. R., 177, *185*
Clore, G. L., 21, *32*, 305, *323*
Cobb, C. D., 302, 305, *323*
Cobb, M. V., 88, 92, 95, *123*
Coetzee, C., 311, *320*
Coffman, C., 269, 275, *278*
Cohen, J., 126, 127, 128, 131, 133,
    136, *137*, *139*
Cohen, P. R., 306, *320*
Colbert, A. E., 203, *209*
Coleman, S., 131, *138*
Collaborative for Academic, Social,
    and Emotional Learning,
    130, *137*
Collins, A. M., 305, *323*
Collins, V. L., 312, *321*
Columbo, J., 164, *183*
Conger, J. A., 204, *207*
Connelly, S., 203, *207*
Conte, J. M., 60, 74, 75, 240, *257*,
    303, 309, *320*, 326, 333,
    342
Conway, J., *279*
Cooper, C. L., 328, *342*
Cooper, J., 142, 154, *159*
Cooper, J. T., 12, 13, 14, *35*, 61, 65,
    72, *76*, 195, *210*, 246, *261*,
    303, 304, 310, *324*, 332,
    343
Cooper, R. K., 190, 195, *207*

Cordes, C. L., 218, *232*
Corey, S., 50, *56*
Corley, R., 164, *184*
Cornelius, S. W., 249, *257*
Costa, P. T., 179, *183*
Coston, T. D., 154, *159*
Côté, S., 202, 204, *209*, 310, 312, 314, *322*
Cox, T. H., 200, *207*
Coy, K. C., 8, *33*
Crane, G. W., 105, *118*
Crawford, J. R., 166, *183*
Creed, P. A., 200, *207*
Creque, R. E., Sr., 241, *259*
Cronbach, L., 6, *31*, 89, 103, 105, 107, 108, *118*, 168, 181, *183*
Cross, B., 23, *32*
Cummins, R. A., 291, *298*
Cyphers, L. H., 165, *183*

D

Dasborough, M. T., 203, *207*
Datnow, A., 135, *138*
Daus, C. S., 38, *56*, 68, *74*, 191, *206*, *207*, 302, 304, 309, 311, 312, 313, 314, 315, 319, *320*, *321*, 332, 333, 339, 340, 341, *342*
Davidshofer, C. O., 68, *76*, 236, *259*
Davies, M., 5, 29, *32*, 38, *56*, 68, *74*, 223, *232*, 240, *257*, 303, 309, 310, *321*
Davis, M. H., 19, *32*
Dawda, D., 13, *32*, 56, 64, *74*
Day, A. L., 14, *34*, 64, 73, 74, *76*, 195, *207*, 242, 244, 246, 255, *257*, *259*, 309, *321*, 332, 339, 342
De Fruyt, F., 238, *260*
Dean, F. P., 19, *31*
Deary, I. J., 166, 169, 170, 176, *183*
DeFries, J. C., 163, 164, *182*, *184*
DeGroot, A. D., 167, *183*
deMille, R., 83, 106, 111, 114, 116, *117*, *121*
Denham, S. A., 8, *32*
Denisi, A. S., 304, *321*
Der, G., 170, 176, *183*
Derksen, J., 64, *75*, 85, *118*, 255, *257*

DeSousa, R., 306, 307, *321*
Detweiler, J. B., 20, 21, *34*
Devine, I., 200, *209*
Devine, J., 131, *137*
DeVos, G., 273, *279*
Dewey, J., 84, 85, *118*
Dewey, J., 128, *137*
Diehl, M., 249, *257*
Diener, E., 287, *298*
Digman, J. M., 271, 278
DiLalla, L. F., 165, *183*
Dilchert, S., 168, *184*, 236, 251, 252, 253, 254, 255, *257*, *259*, 261
Dineen, B. R., 225, *232*
Dinesh, D., 318, *321*
DiPaolo, M. T., 216, *233*, 305, *323*
Dodson, J. D., 340, *344*
Donaldson-Feilder, E. J., 24, *32*
Dornheim, L., 12, 13, 14, *35*, 61, 65, 72, *76*, 142, 154, *159*, 195, *210*, 246, *261*, 303, 304, 310, *324*, 332, *343*
Doty, G., 42, *56*
Dougherty, T. W., 199, 200, *207*, *210*, 218, *232*
Douglas, C., 202, *210*
Drake, C. A., 104, *118*
Dreher, G. F., 200, *210*
Druskat, V. U., 190, 198, *207*, 244, 255, *262*, 273, *278*
Dubin, R., 215, *232*
Dulewicz, V., 73, 75, 201, *207*, 213, *232*
Dunnette, M. D., 226, *233*, 284, *298*
Dutton, J., 135, *139*
Dweck, C. S., 145, *157*
Dwyer, K., 131, *138*

E

Eagly, A. H., 339, *342*
Earles, J. A., 237, 256, *260*
Eddleston, K. A., 200, *207*
Edens, P. S., 229, *232*
Edwards, J. R., 328, *342*
Eimecke, V. W., 99, 105, *118*, 119
Ekman, P., 15, *33*, 193, *207*, 305, 321
Ekstrom, R. B., 88, *119*

Elias, M. J., 25, *32*, 126, 129, *137*, *138*
Emmerling, R. J., 38, 39, 48, 49, *56*, 199, *207*
Emo, A. K., 29, *33*
Endler, N., 21, *32*
Engle, R. W., 236, *262*
Epstein, S., 20, *32*
Erez, M., 111, *119*
Ettorre, B., 286, 289, *298*
Eysenck, H. J., 292, *298*

F

Fagan, J. F., 165, *183*
Fairchild, G., 289, 290, *298*
Feldman, D. C., 193, *209*
Feldman, J., 165, *184*
Ferris, G. R., 202, *210*
Festinger, L., 266, *278*
Feyerherm, A. E., 24, *32*
Fidell, L. S., 304, 319, *324*
Fiedler, F. E., 204, *207*
Field, H. S., 224, *232*
Finn, C. E., 290, *298*
Finnegan, E. B., 178, *184*
Fish, H. L., 99, *119*
Flemming, E. G., 96, *119*
Flynn, J. R., 180, *183*
Foley, J. M., 107, 110, 111, 122, *123*
Ford, G., 176, *183*
Ford, J. K., 73, 75, 228, *233*
Ford, M. E., 109, *119*
Forgas, J. P., 306, 307, *321*
Forret, M. L., 199, *207*
Forsythe, G. B., 162, 175, 178, *185*, 248, 249, 250, *261*
Fox, H. C., 169, *183*
Fox, S., 199, 200, *207*, 248, 257, 273, *279*, 330, *343*
Francis, M. E., 18, *34*
Frank, G., 49, *56*
Frazier, K., 156, *157*
Frederickson, N., 25, *32*, 126, *138*, 141, 142, 143, 153, *158*, 242, 243, *260*
French, J. W., 88, *119*
Freud, S., 128, *137*
Frey, K. S., 129, *137*
Freyd, M., 92, 94, *117*, *119*

Friesen, W. V., 193, *207*, 305, *321*
Frijda, N. H., 193, *208*, 308, *321*
Fryer, D. H., 105, *119*
Fulker, D. W., 163, 164, 165, *182*, *183*, *184*
Fullam, A., 310, *321*
Funke, G., 29, *33*
Furnham, A., 5, 12, 13, 14, 21, 22, *32*, 34, 141, 142, 143, 145, 148, 151, 153, 154, 156, *157*, *158*, 198, *207*, 240, 241, 242, 243, *260*, 294, *298*

G

Gabrriel, C., 176, *185*
Gaddis, B., 203, *207*
Gall, M., 312, *322*
Galton, F., 173, *183*
Gardner, H., 128, *137*, 37, 41, *56*, 81, 142, 152, *158*, 162, 175, *183*,
Garrett, H. E., 94, 98, *119*
Gast-Rosenberg, I. F., 237, 238, *260*
Gatewood, R. D., 224, *232*
Geddes, D., 314, *321*
Geher, G., 15, *32*, 85, *121*, 305, *323*
George, J. M., 197, 202, *208*, 219, 222, *232*, 234, 307, 311, *321*
George, P. S., 133, *137*
Gerhardt, M. W., 273, *279*
Gerits, L., 255, *257*
Ghiselli, E. E., 237, *257*
Gibbs, N., 134, 135, *137*, 205, *208*, 302, *321*
Gibson, D. E., 200, *208*
Gignac, G., 63, *76*, 309, *323*
Giles, S. J. S., 312, *321*
Giles, T. R., 194, *209*
Gilliland, A. R., 94, 99, *119*
Gillis, C., 190, *208*
Glasser, W., 132, *137*
Glomb, T. M., 313, *321*
Goff, S., 252, *260*
Goh, A., 15, *33*
Gohm, C. L., 21, *32*
Golden, C. J., 12, 13, 14, *35*, 61, 65, 72, *76*, 142, 154, *159*, 195,

210, 246, *261*, 303, 304,
310, *324*, 332, *343*
Goldman, S., 12, 26, 34, 142, *159*
Goldstein, I. L., 73, *75*
Goleman, D., xii, *xiii*, 4, 6, 23, 25, 26,
32, 35, 38, 39, 41, 42, 43,
48, 49, *56*, 60, 64, 70, 73,
74, *75*, 132, *138*, 190, 192,
194, 195, 198, 201, 204,
205, *208*, 213, 217, 227,
232, 233, 240, 244, 245,
257, *258*, 263, 274, *278*,
284, 287, 294, *299*, 302,
303, *321*, 326, 328, 333,
342, 343
Gossen, D., 132, *138*
Gottfredson, L. S., 170, 178, *183*,
249, 253, 255, 256, *258*
Gough, H. G., 109, *119*, 273, *278*,
279
Gowing, M. K., 68, *75*
Graf, I. K., 200, *210*
Graham, T., 19, *32*
Grandey, A. A., 219, *232*, 314, *321*,
330, *343*
Greaves, J., 42, *56*
Greenberg, J., 228, *233*
Greenberg, M. T., 25, *32*, 126, 129,
137, 138
Greeson, C., 154, *159*
Grewal, D., 312, *322*
Grigorenko, E. L., 248, *258*, 162,
175, 177, 178, *183, 185*
Gross, M. L., 105, *119*
Grosvenor, E. L., 94, *119*
Grubb III, W. L., 178, *184*
Guidry, B. N., 286, 288, 289, *298*
Guilford, J. P., 82-83, 88, 96, 106,
107, 111, 114, 116, *117,
119, 121*, 236, *258*
Guion, R. M., 99, 108, *119*, 214, 221,
226, *233*, 235, *258*
Gur, R. C., 193, *208*

H

Haggerty, D. J., 72, *76*, 142, 154, *159*,
195, *210*, 246, *261*, 303,
304, 310, *324*, 332, *343*
Haith, M. M., 165, *182, 183*

Hakel, M. D., 238, 239, 256, *260*
Hakstian, A. R., 69, *74*
Hall, L., 12, 13, 14, *35*, 61, 65, 72,
76, 142, 154, *159*, 195, *210*,
246, *261*, 303, 304, 310,
324, 332, *343*
Hall, M. W., 129, *138*
Hall, W. B., 273, *279*
Hamilton, V., 193, *208*
Hammer, M., 269, *279*
Handa, J., 270, *279*
Hare, R. D., 271, *279*
Harquail, C. V., 200, *207*
Harris, A., 311, *321*
Harris, J. I., 241, *259*
Hart, S. D., 13, *32*, 56, 64, *74*
Hartel, C. E. J., 23, 27, *31*, 32, 44,
55, 190, 191, 196, *208*
Hartigan, J. A., 236, 237, *258*
Hartman, B. J., 108, *119*
Hartman, N. S., 178, *184*
Hartmann, G. V., 98, *121*
Hartsfield, M. K., 244, *258*
Harvard Business Review Online,
274, 275, *279*
Harvey, J. H., 286, *299*
Hatch, T., 135, *138*
Hay/McBer, 227, *232*
Haynes, N. M., 129, *137*
Hedlund, J., 162, 175, 178, *185*,
247, 248, 249, 250, 254,
258, 261
Heggestad, E. D., 17, *30*, 240, 256
Helton-Fauth, W., 203, *207*
Henry, E. R., 105, *119*
Henry, P. J., 177, *183*
Hepner, H. W., 104, *119*
Herrnstein, R. J., 38, 41, 55, 56,
161, 174, *183*, 239, *258*
Hersey, P., 204, *208*
Hezlett, S. A., 238, *258*
Higgs, M., 24, *32*, 73, *75*, 201, *207*,
213, *232*
Hilgard, E. R., 306, *321*
Hirsh, H. R., 238, *258*
Hochreich, D. J., 110, *120*
Hochschild, A. R., 193, *208*, 313,
314, *321*, 330, *343*
Hoepfner, R., 107, *119*
Hofstede, G., 116, *119*
Hogan, J., 265, 273, *279*

Hogan, M. J., 14, *34*, 242, *260*
Hogan, R., 265, 271, 273, *279*
Holland, J. L., 264, 273, *279*
Hollander, S., 65, *76*
Hooper, G. S., 196, *208*
Horn, J., 163, *184*
Horvath, J. A., 162, 175, 178, *185*,
    248, 249, 250, *261*
House, R. J., 204, *208*
Huang, S. H. S., 14, *31*, 66, *74*
Hull, C. L., 93, *119*
Humphrey, R. H., 204, *208*
Hunt, T., 82, 93, 95, 97, *119*, *121*
Hunter, J. E., 41, 57, 70, 71, 72, *75*,
    76, 111, 112, *120*, *122*, 197,
    210, 215, *233*, 235, 237,
    238, 239, 241, 252, 254,
    258, *260*, 272, *279*, 289, *299*
Hunter, R. F., 71, *75*, 112, *120*, 215,
    233, 235, 237, 254, *258*

I

Ickes, W., 19, *32*
Ilies, R., 203, *208*, *209*, 273, *279*
Indersmitten, T., 193, *208*
Isen, A. M., 199, *208*, 305, 306, 308,
    320, *322*

J

Jackson, C. J., 198, *207*
Jackson, D. N., 102, 108, *120*, *122*,
    272, *280*
Jackson, S., 131, *138*
Jackson, V. D., 100, *120*
Jacobson, J. W., 291, *299*
Janovics, J., 254, *258*, 315, *322*
Jedlicka, C., 154, *159*
Jencks, C., 168, 172, *184*
Jenness, A., 96, *120*
Jensen, A. R., 173, *184*, 236, 238,
    239, 254, *258*
Johnson, C. A., 308, 311, *324*
Johnson, D. T., 108, *120*
Johnson, D. W., 129, *138*
Johnson, H. M., 339, *343*
Johnson, R. T., 129, *138*
Joncich, G. M., 86, *120*
Jones, W. H. S., 127, *138*

Jordan, P. J., 27, *32*, 190, 191, 194,
    195, 196, 197, 202, *206*,
    208
Joseph, J., 171, *184*
Judge, T. A., 198, 200, 203, *206*,
    208, *209*, 273, *279*

K

Kadis, J., 312, *322*
Kaess, W. A., 102, *120*
Kahneman, D., 267, *279*
Kahnwieler, W. M., 228, *233*
Kammeyer-Mueller, J., 200, *209*,
    313, *321*
Kanfer, R., 23, *33*
Kanungo, R. N., 204, *207*
Kaplan, R. M., 68, *75*
Karlin, L., 102, *120*
Karp, J., 135, *138*
Kassin, S. M., 110, *120*
Katzko, M., 64, *75*, 85, *118*, 255,
    257
Kaufman, A. S., 37, *57*
Kaufman, J. C., 37, *57*
Kausilas, D., 200, *209*
Kaye, C. B., 135, *138*
Kayes, D. C., 198, *207*
Keating, D. P., 109, *120*
Kehoe, J. F., 215, *233*, 241, 253, *258*
Kelley, T. L., 92, 93, *120*
Kellogg, W. N., 94, *119*
Kelly, J. R., 197, *209*
Kerlinger, F. N., 15, *32*
Kessler, R., 129, *137*
Kihlstrom, J. F., 5, *33*
Kilduff, M., 198, *209*
Kim, J., 304, *321*
King, D. B., 90, *123*
Kitson, H. D., 94, *120*
Klahr, D., 215, *233*
Kleiner, A., 135, *139*
Klimoski, R. J., 23, *33*, 336, *343*
Kobe, L. M., 201, *209*
Kochanska, G., 8, *33*
Kooken, K., 15, *33*
Kouzes, J., 312, *321*
Kraiger, K., 228, *233*
Kraimer, M. L., 200, *210*
Kramer, I., 64, *75*, 85, *118*
Kraus, L. A., 19, *32*

Kriete, R., 133, *138*
Kruml, S. M., 314, *321*
Kuhn, T., 293, *299*
Kuiper, N. A., 110, *120*
Kuncel, N. R., 238, *258*

L

Laird, D. A., 94, 99, *120*
Laird, J. D., 306, *322*
Landy, F. J., 60, 75, 83, *120*, 192,
    209, 240, *259*, 309, 316, *322*
    325, 326, 333, *343*
Lane, R. D., 15, *33*
Lanier, P. A., 286, 288, 289, *298*
Lanyon, R. I., 109, *120*
Latham, G. P., 199, *210*
Lavine, C. L., 301, *322*
Law, K. S., 61, 65, 75, 77, 115, *120*,
    243, 244, 254, 255, *262*,
    326, 327, 332, 333, 339,
    341, *343*, *344*
Lawson, R. B., 229, *233*
Lazarus, R. S., 20, 22, *33*, 286, 287,
    295, *299*, 306, *322*
Leeper, R. W., 306, *322*
Lemmon, H., 166, *183*
Lennox, R. D., 202, *209*
LeRoux, J., 15, *33*
Leuner, B., 142, *158*
Levine, E. L., 237, *259*
Lewin, K., 50, *57*
Liden, R. C., 200, *210*
Lievens, F., 336, *343*
Lilienfeld, S. O., 50, *57*
Lilienthal, R. A., 237, *259*
Linn, R., 238, *259*
Little, I. S., 64, *76*, 195, *210*, 213,
    233, 242, 243, *259*
Locke, E. A., 71, 75, 192, *209*, 240,
    259, 309, *322*, 325, 326,
    341, *343*
Loehlin, J. C., 271, *279*
Logan, R. K., 268, 269, *279*
Lohr, J. M., 50, *57*
Lopes, P. N., 21, *33*, 66, 67, *76*, 199,
    202, 204, *209*, 243, *259*,
    310, 311, 312, 314, *322*, *323*
Lord Kelvin, 59, *75*
Lord, R. G., 23, *33*

Lorge, I., 98, *121*
Lubinski, D., 181, *184*
Lucas, T., 135, *139*
Lucier, C., 270, *279*
Lull, H. G., 84, *121*
Luthans, F., 198, *210*
Lynn, A. B., 42, *57*
Lynn, S. J., 50, *57*
Lyubomirsky, S., 286, 295, *299*

M

MacCann, C., 4, 5, 15, 16, 29, *33*,
    60, 67, *75*, 255, *262*
Mack, D. A., 222, *233*
MacKinnon, D. W., 273, *279*
Majeski, S. A., 241, 242, *259*, 260
Malouff, J. M., 12, 13, 14, *35*, 61, 65,
    72, *76*, 154, *159*, 195, 197,
    210, 246, *261*, 303, 304,
    310, *324*, 332, *343*
Mandell, B., 244, *259*
Mankin, D., 273, *279*
Manocha, R., 63, *76*, 309, *323*
Markiewicz, D., 200, *209*
Markus, H., 306, *324*
Martin, G., 157, *158*
Mathews, J., 289, *299*
Matouffi, J., 142, 154, *159*
Matsumoto, D., 15, *33*
Matthews, G., 4, 5, 6, 8, 10, 11, 14,
    15, 16, 17, 18, 20, 21, 22,
    23, 24, 25, 26, 27, 29, *33*,
    34, *35*, 38, 39, 59, 60, 63,
    67, 68, 69, 70, 75, *76*, 82,
    85, 95, 108, *121*, *122*, 144,
    151, *158*, 162, 176, *184*,
    239, 240, 241, 243, 245,
    246, 247, 254, 255, *259*,
    260, *262*, 287, 294, *299*,
    303, 309, 310, *322*, *323*,
    326, 336, 338, *343*, *344*
May, G. L., 228, *233*
Mayer, J. D., 4, 6, 11, 12, 13, 14, 15,
    16, 17, 26, *31*, 33, 34, 37,
    39, 42, 43, *57*, 62, 66, 67,
    69, 72, 74, 75, *76*, 85, 112,
    121, 142, 144, 152, 153,
    158, *159*, 175, 179, *184*,
    190, 191, 192, 193, 194,

196, 197, 202, 204, 205,
209, 216, 217, 227, *233*,
240, 242, 243, 246, 247,
255, *257, 259, 260*, 296,
299, 303, 304, 305, 306,
307, 309, 310, 311, *320*,
*322, 323, 326, 327, 328,
329, 332, 333, 334, 335,
339, 341, 342, 343*
Mayer, R. E., 291, *299*
Mazur, L., 288, *299*
McClatchey, V. R., 94, *121*
McClearn, G. E., 164, *184*
McCrae, R. R., 6, *33*, 179, *183*
McDaniel, M. A., 178, *184*
McGregor, D., 89, *121*
McGuiness, J., 109, *118*
McHenry, J. J., 237, *257*
McIntyre, R. M., 44, *57*
McKee, A., 42, *56*, 201, 204, *208*,
244, *258*
McKenley, J., 65, *76*
McKenney, D., 66, *74*
McMullin, R. E., 194, *209*
McNeely, C. A., 131, *137, 138*
Mediratta K., 135, *138*
Meehl, P. W., 6, *31*, 89, *118*
Megerian, L. E., 201, 202, *209, 210*,
244, *261*
Mehra, A., 198, *209*
Melamed, T., 200, *209*
Melburg, V., 110, *122*
Menon, P. E., 237, *259*
Meyer, J. P., 193, *206*
Michael, W. B., 108, 111, *122*
Miller, J. A., 340, *343*
Miller, M. G., 306, *323*
Miller, T., 198, *207*
Minski, P. S., 14, *34*, 66, *76*
Moore, B. V., 98, *121*
Moore, H., 98, *121*
Morgeson, F. P., 178, *184*
Morris, J. A., 193, *209*, 307, 308, *323*
Moscoso, S., 238, *260*
Moss, F. A., 82, 94, 95, *121*
Mostert, M. P., 291, *299*
Motowidlo, S. J., 226, *233*, 244, *256*
Mount, M. K., 198, *206, 209*
Mueller, C. W., 304, *321*
Mulhall, L., 133, *139*
Mulick, J. A., 291, *299*

Munz, D. C., 202, *210*
Muraven, M., 307, *320*
Murphy, J., 135, *138*
Murphy, K., 49, 51, 52, *57*, 68, *76*,
236, 239, 253, *259*, 287,
288, *299*
Murray, C., 38, 41, *55*, 56, 161, 169,
174, *183, 184*, 239, *258*,
308
Muzushima, K., 273, *279*
Myors, B., 51, 52, *57*

N

Narayanan, L., 237, *259*
National Council on Measurement in
Education, 6, *30*, 71, 74
Nelson, D. L., 222, *233*
Nesselroade, J. R., 164, *184*
Nettelbeck, T., 16, *35*
Neubert, M. J., 203, *209*
Neuringer, C., 109, *118*
Newcombe, M. J., 202, *210*
Newsome, S., 14, *34*, 64, *76*, 242,
259
Nexlek, J. B., 199, *209*, 310, 312,
322
Nicol, A. A. M., 24, *31*
Noe, R. A., 73, *76*, 225, *232*
Nonnemaker, J. M., 131, *138*
Northrop, L. C., 238, *258*
Nystrom, L. E., 128, *139*

O

O'Brien, M. U., 25, *32*, 126, *138*
O'Connor, R. M. Jr., 64, *76*, 195,
210, 213, *233*, 242, 243,
259
O'Sullivan, M., 82, 106, 107, 111,
114, 116, *117, 119, 121*
O'Connell, B. J., 328, *344*
Offermann, L. R., 195, 197, *210*
Office of Elementary and Secondary
Education, 128, *138*
Olatoye, S., 135, *139*
Oliver, R. A. C., 96, *121*
Ollendick, T. H., 50, *56*
Omwake, K. T., 82, *121*

Ones, D. S., 168, *184*, 236, 238, 241, 251, 252, 253, 254, 255, *257*, *258*, *259*, *261*
Opton, E. M., Jr., 306, *322*
Organ, D. W., 305, *323*
Orr, D. B., 109, *121*
Ortony, A., 305, *323*
Osburn, H. G., 237, *257*
Osher, D., 131, *138*
Osipow, S. H., 111, *121*
Osterman, K. F., 131, *138*
Outerbridge, A. N., 252, *260*

P

Palfai, T., 142, *159*
Palmer, B. R., 63, *76*, *323*
Palmer, E., 318, *321*
Panksepp, J., 8, *34*
Park, R. L., 285, *299*
Parker, J. D. A., 14, 21, *32*, 34, 241, 242, *259*, *260*
Patton, W., 200, *207*
Paul, A. M., 66, *76*, 271, *279*
Pauwels, B. G., 286, *299*
Pearlman, K., 237, *259*, *260*
Pedersen, N. L., 164, *184*
Pennebaker, J. W., 18, *34*
Pérez, J. C., 12, *34*
Pescosolido, A. T., 244, 255, *262*
Pesuric, A., 228, *233*
Petrides, K. V., 5, 12, 13, 14, 21, 22, *32*, *34*, 141, 142, 143, 153, 154, *157*, *158*, 240, 241, 242, 243, *260*
Petrilli, M. J., 290, *298*
Pherwani, S., 244, *259*
Phillips, D. A., 128, *139*
Phillips, J. M., 224, *233*
Phillips, K., 165, *183*
Pintner, R., 89, 94, 97, *121*
Plomin, R., 164, 165, 180, *183*, *184*, *185*
Pluta, P., 71, 72, *77*, 241, 247, *261*
Poffenberger, A. T., 83, 95, *121*
Pons, M. M., 195, *210*
Posner, B., 312, *321*
Prati, L., 202, *210*
Price, L. A., 88, *119*
Prior, M. P., 291, *298*
Pyryt, M. C., 107, *122*

Q

Quick, J. C., 222, *233*
Quinlan, D. M., 15, *33*

R

Raider, E., 131, *138*
Reardon, R., 111, *122*
Reddon, J. R., 272, *280*
Ree, M. J., 68, *76*, 179, *184*, 237, 238, 240, 256, *260*, *261*
Reeve, C. L., 238, 239, 256, *260*
Rehberg, R. A., 172, *184*
Reiter-Palmon, R., 201, *209*
Renz, G. L., 224, *232*
Resnik, H., 126, *138*
Resnik, L. B., 129, *138*
Rhee, K., 39, *56*, 60, 74, 112, *117*, 326, 333, *342*
Rhodes, E., 154, *159*
Rice, B., 111, *122*
Rice, C. L., 24, *32*, 313, 315, *323*
Rickers, J. D., 201, *209*
Riess, M., 110, *122*
Rilling, J. K., 128, *139*
Rinehart, P. M., 131, *137*
Roberts, R. D., 4, 5, 6, 8, 10, 11, 14, 15, 18, 20, 21, 22, 23, 24, 25, 26, 27, 29, *30*, *32*, 33, *34*, 35, 38, 39, *56*, 59, 60, 63, 66, 67, 68, 69, 70, *74*, 75, *76*, 82, 85, 95, 108, *121*, *122*, 144, 151, *158*, 162, 176, *184*, 223, *232*, 239, 240, 241, 243, 245, 246, 247, 254, 255, *257*, *259*, *260*, *262*, 294, *299*, 303, 309, 310, *321*, *322*, *323*, 326, 336, 338, *343*, *344*
Rodgers, R., 289, *299*
Rodin, J., 306, *323*
Rolland, J. P., 238, *260*
Romney, D. M., 107, *122*
Ronning, M. M., 82, *121*
Rose, S., 165, *184*
Rosenfeld, P., 110, *122*
Rosenthal, R. E. R., 172, *184*
Ross, L., 266, *279*
Roth, P. L., 238, *260*

Rothstein, M., 272, *280*
Rotundo, M., 313, *321*
Rowe, D. C., 171, *184*
Rubin, M. M., 311, 312, 313, 315, *321, 323*
Rubin, R. S., 202, *210*
Ruch, F. L., 104, *122*
Ryan, K., 305, *323*

S

Saal, F., 49, *57*
Saarni, C., 10, *34*
Saccuzzo, D. P., 68, *75*
Sackett, P. R., 177, *184*, 238, *260*
Saklofske, D. H., 14, 22, *31*, 34, 66, 74, 76
Saks, A. M., 223, *232*
Sala, F., 12, *34*, 60, 61, 63, *74*, 76, 112, *122*, 303, *323*
Salas, E., 228, *233*
Salgado, J. F., 238, *260*
Salovey, P., 4, 6, 11, 12, 13, 14, 15, 16, 20, 21, 26, *33*, 34, *35*, 37, 39, 42, 43, *57*, 62, 66, 67, 69, 71, 72, *74*, 75, *76*, 85, 112, *121*, 128, 131, 133, *136*, *139*, 141, 142, 144, 152, 153, *158*, *159*, 175, *184*, 190, 191, 192, 193, 194, 196, 197, 199, 202, 204, 205, *209*, 216, 217, 227, *233*, 240, 243, 246, 247, 255, *259*, *260*, 296, *299*, 303, 304, 305, 306, 307, 309, 310, 311, 312, 314, *322*, *323*, *324*, 326, 327, 328, 329, 332, 333, 334, 335, 339, 341, *343*
Sandy, S., 131, 133, *136*
Sanfey, A. G., 128, *139*
Sass, M., 195, 197, *210*
Saul, K., 312, 313, 314, 315
Sawaf, A., 190, 195, *207*
Schaap, P., 311, *320*
Schaie, K. W., 249, *257*, *262*
Schmidt, F. L., 41, *57*, 70, 72, *76*, 111, 112, *122*, 197, *210*, 235, 237, 238, 239, 241, 252, 253, 254, *258*, *259*, 260

Schneck, M. R., 98, *119*
Schuettpelz, E., 197, *210*
Schulte, M. J., 68, *76*, 240, *261*, 179, *184*
Schulze, R., 18, 23, 29, *33*, 34
Schutte, N. S., 12, 13, 14, *35*, 61, 65, 72, *76*, 142, 154, *159*, 195, 197, *210*, 246, *261*, 303, 304, 310, *324*, 332, *343*
Schütz, A., 199, *209*, 310, 312, *322*
Schuyt, R., 270, *279*
Schwab-Stone, M. E., 129, *137*
Schwartz, A. A., 291, *299*
Schwartz, G. E., 15, *33*
Schwartz, M. M., 102, *120*
Schwartz, T., 213, *233*, 275, *279*
Schwarz, N., 308, *323*
Seal, C., 195, 197, *210*
Sechrest, L., 102, *122*
Seligman, M. E. P., 152, *159*, 266, *280*
Sellin, I., 199, *209*, 310, 312, *322*
Senge, P., 135, *139*
Sergiovanni, T., 132, *139*
Shane, G. S., 237, *260*
Shanley, L. A., 107, *122*
Shea, D. L., 181, *184* __
Sheddan, B. R., 99, *122*
Shen, Z., 229, *233*
Shonkoff, J. P., 128, *139*
Shriver, T. P., 129, *137*
Shuter-Dyson, R., 176, *185*
Simon, H. A., 215, *233*, 307
Simon, T., 162, *182*
Simonton, D. K., 200, *210*
Simunek, M., 65, *76*
Sitarenios, G., 67, 72, *76*, 112, *121*, 227, *233*, 255, *259*, 296, *299*, 327, 329, 333, 335, *343*
Slaski, M., 24, 25, *35*, 64, 73, 76, 77, 201, *207*, 245, *261*
Smart, L., 19, *31*
Smith, B., 135, *139*
Smith, H. C., 99, *122*
Smith, P. C., 226, *232*
Smith, R. K., 312, 313, 315, *321*
Snook, S. A., 162, 175, 178, *185*
Snow, R., 168, 181, *183*
Snyder, M., 266, *280*
Snyder, S. D., 108, 111, *122*

Song, L., 61, 65, *75*, 115, *120*, 332, 333, *343*
Sosik, J. J., 201, 202, *209*, *210*, 244, *261*
Spearman, C., 6, *35*, 83, 92, *122*, 161, *185*, 236, *261*
Spector, P. E., 199, 200, *207*, 237, 248, *257*, *259*, 328, 330, *343*, *344*
Spencer-Bowdage, S., 21, *32*
Spinath, F. M., 180, *185*
Stagner, R., 96, 99, *122*
Stajkovic, A. D., 198, *210*
Stanford Aptitude Seminar, 10, *35*
Stankov, L., 5, 29, *32*, 38, *56*, 68, *74*, 223, *232*, 240, *257*, 303, 309, 310, *321*
Stanley, J. C., 215, *232*
Stanovich, K. E., 267, *280*
Starr, J. M., 166, 169, *183*
Stein, S., 87, 97, 99, 104, *123*
Sternberg, R. J., 128, *139*, 162, 175, 177, 178, *183*, *185*, 247, 248, 249, 250, 251, 252, 254, *258*, *261*, *262*
Stevenson, H. W., 181, *185*
Stigler, J. W., 181, *185*
Stewart, G. L., 198, *209*
Stokes, L. W., 268, 269, *279*
Storladen, M., 21, *30*
Stough, C., 63, *76*, 309, *323*
Strang, R., 95, 96, 113, *122*
Straus, R., 21, *33*, 243, *259*
Stroud, L. R., 12, *35*
Sue-Chan, C., 199, *210*
Summerfeldt, L. J., 14, *34*, 242, *260*
Super, D. E., 103, *123*
Swift, D. G., 311, *324*
Switzer, F. S., 238, *260*
Sylwester, R., 128, *139*

T

Tabachnick, B. G., 304, 319, *324*
Taft, R., 102, *123*
Taggar, S., 203, *209*
Taguiri, R., 102, *118*
Taylor, G. J., 12, *35*
Taylor, H. L., 104, *123*
Teachout, M. S., 237, 256, *260*
Tedescho, J. T., 110, *122*

Tenopyr, M. L., 111, *123*
Tesser, A., 306, *323*
Tett, R. P., 272, *280*
Thayer, R. E., 305, 307, *324*
Thompson, L. A., 165, *183*
Thorlakson, A. J. H., 198, 199, *210*
Thorndike, E. L., 37, 83, 84, 85, 86, 87, 88, 89, 92, 95, 97, 99, 101, 104, 109, *123*, 142, 152, *159*, 247, *261*
Thurstone, L. L., 236, *261*
Tice, D. M., 307, *320*
Tiffin, J., 104, *123*
Tisak, M. S., 109, *119*
Tomkins, S., 306, *324*
Torgerson, W. S., 17, *35*
Travaglione, A., 23, *32*
Trinidad, D. R., 311, *324*
Troth, A. C., 195, 196, 197, *208*
Tse, B., 202, 203, 204, *206*, 311, *320*
Turvey, C., 12, 26, 34, 142, *159*
Tyler, P., 238, *260*

U

Uchida, H., 15, *33*
Unger, J. B., 311, *324*
Upshall, C., 94, *121*

V

Van Rooy, D. L., 15, 24, *35*, 38, 41, 42, 44, 48, 49, *58*, 63, 67, 68, 69, 70, 71, 72, 77, 112, *123*, 240, 241, 242, 246, 247, 254, *261*, 294, *299*, 303, 309, 310, *324*
Van Tassel, J. D., 318, *324*
Van Vianen, A. E. M., 225, *234*
Vasilopoulos, N. L., 195, 197, *210*
Veiga, J. F., 200, *207*
Verbruggen, A. B., 255, *257*
Vince, R., 223, *234*
Vincent, C., 156, *158*
Viney, W., 90, *123*
Viswesvaran, C., 15, 24, *35*, 38, 41, 42, 44, 48, 49, *58*, 63, 67, 68, 69, 70, 71, 72, 77, 112, *123*, 168, *184*, 236, 240,

241, 243, 246, 247, 252,
254, *259*, *261*, 294, *299*,
303, 309, 310, *324*
Viteles, M. S., 98, *123*

W

Wagner, R. K., 162, 175, 178, *185*,
248, 249, 250, 252, *261*,
262
Walberg, H. J., 129, 130, *139*
Walker, R. E., 107, 110, 111, *122*,
123
Walsh, W. B., 111, *121*
Wang, C. K. A., 96, *123*
Wang, M. C., 25, 26, *35*, 129, 130, *139*
Wanous, J. P., 224, *234*
Warner, R. M., 15, *32*, 240, 243, *257*,
311, 332, 339, *342*
Warwick, J., 16, *35*
Watson, M., 132, *139*
Watson, W. W., 224, *232*
Wayne, S. J., 200, *210*
Wechsler, D., 103, *123*
Wedeck, J., 101, *123*
Weisinger, H., 24, *35*
Weissberg, R. P., 25, 26, *32*, 35, 126,
129, 130, *137*, *138*, *139*
Wendorf, G., 154, *159*
Werner, M. W., 203, *208*
West, R. F., 267, *280*
Westermann, M., 316, *324*
Whalley, L. J., 166, 169, *183*
Wheelock, A. K., 316, *324*
White, K. R., 163
Whitely, W., 200, *210*
Whiteman, M. C., 169, *183*
Wigdor, A. K., 236, 237, *258*
Wilczenski, F. L., 135, *139*
Wilhelm, O., 236, *262*
Williams, W. M., 162, 175, 178, *185*,
248, 249, 250, *261*
Willis, S. L., 249, *257*, *262*
Wilson-Cohn, C., 15, *33*
Wise, L. L., 237, *257*
Witmer, L. R., 99, *122*, 128, *139*
Witryol, S. L., 102, *120*
Wolfe, R. N., 202, *209*

Wolff, S. B., 190, *207*, 244, 255, *262*,
274, 278
Wong, C. S., 61, 65, *75*, 77, 115, *120*
Wong, C. S., 243, 244, 254, 255,
262, 326, 327, 332, 333,
339, 341, *343*, *344*
Wong, P. M., 65, *77*
Wood, L. M., 241, *259*
Woodrow, H., 96, *123*
Woodyard, E., 88, 92, 95, *123*
Woolery, A., 12, *35*

Y

Yee, A., 15, *33*
Yerkes, R. M., 340, *344*
Young, P. V., 98, *123*
Young, P. T., 306, *324*
Yrizarry, N., 15, *33*

Z

Zachary E., 135, *139*
Zajonc, R. B., 306, *324*
Zapf, D., 218, *234*
Zedeck, S., 51, 52, *56*
Zeidner, M., 6, 17, *35*
Zeidner, M., 20, 21, *35*
Zeidner, M., 5, 6, 8, 10, 11, 14, 15,
18, 20, 21, 22, 24, 25, 26,
27, 29, *30*, *33*, 35, 38, 39,
59, 60, 63, 66, 67, 68, 69,
70, *75*, 82, 85, 95, 108, *121*,
122, 144, 151, *158*, 162,
176, *184*, 239, 240, 241,
243, 245, 246, 247, 254,
255, *259*, 260, *262*, 287,
294, *299*, 303, 309, 310,
322, *323*, 326, 336, 338,
343, *344*
Zerbe, W. J., 23, *31*, 44, *55*
Zhou, J., 222, *234*
Ziegler, S., 133, *139*
Zins, J. E., 25, 26, *35*, 126, 129,
130, *137*, *138*

Subject Index

A

Abstract intelligence, 85–90
Academic performance, 242–243,
    253
Action research, 50
Adverse impact, 236, 238–239, 246
American Express, 213, 220, 229
Assessing Emotions Scale, 303, 304

B

Bandwagon effect, 301
Behaviorism, 272
Bias, 239
Big Five, see Personality

C

California Psychological Inventory,
    272–273
Career success, 198–201
Cleary Regression Model, 239
Coaching, 228–229
Cognition, 306–307

Cognition of behavioral relationships
    (CBR), 107–108
Cognitive ability, see Intelligence
Collaborative of Academic, Social,
    and Emotional Learning
    (CASEL), 25
Consensual decision making,
    318–319
Contextual behavior, 244
Creativity, 222, 308
Cultures, 43–54
    Practice-driven, 43–54
    Science-driven, 43–54
    Values, 45–46
    Criteria, 46–47
    Audience, 47–48
Customer service, 218–221, 313–314

D

Decision making, 267, 308
Drug use, 311

E

Emotion, 217–223, 306–308, 335

positive emotion, 220–221, 308, 335

negative emotion, 217–219, 308, 335

Emotion facilitation, 193, 216, 222

Emotion management, *see* Emotion regulation

Emotion perception, 193, 216, 220, 332, 334, 335–337, 340

Emotion regulation, 8–9, 194, 216, 220, 228, 307, 313–314, 329, 330–331, 332, 334, 336–338, 340

Emotion understanding, 193–194, 216, 220, 228, 332, 334

Emotional Accuracy Research Scale (EARS), 15

Emotional Competence Inventory (ECI), 12, 60–61, 63, 227, 303–304

Emotional demands, 223–225, 230

Emotional exhaustion, 339

Emotional intelligence

alternative to g, as, 175–176, 178–179

applications, 23–25

construct validity, 331, 334

criterion-related validity, 331–332, 339

debate and controversy over, 38–42

definition, 6–10, 39–41, 217, 326–333, 346–348

face validity, 315–317

definition, 315

group differences, 72–73, 245–247

history of, 81–123

in educational and school psychology, 25,

in classrooms and schools, 125–139

in the workplace, 42, 48–49

incremental validity, 242–243, 338–339

measures, 10–18, 59–77, 115–116, 153–155, 304, 333–338, 346–348

ability-based tests, 14–16

assessment center, 337

comparability of, 68

consensus scoring, 15, 67

cultural differences, and, 116

expert scoring, 15, 66–67

factor analysis, 153–154

faking on, 72–73

guidelines, 11

interpersonal simulation tests, 336–338

meta-analyses of, 70–73

multidimensionality, 153–155

paper-and-pencil, 334–336

personality-based tests, 69

scoring, 348

validity, 70–73, 115

models, 1, 39, 42, 144, 192–194, 216, 240–248, 254–255, 302–310, 316, 328–329, 332, 346–347, 351, 354

ability models, 1, 42, 144, 240–248, 254–255, 302–310, 316, 328, 332, 347–348, 351, 354

Coleman model of, 39

expansive models of, 1

Mayer-Salovey model of, 39

mixed model, 240–248, 254, 302–304, 328, 332, 346–347, 351, 354

trait models, *see* mixed model

myths of, 26–29

popularity of, 141–159

predictive validity, *see* criterion-related validity

questionnaires for, 12–14

stress, and, 20–23

trait-based, 144

Emotional Intelligence Scale (EIS), 61, 65–66

Emotional knowledge and skills, 8–9

Emotional labor, 219, 313–315, 329–330, 339

deep acting, 315, 330

definition, 313–314, 329–330

surface acting, 315, 330

Emotional quotient, 39, 145, 156–157

Emotional Quotient Inventory, 12–14, 16, 61, 63–65, 227, 242, 304, 310, 332

Errors, 51–52

Type I, 51–52

Type II, 51–52

Ethical issues, 52–54

Ethical Principles of Psychologists and Code of Conduct of, 4, 53

F

Fads, 263–278, 283–298

definition, 284–285

diagnosing, 291–295
education fads, 290–291
    discovery learning, 291
    facilitated communication, 291
life cycle, 286
management fads, 288–290
    Management by Objective, 289,
        318
    Total Quality Management, 289
    Quality Circles, 289
psychology fads, 286–288
    graphology, 287–288
    positive psychology, 286–287
Functionalism (versus structuralism),
    90

G

g, see Intelligence
General mental ability, see Intelligence
Group performance, see Team perfor-
    mance

H

Holland model of occupational types,
    264–265
Human resource practices, 214–215

I

Information processing, 8–9
Internet, 268
Intelligence, 17, 70, 72, 85–92, 145,
    156–157, 161–185, 235–247,
    251–256, 328, 349–352
    alternatives to, 174–179
    continuity of, 163–166
    definition, 236
    different types of, 85–90
    education, and, 180–181
    g, 17, 70, 72, 91, 161–185
    group differences, 238–239
    heritability of, 171, 239
    idiographic complexity of, 170–171
    malleability of, 166–168, 180,
        238–239
    positive manifolds, and, 162–163
    quotient (IQ), 145, 156–157,
        163–166, 170
        prior to birth, 163
        from conception to adult,
            163–165
    from childhood to adult,
        165–166
    race and class, and, 173–174
    social relevance of, 168–170
    social policy, and, 171–173
    statistical theories of, 91–92

J

Japanese and Caucasian Brief Affect
    Recognition Test
    (JACBART), 15
Job analysis, 214, 223–224, 340
Job performance, 24–25, 48,
    194–198, 215, 217–222,
    227, 235–239, 243–245,
    253, 255, 312–313, 339
Job satisfaction, 24, 313

K

Knowledge era, 268

L

Leadership, 201–204, 227, 244–245,
    311–312
    transformational leadership,
        201–204, 244–245,
        311–312
Learning community, 131–135
Levels of Emotional Awareness Scale
    (LEAS), 15
Loyalty, 268–269

M

Managers, 219, 269, 276
Mayer-Salovey-Caruso Emotional In-
    telligence Test (MSCEIT),
    12–13, 15–16, 26, 67–68,
    153, 176–177, 178–179,
    227, 242, 254, 304–305,
    309, 315, 332–333, 335,
    339, 341
    reliability, 309
    validity, 309–310, 332
        criterion-related validity, 332
        discriminant validity, 309–310
        incremental validity, 332

Mental health, 311
Mentoring, *see* Coaching
Meta-analysis, 237, 241, 242, 246,
    252, 253, 271–272, 289
Multifactor Emotional Intelligence
    Scale (MEIS), 12–15, 26,
    66–67, 304
Myers-Briggs Type Indicator, 272, 277

N

Nature (versus nurture), 90–91
Nurture (versus nature), 90–91

O

Organizational analysis, 230
Organizational change, 222–223,
    229–230
Organizational citizenship behavior,
    305, 339

P

Personality, 198, 201–203, 240–245,
    254, 264–268, 270–277,
    309–310, 332–333, 341, 350
bidirectionality, 272
Big Five, 5, 14, 16, 22, 63, 64, 65,
    66, 67, 68, 72
extraversion, 265
measures, 273–274
    Edwards Personal Preference
        Schedule (EPPS), 143
    NEO Personality Inventory-Re-
        vised (NEO-PI-R), 143
single-trait personality theories,
    151–156
Practical intelligence, 247–255
definition, 248
incremental validity, 253
tacit knowledge, 248–252
    definition, 249
    measures, 250
Problem solving, 222, 308
Promotion, 225–227
Psychological ability, 101–102,

R

Realistic job previews, 224–225

Recruitment, 224–225
Reliability, 1, 309

S

Selection, 225–227, 235–236, 253
high fidelity measures, 225–226
low fidelity measures, 226–227
Self-assessment, 225
Self-Assessment Questionnaire
    (SAQ), 63
Self-Report Inventory (SSRI), 12–14,
    16
Social and emotional education
    (SEE), 126–136
Social desirability, 244–245
Social intelligence, 37, 84–105,
    107–113, 247
emergence of, 84–92
in the 1920s, 92–95
in the 1930s, 95–105
measures, 92–105
    Ability to Sell Test, the 104,
        112–113
    Chapin's Test of Social Insight,
        100–101, 109,
        112–113
    Cognition of Behavioral Rela-
        tionships (CBR) tests,
        107–108, 111,
        112–113
    George Washington Test, the,
        93–94, 95–99, 103
    Gilliland Measure of Sociabil-
        ity, 94, 112–113
    Jackson Test of Social Profi-
        ciency, 100, 112–113
Socialization, 228–229
Stress, 222, 314
Structuralism (versus functionalism),
    90
Subject matter experts, 224

T

Team performance, 24, 314
Temperament, 8–9
Training, 213, 218, 227–229,
    263–266
affective training, 228
cognitive training, 227–228
interpersonal training, 229

skill-based training, 227–228
Trait Emotional Intelligence Question-
     naire (TEIque), 12
Trait Meta-Mood Scale (TMMS),
     12–13, 16

U

Utility, 23–25

V

Validation, 18–23, 153
Validity 1, 5, 64–66, 315–317
   concurrent, 317
   criterion-related, 317

face, 315–316
of EIS, 65–66
of EQ-I, 64,
of George Washington Test of So-
     cial Intelligence, 96–97
of MSCEIT, 67–68
of WEIS, 67
of WLEIS, 65,
predictive, 317

W

Wong and Law Emotional Intelligence
     Scale, 61, 65, 332–333, 339
Work performance, see Job perfor-
     mance